The Big Book of Fashion Illustration

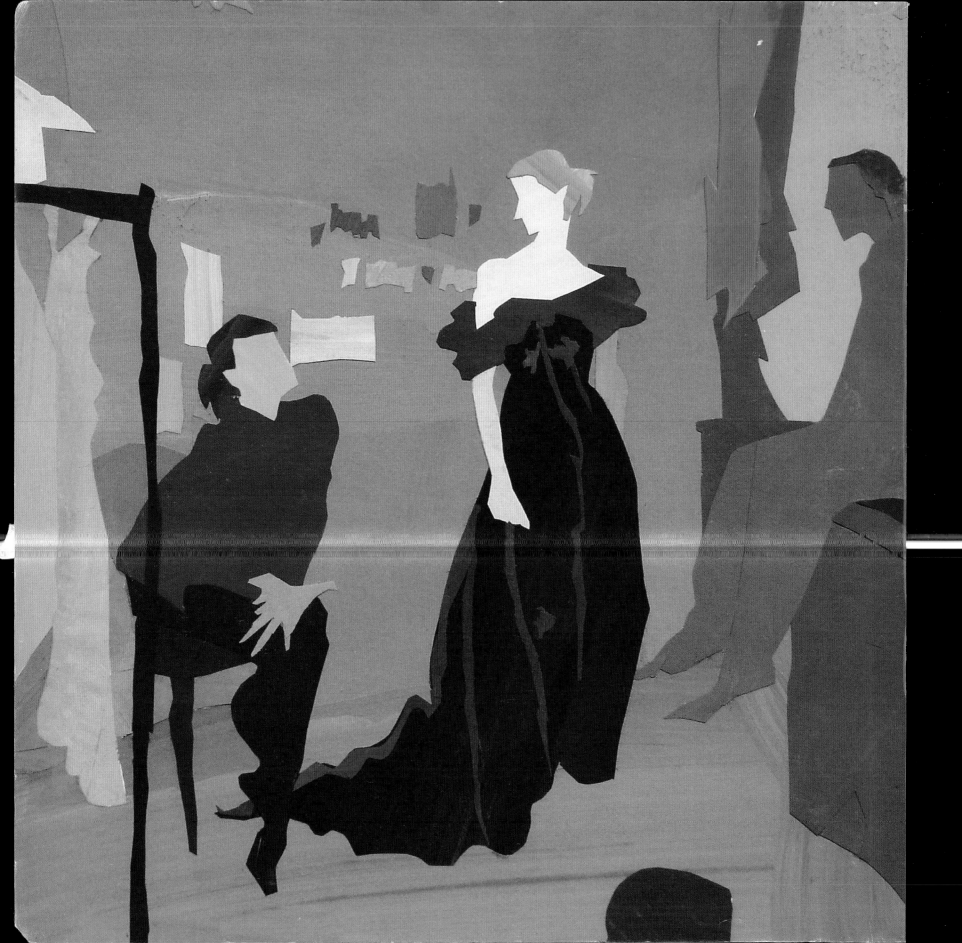

The Big Book of Fashion Illustration

Martin Dawber

BATSFORD

This book is in memory of my father, James Samuel Dawber,
and offered with love to my mother, Betty, and my sister, Carole.

'Fashion is not something that exists in dresses only. Fashion is in
the sky, in the street; fashion has to do with ideas, the way we
live, what is happening'
'Coco' Chanel (1883–1971)

First published in the United Kingdom in 2007 by
Batsford
10 Southcombe Street
London W14 0RA

An imprint of Anova Books Company Ltd

ISBN-13: 9780713490459

A CIP catalogue record for this book is available from the British Library.

15 14 13 12 10 09 08
10 9 8 7 6 5 4

Reproduction by Anorax Imaging Ltd, Leeds
Printed by SNP Leefung Ltd, China

This book can be ordered direct from the publisher at the website:
www.anovabooks.com, or try your local bookshop

Distributed in the United States and Canada by Sterling Publishing Co.,
387 Park Avenue South, New York, NY 10016, USA

Front cover:
Terence Lawlor
Carlotta/The Vanities (2006)
Collage

Title page:
Janis Salek
Atelier (2006)
Collage using hand-painted papers

Opposite:
Sonya Suhariyan
Accessories (2006)
Ink/Watercolour/Pen

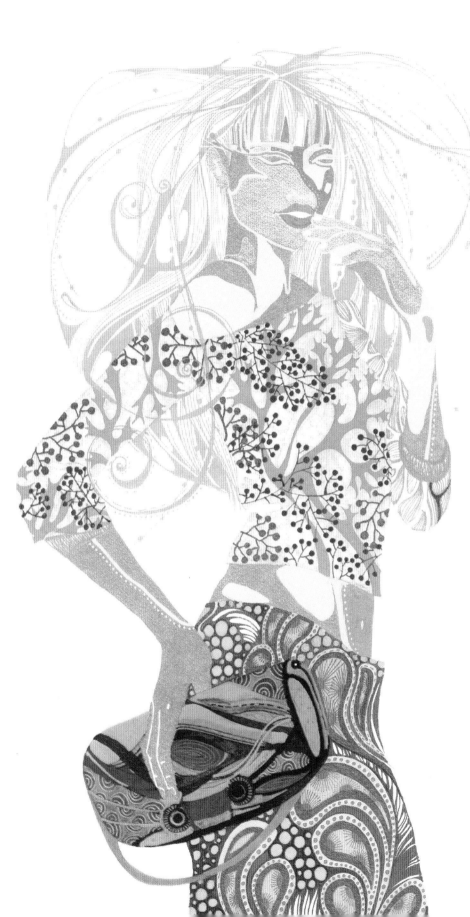

Contents

FOREWORD

Fashion illustration these days is said to be as rare as a snow leopard. To smoke out the images in this exciting book, Martin Dawber has become a kind of Pied Piper eliciting, with a secret digital pitch, the cutting-edge visions of hundreds of snow leopards from all over the world.

Encountering his artists in the light of monitors, at the foot of fashion runways, on the streets of Paris and in the pages of little-known magazines, he found fashion art alive and well – and yet much changed. The artists of today do not just portray fashion in beautiful isolation. They transpose it – with seamless integration – into contemporary lifestyle.

The globalization of all design areas, such as home-style, travel and sports, are revealed in this book. The viewer's identification of these elements, which draws them in with welcome recognition, is made more delightful by the art of the illustrator. Coffee at Starbucks, skateboard ramps, Shoe Fest at Barney's, and even the bedroom, all provide a new stage for the daily interaction of fashion and lifestyle.

This is in front of us everyday, but it is the special terrain of the fashion illustrator to orchestrate and edit the clearest punch. These innovators inspire through their unique expressions – unsurprisingly, they are at the forefront of dictating new trends.

The book's other thread, significant as it ever was, is fashion illustration's most important element – drawing. This is still tantamount, whether the artist is using a Number 4 pencil or a Wacom tablet. Line, like the baton of a skilled maestro, takes the viewer throughout this book. Throughout history, the skilled use of line has earned the credential of being one of the most effective artistic methods used to convey emotion. The confluence of hands-on materials and the latest digital programs results in the increase of fashion illustration being chosen over photography.

The diversity of artwork is also augmented by the fact that these artists come from many cultures and countries. After a while, the reader eagerly attempts to identify the roots of each illustrator and is rather startled to find that East has been busy meeting West.

The fashion illustrator's skill at creating a seductive environmental perfume is joined by an ability to quickly sketch character, to depict emotion and attitude by imposing style. It is here that style from within – or attitude, a major earmark of the fashionistas – ranges from heartbroken women to bored sprawling youth, or angry bad boys flying around the hood like a pack of hornets.

Born of a generation of artists deeply influenced by comic books, music videos and cartoons, the multi-vantage point often enlivens the illustration, inviting the viewers to participate as opposed to keeping them at a distance behind the velvet ropes. For page after page sexuality is brazenly flaunted when needed, creating at times a privileged voyeuristic seat for the viewer, but more often sensuality prevails. This is fashion illustration at its best, incorporating every weapon of seduction. Hang on to your hats and wallets – these formerly endangered artists are out to get you!

Karen Santry, Associate Professor, Fashion Institute of Technology, New York
Executive Vice President, Fashion Art Bank Inc. (USA and Japan)

Giulio Iurissevich
Cry Me a River (2006)
Adobe Illustrator/Adobe
Photoshop

INTRODUCTION

It's life, Jim, but not as we know it,
not as we know it, Captain
'Star Trekkin'
by The Firm (Lister/John O'Connor)

To paraphrase Mr Spock, fashion illustration has been turned around during the past decade and re-invented for today's more visually conscious audience. Benefiting from its reawakening as the foremost barometer of contemporary lifestyle it remains unique in its ability to articulate fashion.

Berlin-based designer Lulu feels we are experiencing an illustration revolution. '20 years ago, photography was the main media used in fashion magazines. Only a few illustrators worked as commercial artists. It all came back with *Wallpaper** magazine – Tyler Brûlé made it possible. He started to use illustration again like magazines had in the 50s'.

Unquestionably, illustration has elbowed itself back into the limelight after only being tolerated in the shadows of photography's monopoly. Indeed, photography's dominance is equally under threat, as current technological advances bring their individual techniques closer together. UK-based illustration duo, Jacqui Paull and Carl Melegari, who combine both photography and illustration in their artwork, prefer the term 'reportage image-makers'. 'We like to fuse the two elements together to achieve our goal. It is more innovative and exciting. We mix a combination of techniques – photography, hand-drawn elements, Xerox, flat graphics – all collaged together using Photoshop to give a more individual approach. We are influenced by fashion and street culture but like to use our observational skills, so to label oneself as purely a 'fashion illustrator' today would not be totally true'.

The ivory-tower exclusivity that cloaked preceding exponents has been replaced with a steady fix of fashion 'in yer face' – shaking off the mothballs of convention in a heady mix of editorial Esperanto and exhibitionism. 'Fashion is more important today than ever' states Australian artist, Vincent Agostino, 'because as the world becomes more populated we will strive to be more individual. Fashion will always give us an identity. We now have the technologies to help us explore the past and future in new ways'. Similarly, Hungarian artist Naomi Devil reveals 'in my work I am interested in how young people find a way of self-expression through the extreme vogues of fashion. Their creativity is an elemental part of my work. The quality of my illustration has changed, because the clothes we have to illustrate have become more eye-catching, more colourful'.

For too long art students were force-fed the misconception that there was an accepted stereotype passing itself off as the elongated, nine-head-length norm. Fashion has never supported the notion of normality – its function is to innovate and revolutionize – so why should its graphic representation resist change and stick so closely to an accepted template? Fashion illustration is never solely about the minutiae of garment construction – it is painted in broader brushstrokes and equally concerned with mood, emotion and, above all else, style.

UK university graduate Gemma Waite concurs: 'When you say 'fashion illustration' people always conjure up images of 1940s-style sketches with long, tall legs – fashion illustration is always changing!'. This is a view that Dutch illustrator Irene Jacobs, alias *I'm JAC*, agrees with: 'In my

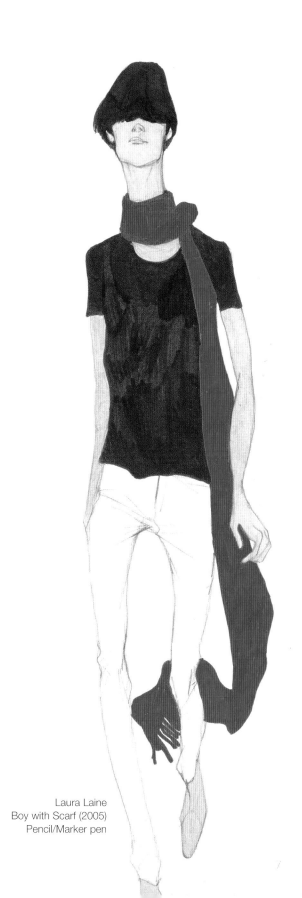

Laura Laine
Boy with Scarf (2005)
Pencil/Marker pen

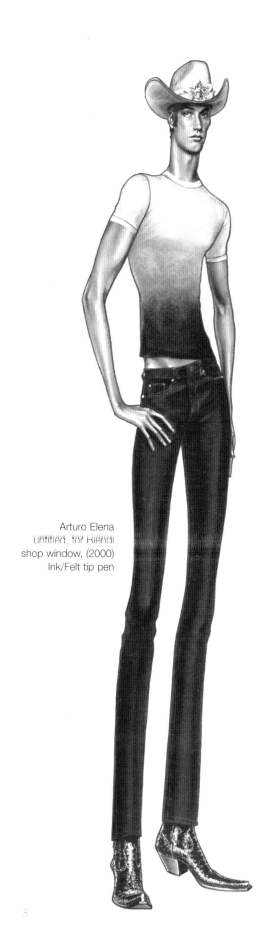

Arturo Elena
Untitled, for Bikkit
shop window, (2000)
Ink/Felt tip pen

experience illustration styles change every season, just like fashion or interior and graphic design'. The once-exclusive club that barred all non-members now flashes an 'All Welcome' sign over the door. *The Big Book of Fashion Illustration* has flung its net wide, embracing the documentary photo-realism of Yusuke Saitoh (Japan) and Mayrhosby Yeoshen (Venezuela) in contrast to the impressionistic approach of Noumeda Carbone (Italy) and Margot Mace (France). The cleanly articulated pixels of Arthur Mount (USA) and Daniel Chen (Canada) clash with the baroque digital rhythms of Kosmas Apatangelos (Greece) and Ella Tjader (Lithuania). All are adopted along with the tactile fabrications of Borja Uriona (Spain) and Lys Wilcox (USA).

Widening of the doors of participation means newer exponents of fashion illustration are bringing their own personal baggage into the ever-expanding frame, fuelling a visual crossover culture.

California collage artist Christy McCaffrey comments that 'fashion is always going to be important to people. It is the most obvious expression of who you are. How are designers going to explain their vision without a drawing? It remains the most convincing explanation, showing the thought process behind the fashion. A photograph only reflects the end result, the reality'. Of her own distinctive approach, she adds: 'it is important to get the look of the clothing right because it can tell so much about a person. Whether a goth or a jock you have a sort of uniform that explains this. I have always tried to represent that in a believable way'.

During the 20th century, fashion illustrators endured a bumpy ride. Today they are fluent in an unorthodox language that, while encouraging a radical re-think, is fully aware of its rich aesthetic lineage. For Barcelona illustrator Oscar Gimenez, 'fashion has changed a lot. Nowadays it covers a variety of trends. Fashion illustration has evolved from a close-to-reality representation to now capturing the essence of our time in a variety of styles'.

The niche bubble that often pigeon-holed last century's exponents of fashion illustration in their silver-service exclusivity zone, and nearly forced its extinction, has been exploded, exploited and reinvented for this new generation. Claudio Parentela (Italy) subverts the prototype with caricatured illustrations in total contrast to the Art Nouveau outlines from Wai (Japan) – both equally individual and valid treatments of the form.

Now there is an inspirational freedom of expression that challenges each and every illustrator to roll the dice and, by rising to the challenge, push their work to the limit. Tokyo-born illustrator Yuko Shimizu affirms from his New York studio, that the 'possibilities are limitless. The only limit is that of our imagination and creativity'. A view supported by Russian artist Sonya Suhariyan; 'It is now possible to draw everything – illustration gives free rein to your imagination'.

Formal recognition has improved with wide-reaching exhibitions acknowledging their output alongside that of more mainstream artists. As part of the Amsterdam International Fashion Week 2006, 48 illustrators were presented in *How Do You Do? Deconstructing Illustration*. Across the world at the Alliance Francaise in Bangalore, there was *Traits Très Mode*, an exhibition featuring contemporary French fashion illustration. Solo retrospectives are on the increase. London played host to the dramatic illustrations of David Downton (*Couture Voyeur*) while in Hamburg, the pop-inspired graphic illustrator Jasper Goodall, blazed in his own five-year retrospective (*God of Illustration*).

As 'fast fashion' became the drip feed for today's consumer fashion victim, technological advances have given illustrators access to a fashion awareness that speaks a different language from two decades ago. 'Catwalks' are no longer restricted to salons in Paris and Milan – video streaming the latest pop icon can have more direct impact on contemporary style.

Australian fashion designer and illustrator John Prikryl admits that historically 'illustrating within the fashion industry was generic across the board. Technological advances have changed the meaning of the term 'fashion illustration'. Technology has opened doors to entirely new worlds of illustration that allows each creator more freedom in media, methods, and so on. The difference is that almost anything can be considered 'fashion illustration' these days'.

In *The Big Book of Fashion Illustration*, illustrators are fully in tune with this new frequency and articulate their reactions in directions that are exciting and innovative. While some remain exponents of traditional media, others epitomise the PlayStation generation that encountered digital technology at their mother's knee. 'The arrival of computers has had a massive impact', acknowledges UK artist Claire Baker. 'It has allowed illustration to evolve', while Korean illustrator Woonyoung Chang adds that although computers can 'make everything easier, you still have to know how to use your hand. The computer is only a tool like your pen or brush'.

Streetwise Filipino illustrator Jason Jaring maintains 'technology affects everything – commerce, politics, art. Fashion illustrators always want to try out new media. There are things you can do with digital media that you can't do with traditional illustration, but ultimately, software programs are just another medium – they have limits. What is limitless is each artist's own creativity and imagination. The product is more important than the process. If you do it with computer software – great. If you can do it with a pen and paper – cool'.

Increasingly there are illustrators operating like scratch DJs, mixing and sampling everything that comes within their skill arena, whether it be time-honored analog or new-age digital. Boundaries continue to be blurred. Gimenez also acknowledges that 'previously, an illustrator was somebody who could draw. Nowadays many other artists, with skills ranging from photography to graffiti, can produce amazing illustrations. It has broadened the number of resources for the rest of us'.

Be it the spontaneous gesture of graphite hitting paper or a virtual layering of pixels, the challenge is to stretch the envelope in ever-increasing personal and individual reworkings. Their work continues to register as an allegory of contemporary lifestyle.

The Big Book of Fashion Illustration is laid out like a worldwide directory of style, championing a unique assembly of over 250 international artists and illustrators whose loyalties and experience lie within fashion, but no longer feel happy with their 'fashion illustrator' label. They deem it is too limiting a nomenclature – looking over their shoulders rather than to the future. Is the term 'fashion illustration' now passed its own sell-by date? – most prefer to shelter in the inclusive umbrella of 'fashion artist'.

Whatever their eventual classification, I owe a huge debt of gratitude to these featured artists, who were so gracious with their time and generous with their artwork – this book stands testament to their outstanding talent.

Martin Dawber

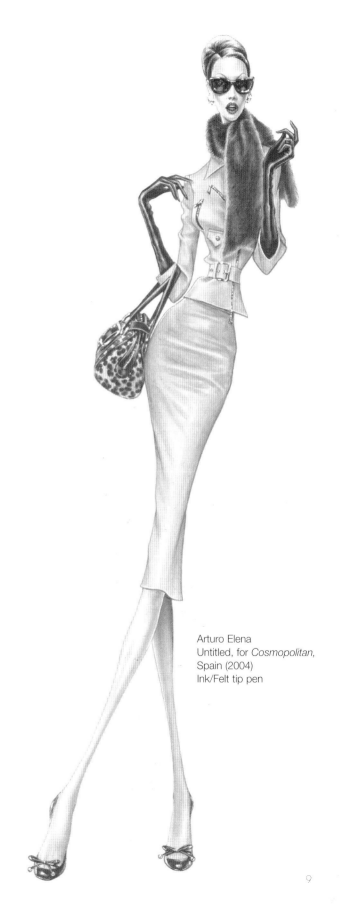

Arturo Elena
Untitled, for *Cosmopolitan*,
Spain (2004)
Ink/Felt tip pen

9

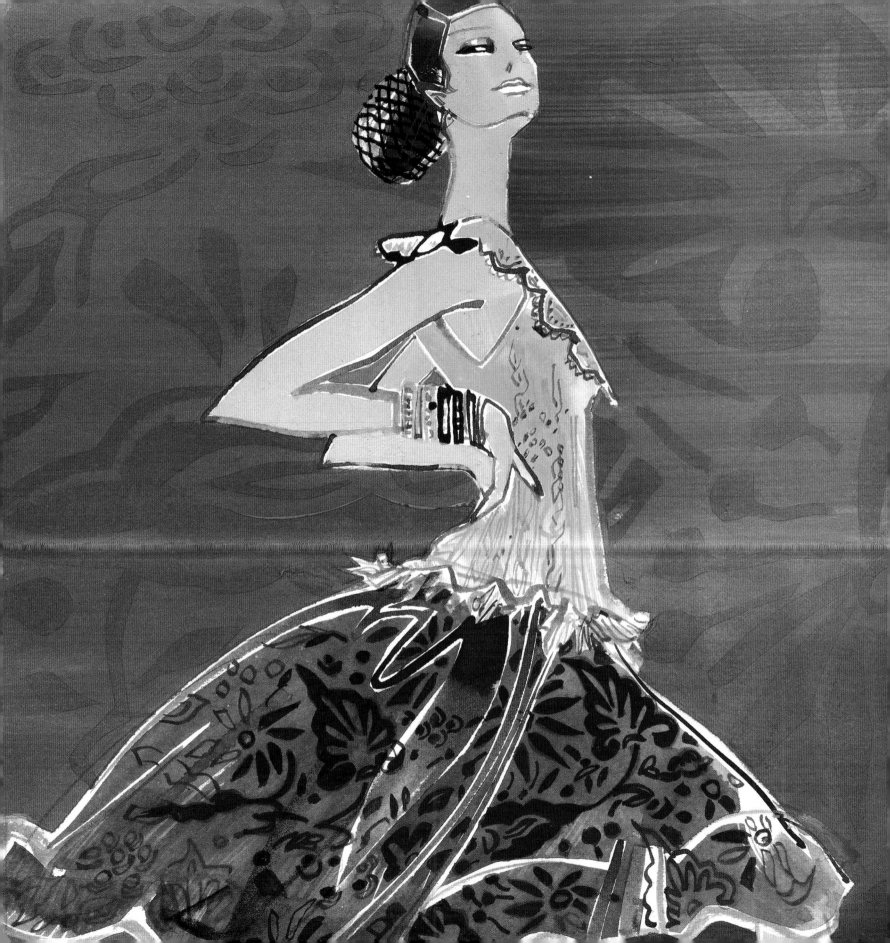

Womenswear

separates knit coats & jackets

eveningwear couture bridal lingerie

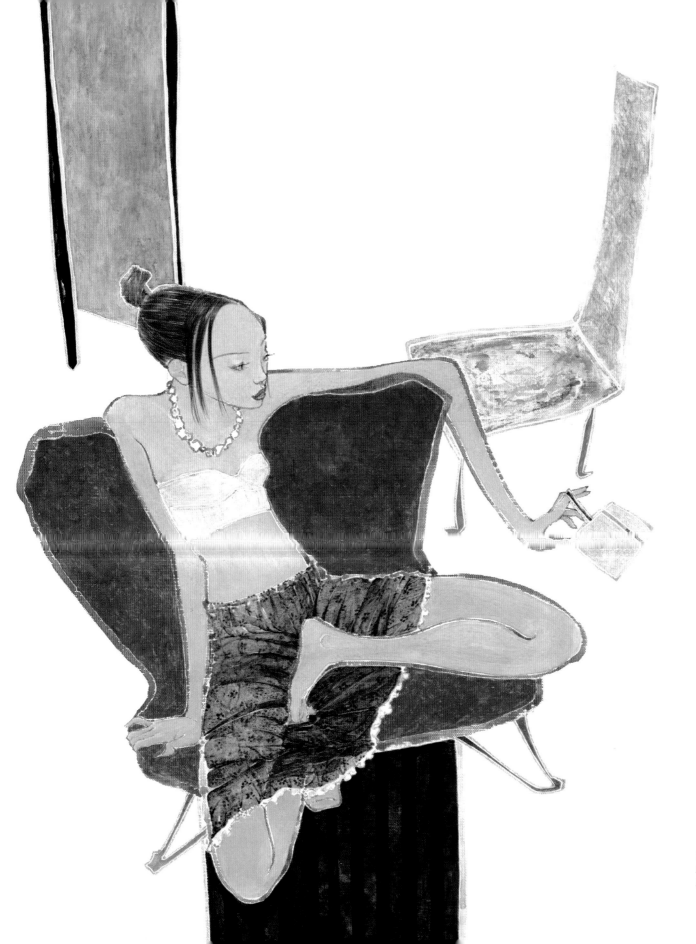

Hayato Jome
A Small Bag (2003)
Acrylic on paper

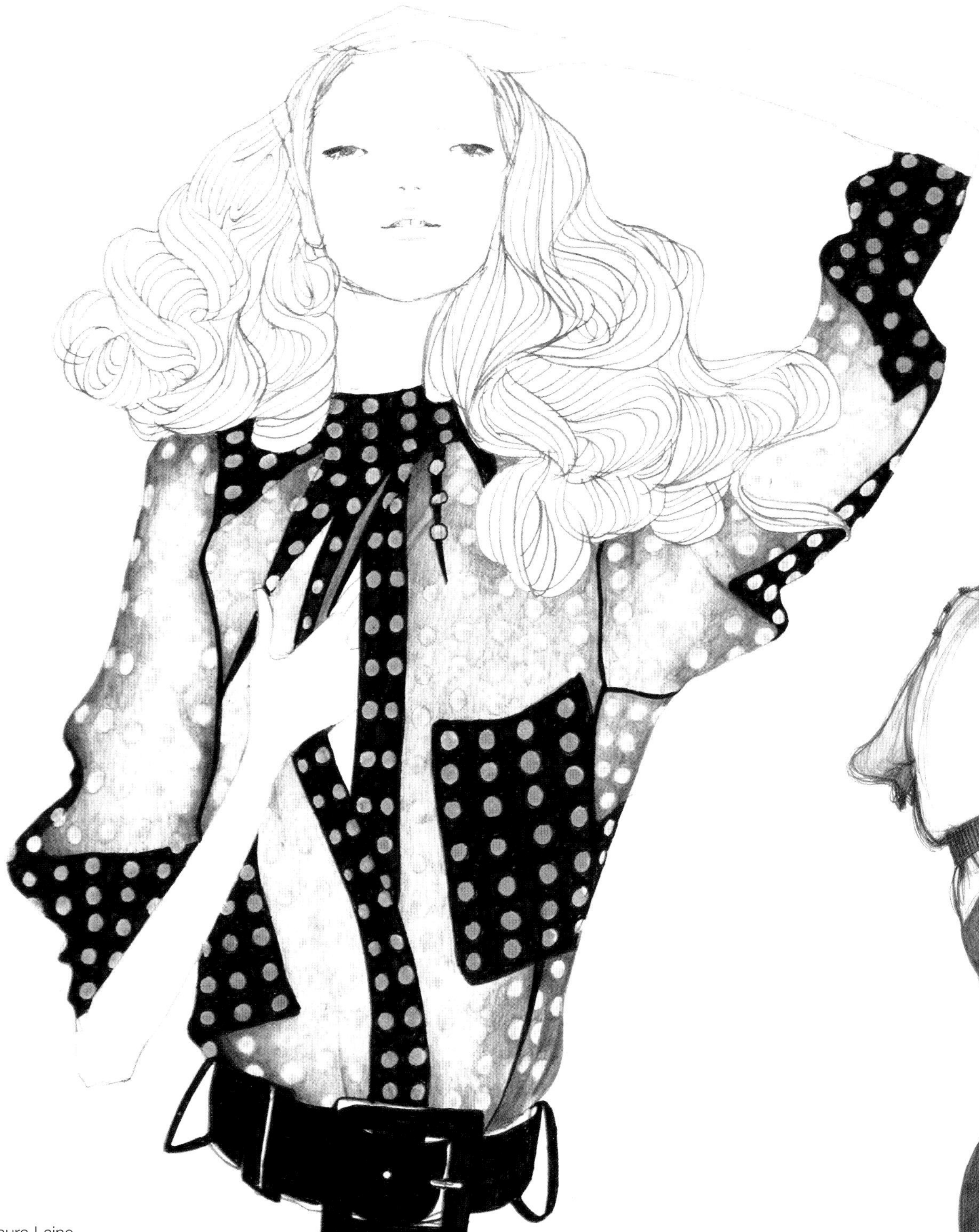

Laura Laine
Girl with Blouse (2005)
Pencil/Marker pen

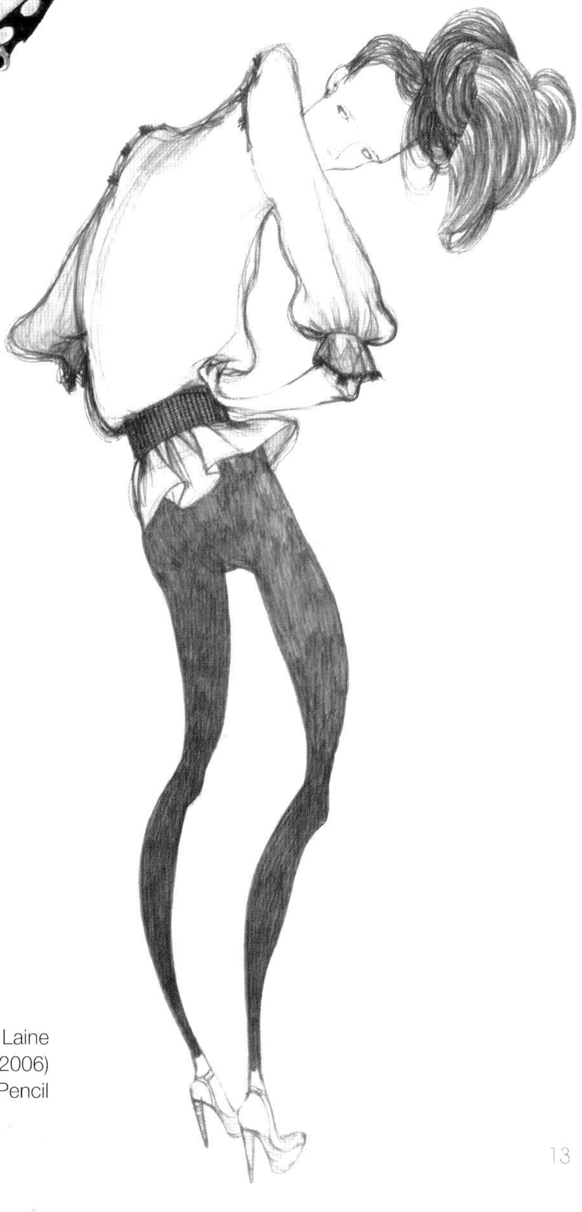

Laura Laine
Untitled (2006)
Pencil

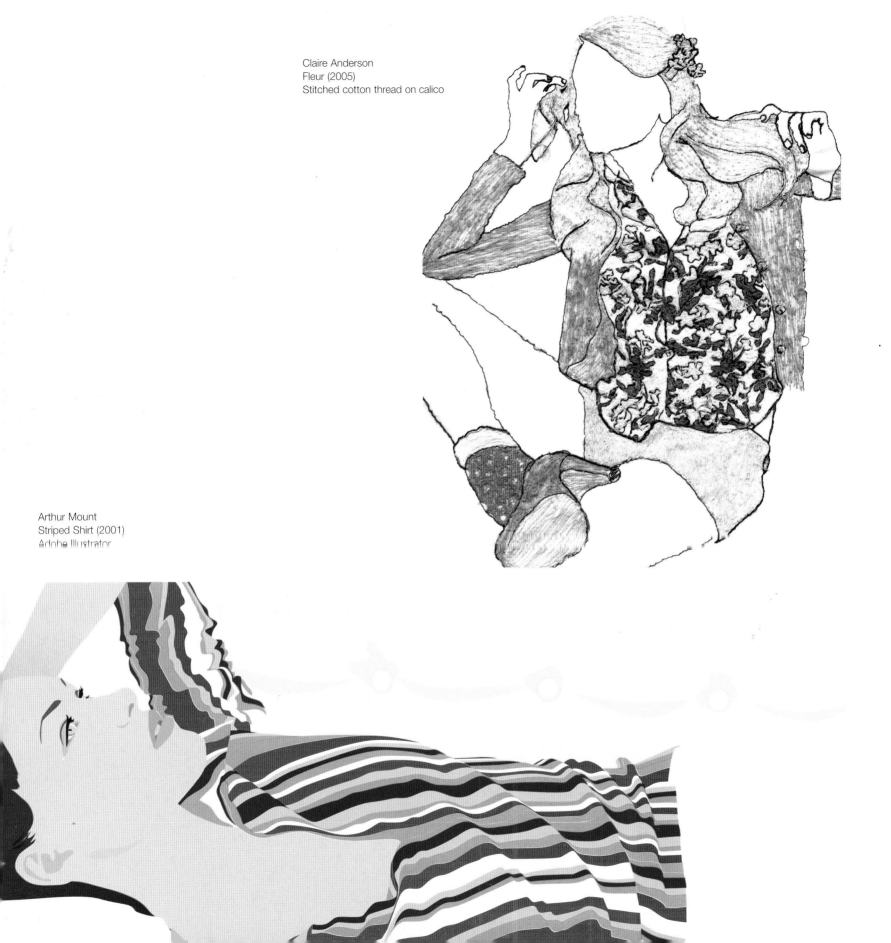

Claire Anderson
Fleur (2005)
Stitched cotton thread on calico

Arthur Mount
Striped Shirt (2001)
Adobe Illustrator

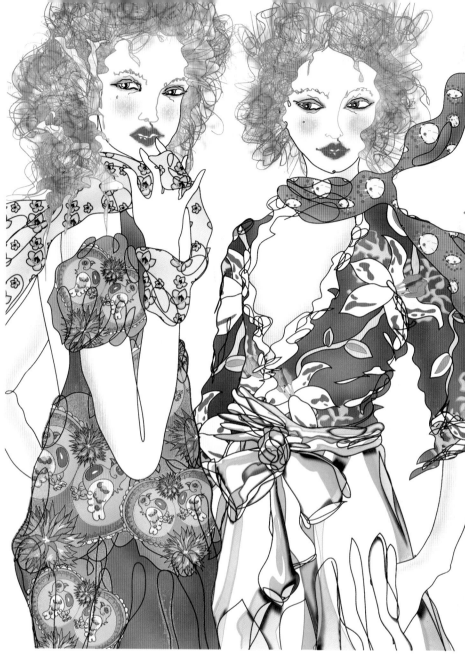

Ella Tjader
Patterns Craze (2005)
Adobe Illustrator/Adobe Photoshop

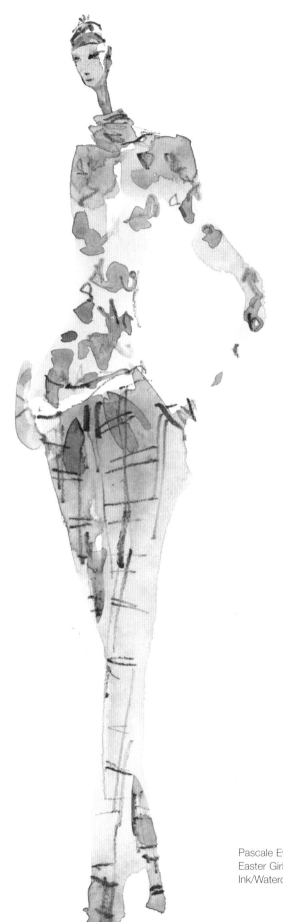

Pascale Evrard
Easter Girl (2006)
Ink/Watercolour/Pencil/Adobe Photoshop

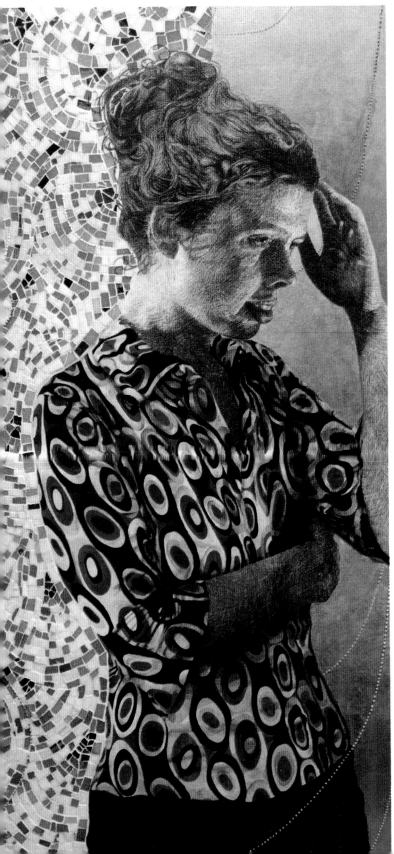

Michael Sibley
Kim (2002)
Oils, glass and gold on plywood

Claire Anderson
Anna and Annabelle (2005)
Stitched cotton thread on calico

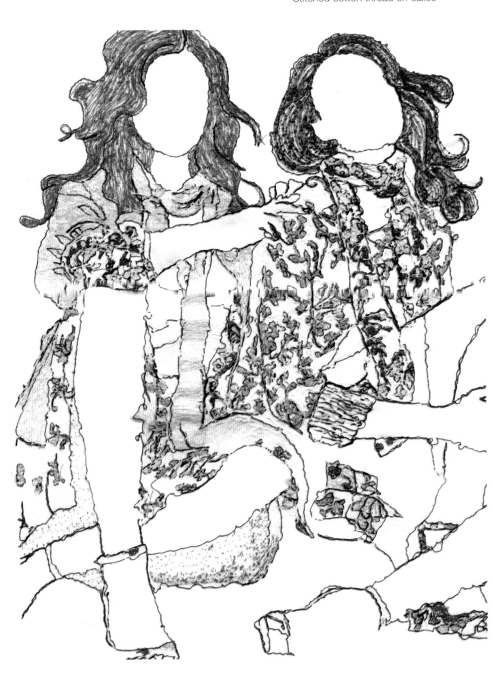

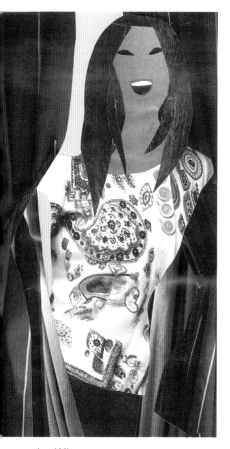

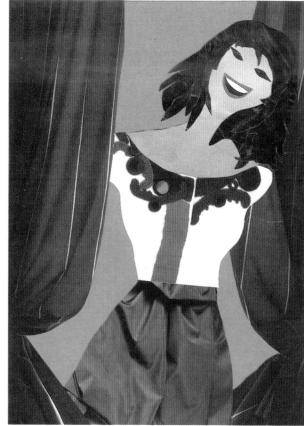

Lys Wilcox
Kimora (2004)
Collage/Cut paper

Lys Wilcox
Carol Ann (2004)
Collage/Cut paper

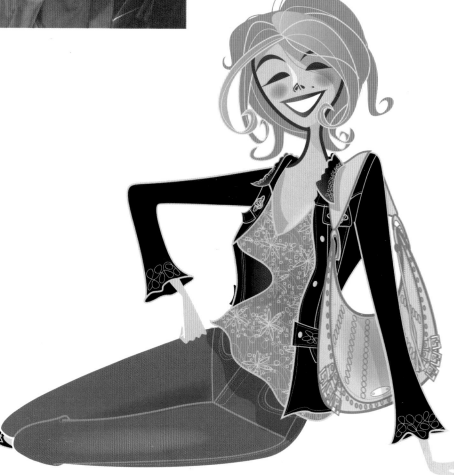

Jonas Bergstrand
Neiman Marcus Womenswear, New York (2005)
Adobe Illustrator/Adobe Photoshop

Nicoletta Mazzesi
Rising (2006)
Adobe Photoshop/Adobe Illustrator

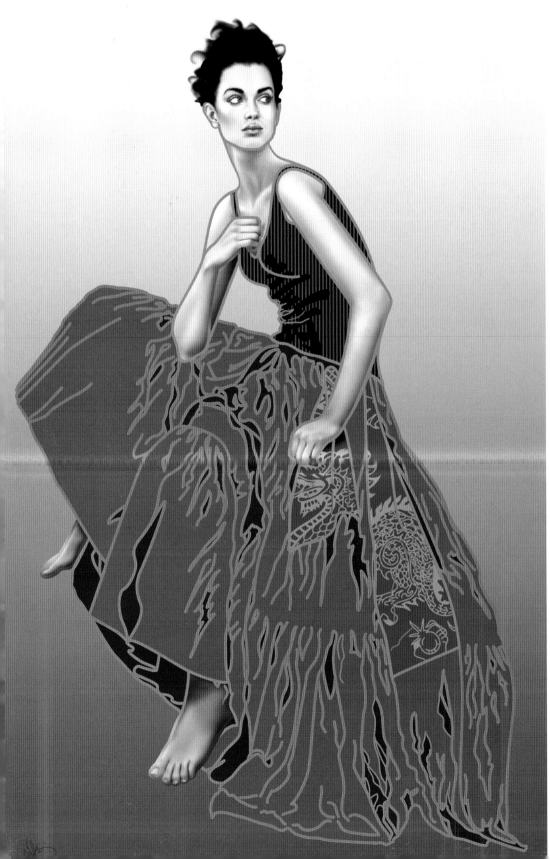

Cecilia Carlstedt
Nordiska Kompaniet (2006)
Pencil/Ink/Adobe Illustrator/
Adobe Photoshop

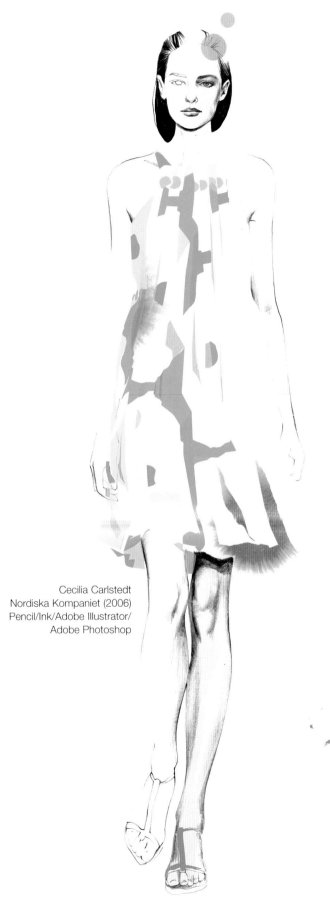

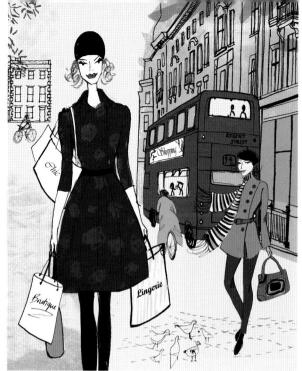

Samantha Wilson
London Shopping (2006)
Paint/Crayon/Ink/Collage/Adobe Photoshop

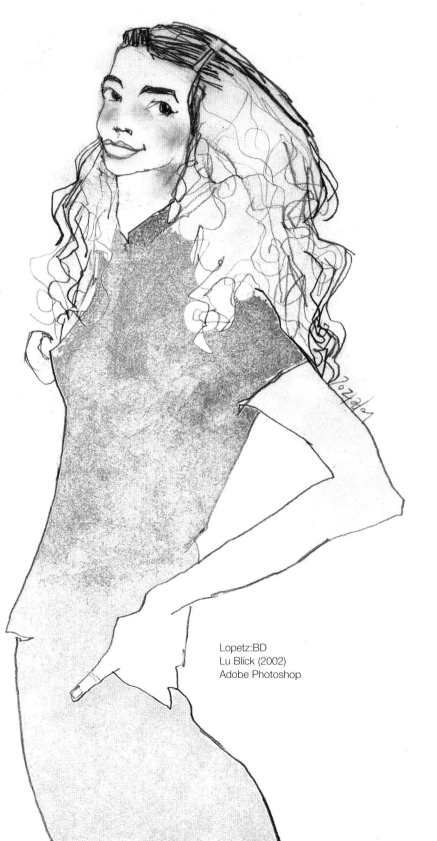

Lopetz:BD
Lu Blick (2002)
Adobe Photoshop

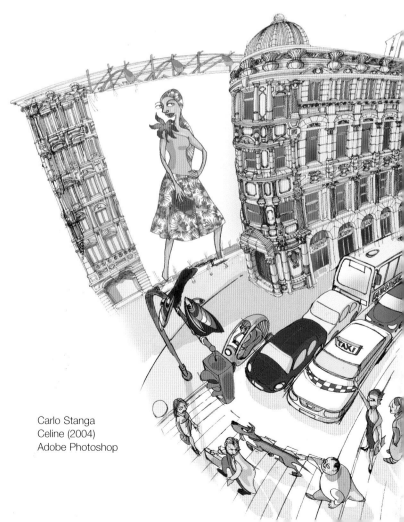

Carlo Stanga
Celine (2004)
Adobe Photoshop

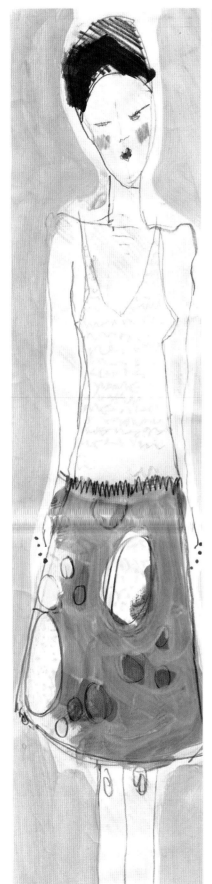

Emily Peach
Untitled (2004)
Paint/Pencil

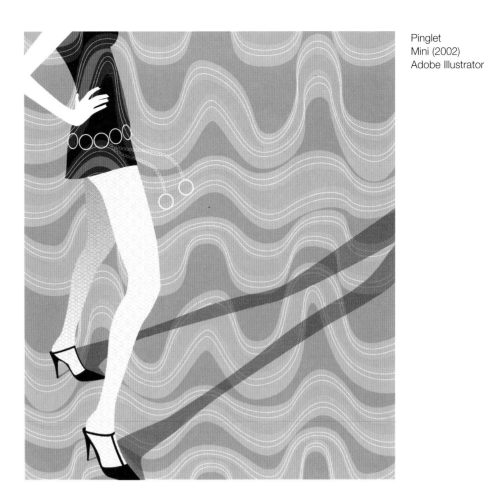

Pinglet
Mini (2002)
Adobe Illustrator

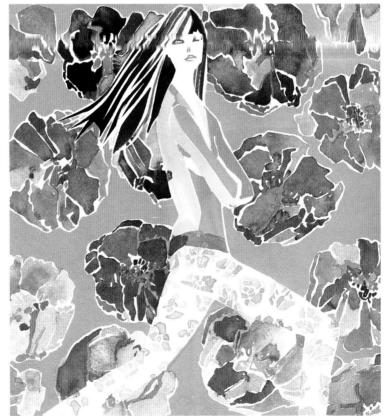

Bil Donovan
MAG Spring (2005)
Ink/Gouache

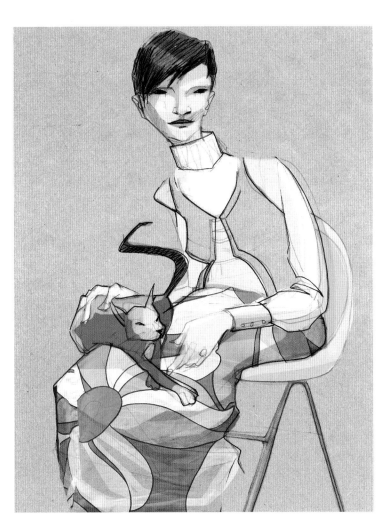

Alex Green
Bernice (2006)
Pencil/Paint/Pen/
Collage/Adobe Photoshop

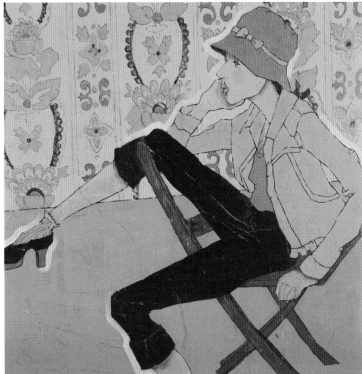

Anna Cangialosi
Waiting (2005)
Acrylic and tissue on wood

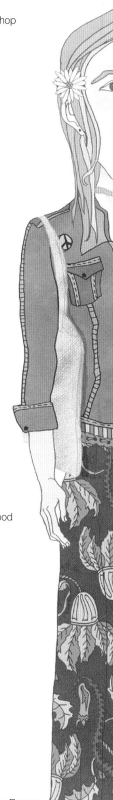

Kim Rosen
Earthy Student (2004)
Ink/Acrylic/Adobe Photoshop

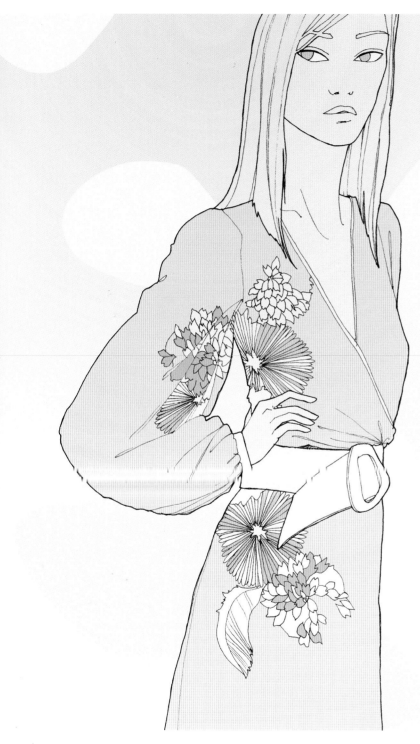

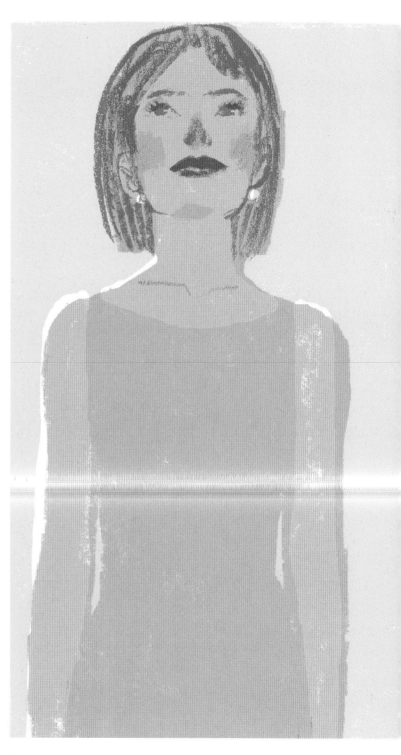

Erica Sharp
Floral Print (2005)
Adobe Photoshop/Adobe Illustrator

Tatsuro Kuichi
Untitled (2002)
Adobe Photoshop

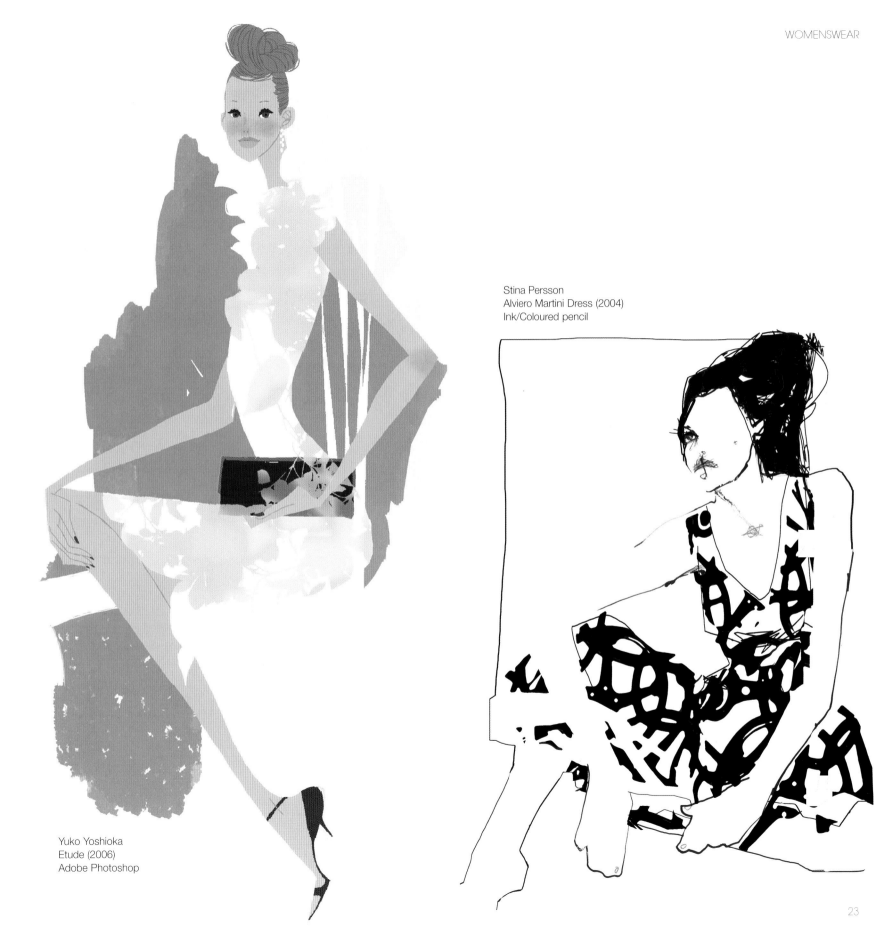

Stina Persson
Alviero Martini Dress (2004)
Ink/Coloured pencil

Yuko Yoshioka
Etude (2006)
Adobe Photoshop

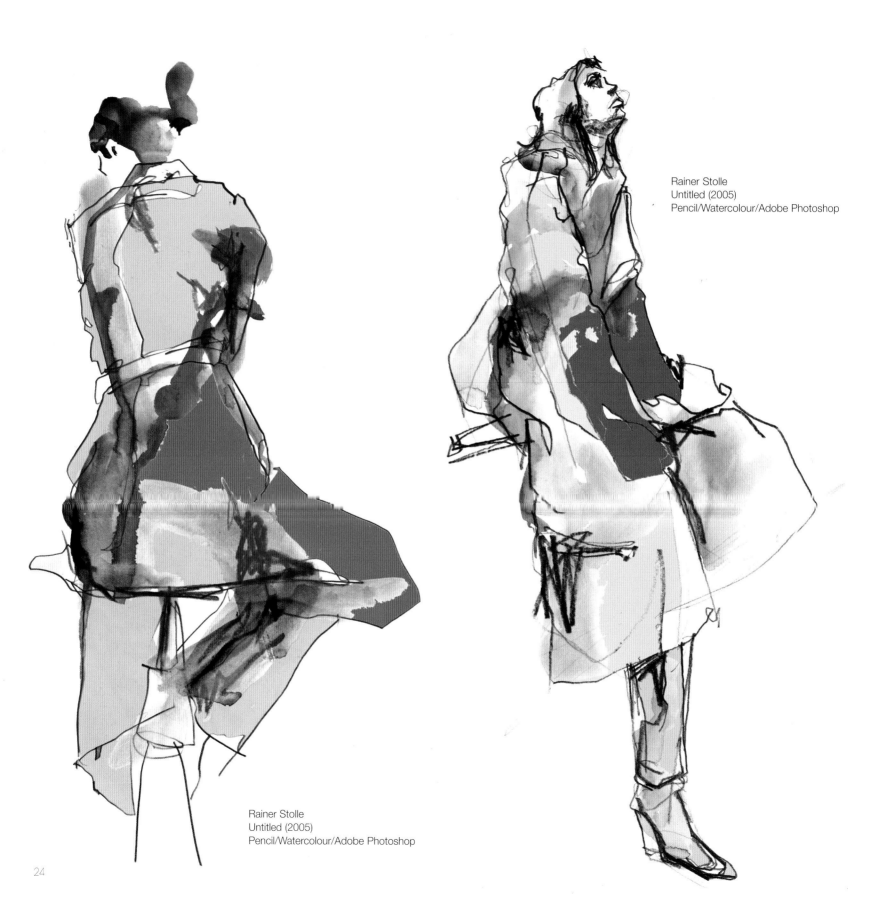

Rainer Stolle
Untitled (2005)
Pencil/Watercolour/Adobe Photoshop

Rainer Stolle
Untitled (2005)
Pencil/Watercolour/Adobe Photoshop

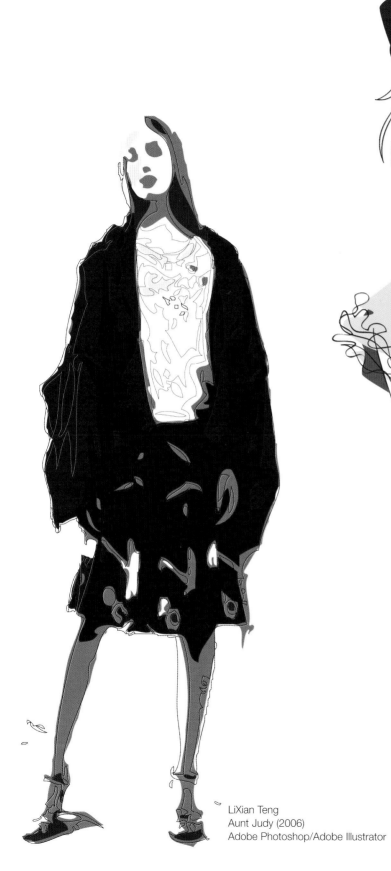

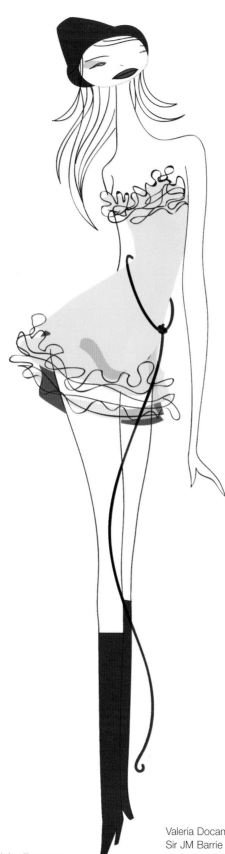

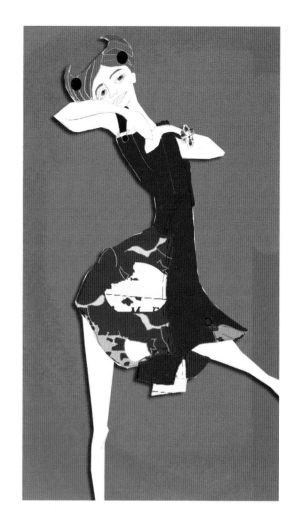

Anna Olivia Jeffcoat
Waste Not, Want Not (2005)
Pencil/Adobe Photoshop

LiXian Teng
Aunt Judy (2006)
Adobe Photoshop/Adobe Illustrator

Valeria Docampo
Sir JM Barrie Style (2005)
Adobe Illustrator

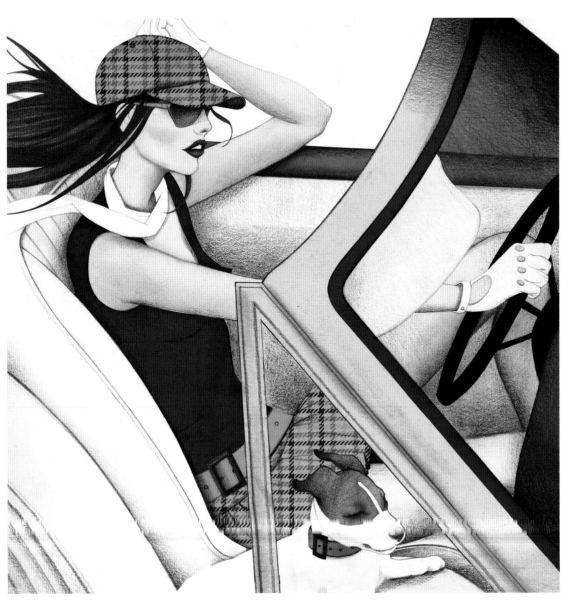

Menisha
Let's Drive! (2005)
Adobe Photoshop

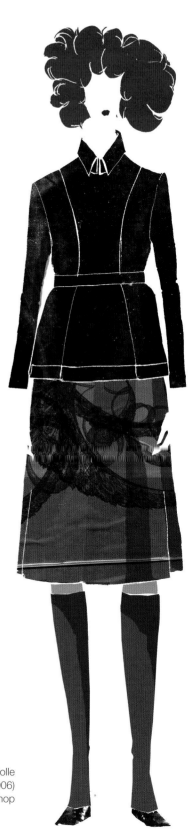

Rainer Stolle
Pressure-sensitive Skin (2006)
Pressure-sensitive tape/Rubber/Pencil/Adobe Photoshop

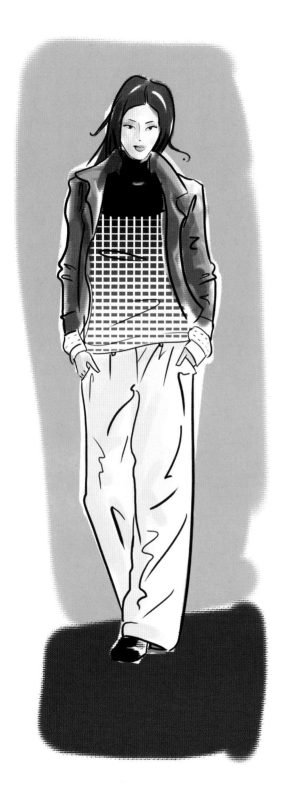

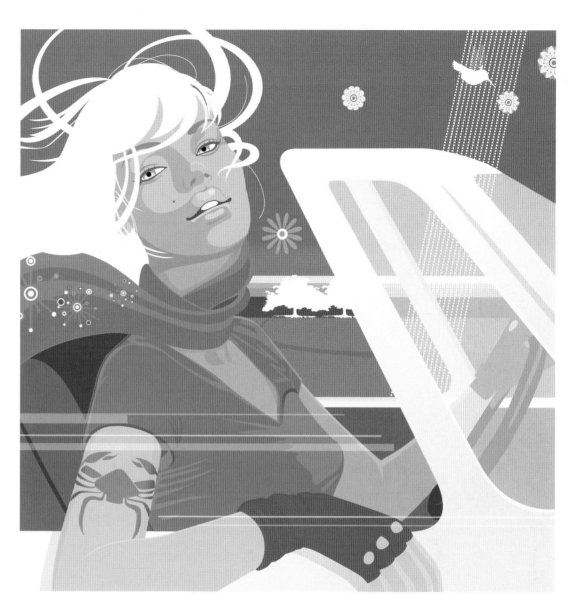

Irene Jacobs
Starsign Cancer (2004)
Adobe Illustrator

Astrid Mueller (Potatomammadesign)
Untitled (2006)
Corel Painter/Adobe Illustrator

27

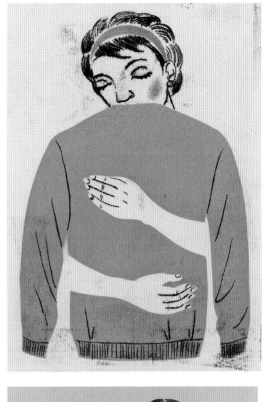

Edel Rodriguez
My Father's Sweater (2005)
Pastel and ink on paper

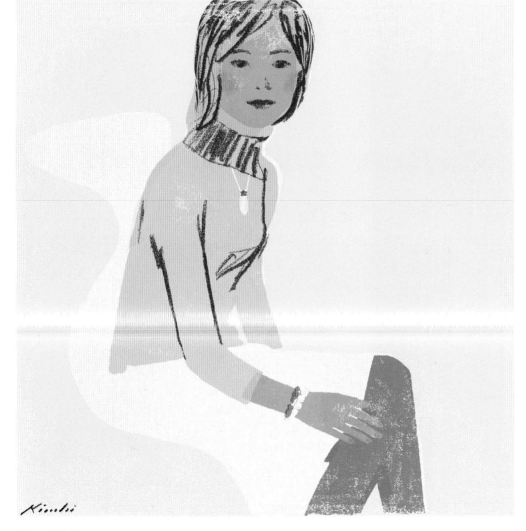

Tatsuro Kuichi
Untitled (2006)
Adobe Photoshop

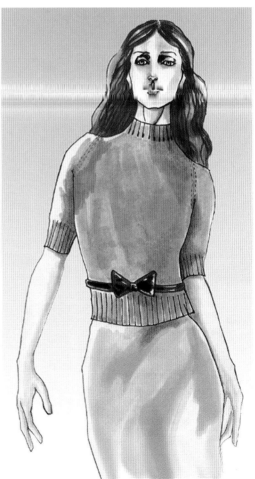

Raissa Gabriel
Scheme Walk (2005)
Ink/Marker pen

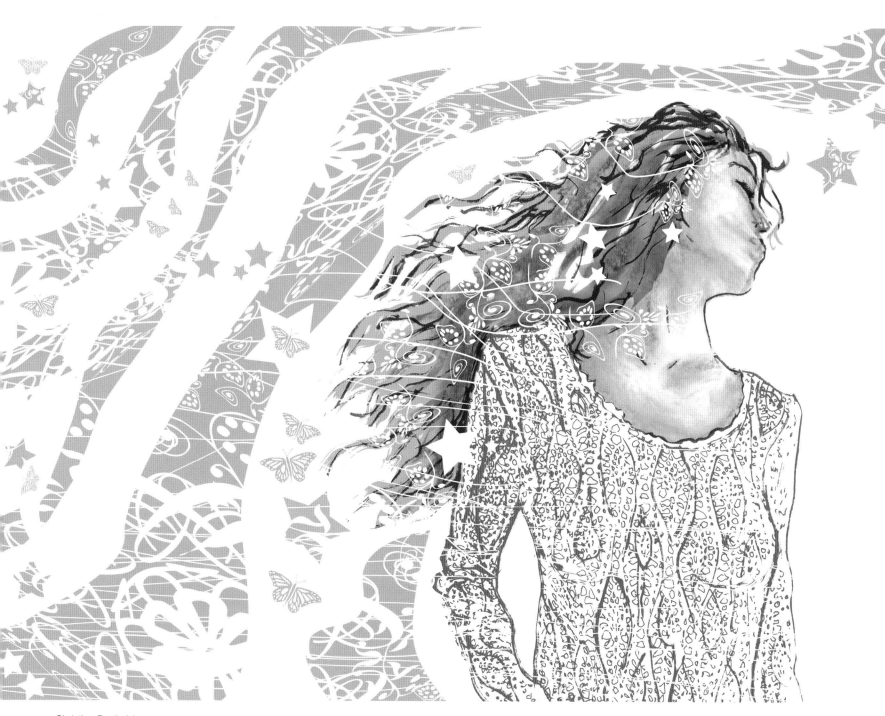

Christian Barthold
Summer Wind (2005)
India ink/Adobe Photoshop/Adobe Illustrator

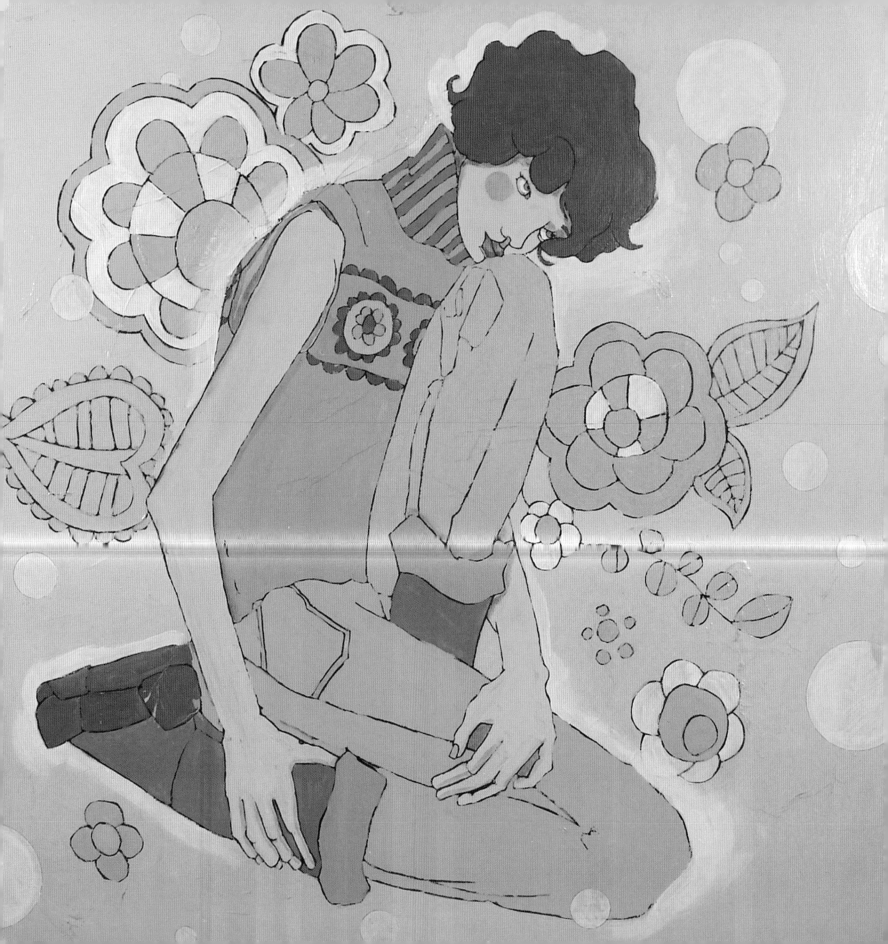

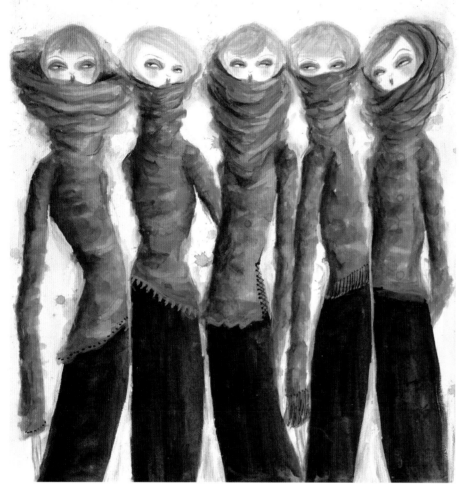

Bella Pilar
Turtles (2005)
Gouache

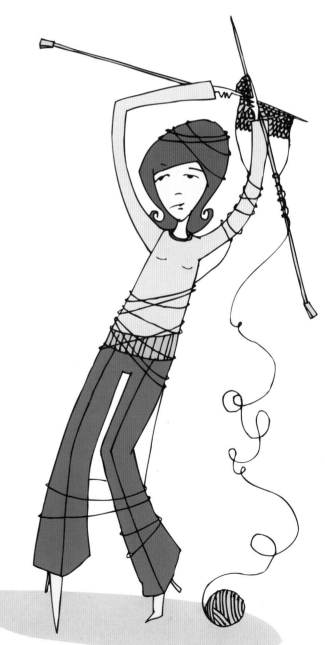

Anna Cangialosi
Portlandia (2006)
Acrylic and tissue on wood

Malena Gagliesi
Fussy Knitting, *Vogue Knitting*, NYC (2003)
Adobe Illustrator

Arturo Elena
Untitled, for *Mujer Hoy* (2005)
Ink/Felt tip pen

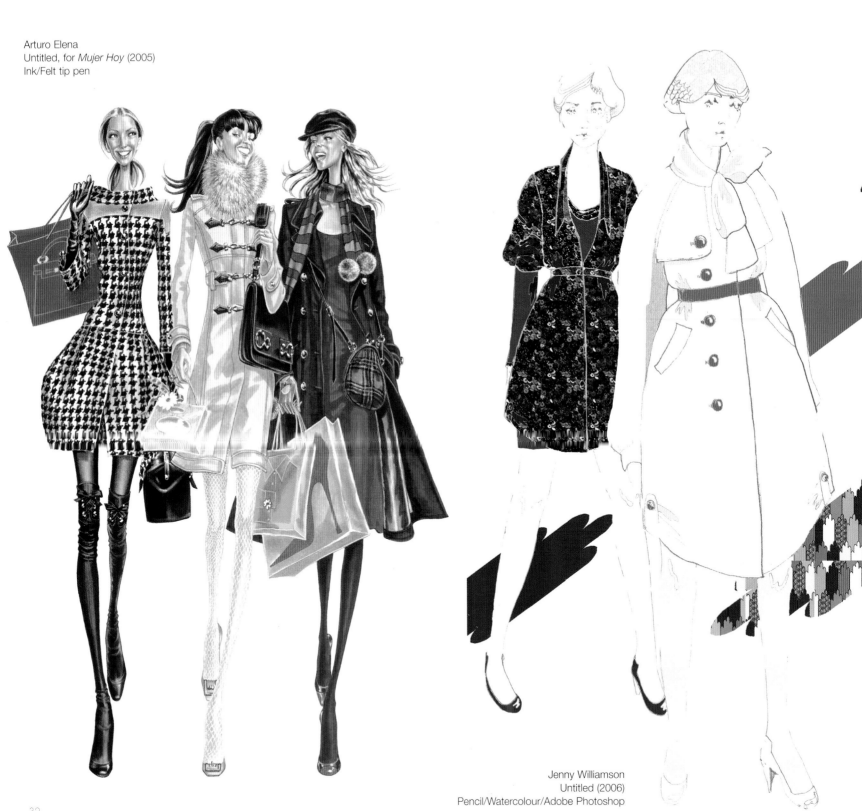

Jenny Williamson
Untitled (2006)
Pencil/Watercolour/Adobe Photoshop

Nicoletta Mazzesi
AVX (2005)
Ink/Adobe Photoshop

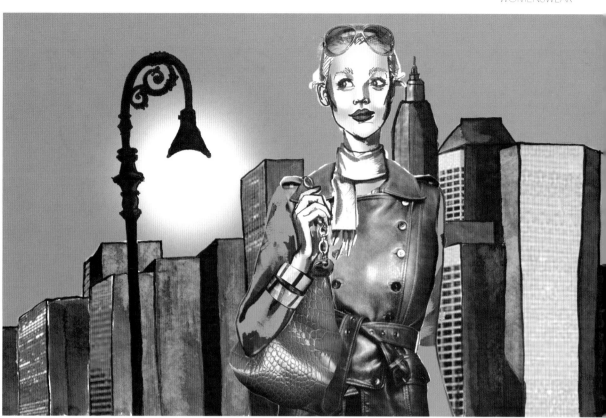

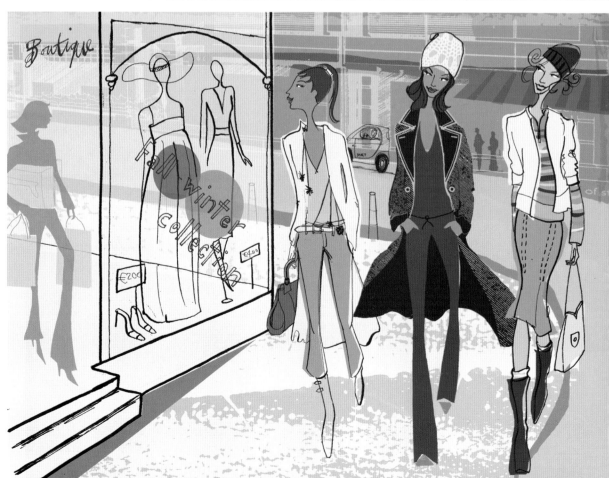

Sam Wilson
Eye Candy (2004)
Pen/Ink/Adobe Photoshop

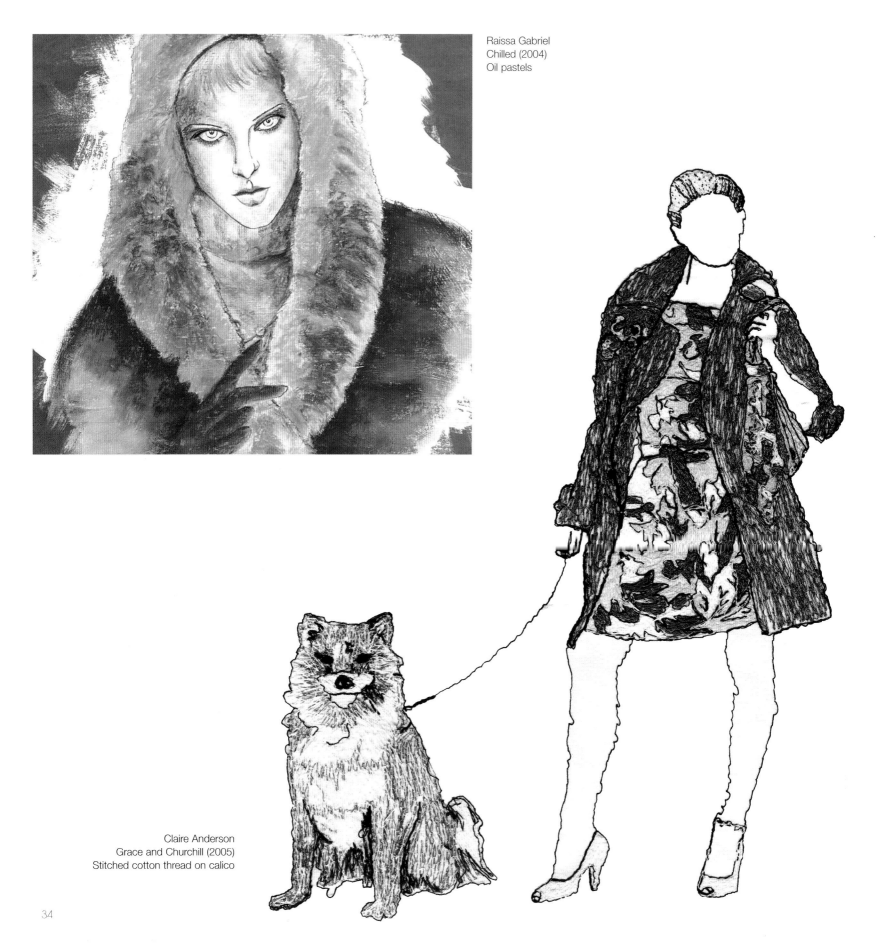

Raissa Gabriel
Chilled (2004)
Oil pastels

Claire Anderson
Grace and Churchill (2005)
Stitched cotton thread on calico

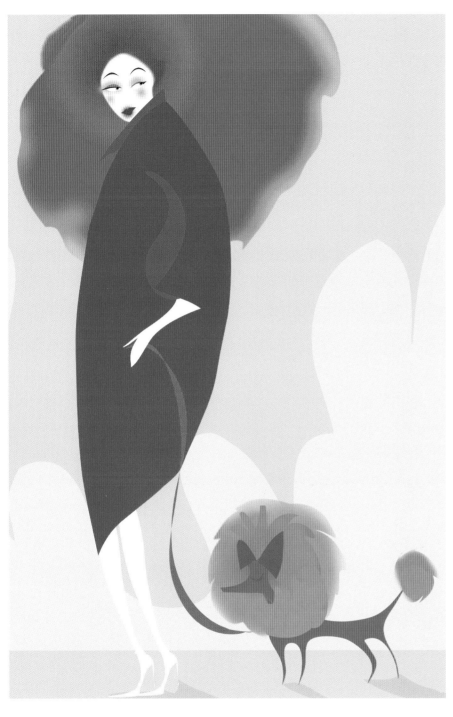

Eva Byrne
Aruba Fall Collection (2005)
Adobe Photoshop

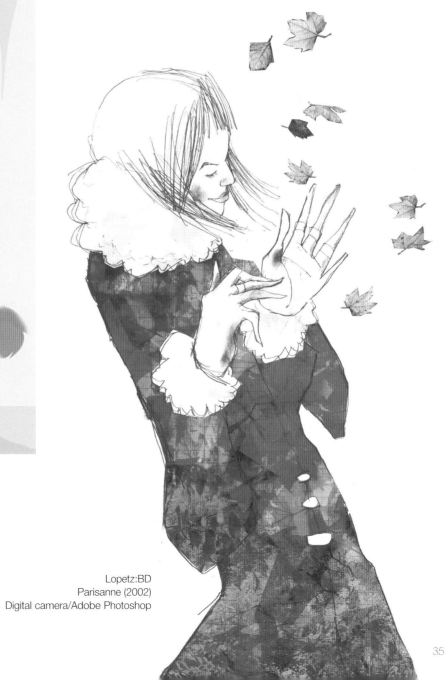

Lopetz:BD
Parisanne (2002)
Digital camera/Adobe Photoshop

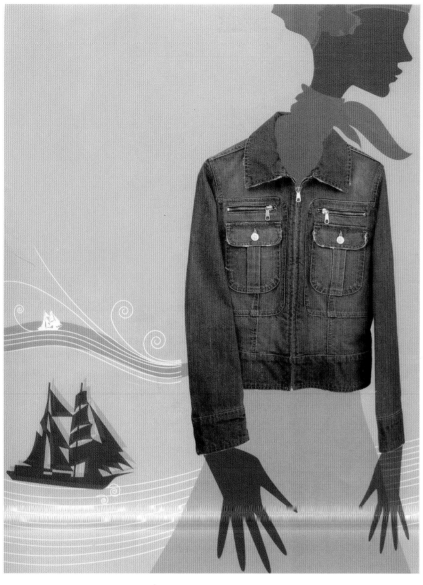

Lulu
Untitled (2003)
Adobe Photoshop/Adobe Illustrator

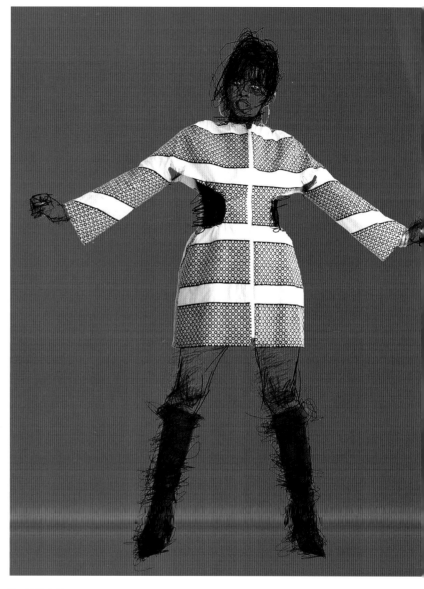

David Knight
Anna in Kente Double Coat by Vusi (2006)
Corel Draw

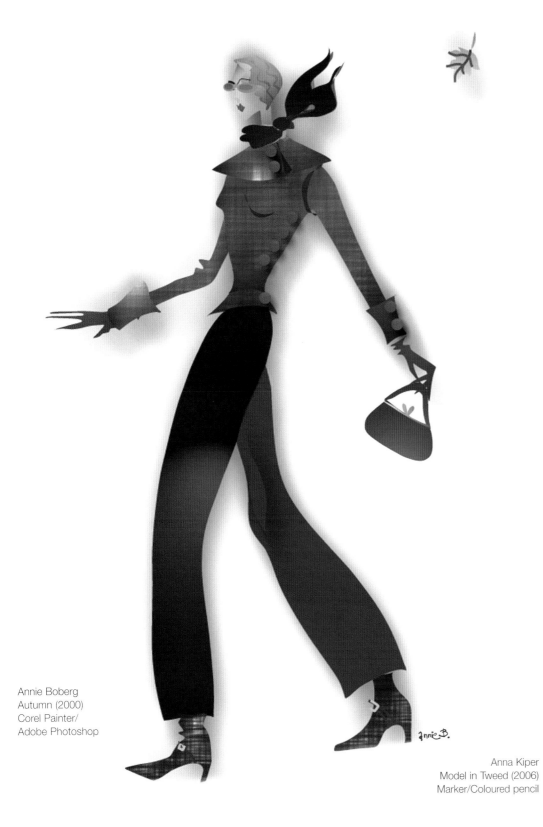

Annie Boberg
Autumn (2000)
Corel Painter/
Adobe Photoshop

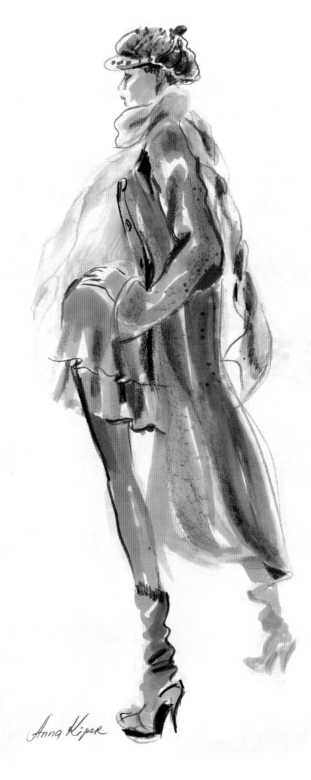

Anna Kiper
Model in Tweed (2006)
Marker/Coloured pencil

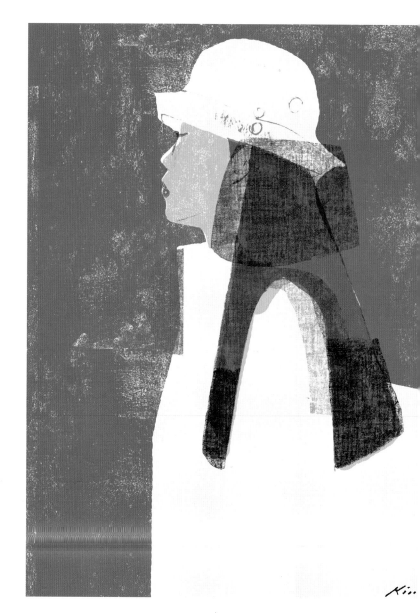

Tatsuro Kuichi
Untitled (2004)
Adobe Photoshop

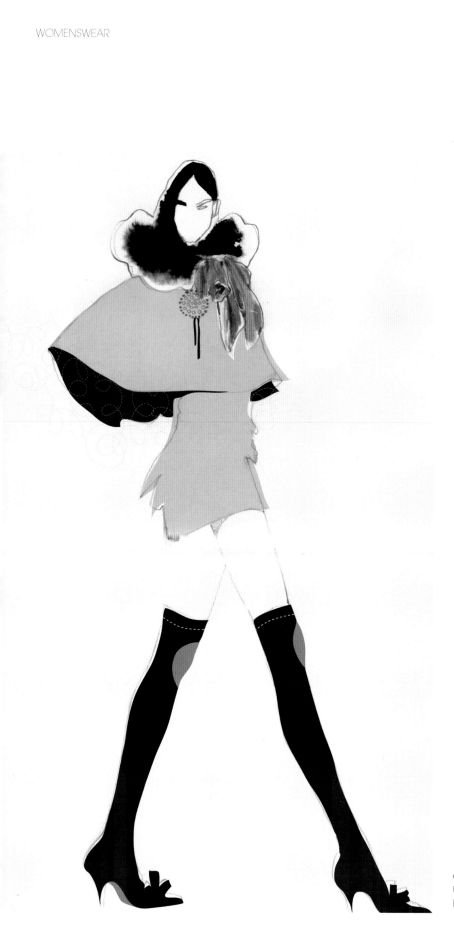

Cecilia Carlstedt
Untitled (2004)
Pencil/Adobe Illustrator

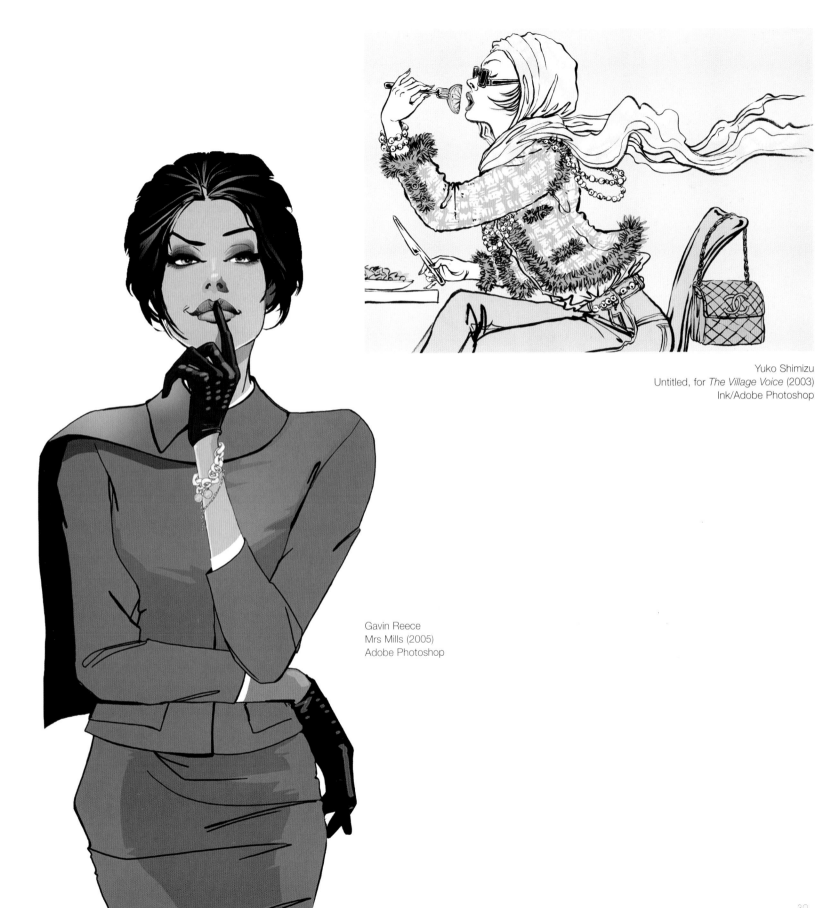

Yuko Shimizu
Untitled, for *The Village Voice* (2003)
Ink/Adobe Photoshop

Gavin Reece
Mrs Mills (2005)
Adobe Photoshop

39

Fhiona Galloway
Salvatore (2006)
Macromedia FreeHand

Andrea Byrne
Cordelia's Corsage (2004)
Watercolour/Ink on paper

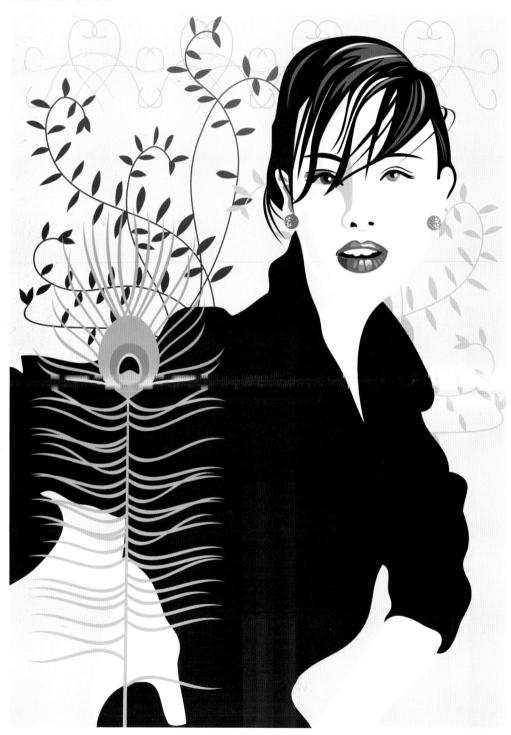

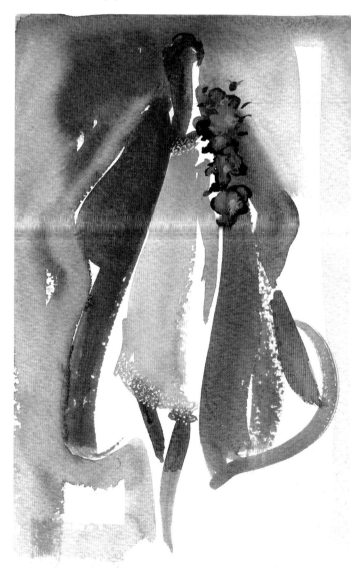

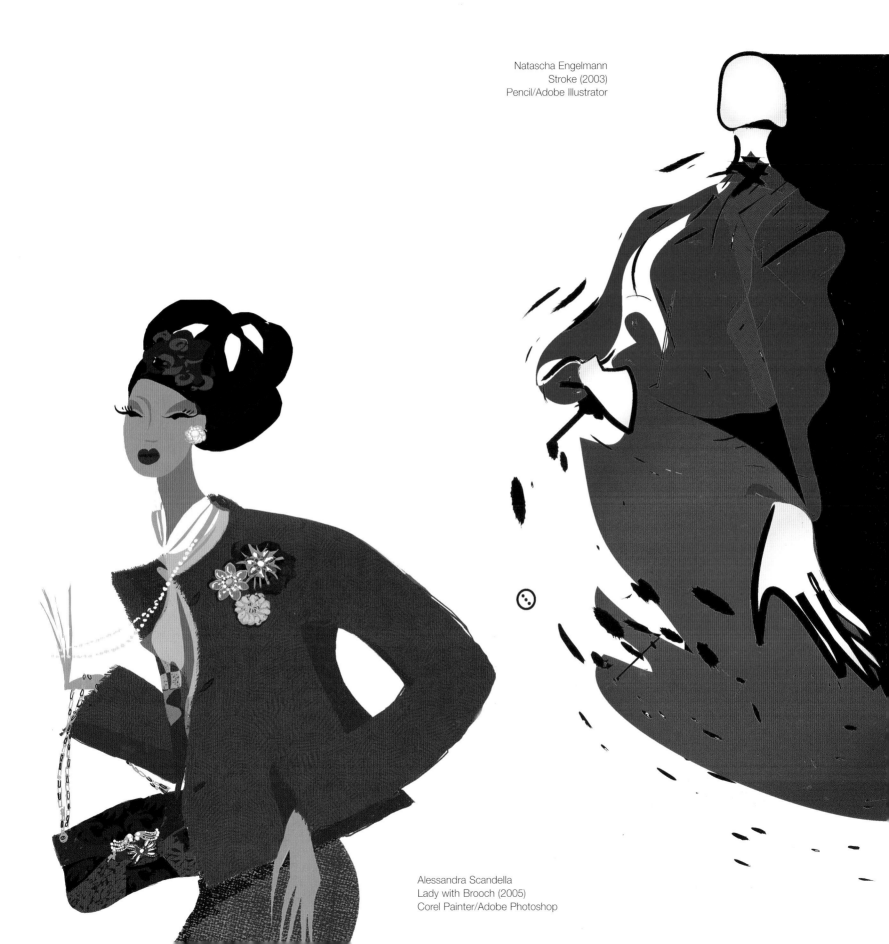

Natascha Engelmann
Stroke (2003)
Pencil/Adobe Illustrator

Alessandra Scandella
Lady with Brooch (2005)
Corel Painter/Adobe Photoshop

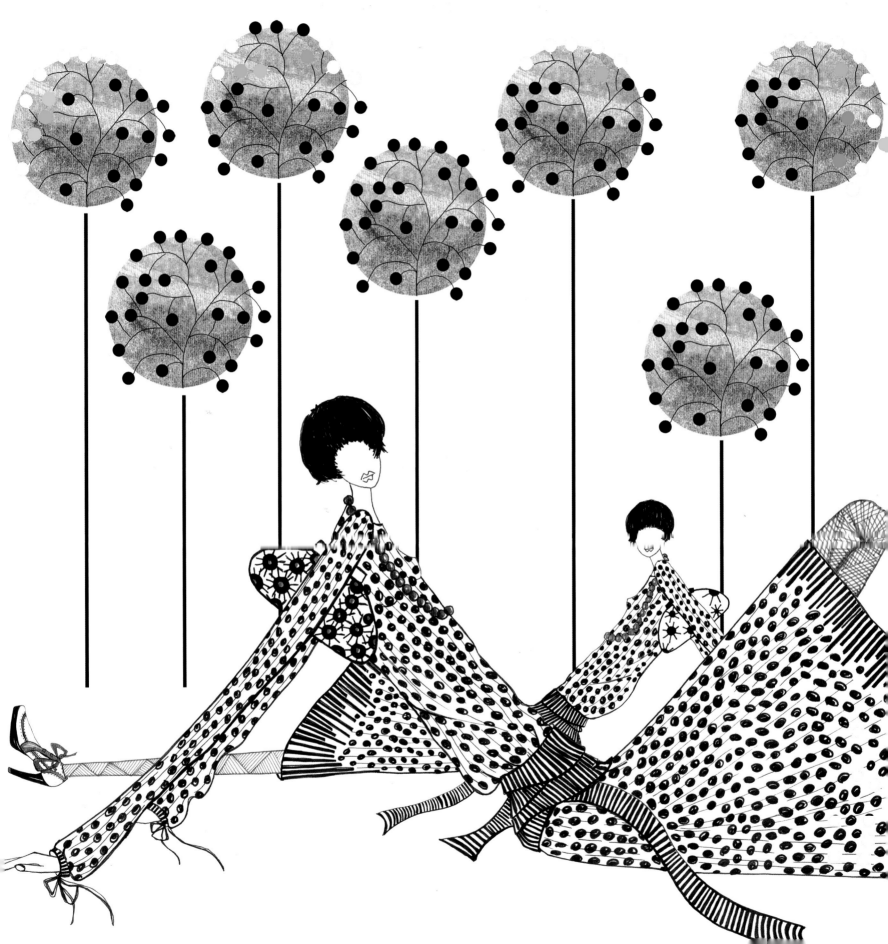

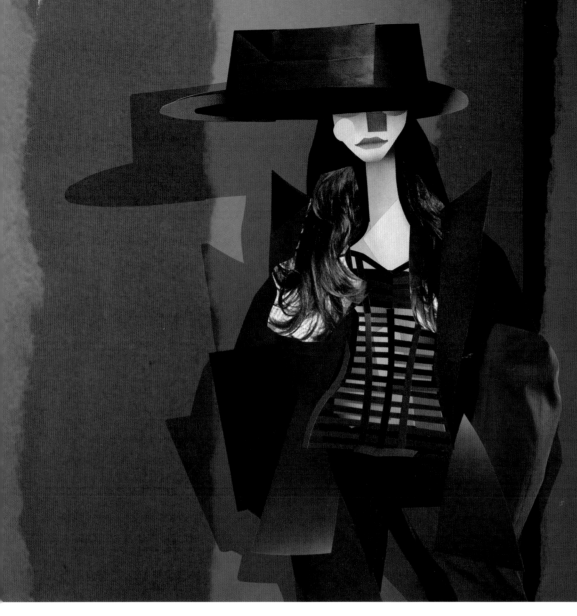

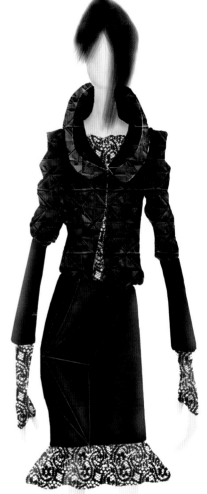

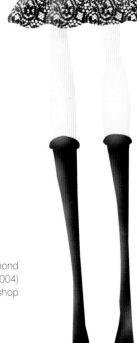

Terence Lawlor
Yamamoto, Fall 2006 (2006)
Collage

Prot Srimekhanond
Untitled (2004)
Adobe Photoshop

Kerstin Wacker
Forest (2006)
Pen/Watercolour/Adobe Photoshop

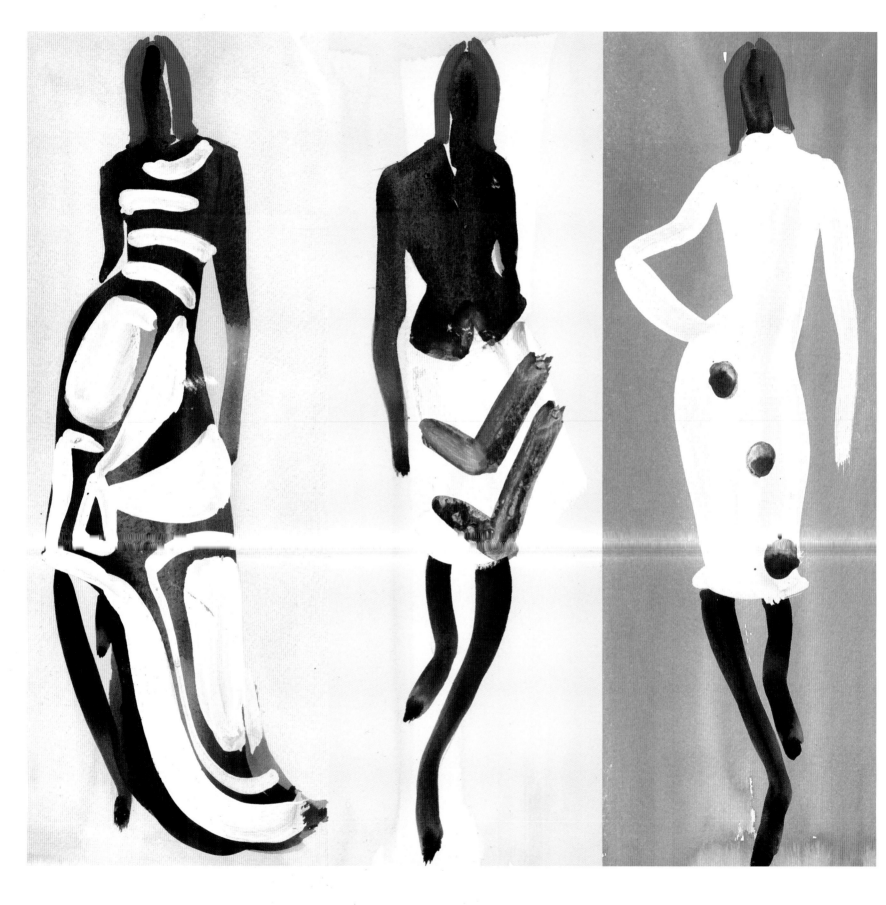

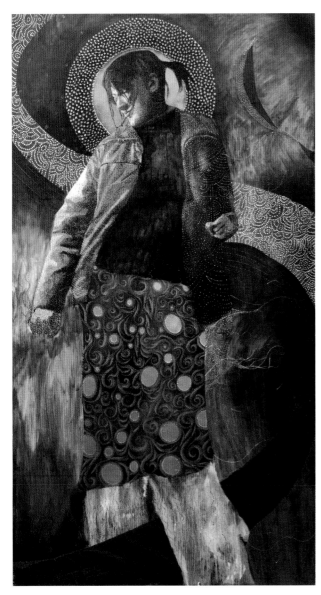

Michael Sibley
Emma (2002)
Oils, acrylic and fabric on canvas

Andrea Byrne
Trinity (2003)
Watercolour/Ink on paper

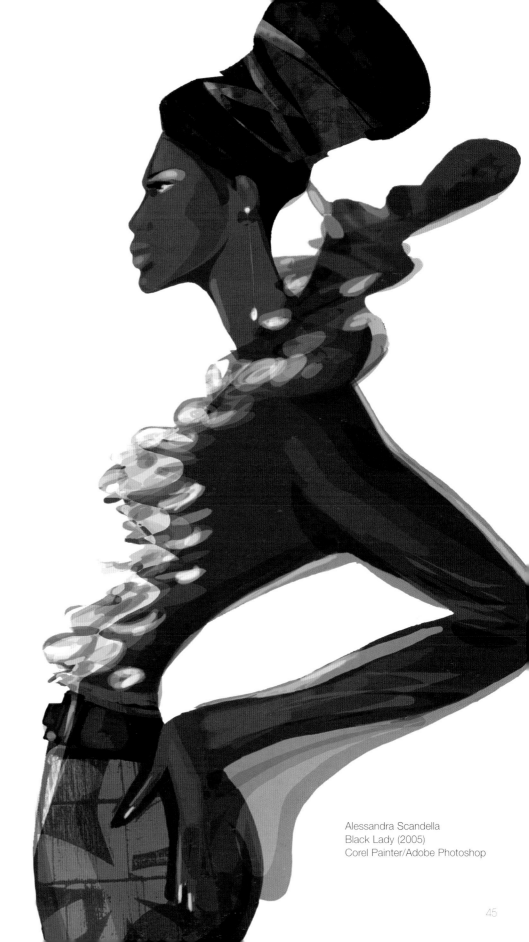

Alessandra Scandella
Black Lady (2005)
Corel Painter/Adobe Photoshop

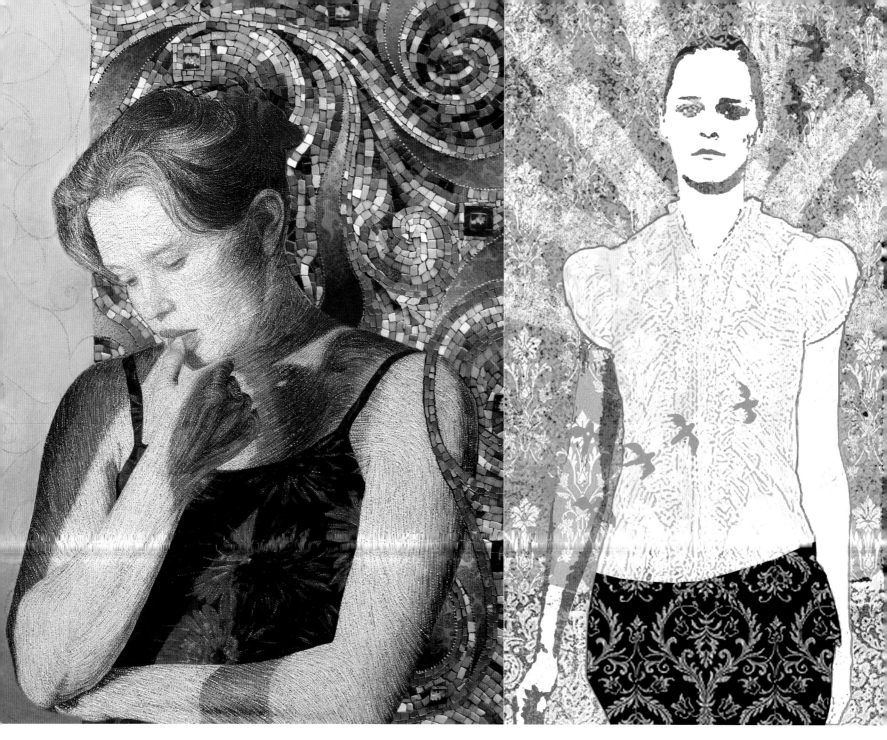

Michael Sibley
Jo (2004)
Oils, glass and gold on plywood

Genevieve Kelly
Morning Sunrise (2005)
Pencil/Collage/Photograph/Adobe Photoshop

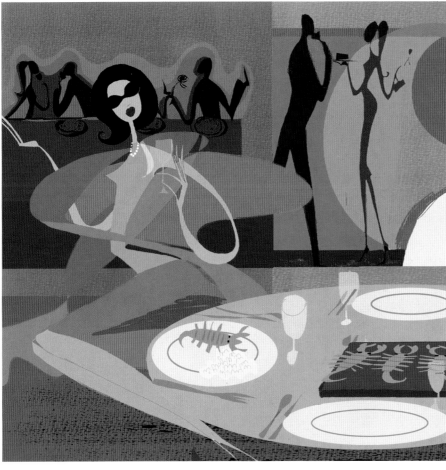

Alessandra Scandella
San Pellegrino (2005)
Corel Painter/Adobe Photoshop

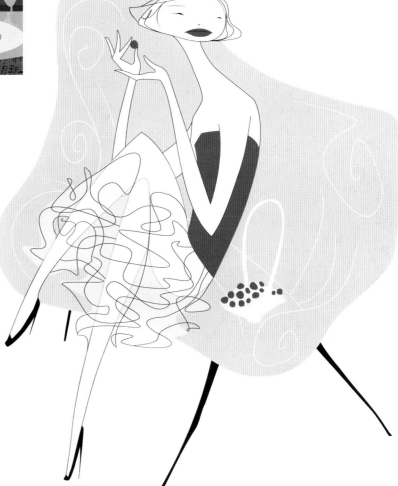

Valeria Docampo
The Taste of Cherries (2005)
Adobe Illustrator

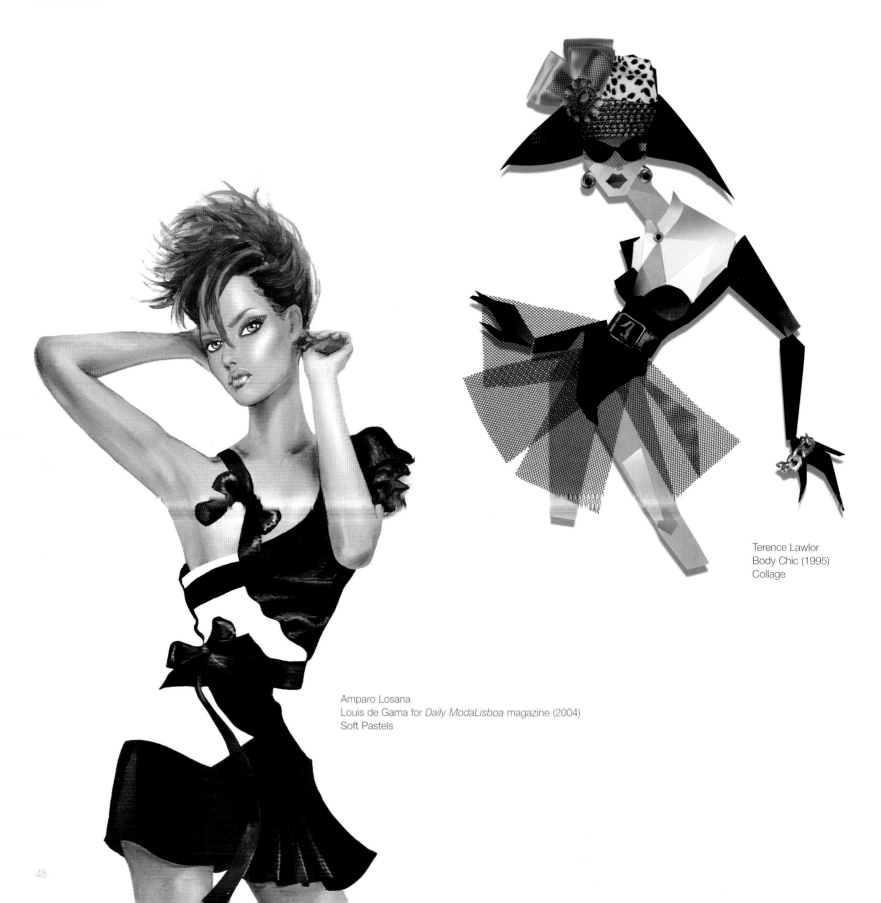

Terence Lawlor
Body Chic (1995)
Collage

Amparo Losana
Louis de Gama for *Daily ModaLisboa* magazine (2004)
Soft Pastels

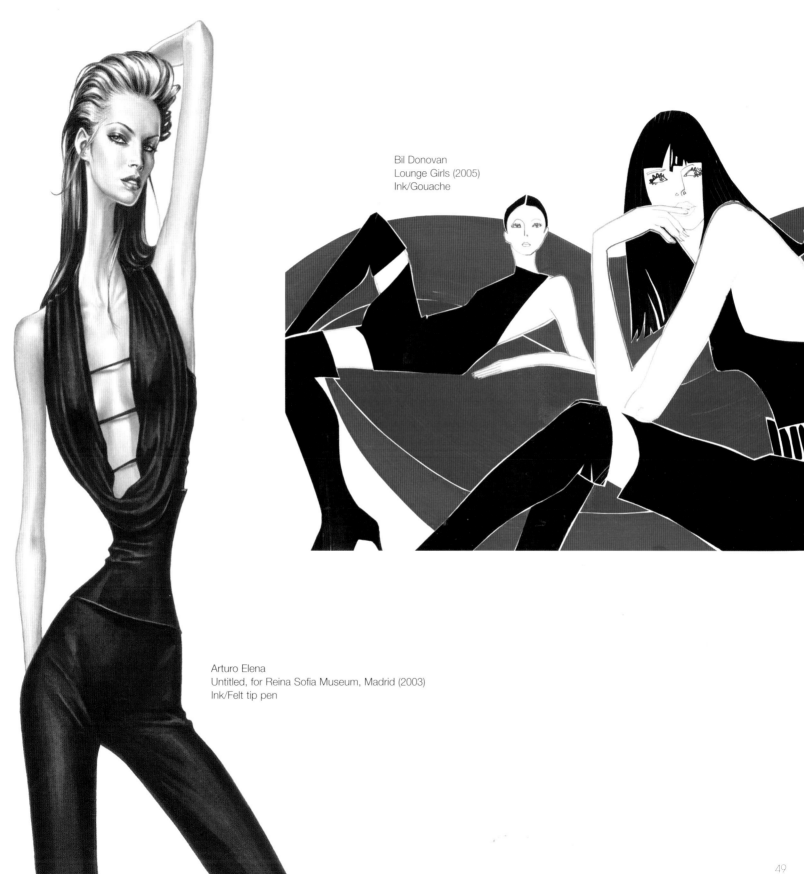

Bil Donovan
Lounge Girls (2005)
Ink/Gouache

Arturo Elena
Untitled, for Reina Sofia Museum, Madrid (2003)
Ink/Felt tip pen

Cybèle
Goddess Five (2003)
Adobe Illustrator

Cybèle
Goddess One (2003)
Adobe Illustrator

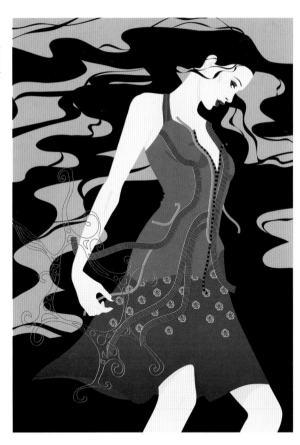

Cybèle
Goddess Four (2003)
Adobe Illustrator

Cybèle
Goddess Two (2003)
Adobe Illustrator

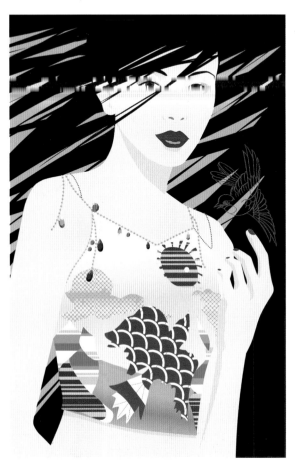

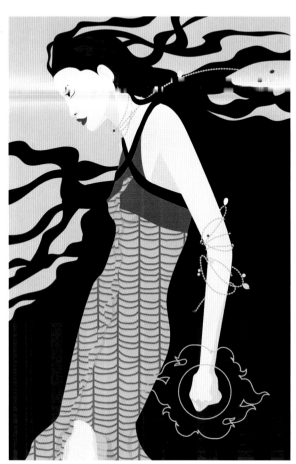

Karen Santry
Bumble Bee Girl Walking
Pugs (2006)
Oil on wood cutouts/Wire

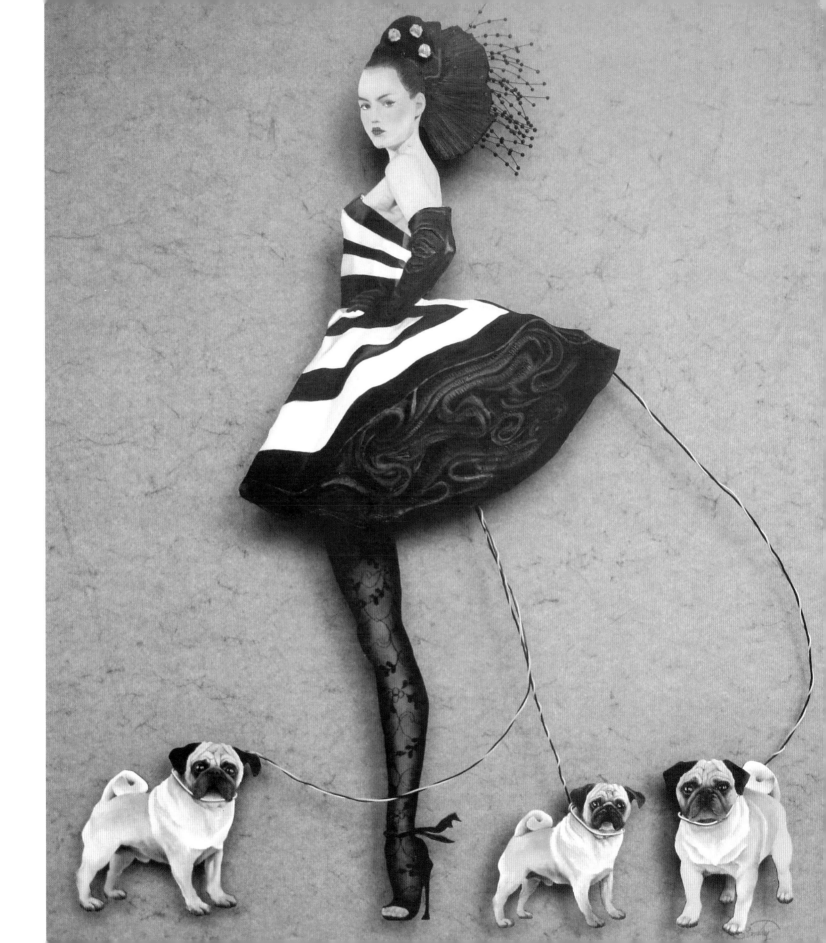

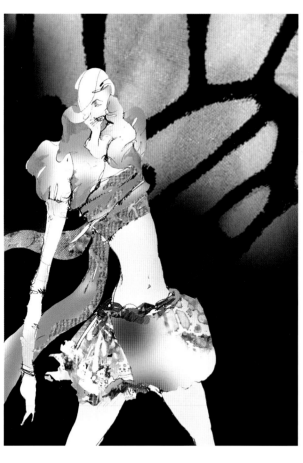

Manna Lai
Butterfly (2005)
Pencil/Adobe Photoshop

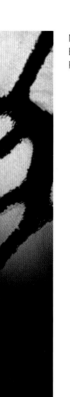

Lopetz:BD
Pink Dress (1994)
Pencil/Crayon

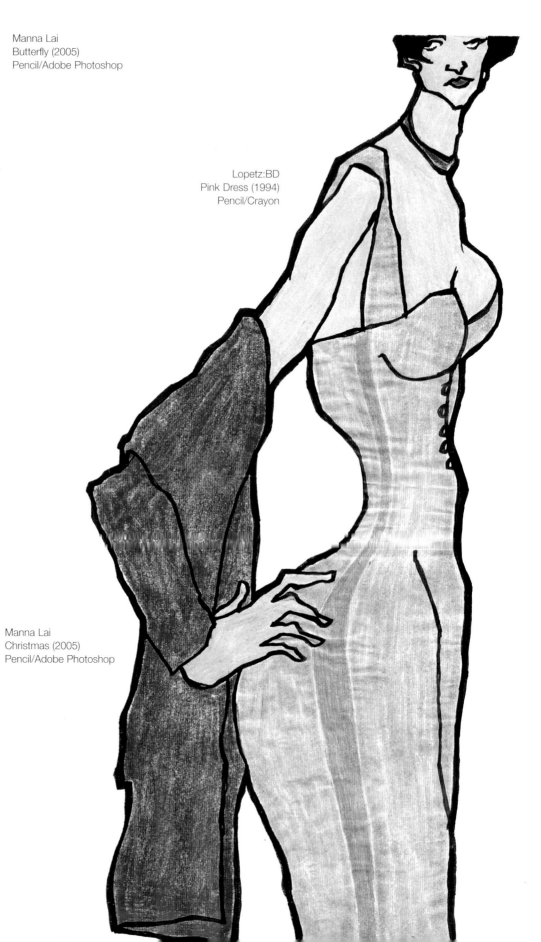

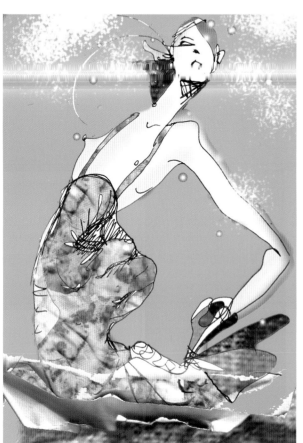

Manna Lai
Christmas (2005)
Pencil/Adobe Photoshop

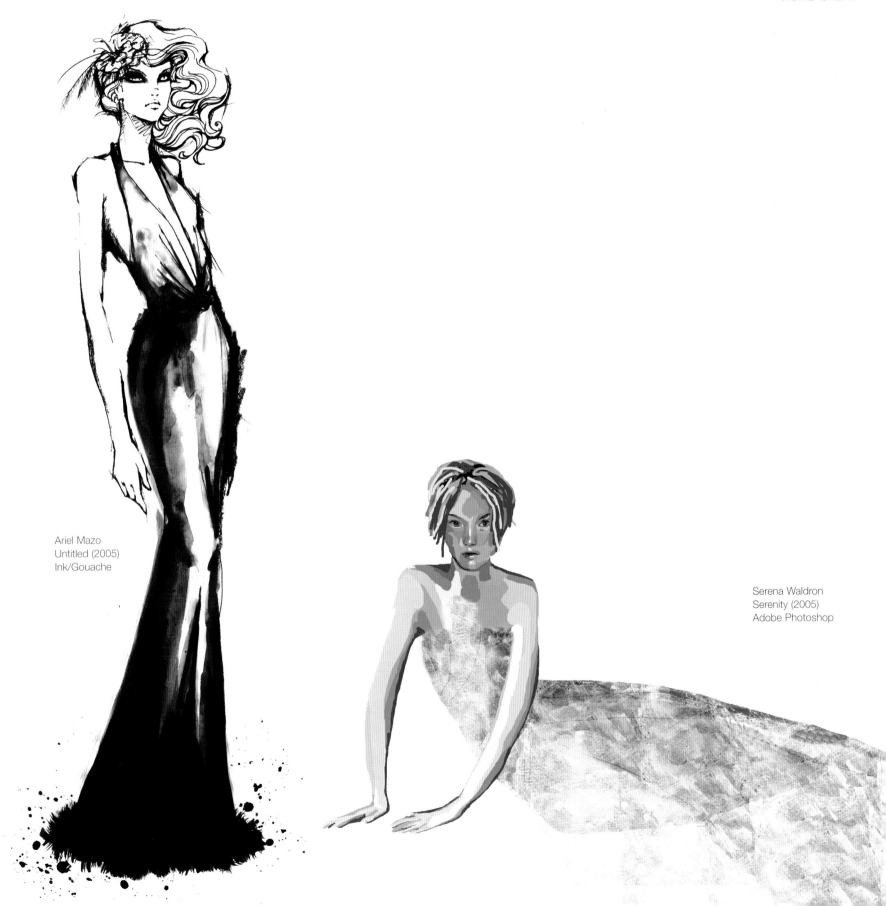

Ariel Mazo
Untitled (2005)
Ink/Gouache

Serena Waldron
Serenity (2005)
Adobe Photoshop

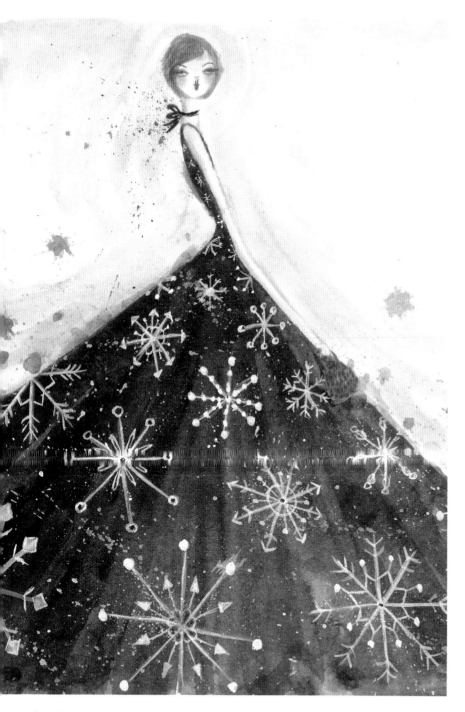

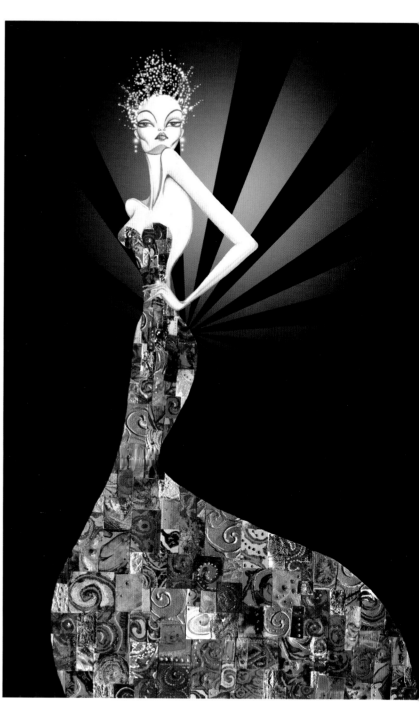

Bella Pilar
Snowflake Gown (2004)
Gouache

Alexander Brooke Smith
Hera (2006)
Mixed-media collage/Watercolour

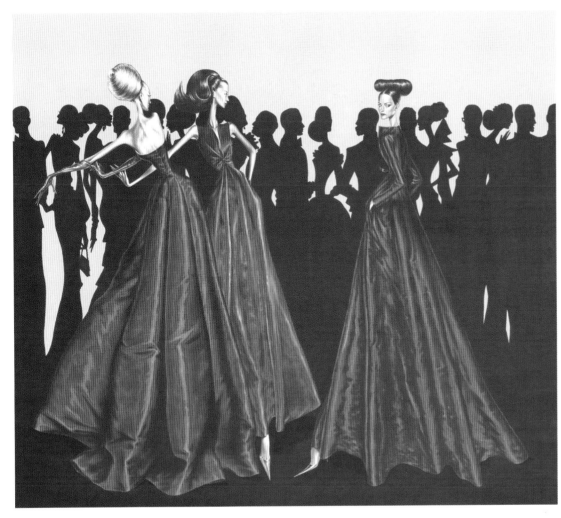

Arturo Elena
Untitled, for Reina Sofia Museum, Madrid (2003)
Ink/Felt tip pen

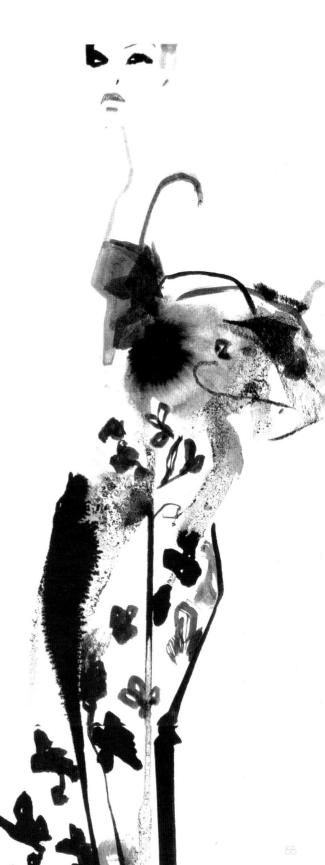

Bil Donovan
Glam Girl (2004)
Ink

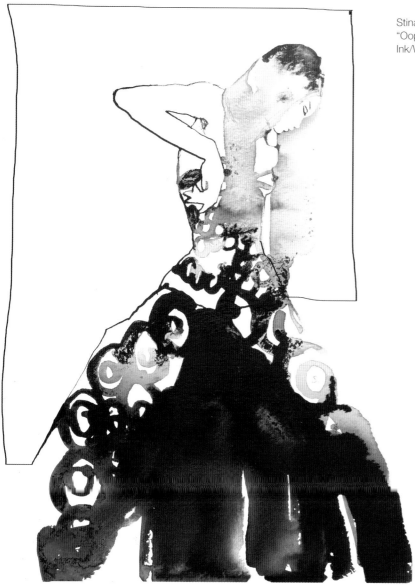

Stina Persson
"Oops!", Versace (2004)
Ink/Watercolour dyes/Adobe Photoshop

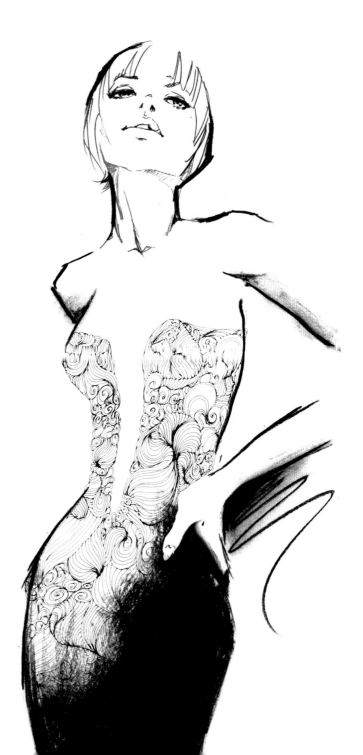

Ariel Mazo
Untitled (2005)
Ink/Pastel

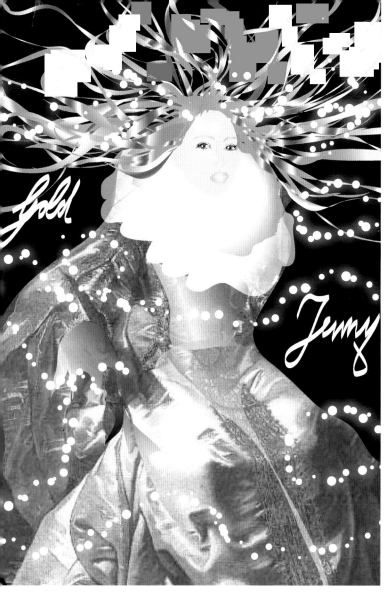

Natascha Engelmann
Goldjenny (2002)
Collage/Adobe Photoshop/Adobe Illustrator

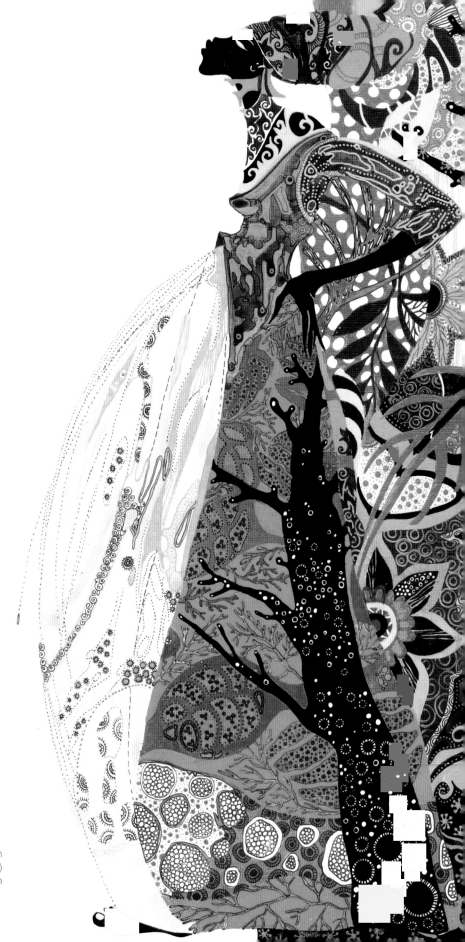

Sonya Suhariyan
Autumn (2005)
Gouache/Acrylic/Felt pen

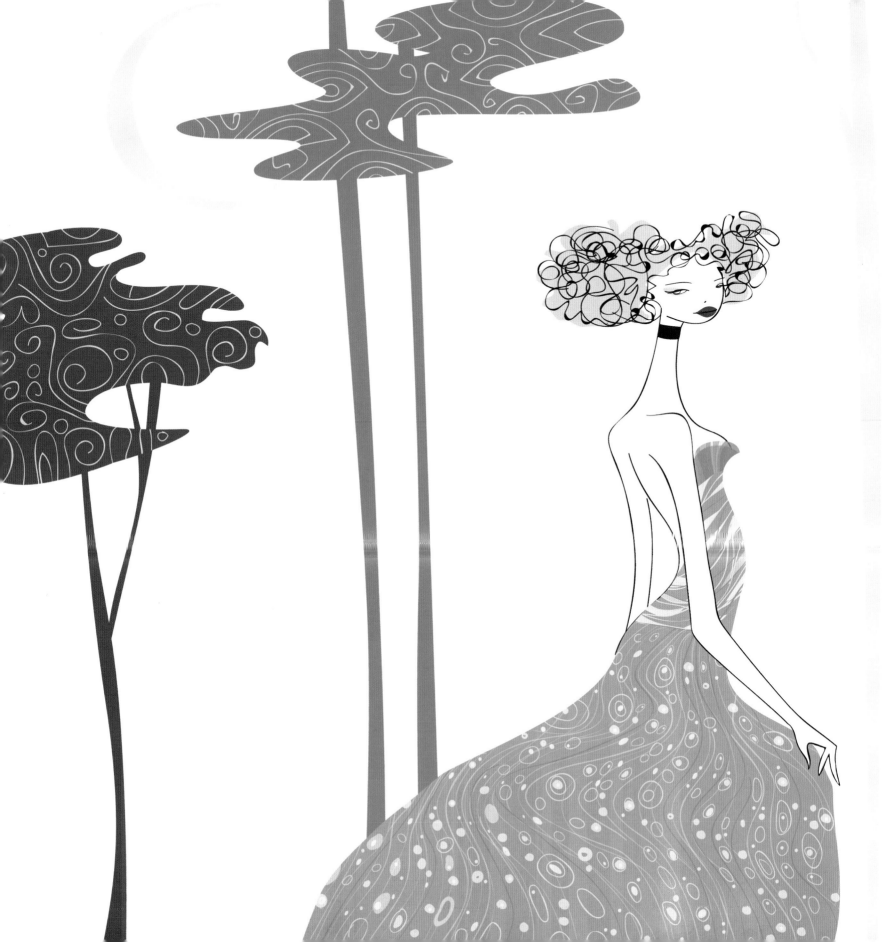

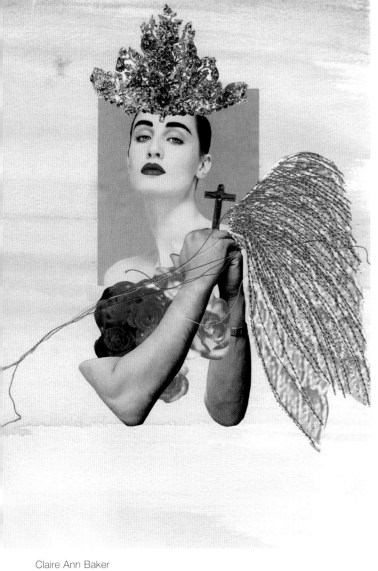

Claire Ann Baker
Edith (2003)
Collage/Gouache/Machine embroidery

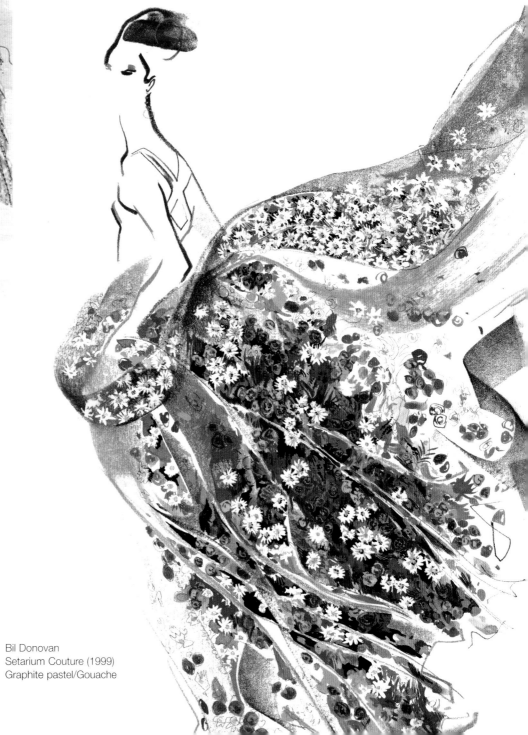

Valeria Docampo
Milky Way Dress (2005)
Adobe Illustrator

Bil Donovan
Setarium Couture (1999)
Graphite pastel/Gouache

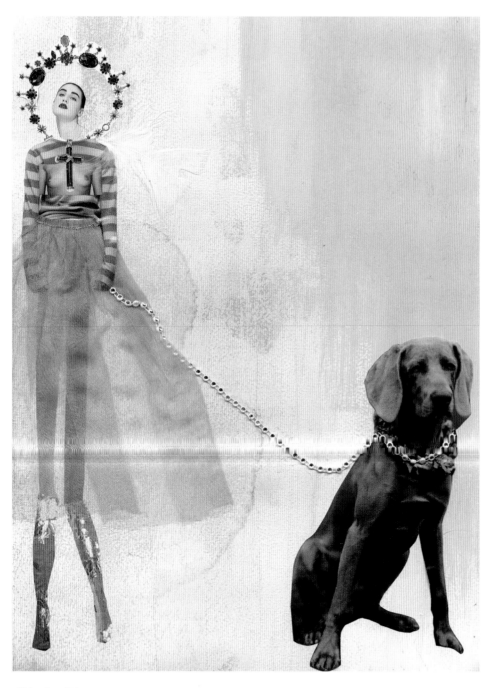

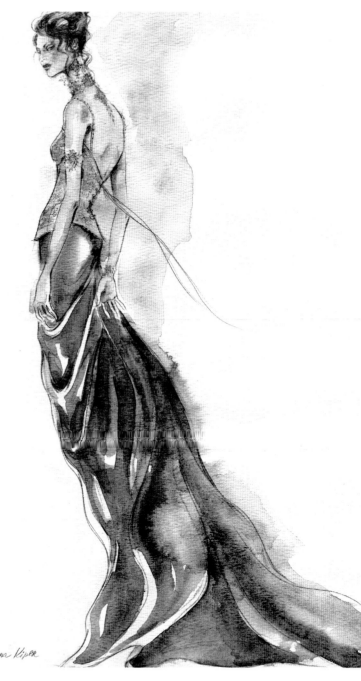

Claire Ann Baker
Tallulah (2003)
Magazine collage/Embellishment

Anna Kiper
Evening Outfit (2000)
Watercolour

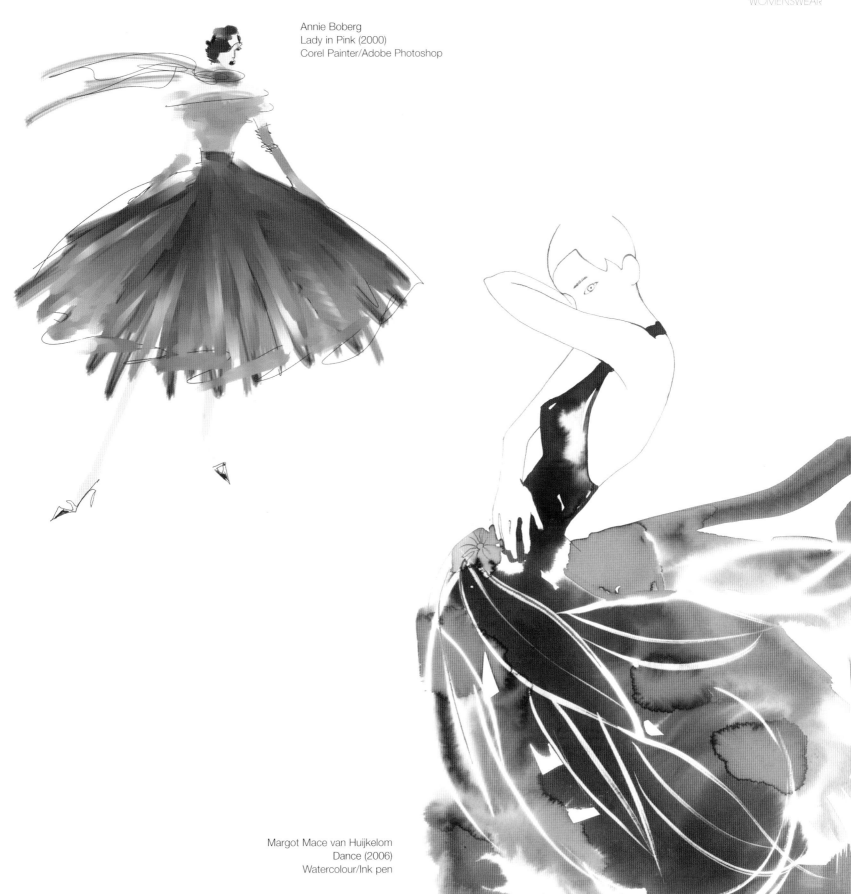

Annie Boberg
Lady in Pink (2000)
Corel Painter/Adobe Photoshop

Margot Mace van Huijkelom
Dance (2006)
Watercolour/Ink pen

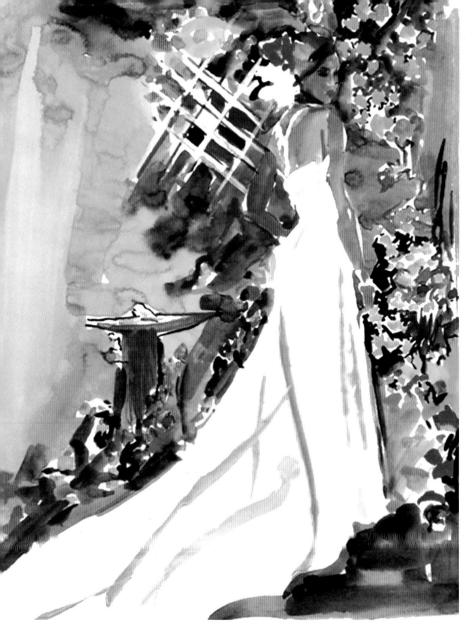

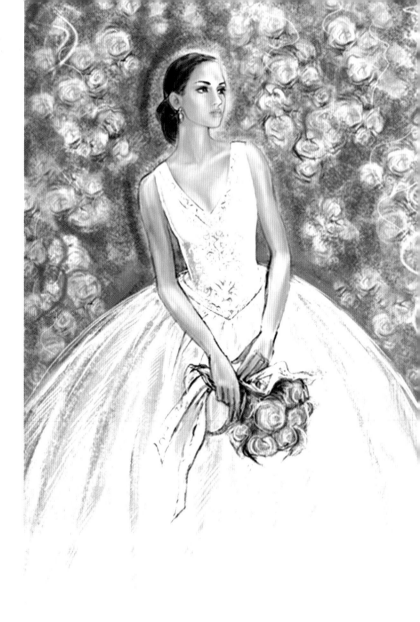

Janis Salek
Wedding Belle (2005)
Watercolour

Marsha Silvestri
Portrait of a Bride with Roses (2004)
Pencil/Pastel/Adobe Photoshop

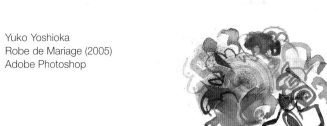

Yuko Yoshioka
Robe de Mariage (2005)
Adobe Photoshop

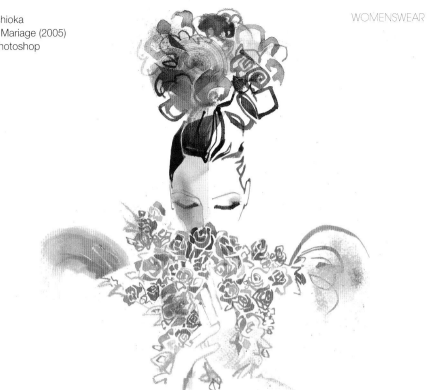

Bil Donovan
Estée Lauder Shopping Bag (1996)
Watercolour

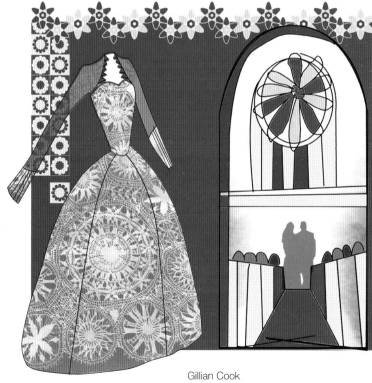

Gillian Cook
Wedding Day (2005)
Adobe Photoshop

Karen Santry
Gangsta Rapper's Daughter Bride (2006)
Oil on rosewood

Jennie Yip
Spring Bride (2006)
Gouache on paper

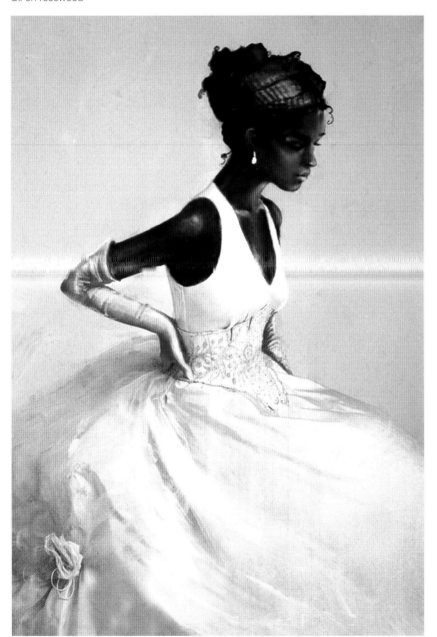

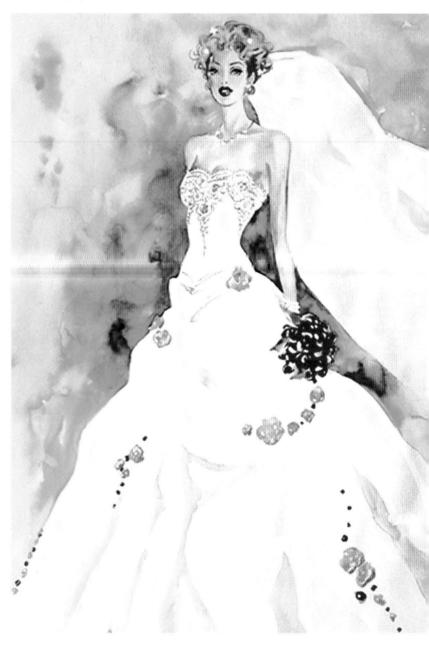

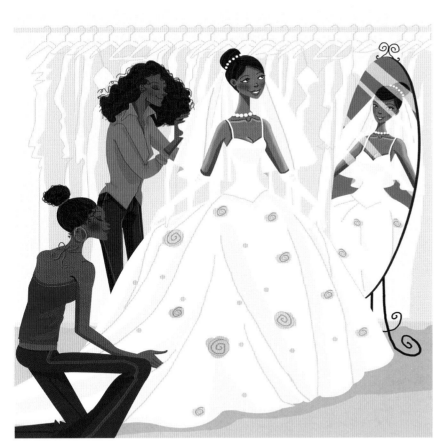

Nina Edwards
Young Bride and Her Sisters (2006)
Adobe Illustrator/Adobe Photoshop

Christophe Lardot
La Panne (2006)
Adobe Photoshop

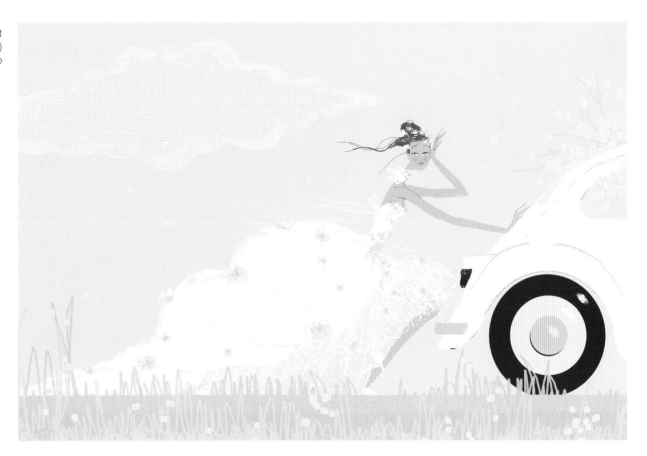

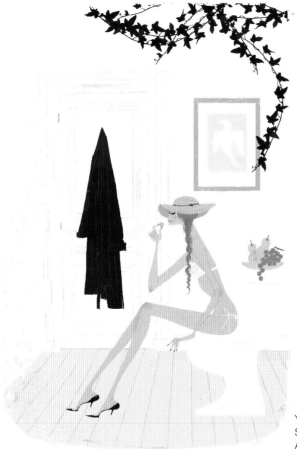

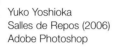

Yuko Yoshioka
Salles de Repos (2006)
Adobe Photoshop

Wai
Lingerie (2004)
Adobe Illustrator/
Adobe Photoshop

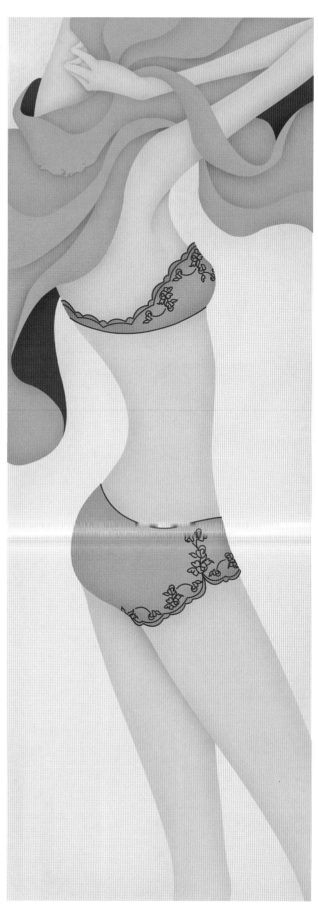

Amparo Losana
D&G (2006)
Adobe Photoshop

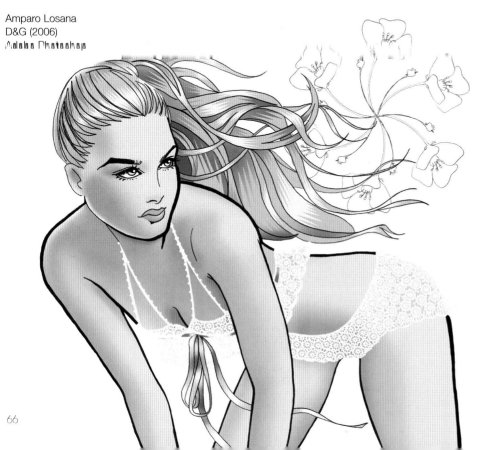

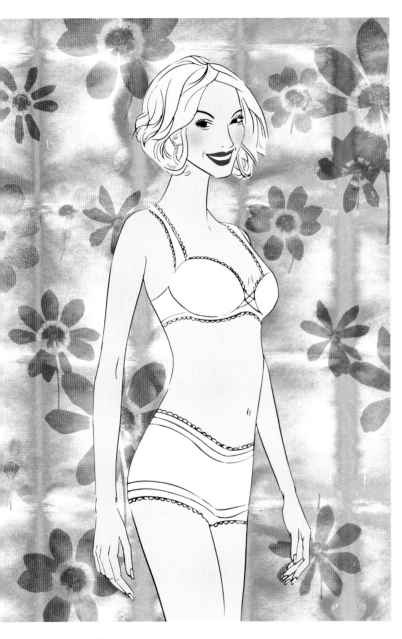

Annabelle J. Verhoye
Vanity Fair (2006)
Chine collé/Adobe Photoshop

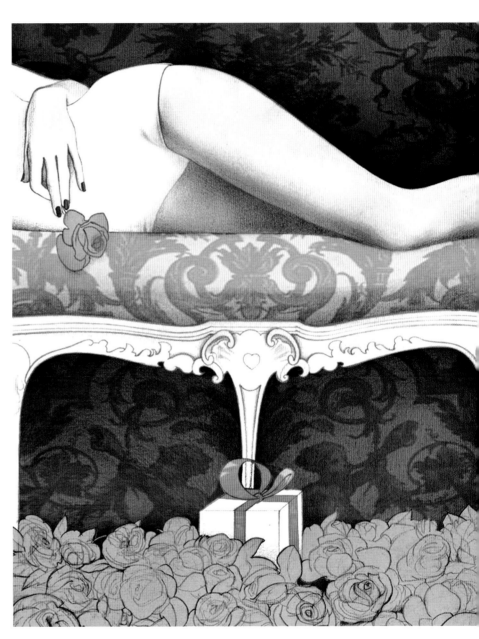

Menisha
Pink Room (2005)
Adobe Photoshop

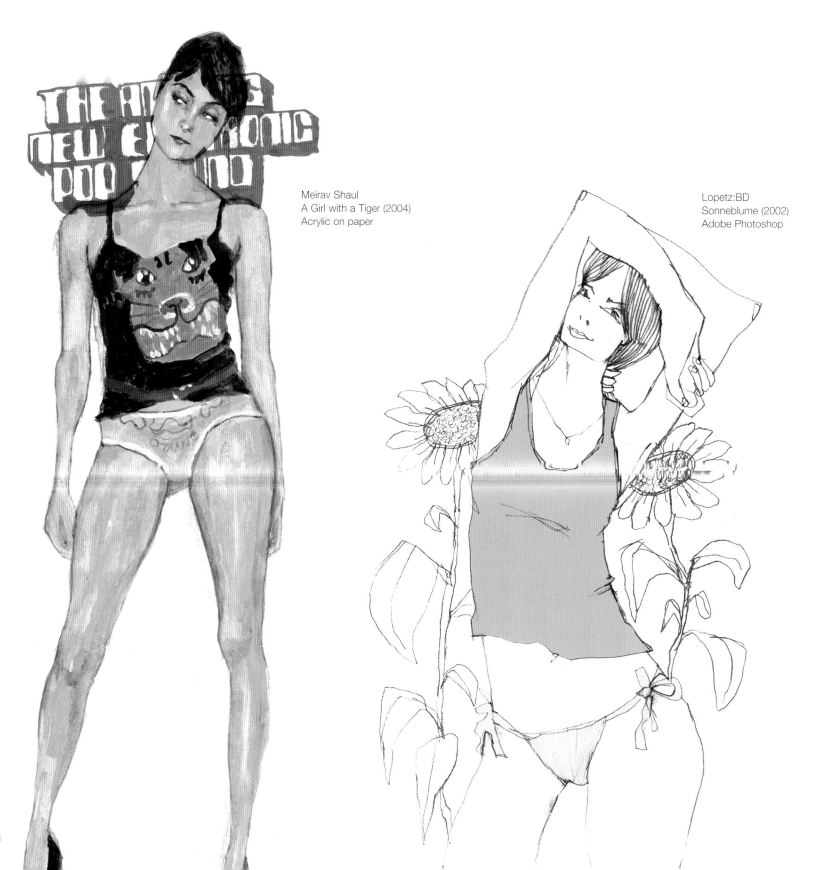

Meirav Shaul
A Girl with a Tiger (2004)
Acrylic on paper

Lopetz:BD
Sonneblume (2002)
Adobe Photoshop

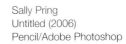

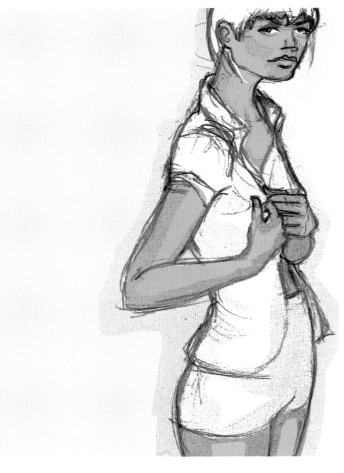

Sally Pring
Untitled (2006)
Pencil/Adobe Photoshop

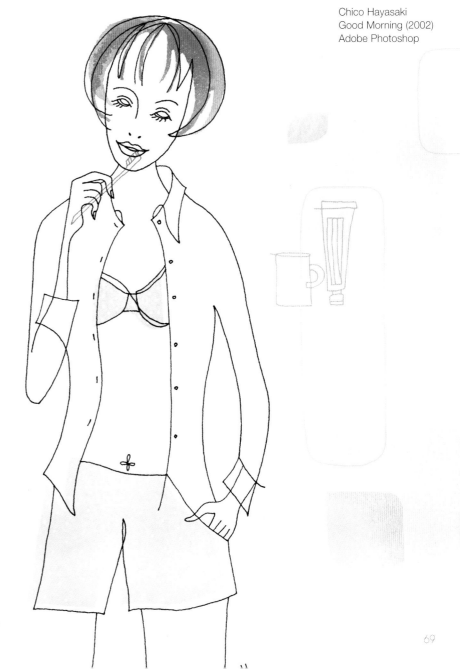

Chico Hayasaki
Good Morning (2002)
Adobe Photoshop

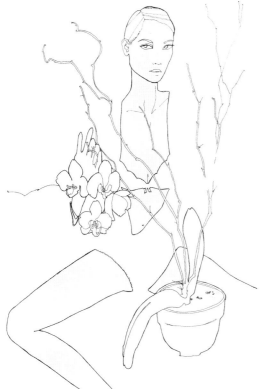

Erica Sharp
Androgyne (2005)
Adobe Photoshop/
Adobe Illustrator

Fhiona Galloway
Sparkle (2005)
Macromedia FreeHand

Arturo Elena
Untitled, for Custo Barcelona (2005)
Ink/Felt tip pen

J. David McKenney
Peepshow (2005)
Ink/Adobe Photoshop

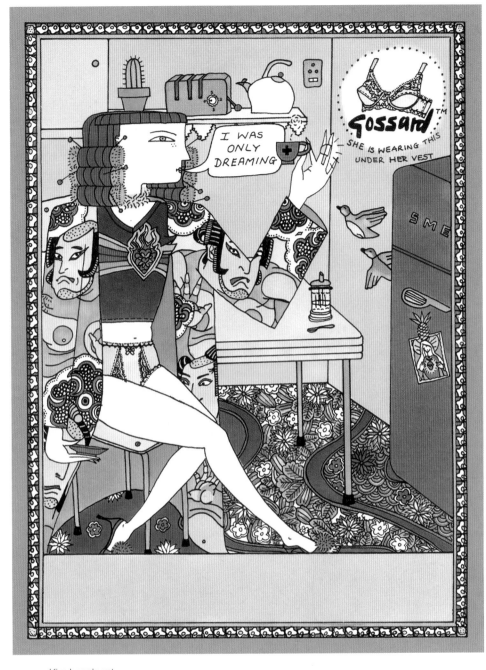

Kim Longhurst
Dream Girl (1998)
Macromedia FreeHand/Adobe Photoshop

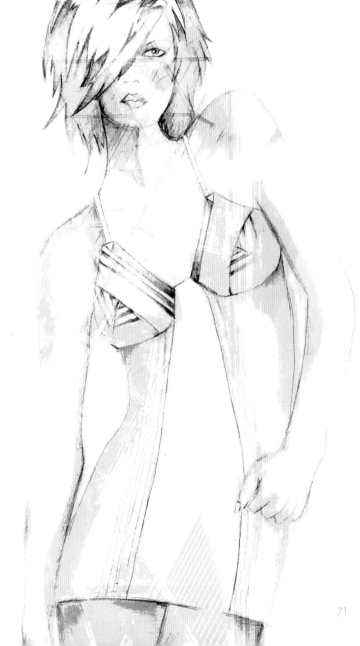

Laura Niles
Subtract Lingerie (2005)
Pencil/Adobe Photoshop

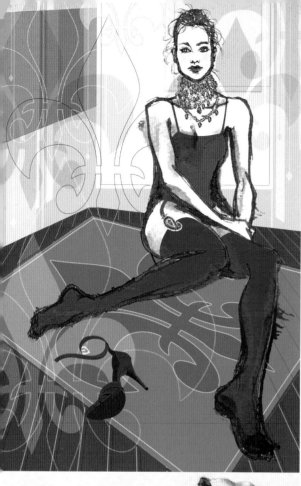

Nicoletta Mazzesi
Dancing Threads (2005)
Ink/Adobe Photoshop/Adobe Illustrator

Borja Uriarte
Lady Chair (2005)
Fabric

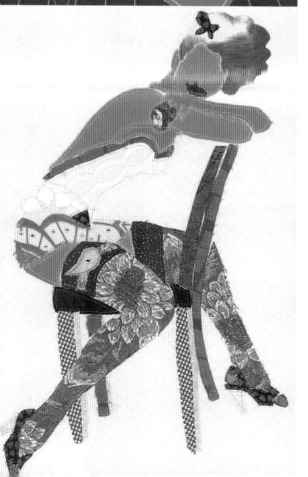

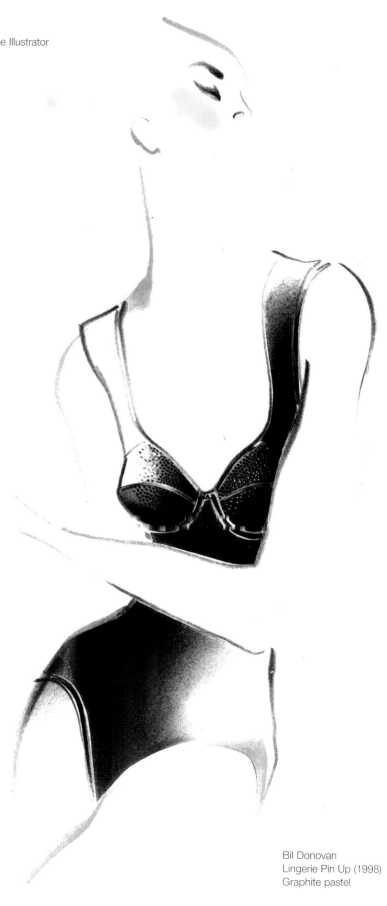

Bil Donovan
Lingerie Pin Up (1998)
Graphite pastel

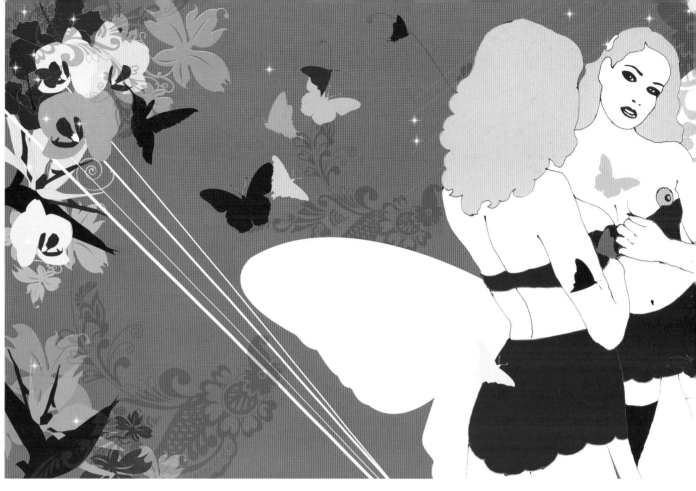

Lucy Allen
Private Commission, Untitled (2005)
Ink pen/Adobe Photoshop

Bella Pilar
Pink Art (2005)
Gouache

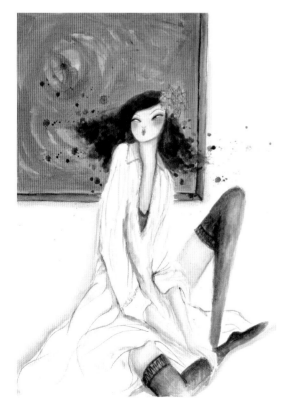

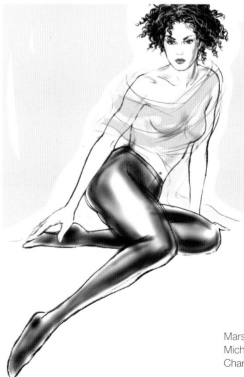

Marsha Silvestri
Michelle in Mermaid Pose (2003)
Charcoal/Adobe Photoshop/Adobe Illustrator

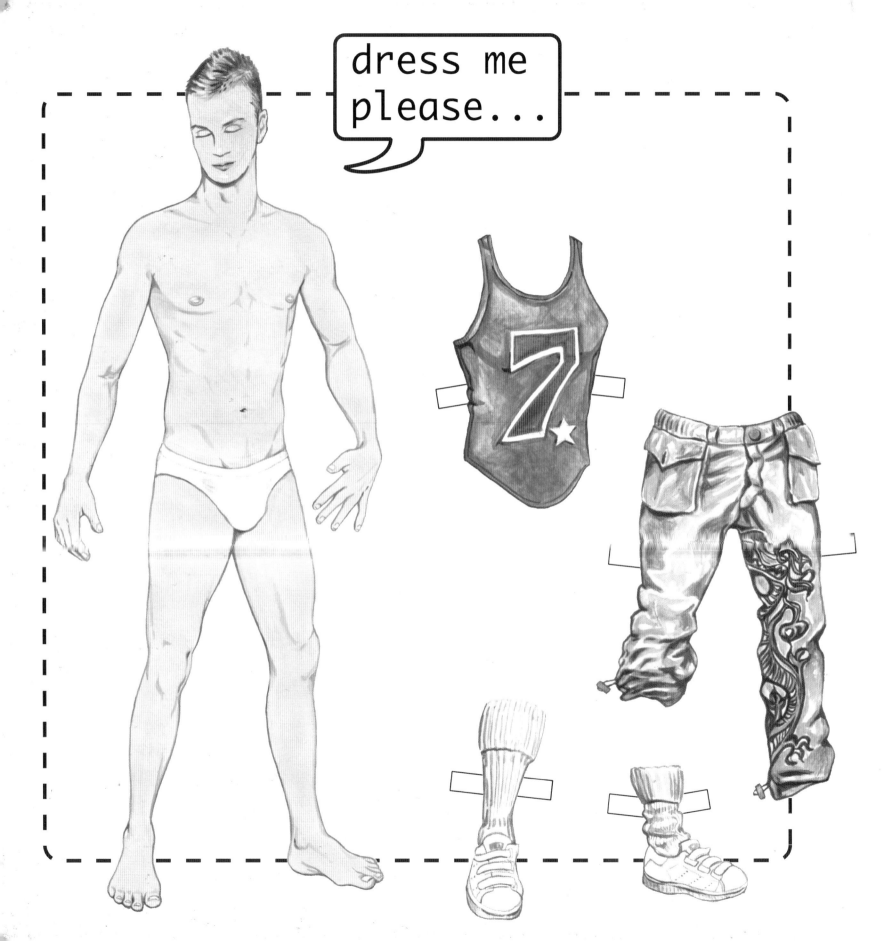

Menswear

tees & shirts   outerwear   knit   casual

neckwear   smart   bespoke   underwear

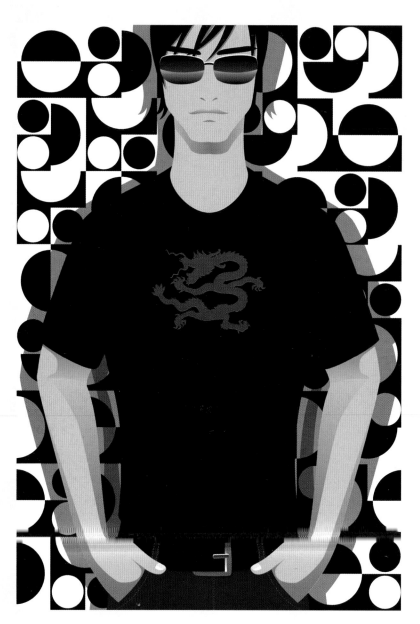

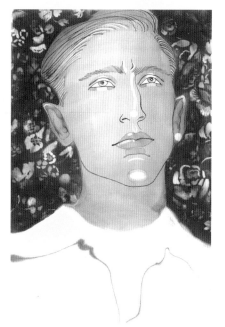

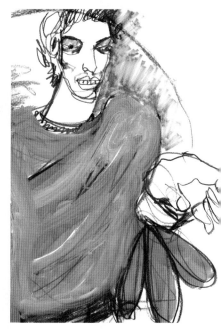

Margot Mace van Huijkelom
Romeo (2006)
Watercolour/Ink pen

James Holman
Disco Micheal (2006)
Graphite/Ink/Pencil/Crayon/Felt tip

Pinglet
Dragon (2002)
Adobe Illustrator

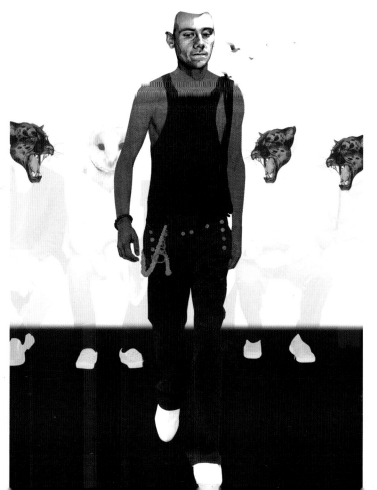

Hellovon
Owl (2005)
Pencil/Photography/
Ink/Adobe Illustrator

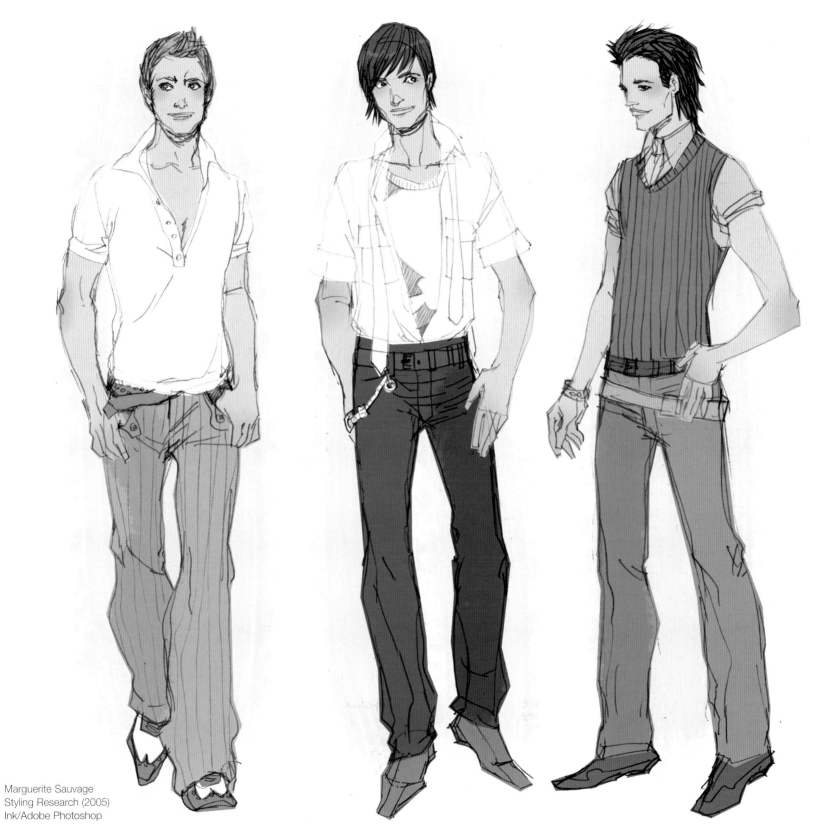

Marguerite Sauvage
Styling Research (2005)
Ink/Adobe Photoshop

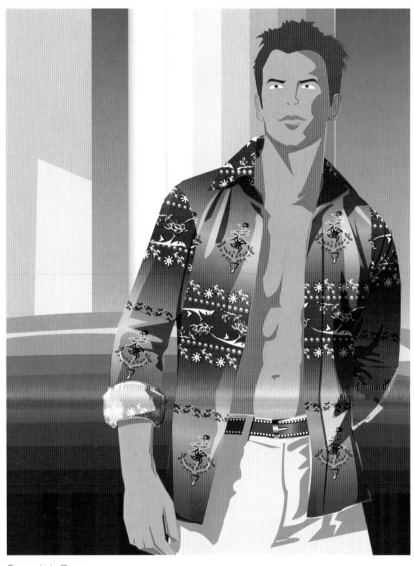

Cesar de la Rosa
Miami Summer (2004)
Adobe Illustrator

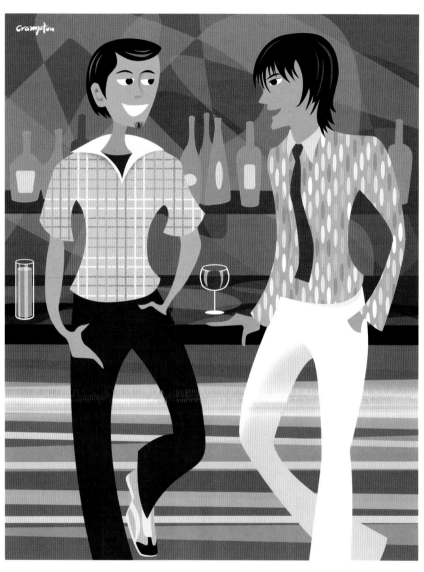

Michael Crampton
Bar Talk (2005)
Adobe Photoshop

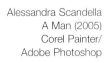

Alessandra Scandella
A Man (2005)
Corel Painter/
Adobe Photoshop

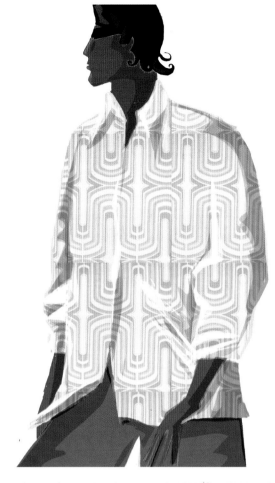

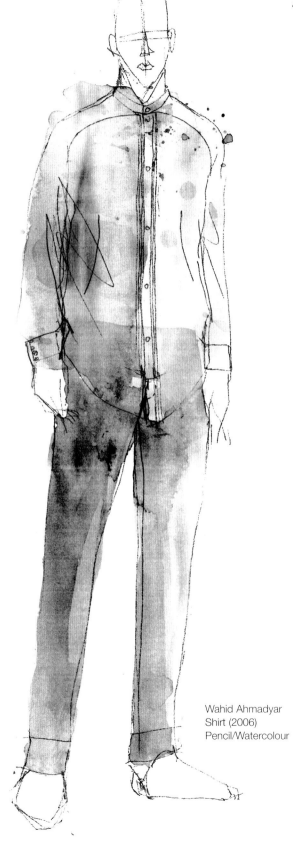

Lopetz:BD
Tom (2002)
Adobe Photoshop

Wahid Ahmadyar
Shirt (2006)
Pencil/Watercolour

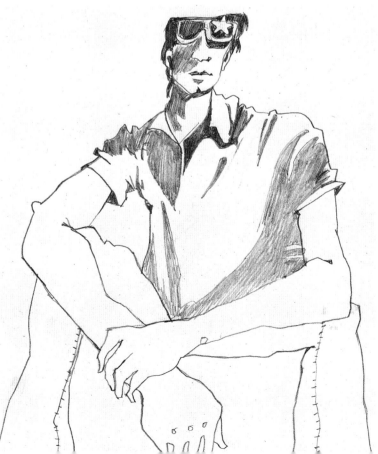

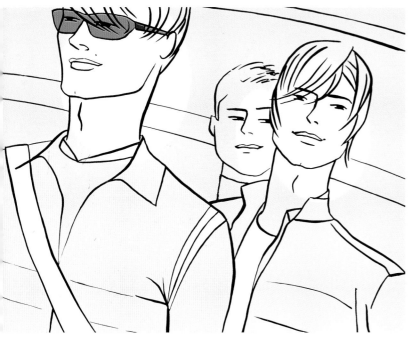

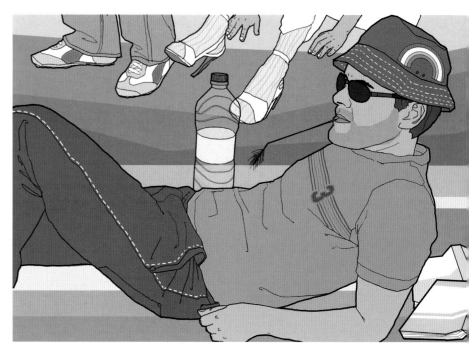

Dorothea Renault
3 Men Arriving (2005)
Adobe Illustrator

Lee Woodgate
The Big Chill (2002)
Adobe Photoshop

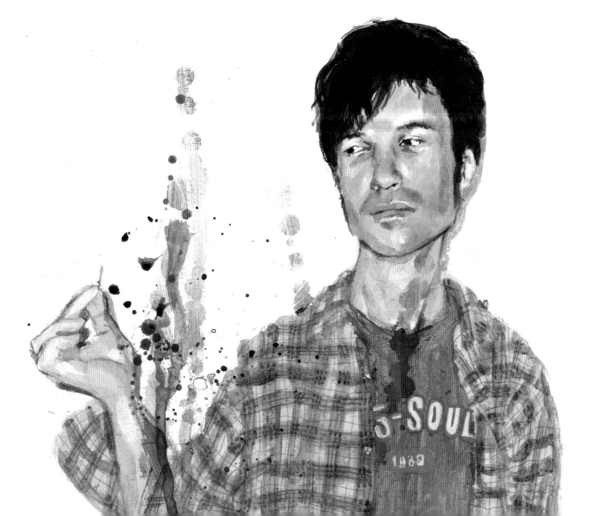

Meirav Shaul
Alon (2004)
Acrylic on paper

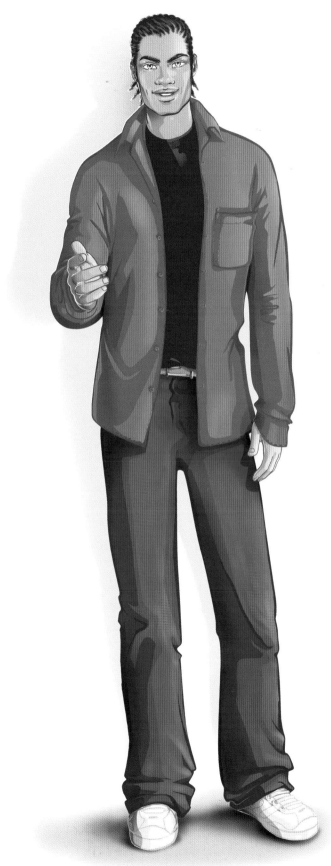

Monica Laita
NY Estate Agency N.1 (2006)
Adobe Photoshop

Irene Jacobs
Untitled, for 'A Man's Guide to Life',
Man magazine (1999)
Adobe Photoshop/Adobe Illustrator

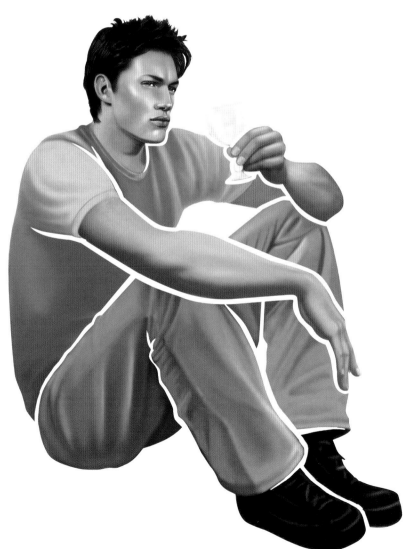

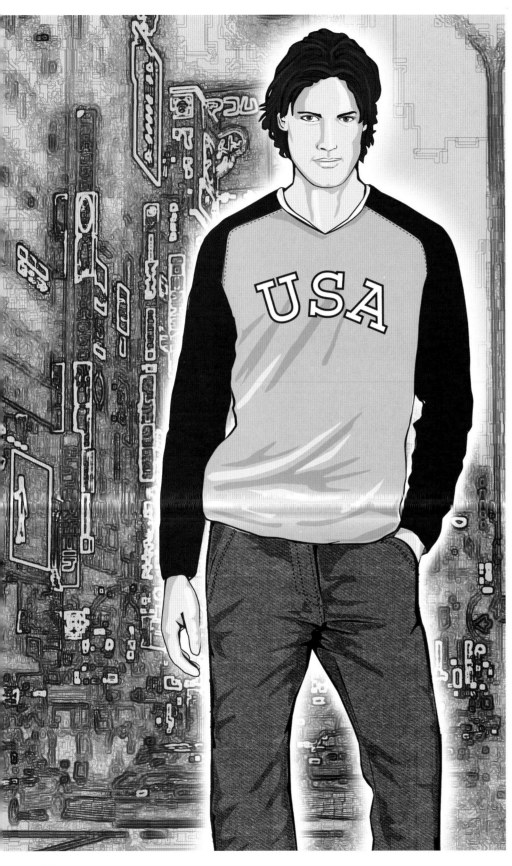

Naomi Austin
Neon City (2006)
Adobe Illustrator/
Adobe Photoshop

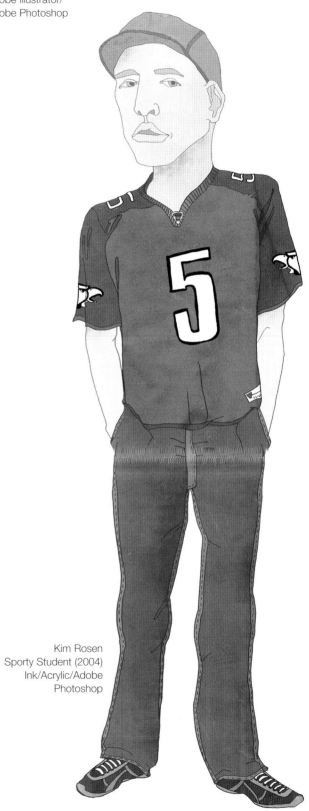

Kim Rosen
Sporty Student (2004)
Ink/Acrylic/Adobe
Photoshop

Jacqui Paull and Carl Melegari
Joey (2006)
Adobe Photoshop

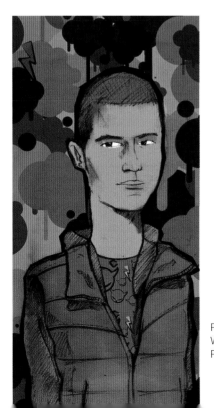

Paul Watmough
We Know (2006)
Pen/Ink/Adobe Photoshop

Kun-Sung Chung
Three Guys (2004)
Adobe Illustrator

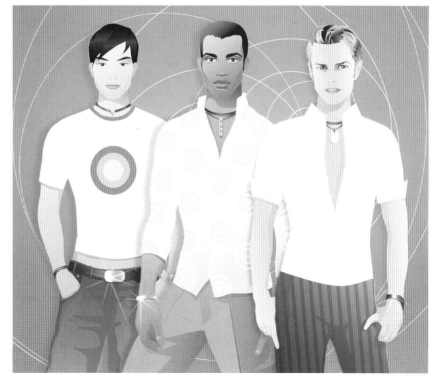

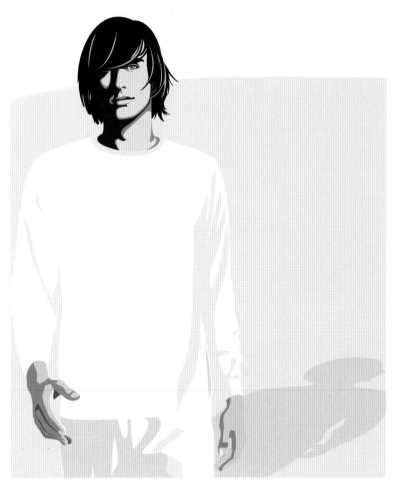

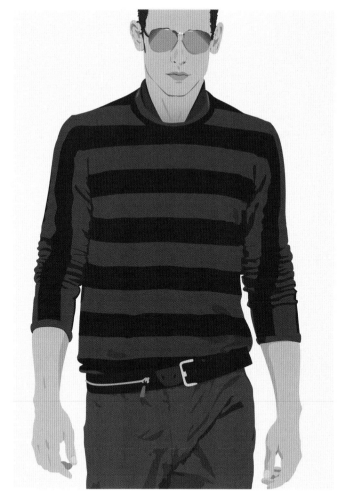

Irene Jacobs
Indulgence 1, for Philips Design (2002)
Adobe Illustrator

Arthur Mount
Jil Sander (2003)
Adobe Illustrator

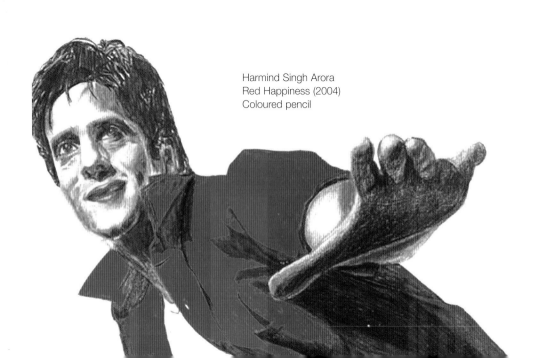

Harmind Singh Arora
Red Happiness (2004)
Coloured pencil

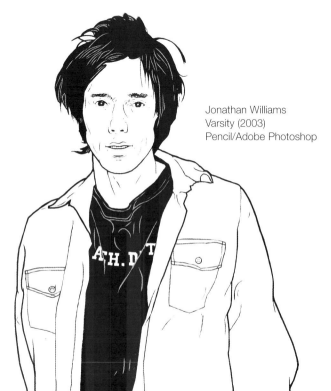

Jonathan Williams
Varsity (2003)
Pencil/Adobe Photoshop

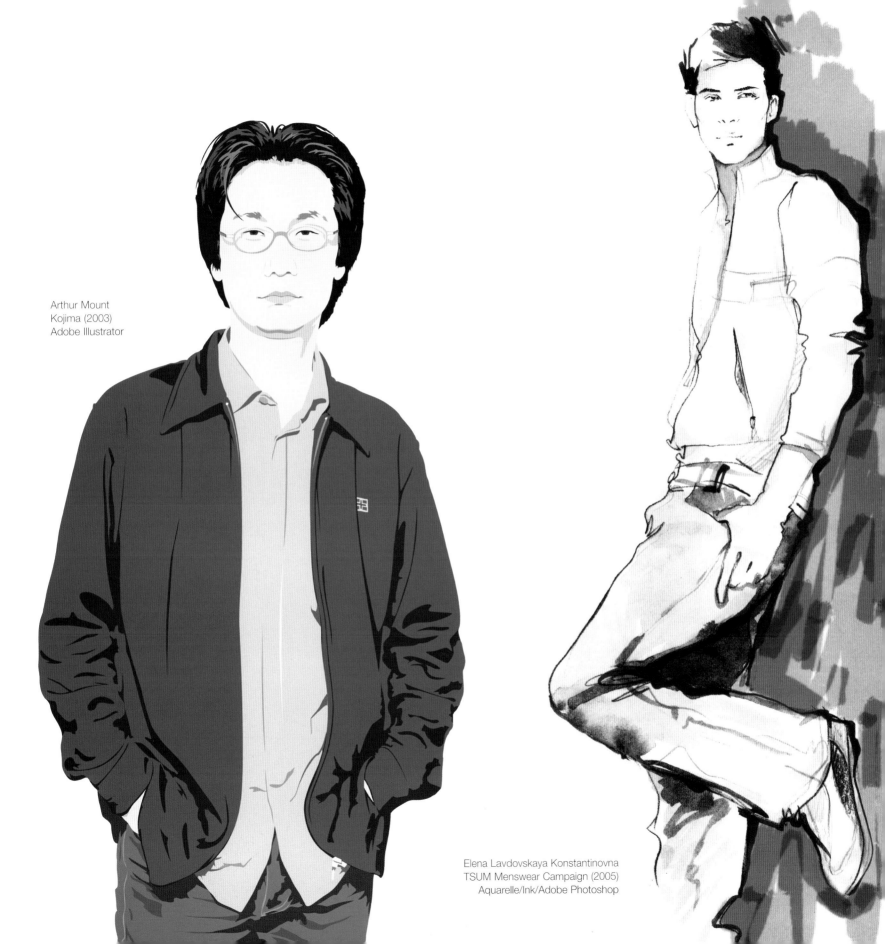

Arthur Mount
Kojima (2003)
Adobe Illustrator

Elena Lavdovskaya Konstantinovna
TSUM Menswear Campaign (2005)
Aquarelle/Ink/Adobe Photoshop

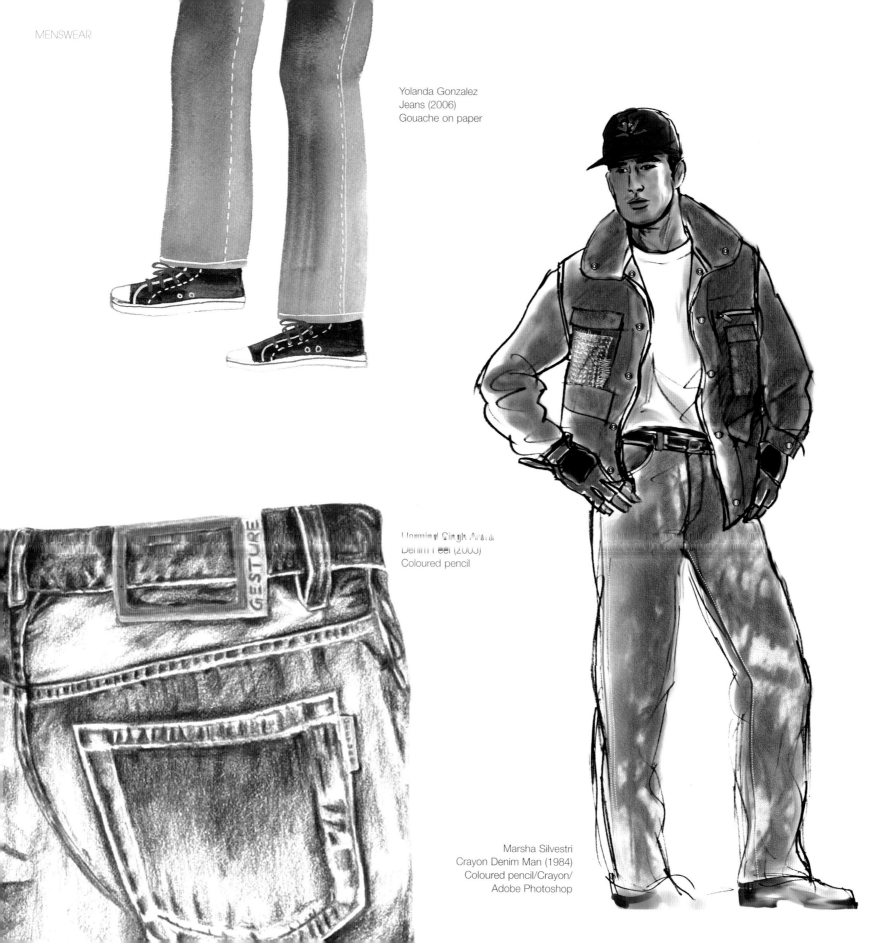

Yolanda Gonzalez
Jeans (2006)
Gouache on paper

Harminder Singh Ahluwalia
Denim Feel (2003)
Coloured pencil

Marsha Silvestri
Crayon Denim Man (1984)
Coloured pencil/Crayon/
Adobe Photoshop

Jamal 'Bam' Tate
Untitled (2002)
Pen/Ink/Adobe Illustrator

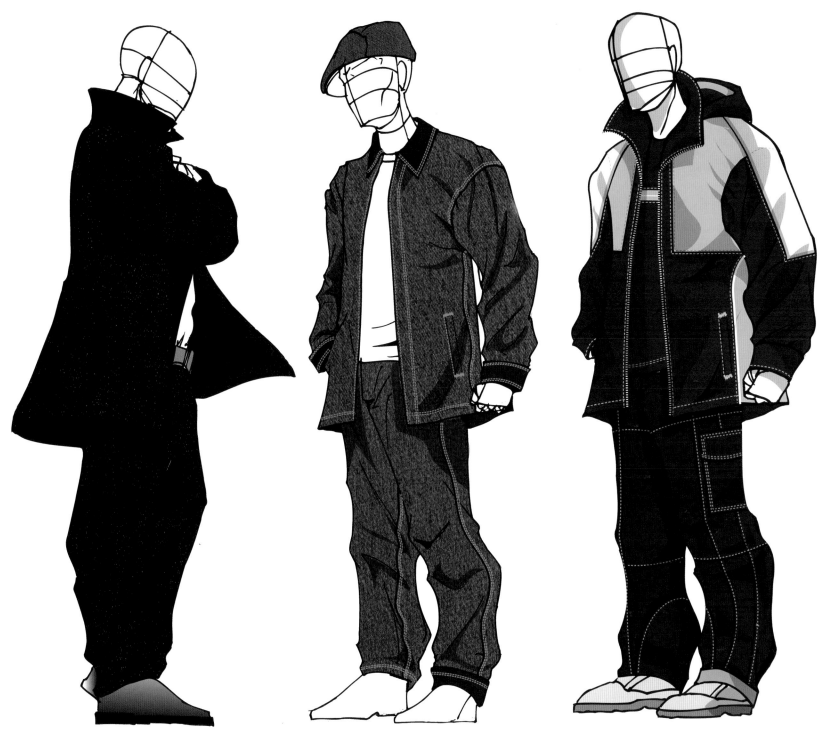

Wahid Ahmadyar
Bomber (2006)
Pencil/Watercolour

Rachel Messenger
Untitled (2006)
Ink/Pencil/Adobe Photoshop

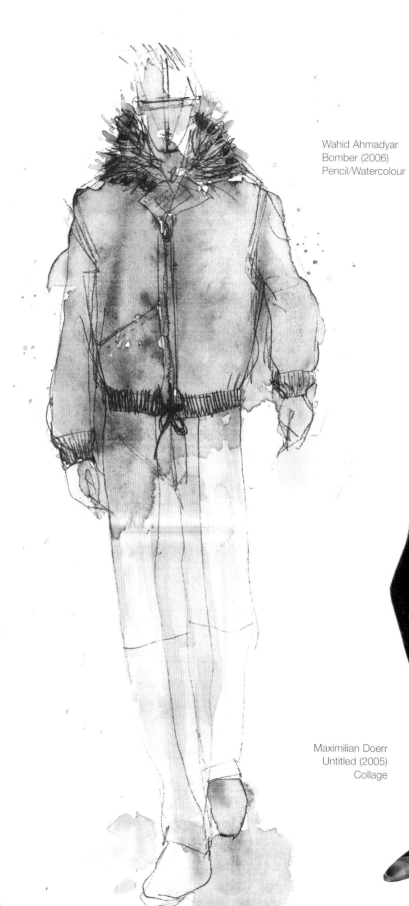

Maximilian Doerr
Untitled (2005)
Collage

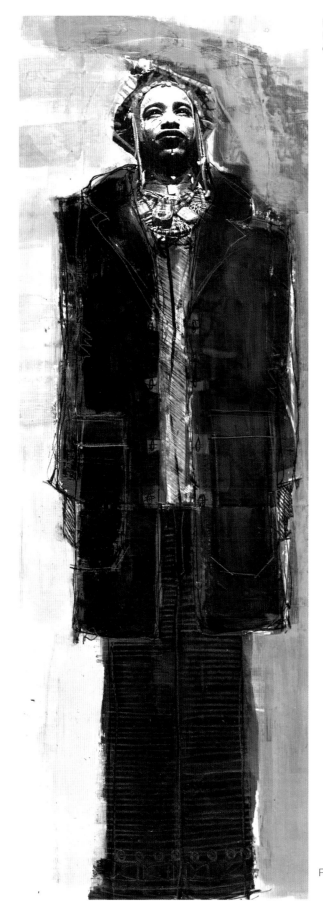

Emily Peach
Big Coat (2004)
Collage/Paint/Chalk

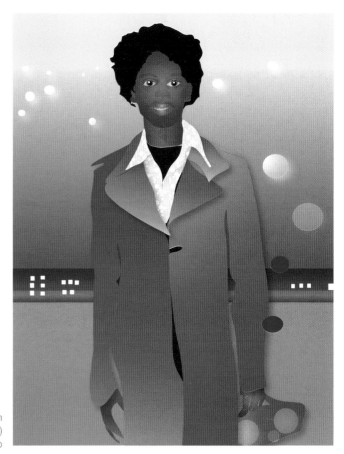

Natascha Engelmann
Ghettoblaster (2000)
Pencil/Adobe Photoshop

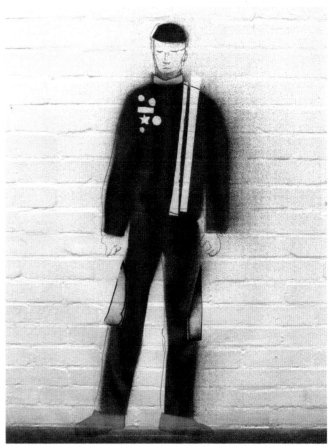

Koichiro Furukawa
Shadow on the Wall (2006)
Pencil/Stencil/Adobe Photoshop

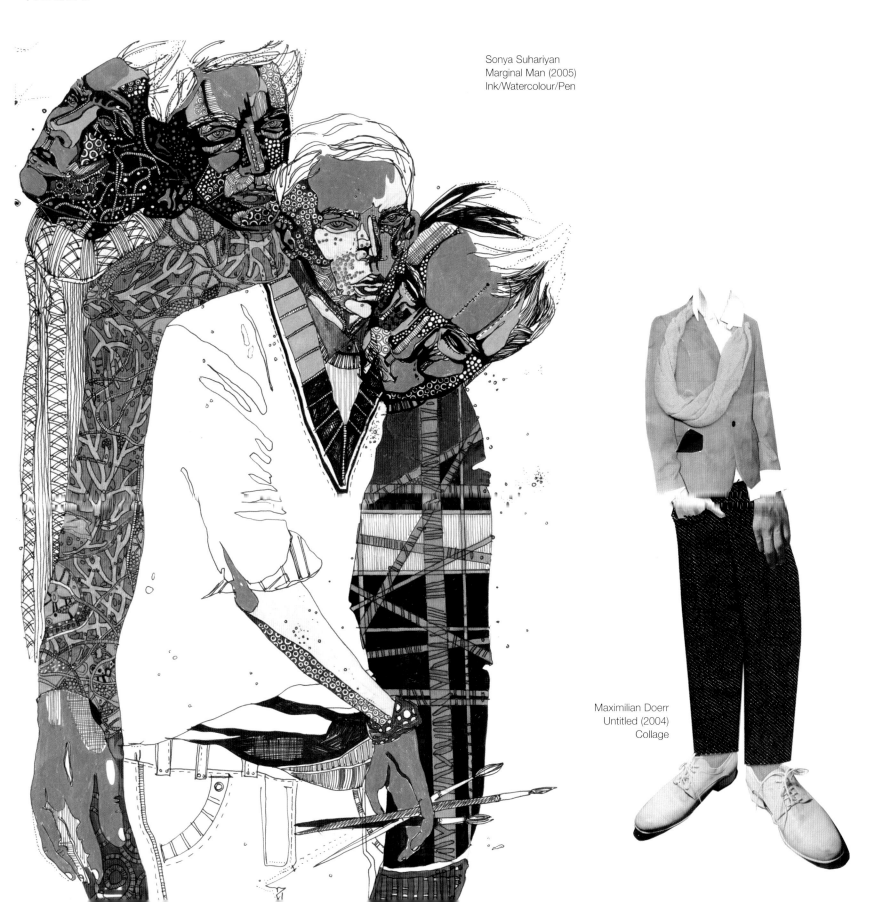

Sonya Suhariyan
Marginal Man (2005)
Ink/Watercolour/Pen

Maximilian Doerr
Untitled (2004)
Collage

Mayrhosby Yeoshen
The Bishounen (2004)
Adobe Photoshop/Corel Painter

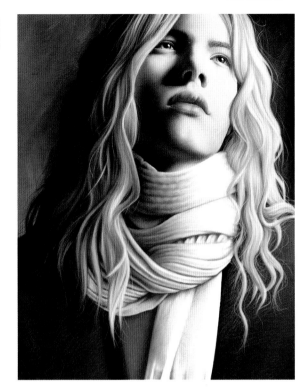

Chico Hayasaki
T-shirt (2003)
Adobe Photoshop

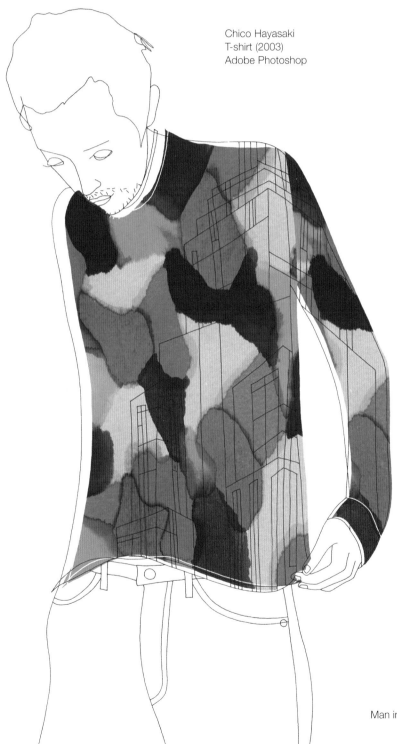

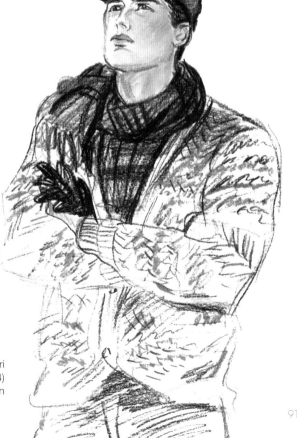

Marsha Silvestri
Man in Hat and Sweater (1984)
Crayola Crayon

91

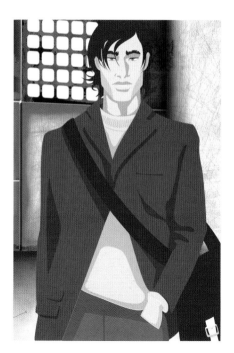

Javier Joaquin
Airbourne Clothes (2004)
Adobe Illustrator

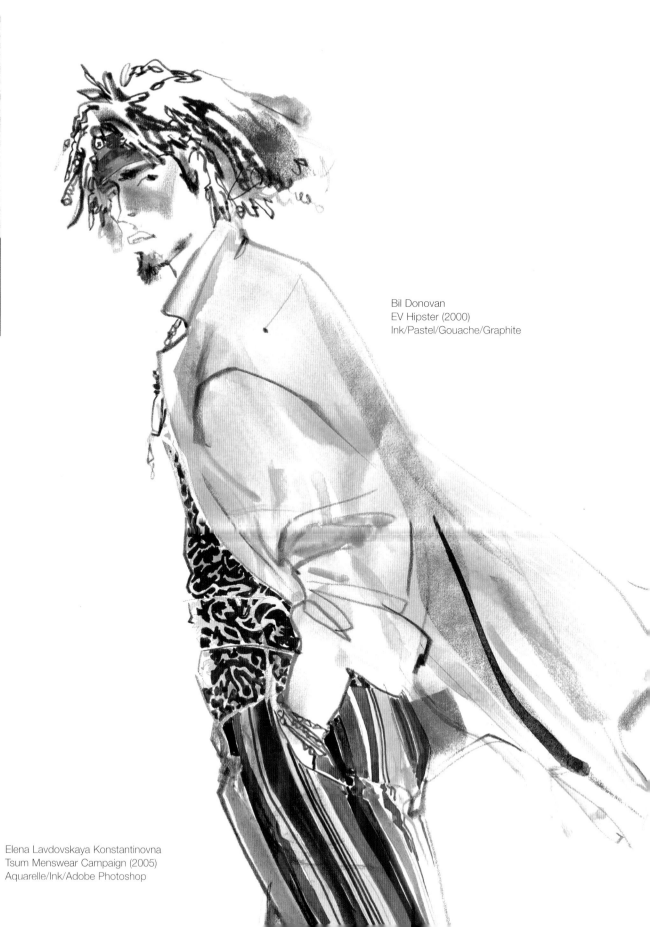

Bil Donovan
EV Hipster (2000)
Ink/Pastel/Gouache/Graphite

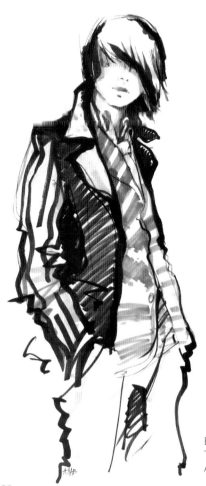

Elena Lavdovskaya Konstantinovna
Tsum Menswear Campaign (2005)
Aquarelle/Ink/Adobe Photoshop

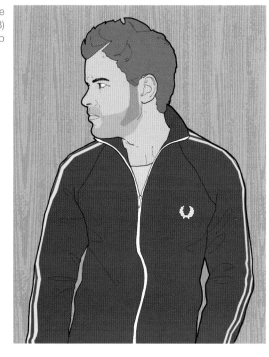

Lee Woodgate
Fred Perry (2003)
Adobe Photoshop

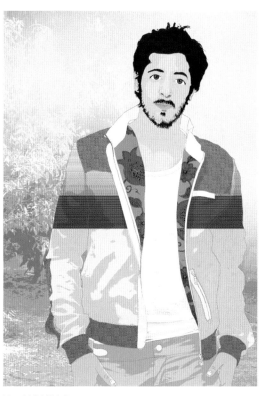

Lior Yefet Tabib
Beard Guy (Self Portrait) (2005)
Adobe Photoshop

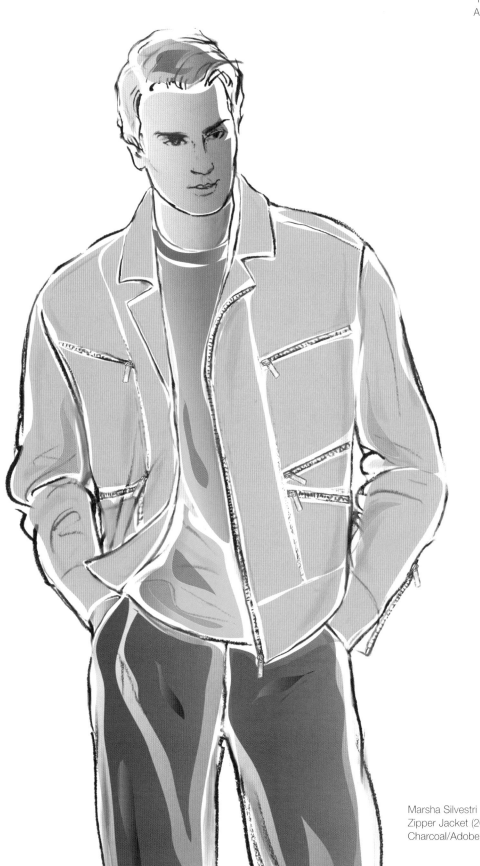

Marsha Silvestri
Zipper Jacket (2003)
Charcoal/Adobe Illustrator

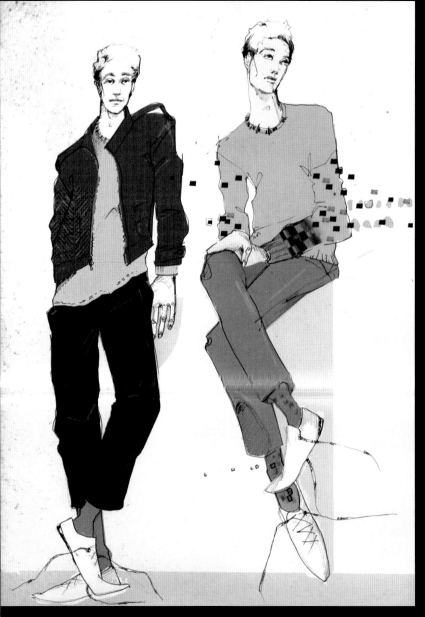

Kaja Jamtli
Untitled (2005)
Pencil/Felt pen/Pen/Adobe
Photoshop/Adobe Illustrator

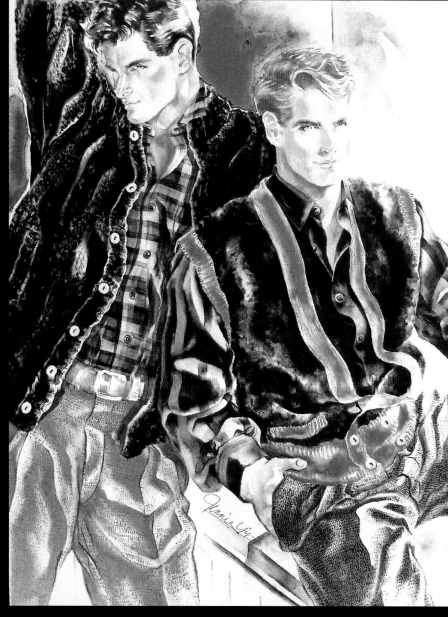

Jennie Yip
Castile Fall (2006)
Gouache on watercolour paper

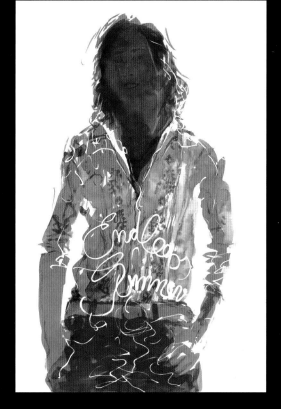

Christian Barthold
Endless Summer (2000)
India ink/Gouache/Adobe
Photoshop

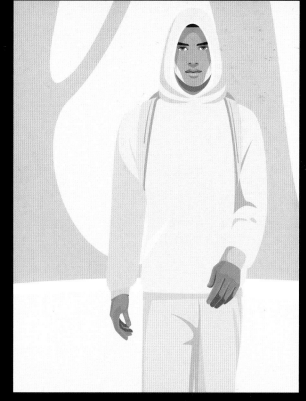

Irene Jacobs
Indulgence 2, for Philips
Design (2002)
Adobe Illustrator

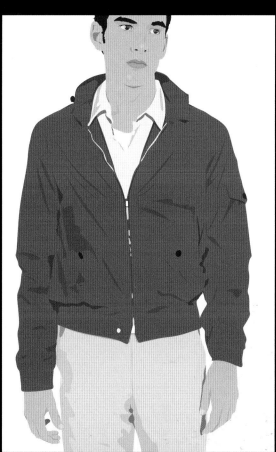

Arthur Mount
Marc Jacobs (2003)
Adobe Illustrator

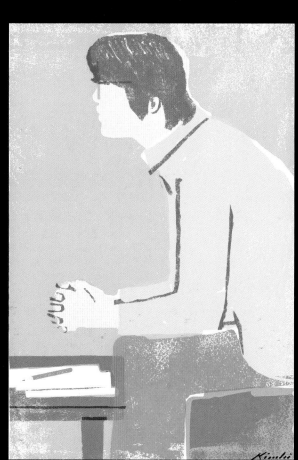

Tatsuro Kuichi
Untitled (2005)
Adobe Photoshop

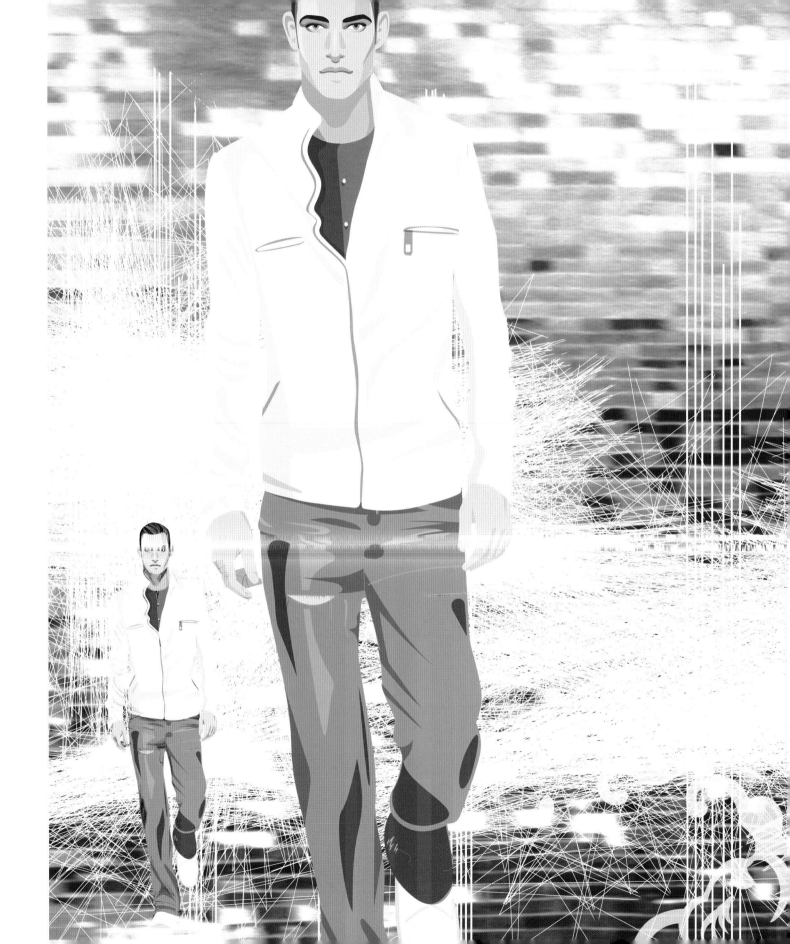

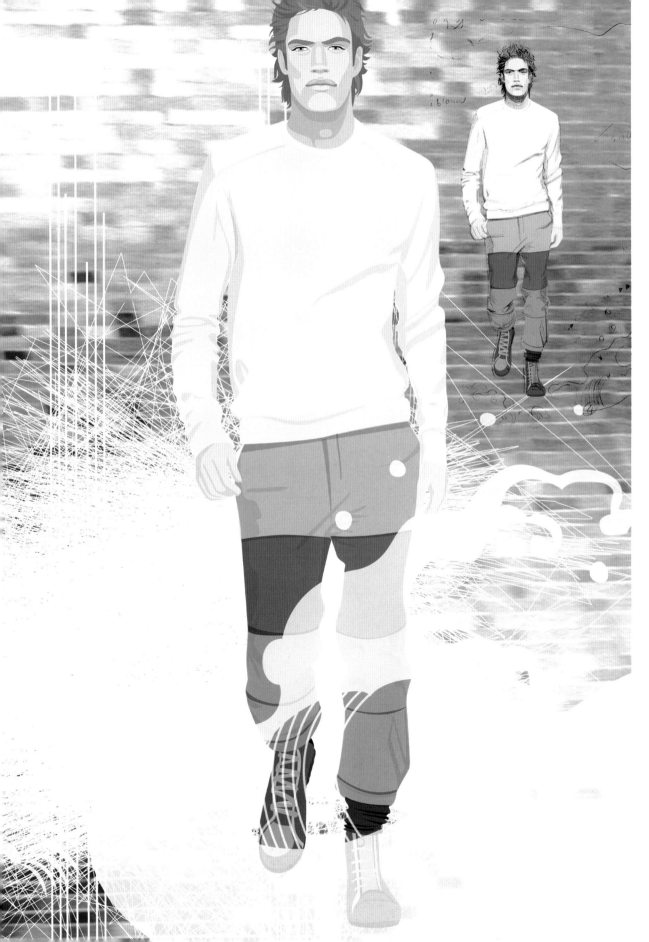

Irene Jacobs
Summer Trends, for *Esquire* magazine (2003)
Adobe Illustrator

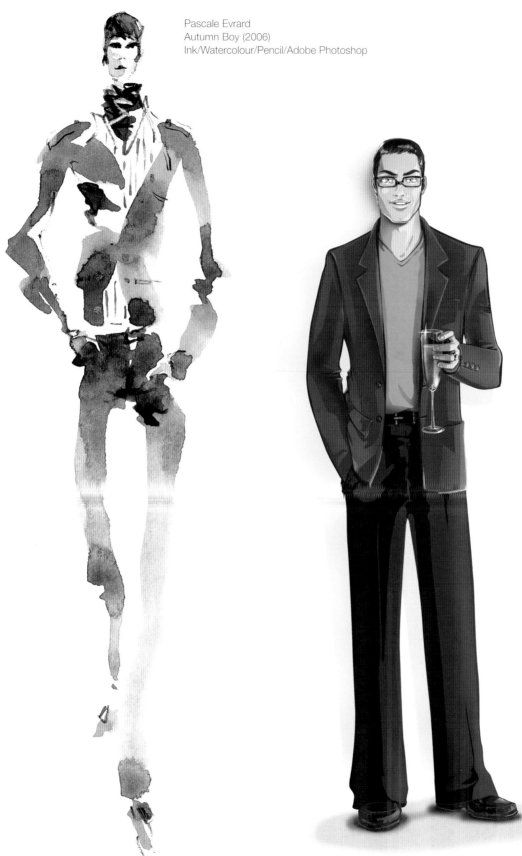

Pascale Evrard
Autumn Boy (2006)
Ink/Watercolour/Pencil/Adobe Photoshop

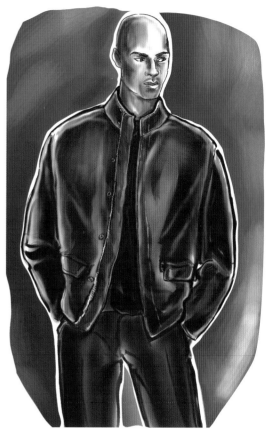

Marsha Silvestri
Brown Zip Jacket (2004)
Charcoal/Adobe Photoshop/Adobe Illustrator

Monica Laita
NY Estate Agency N.2 (2006)
Adobe Photoshop

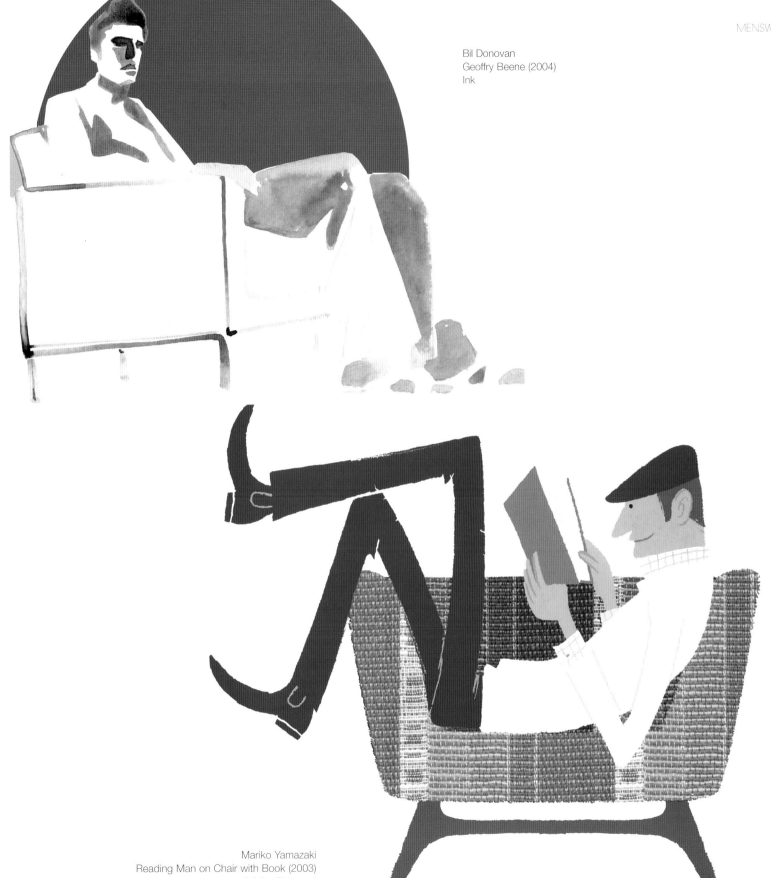

Bil Donovan
Geoffry Beene (2004)
Ink

Mariko Yamazaki
Reading Man on Chair with Book (2003)
Adobe Illustrator

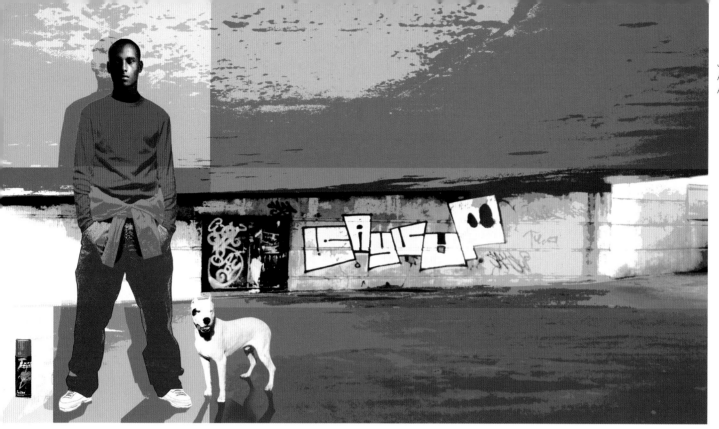

Jacqui Paull and Carl Melegari
Aadel and Rokit (2003)
Adobe Photoshop

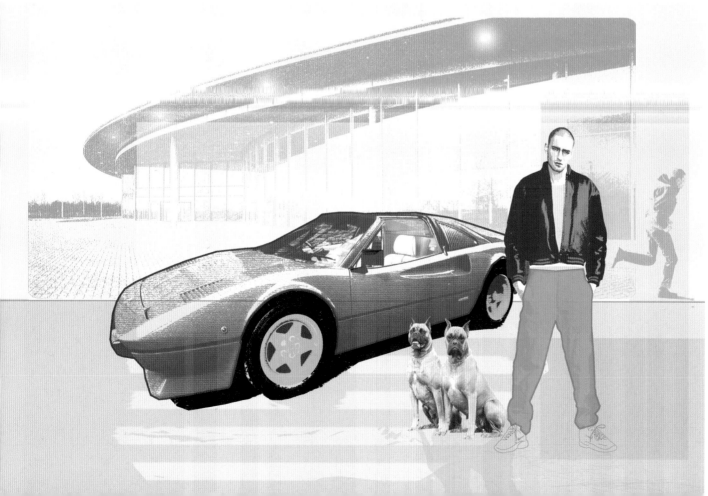

Jacqui Paull and Carl Melegari
Guy's Car (2002)
Adobe Photoshop

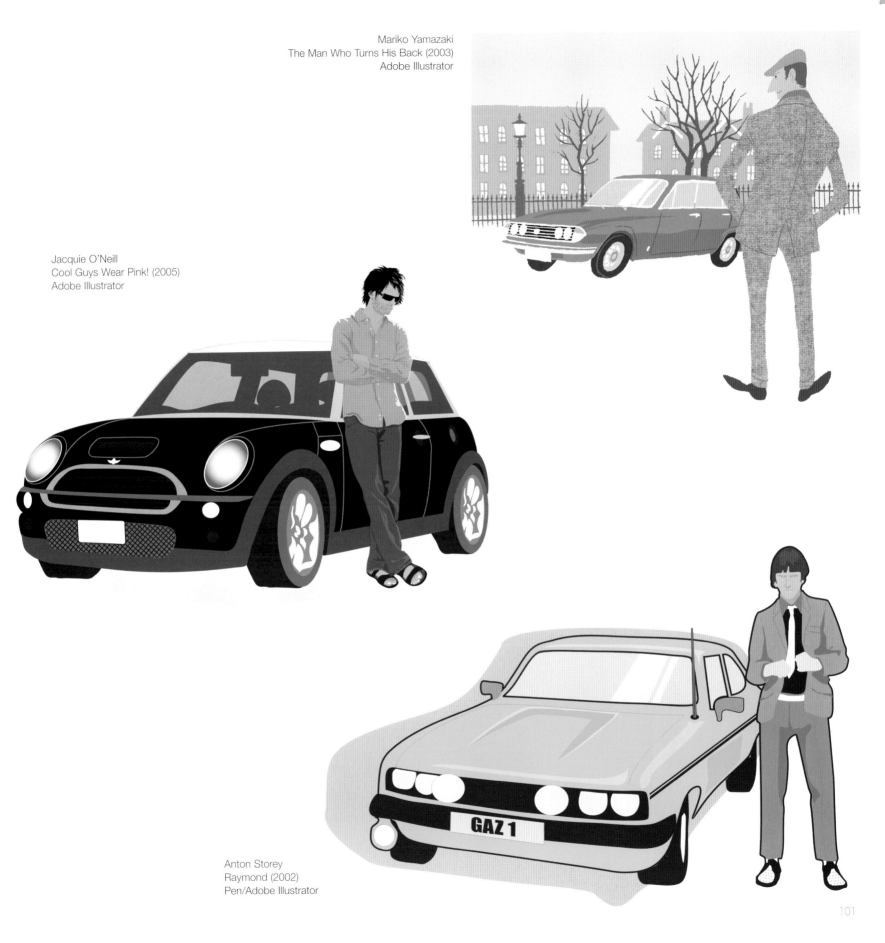

Mariko Yamazaki
The Man Who Turns His Back (2003)
Adobe Illustrator

Jacquie O'Neill
Cool Guys Wear Pink! (2005)
Adobe Illustrator

Anton Storey
Raymond (2002)
Pen/Adobe Illustrator

GAZ 1

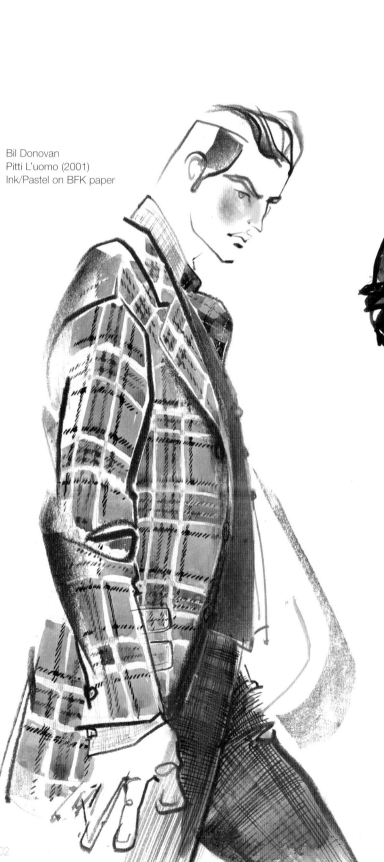

Bil Donovan
Pitti L'uomo (2001)
Ink/Pastel on BFK paper

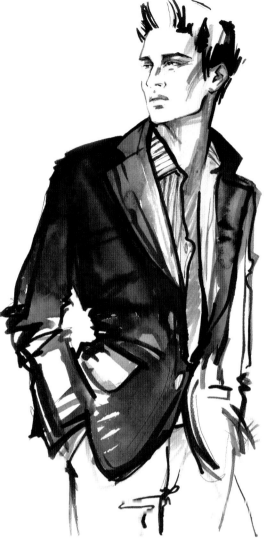

Elena Lavdovskaya Konstantinovna
TSUM Menswear Campaign (2005)
Aquarelle/Ink/Adobe Photoshop

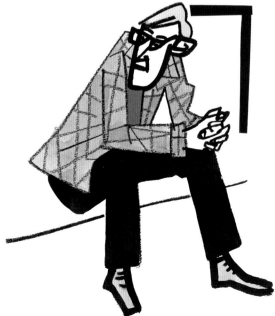

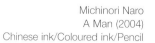

Michinori Naro
A Man (2004)
Chinese ink/Coloured ink/Pencil

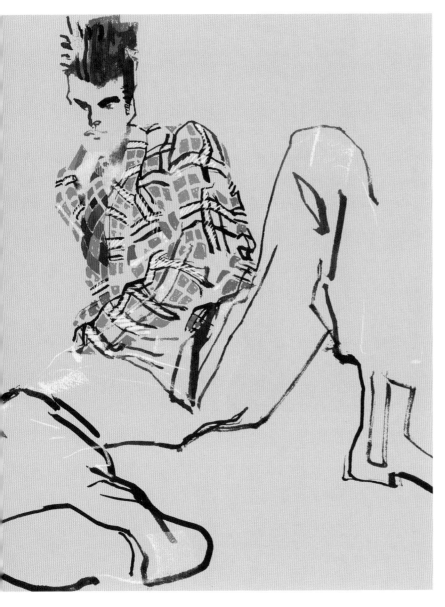

Bil Donovan
Untitled (2000)
Conté/Pastel/Gouache

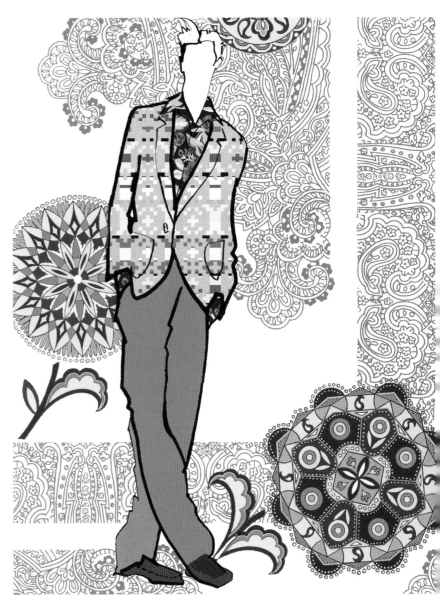

Janis Salek
Parisian Dandy (2006)
Adobe Photoshop

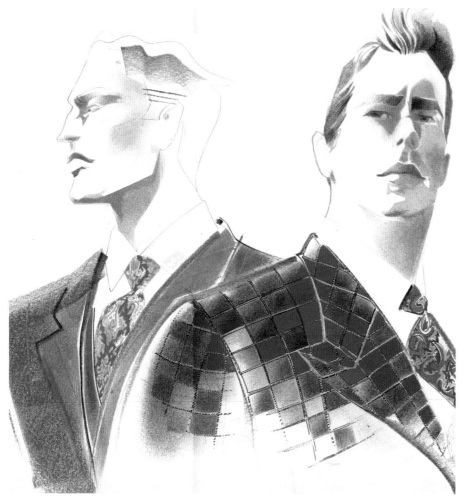

Bil Donovan
Untitled (1999)
Pastel/Gouache

Margot Maas van Huijkelom
An English Man (2006)
Watercolour/Ink pen

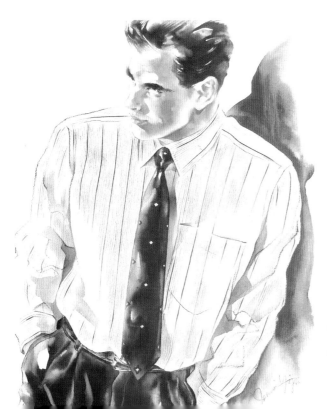

Jennie Yip
Excello Shirts (2006)
Gouache on watercolour paper

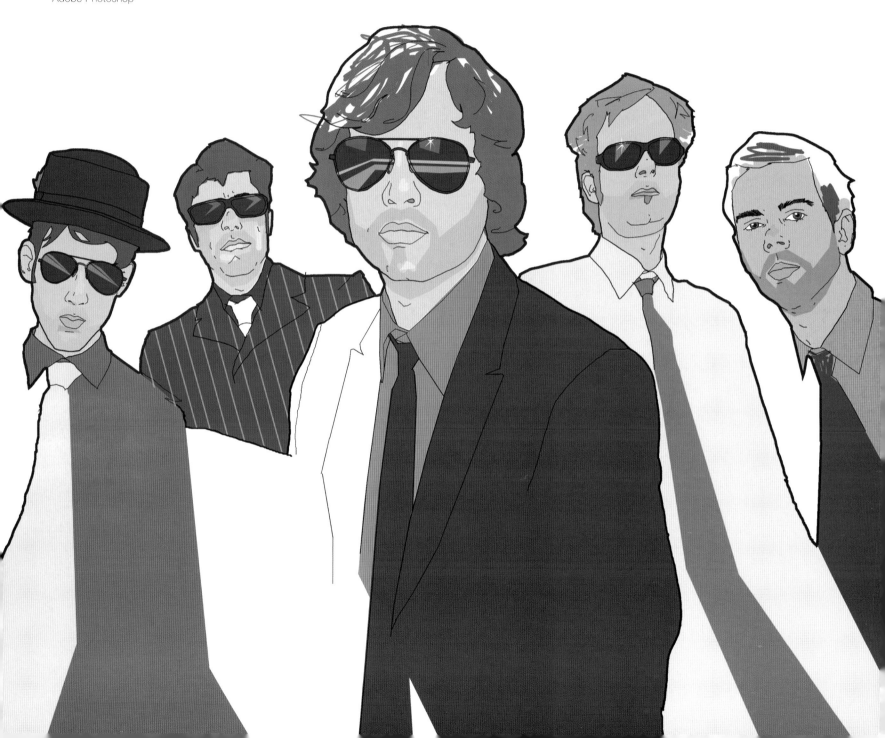

Lee Woodgate
Electric Six (2005)
Adobe Photoshop

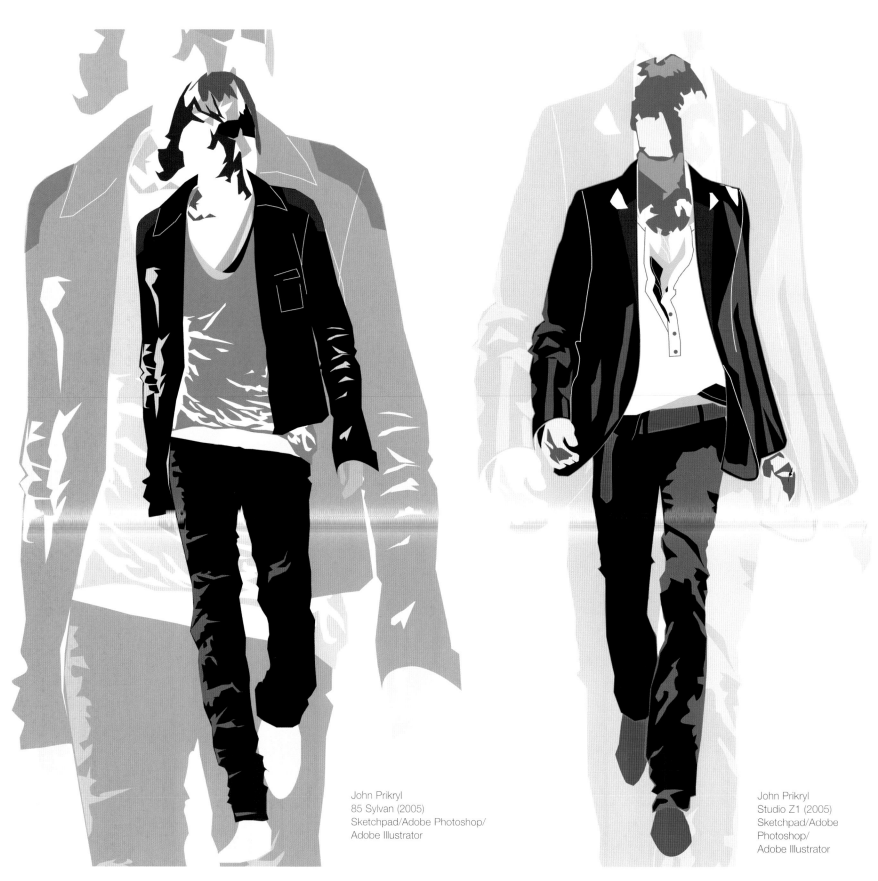

John Prikryl
85 Sylvan (2005)
Sketchpad/Adobe Photoshop/
Adobe Illustrator

John Prikryl
Studio Z1 (2005)
Sketchpad/Adobe
Photoshop/
Adobe Illustrator

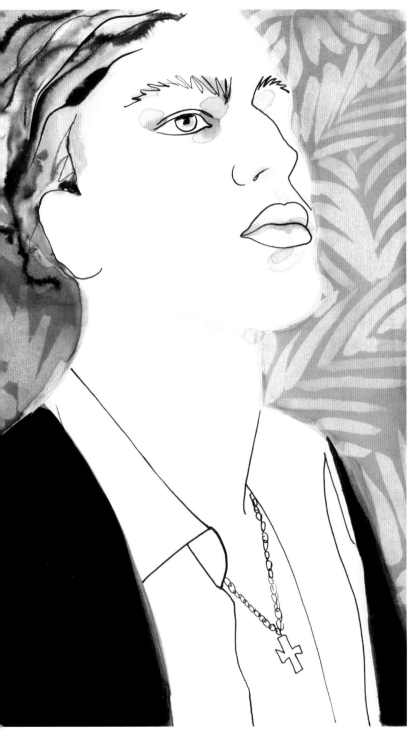

Margot Mace van Huijkelom
Jamel (2006)
Watercolour/Ink pen

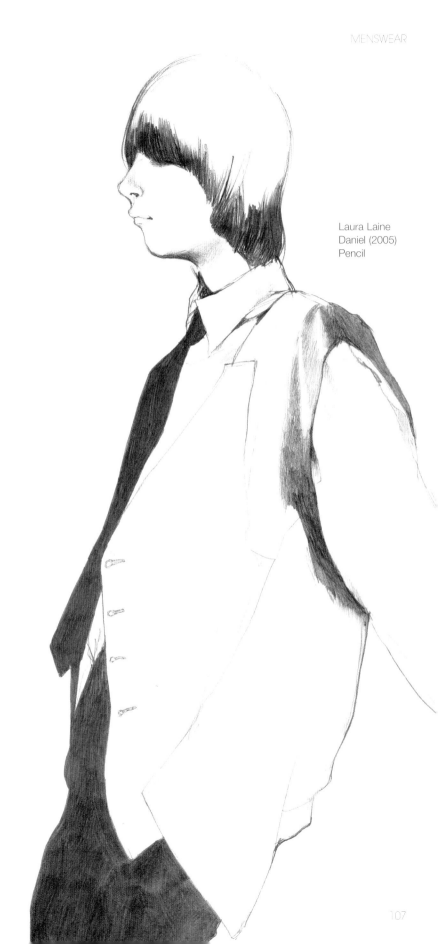

Laura Laine
Daniel (2005)
Pencil

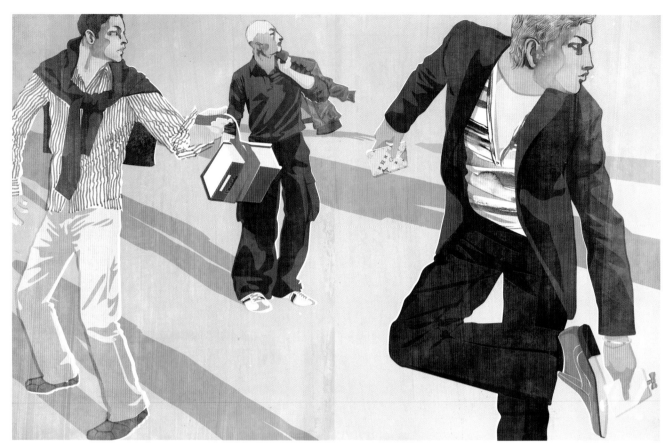

Tina Berning
Männermode (2004)
Felt pen/Watercolour/Vector
Graphic/Adobe Photoshop

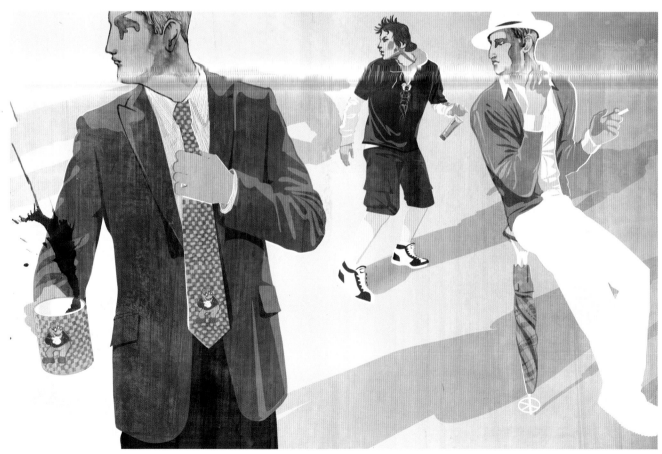

Tina Berning
Männermode (2004)
Felt pen/Watercolour/Vector
Graphic/Adobe Photoshop

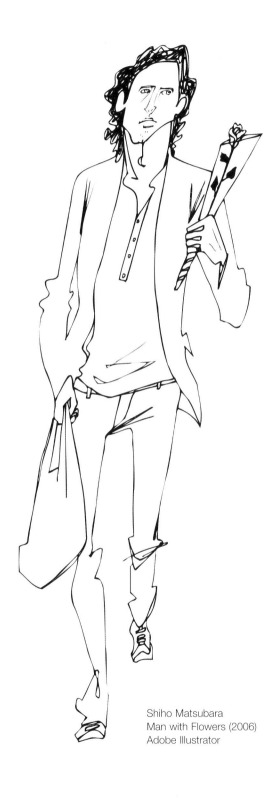

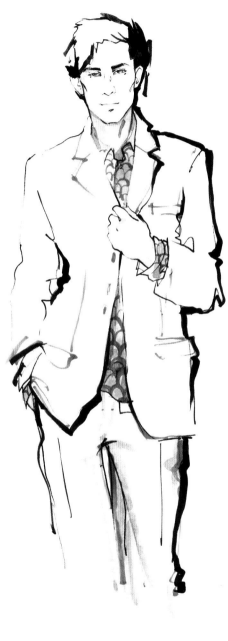

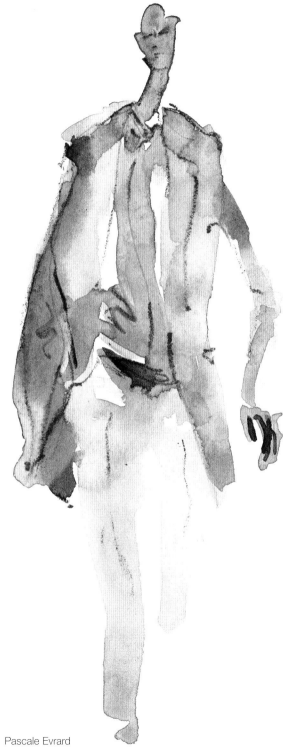

Shiho Matsubara
Man with Flowers (2006)
Adobe Illustrator

Elena Lavdovskaya Konstantinovna
TSUM Menswear Campaign (2005)
Aquarelle/Ink/Adobe Photoshop

Pascale Evrard
Man in Blue Jacket (2006)
Ink/Watercolour/Pencil/Adobe Photoshop

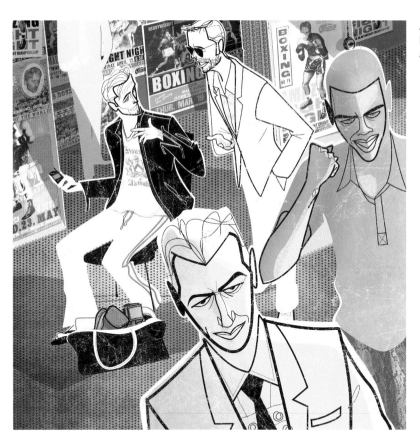

Jonas Bergstrand
Neiman Marcus Menswear, New York (2005)
Adobe Illustrator/Adobe Photoshop

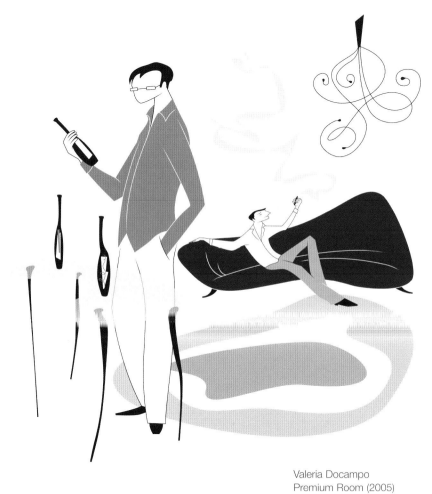

Valeria Docampo
Premium Room (2005)
Adobe Illustrator

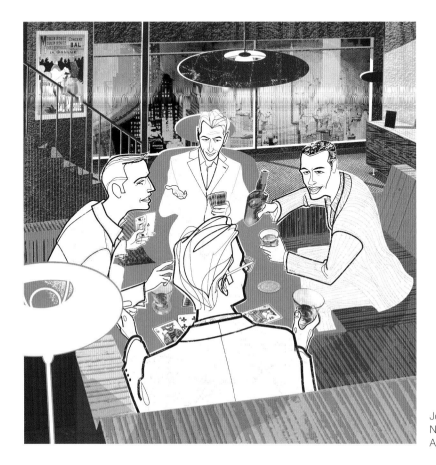

Jonas Bergstrand
Neiman Marcus Menswear, New York (2005)
Adobe Illustrator/Adobe Photoshop

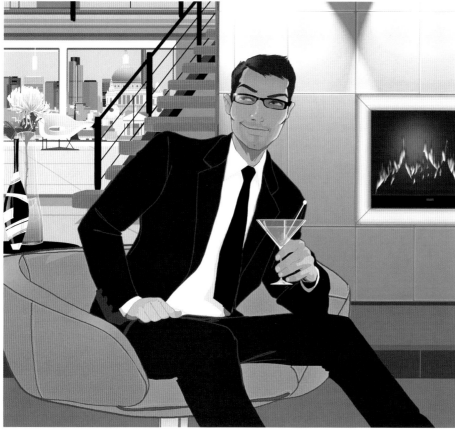

Gavin Reece
Metro Sexual (2003)
Adobe Photoshop

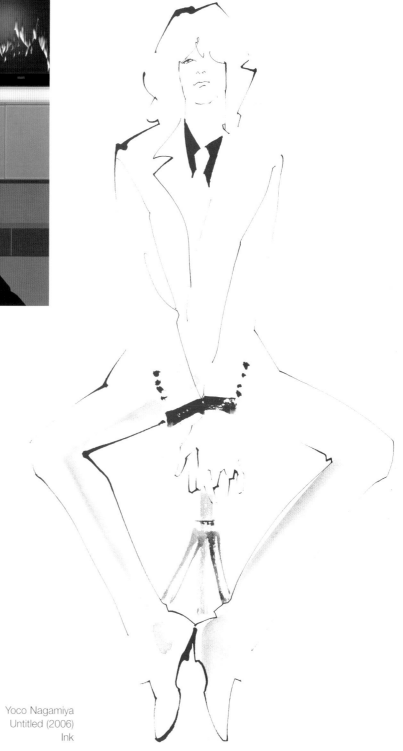

Yoco Nagamiya
Untitled (2006)
Ink

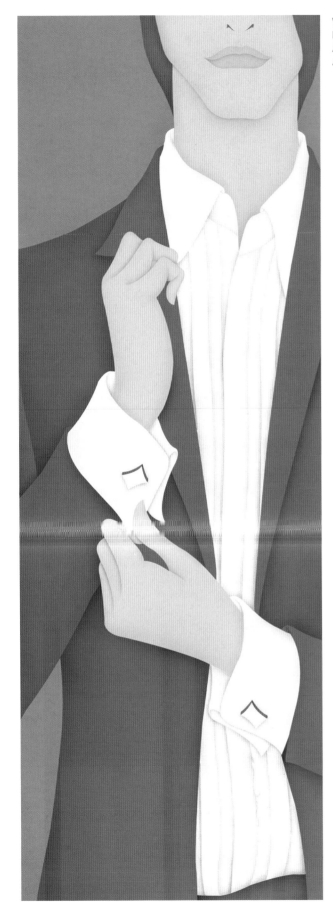

Wai
Dapper (2005)
Adobe Illustrator/
Adobe Photoshop

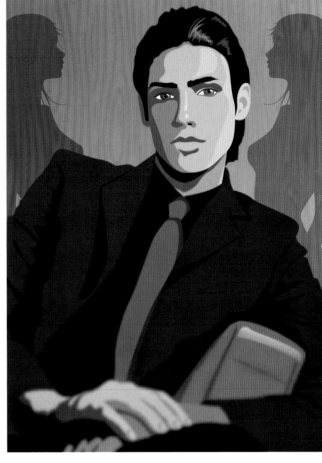

Herman Yap
Cool Dude for Nivea Men (2005)
Macromedia FreeHand/Adobe
Photoshop

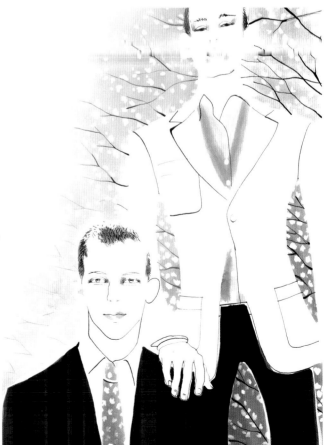

Margot Mace van Huijkelom
Two Guys (2006)
Watercolour/Ink pen

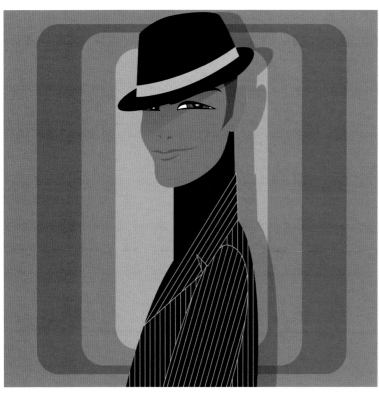

Pinglet
Styleguy (2002)
Adobe Illustrator

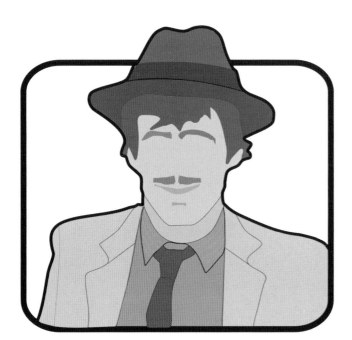

Anton Storey
Untitled (2001)
Pen/Adobe Illustrator

Coburn
Man in White (2006)
Adobe Illustrator

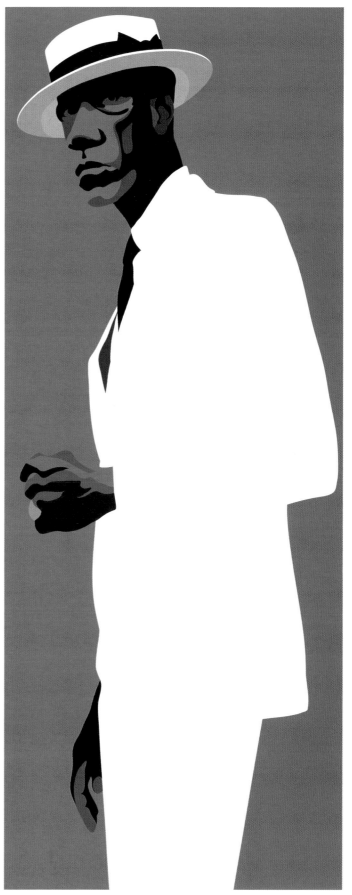

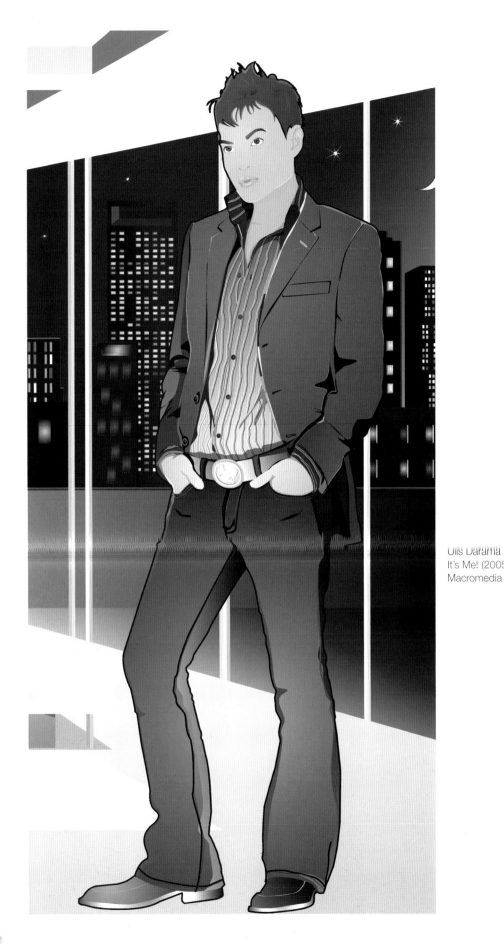

Ulis Darama
It's Me! (2005)
Macromedia FreeHand

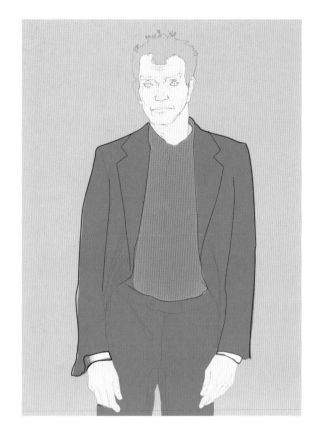

Anton Storey
Bob (2003)
Pen/Adobe Illustrator

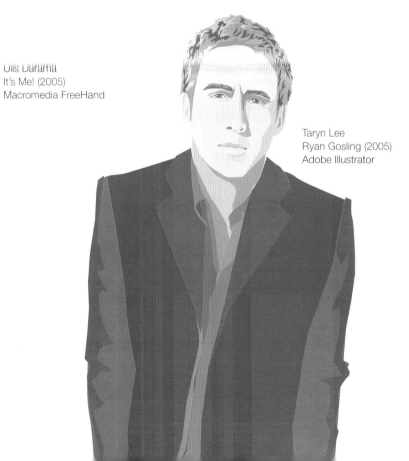

Taryn Lee
Ryan Gosling (2005)
Adobe Illustrator

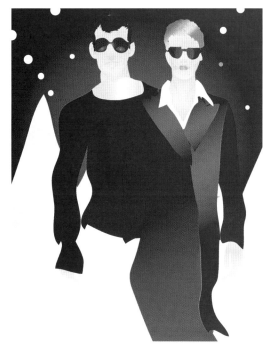

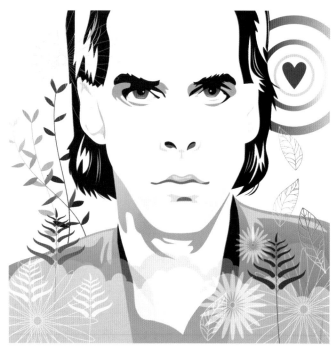

Fhiona Galloway
Nick Cave (2006)
Macromedia FreeHand

Natascha Engelmann
Brotherhood (2004)
Pencil/Adobe Photoshop

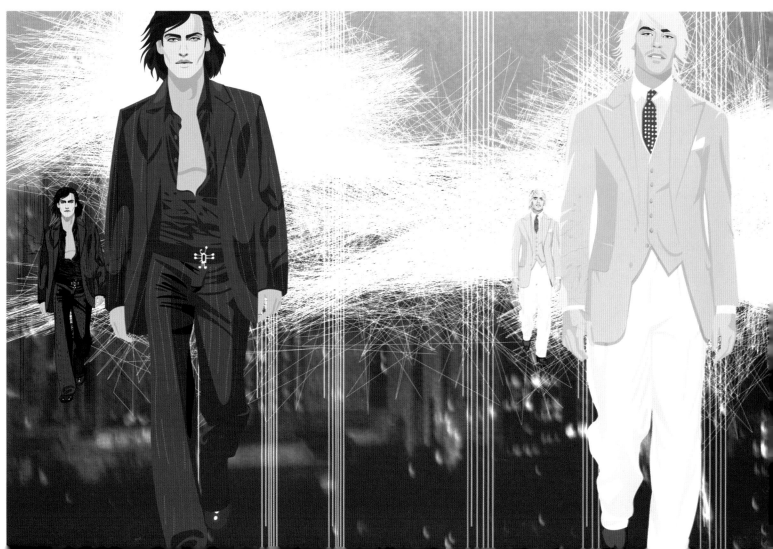

Irene Jacobs
mer Trends, for *Esquire*
magazine (2003)
Adobe Illustrator

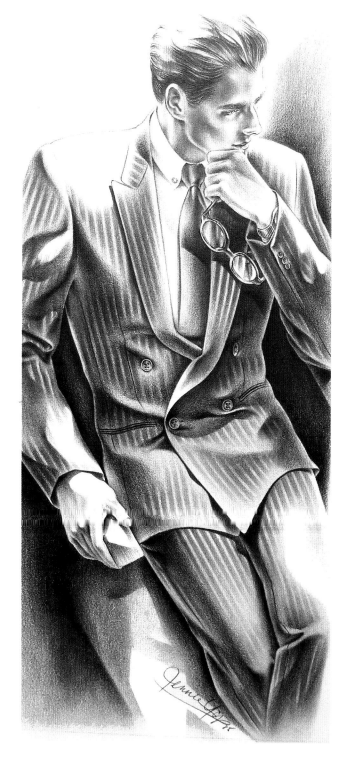

Jennie Yip
Salamandra (2006)
Pencil on paper

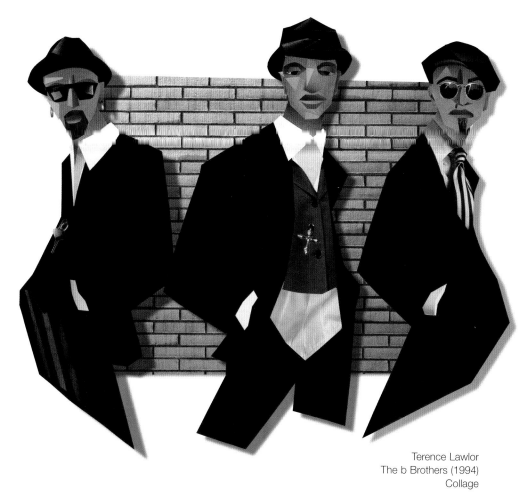

Terence Lawlor
The b Brothers (1994)
Collage

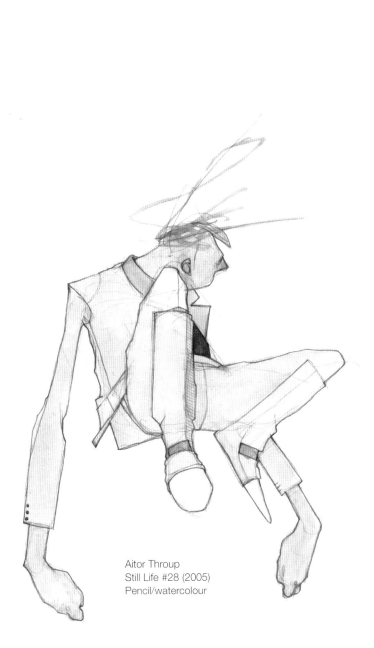

Aitor Throup
Still Life #28 (2005)
Pencil/watercolour

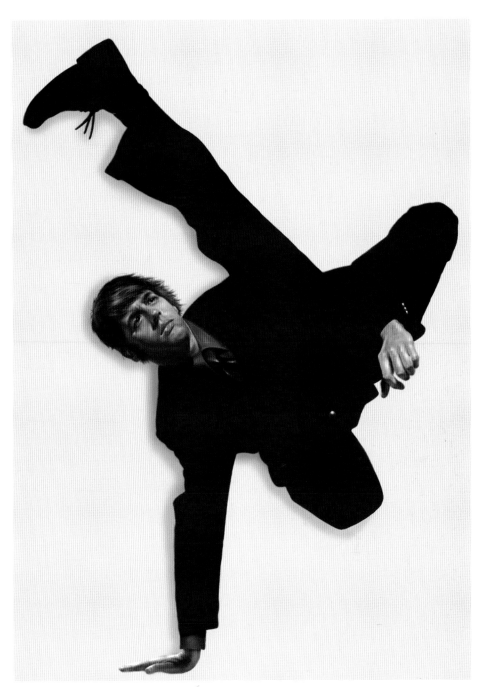

Andrew Smith
Break Down (2006)
Adobe Photoshop

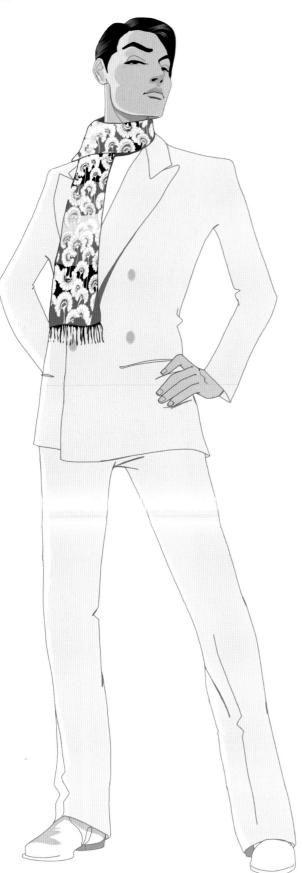

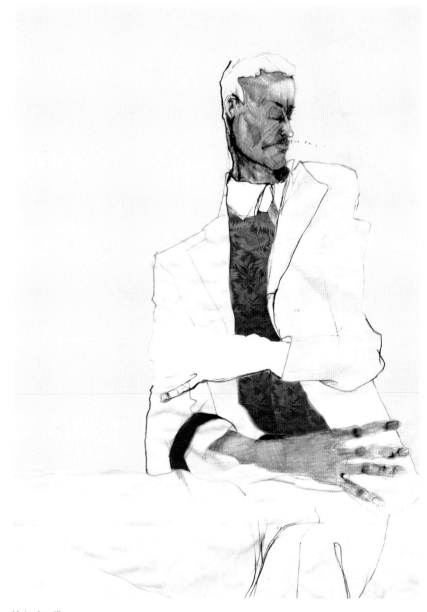

Kaja Jamtli
Reformed White Suit for Andrew Ibi (2006)
Pencil/Pen/Adobe Photoshop/Adobe Illustrator

Gavin Reece
Style Snob (2004)
Adobe Photoshop

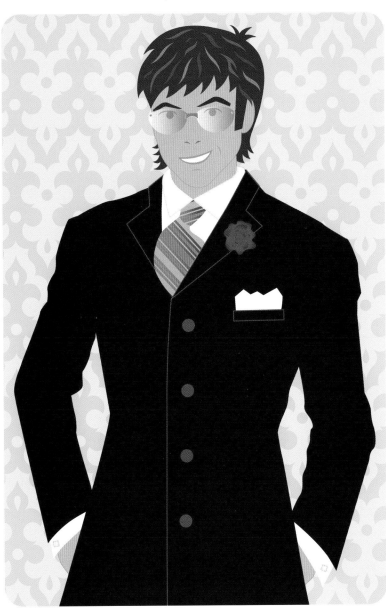

Robert Weiss
The Metrosexual (2004)
Adobe Illustrator

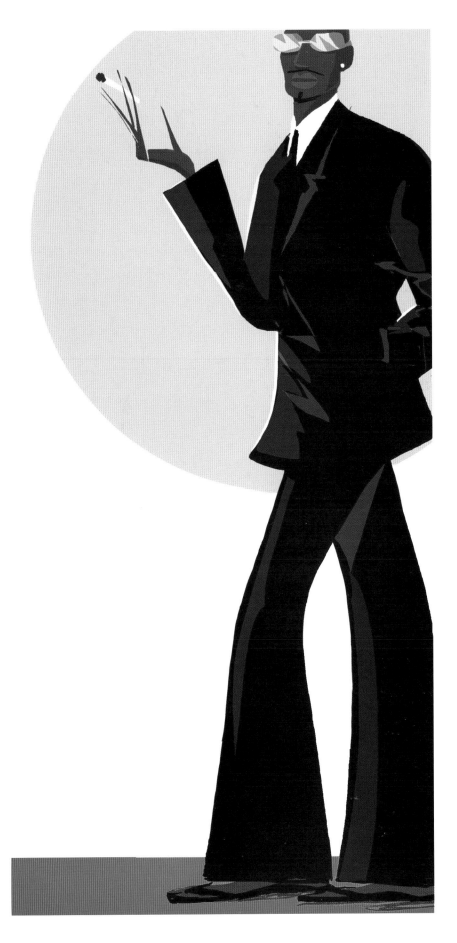

Alessandra Scandella
A Man in Black (2005)
Corel Painter/Adobe Photoshop

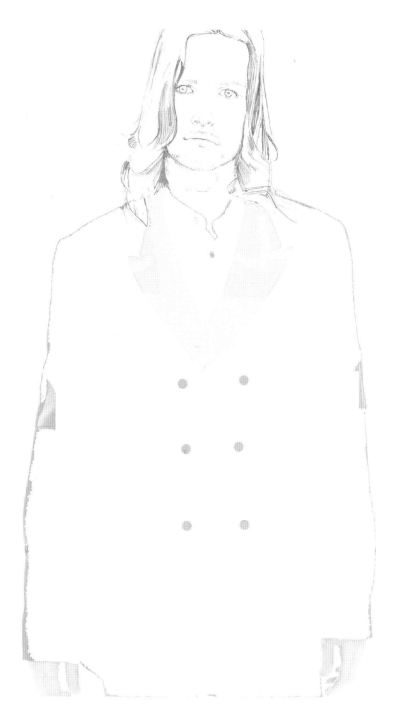

Anton Storey
Erik (2004)
Pen/Adobe Photoshop

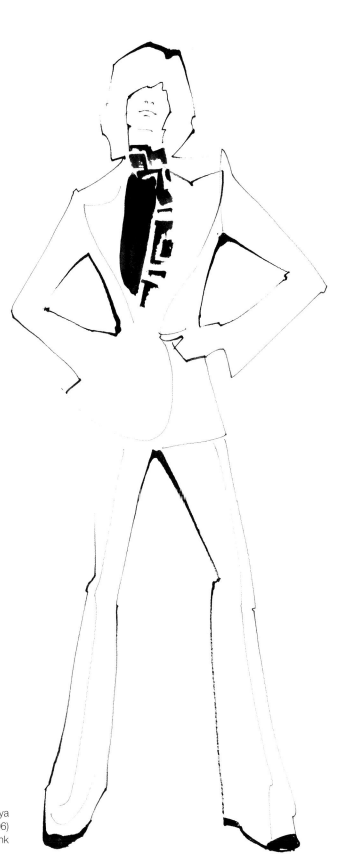

Yoco Nagamiya
Untitled (2006)
Ink

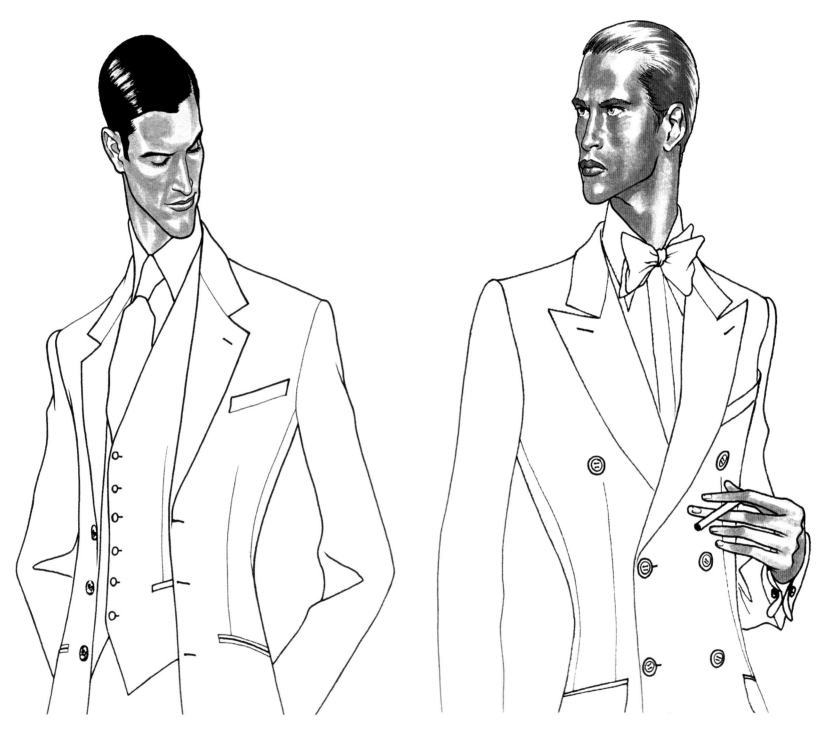

Arturo Elena
Untitled, for Biendi shop window (2001)
Ink/Felt tip pen

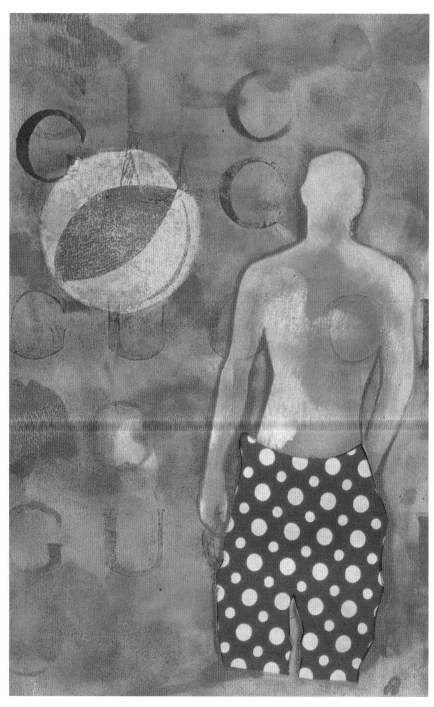

Vincent Agostino
Gucci Summer (2004)
Acrylic/Fabric

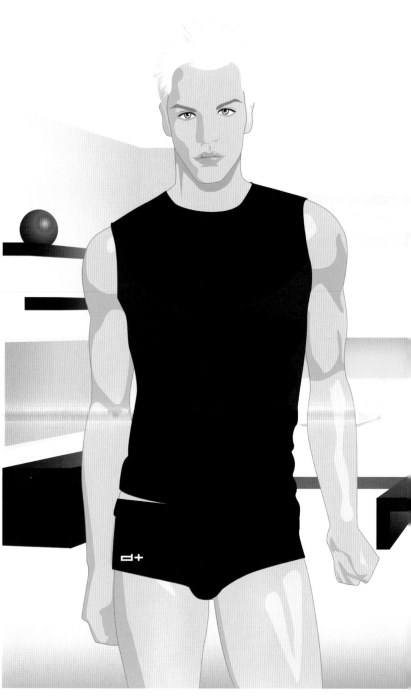

Dilek Peker
Perfect Day (2006)
Adobe Photoshop

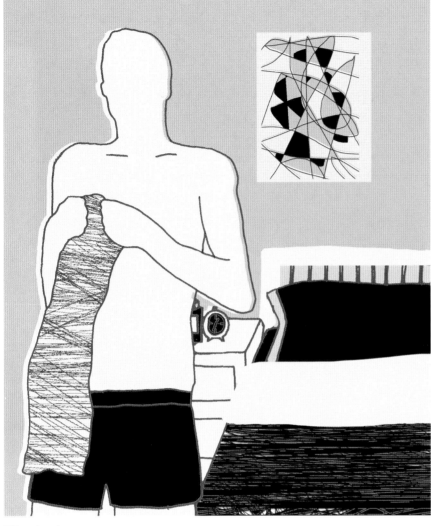

Tiffany Lynch
Bedroom Boy (2006)
Pen/Ink/Adobe Photoshop

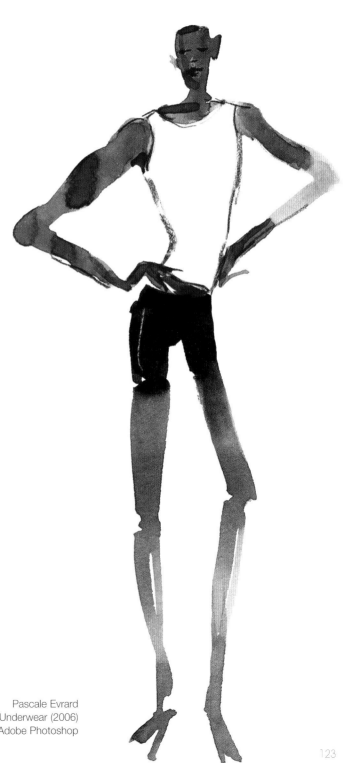

Pascale Evrard
Guy in Underwear (2006)
Ink/Watercolour/Pencil/Adobe Photoshop

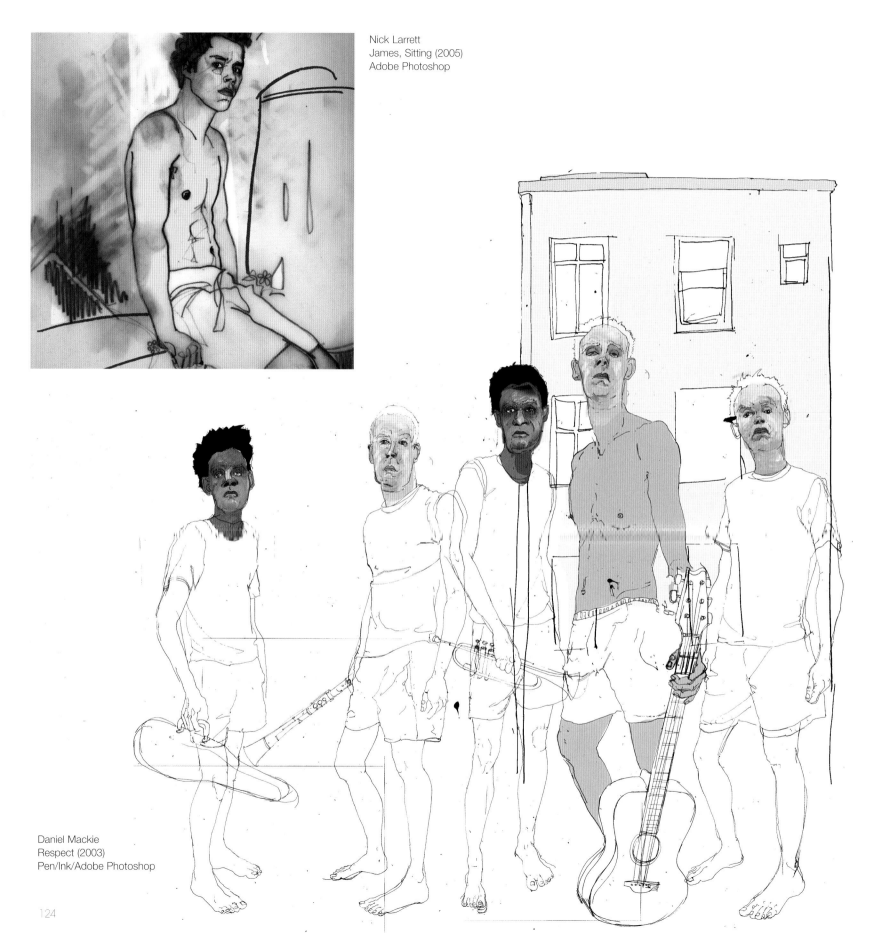

Nick Larrett
James, Sitting (2005)
Adobe Photoshop

Daniel Mackie
Respect (2003)
Pen/Ink/Adobe Photoshop

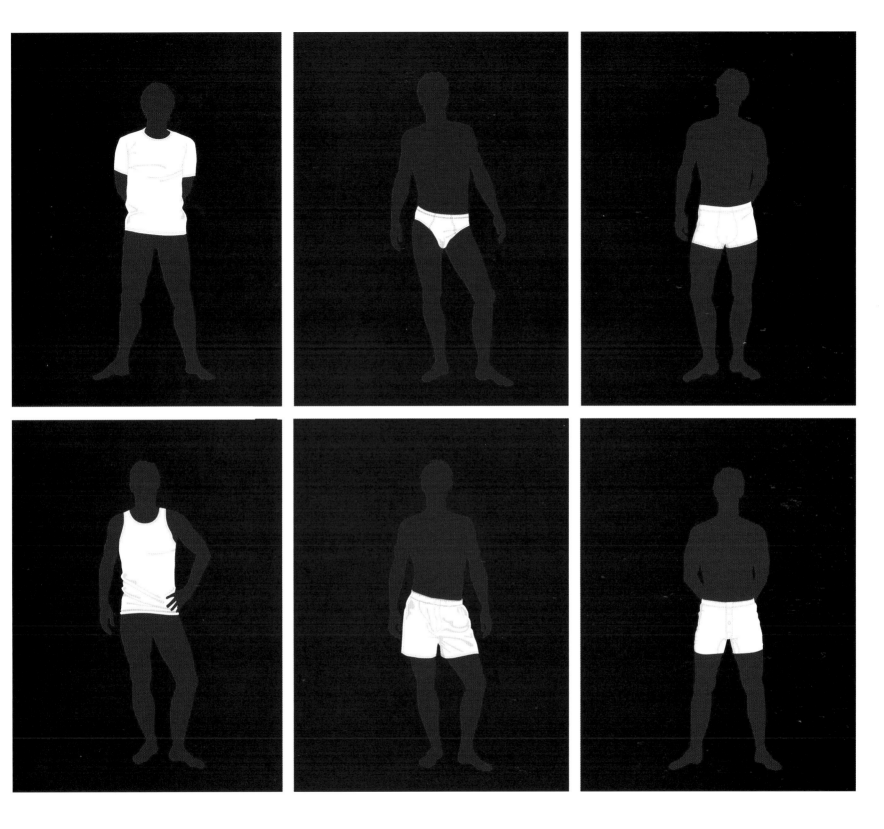

Stuart Holmes
Marks and Spencer, basic range (2003)
Adobe Illustrator

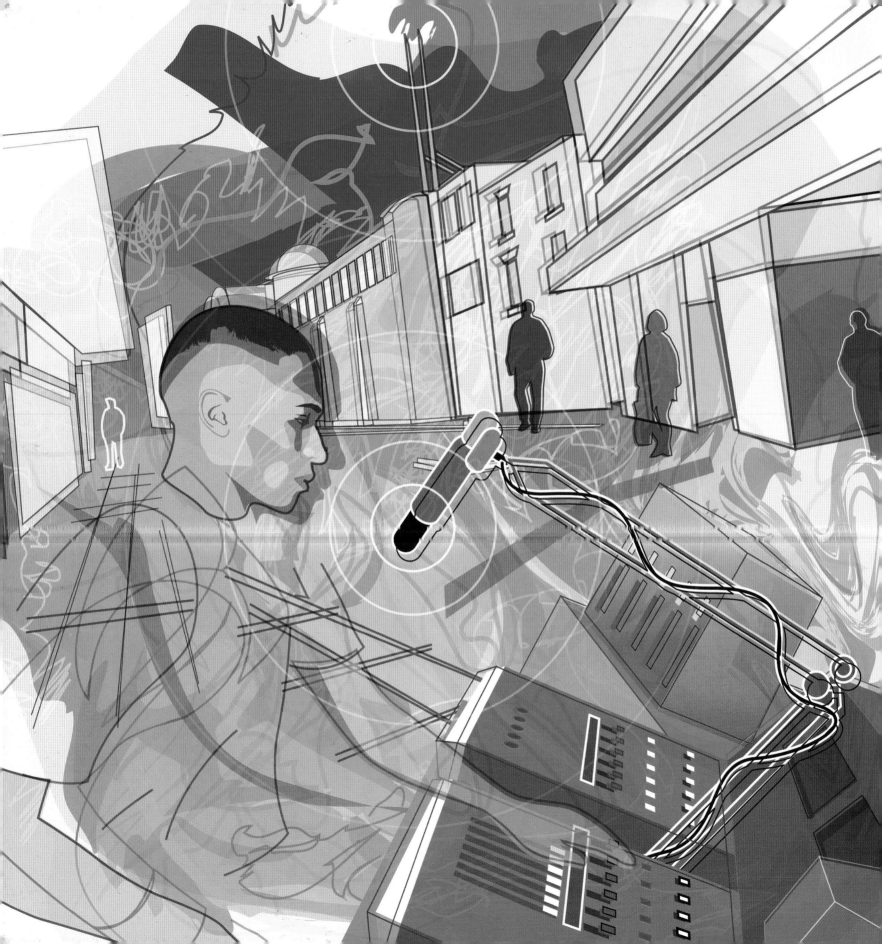

Youth Culture

music clubland tribes & vibes street fashion girls

streetwise guys relationships

Domanic Li
Radio Regen (2003)
Adobe Photoshop

Irene Jacobs
Untitled, for 'A Man's Guide to
Life', *Man* magazine (1999)
Adobe Illustrator

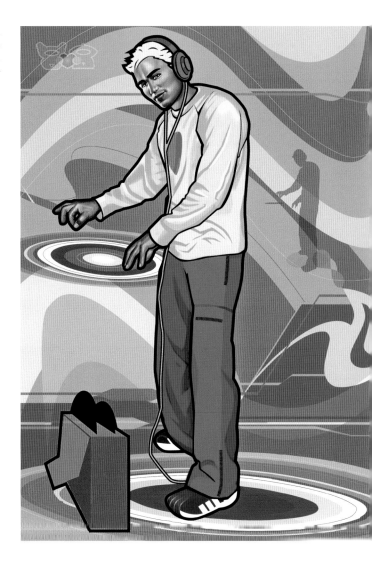

Anton Storey
Untitled (2002)
Pen/Adobe Illustrator

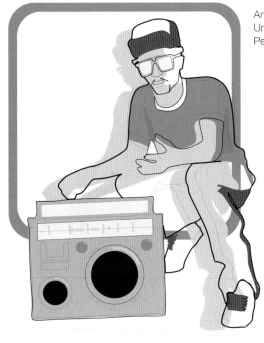

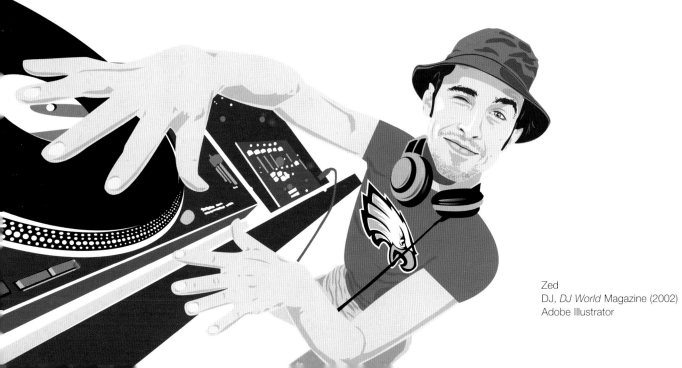

Zed
DJ, *DJ World* Magazine (2002)
Adobe Illustrator

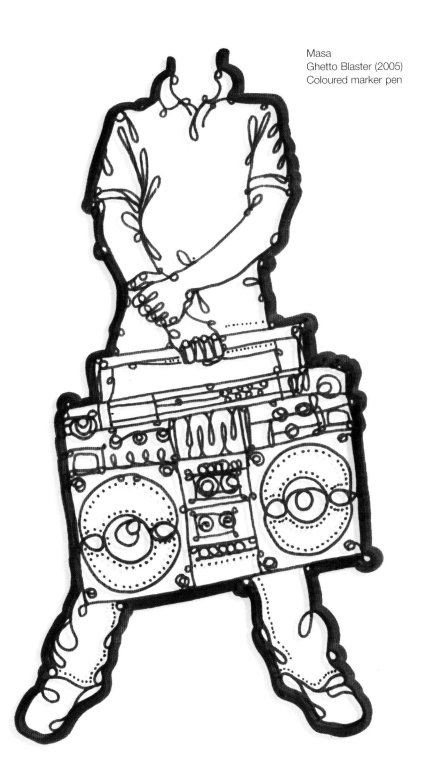

Masa
Ghetto Blaster (2005)
Coloured marker pen

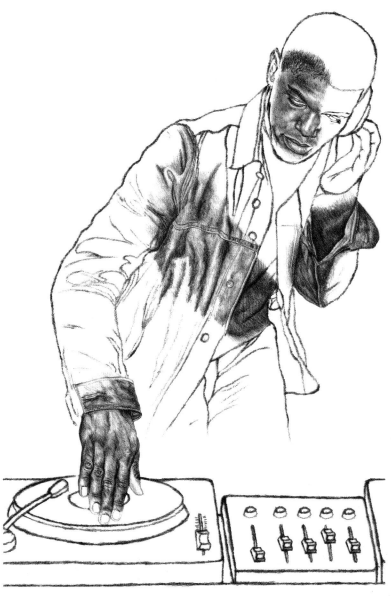

David Nwokedi
Ray (2004)
Pencil/Adobe Photoshop

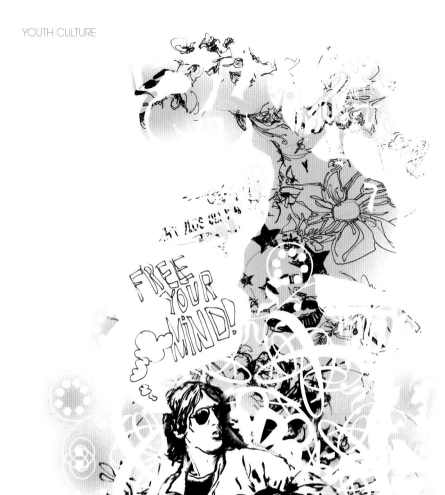

Christian Barthold
Free Your Mind (2006)
India ink/Adobe Photoshop

Jacquie O'Neill
Lost in Music (2005)
Adobe Illustrator CC

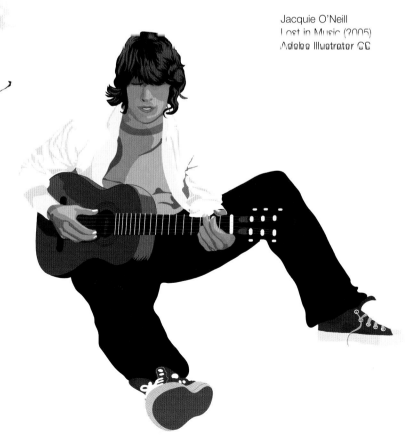

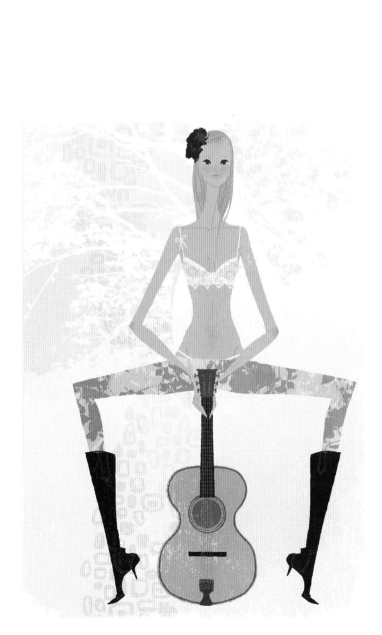

Yuko Yoshioka
Guitare (2006)
Adobe Photoshop

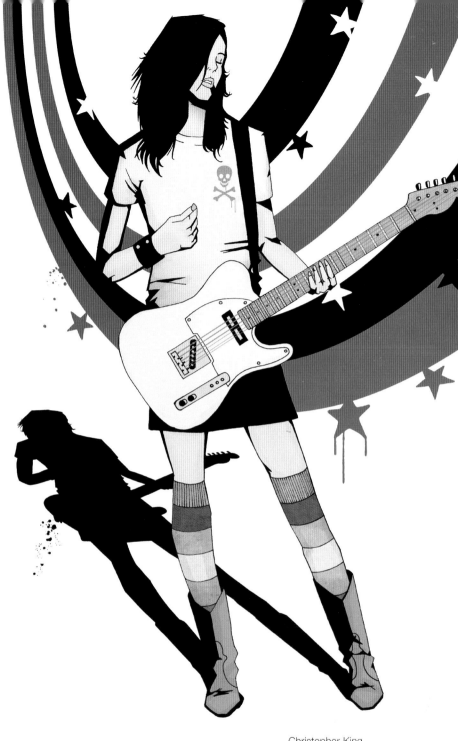

Christopher King
Guitar Girl (2005)
Pen/Ink/Adobe Photoshop

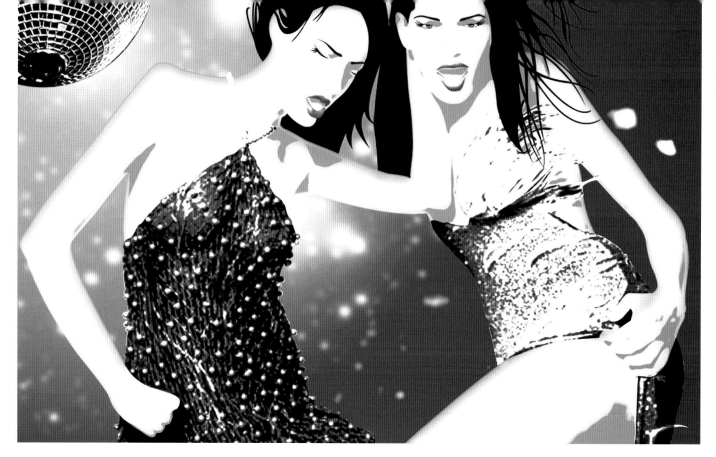

Ewa Brockway
Party Girls (2005)
Adobe Photoshop

Marguerite Sauvage
Pcncil/Adobc Photoshop

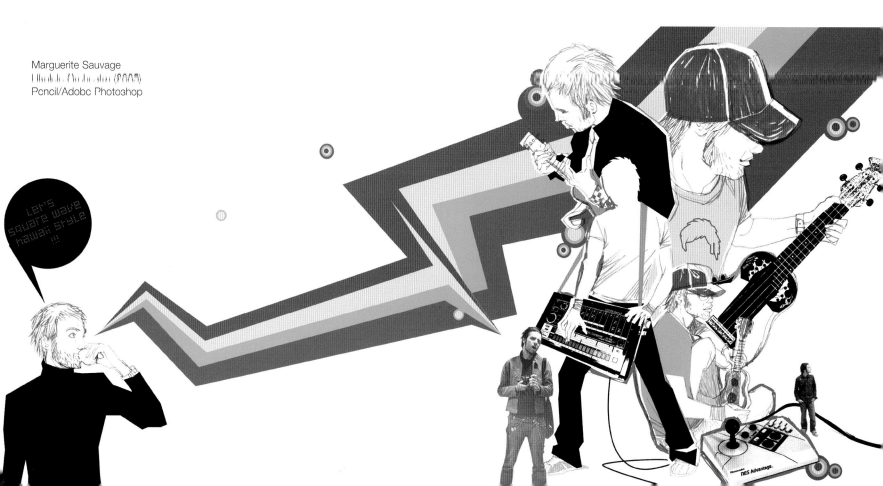

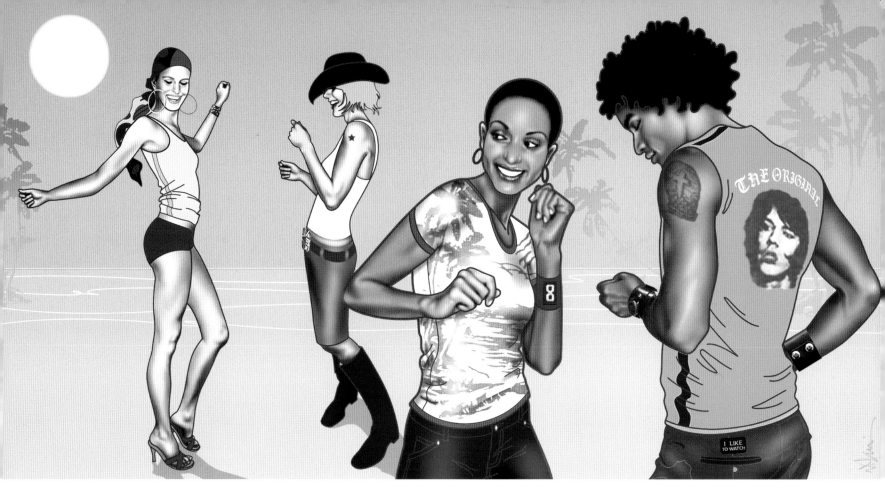

Nicoletta Mazzesi
New Scene (2005)
Adobe Photoshop/Adobe Illustrator

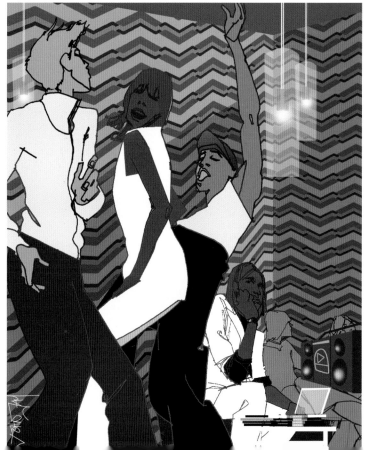

John Jay Cabuay
The Jealous Guy
Pen/Ink/Adobe Photoshop

133

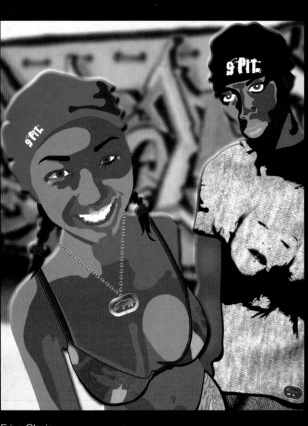

Erica Glasier
Butterfly (2002)
Adobe Photoshop/Adobe Illustrator

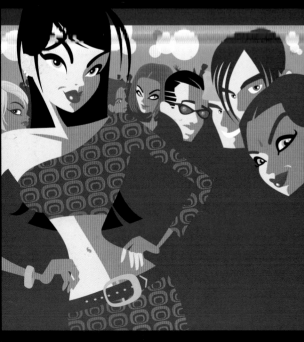

Rian Hughes
Automatic Anthems (1998)
Adobe Illustrator/Adobe Photoshop

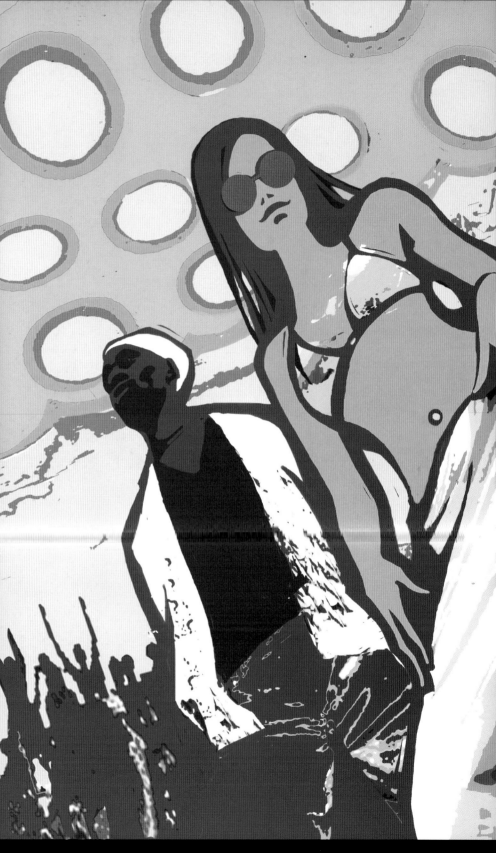

Marcella Peluffo
Beach Party (2005)
Corel Painter

Jeff Mulawka
Clubland (2004)
Adobe Photoshop

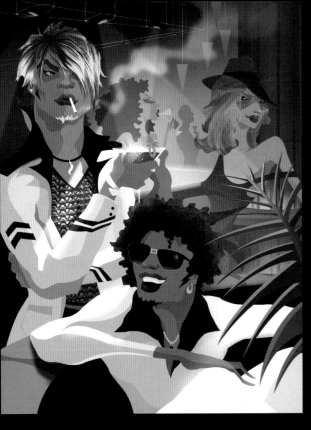

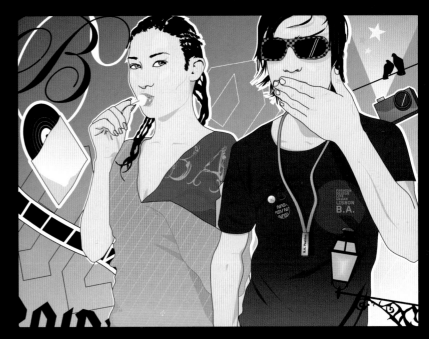

Sofia Dias
Pink Neon Dream (2004)
Macromedia FreeHand

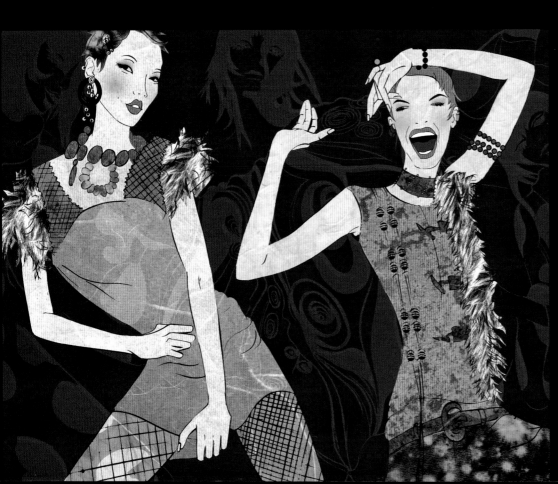

Annabelle J Verhoye
La Samaritaine (2006)
Chine collé/Adobe Photoshop

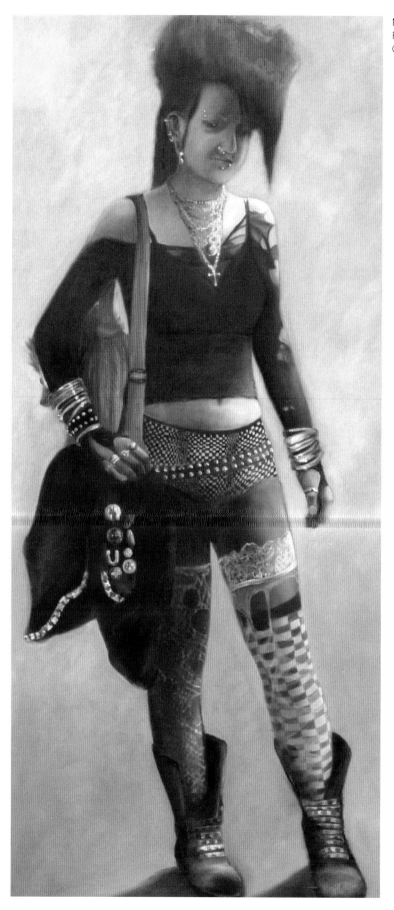

Naomi Devil
Punk (2005)
Oil on canvas

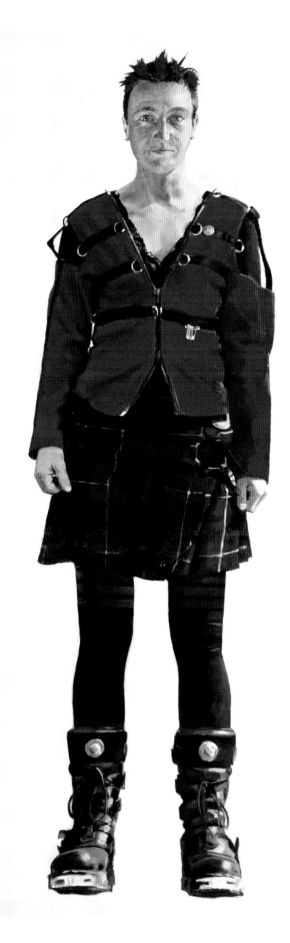

Stuart Mason
Jane (2004)
Oil/Acrylic

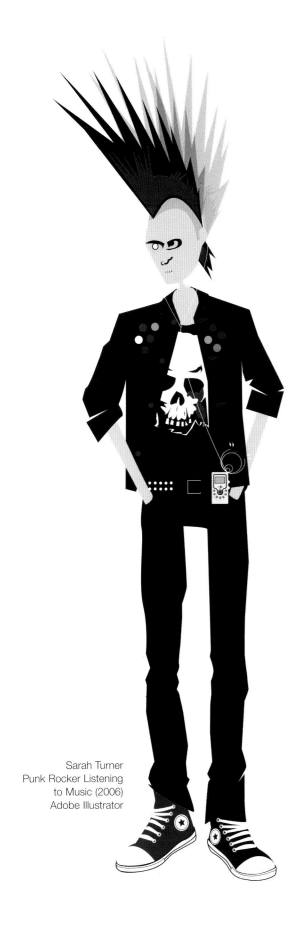

Sarah Turner
Punk Rocker Listening
to Music (2006)
Adobe Illustrator

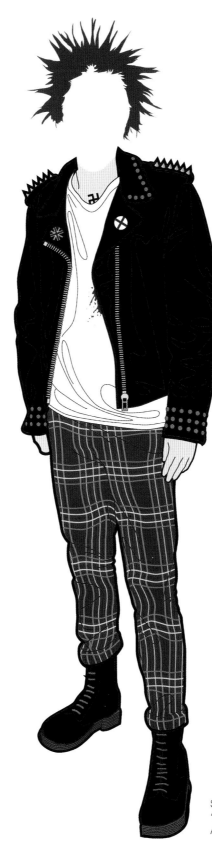

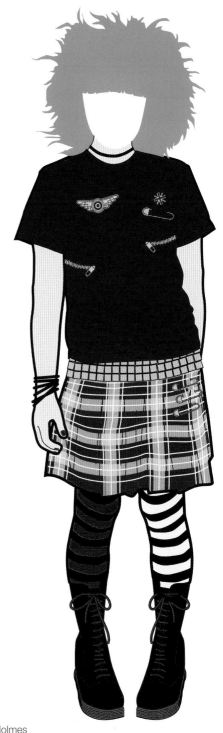

Stuart Holmes
'Punks', for the V&A Museum (2004)
Adobe Illustrator

137

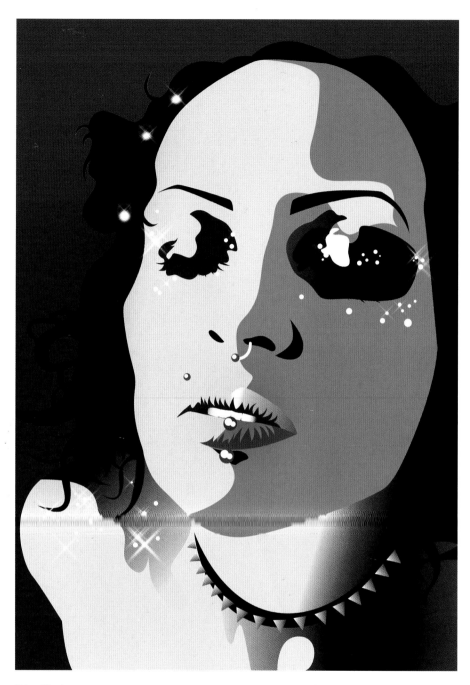

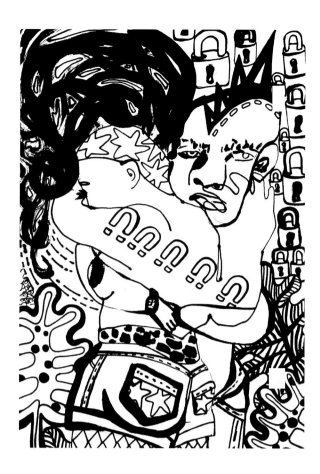

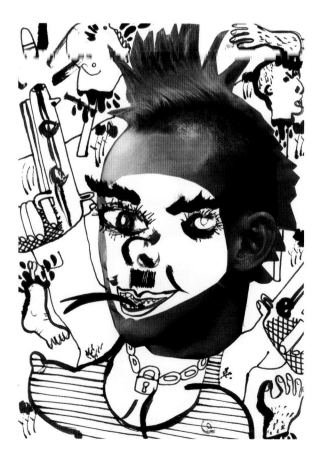

Erica Glasier
Found (2002)
Adobe Illustrator

Claudio Parentela
Untitled (2005)
Ink and pen on paper

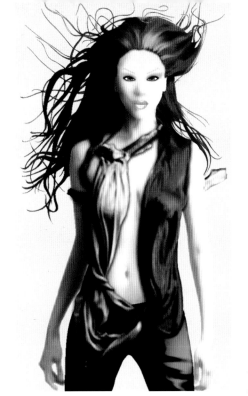

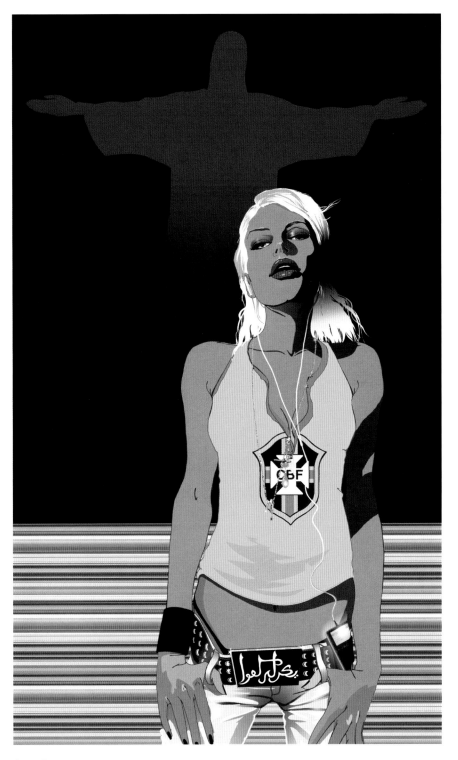

Ewa Brockway
Tyra (2005)
Adobe Photoshop

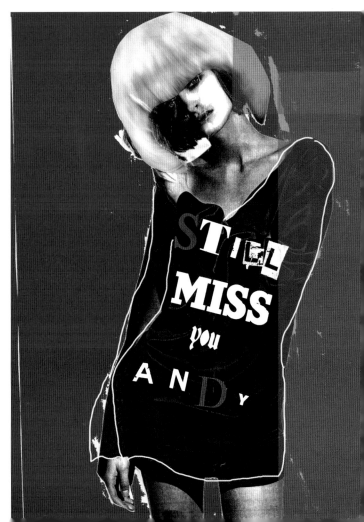

Gavin Reece
Brazilian! (2004)
Adobe Photoshop

Aga Baranska
Blondie (2006)
Collage/Paint/Adobe Photoshop

Giulio Iurissevich
UFO Dictactor (2006)
Macromedia FreeHand/Adobe Photoshop

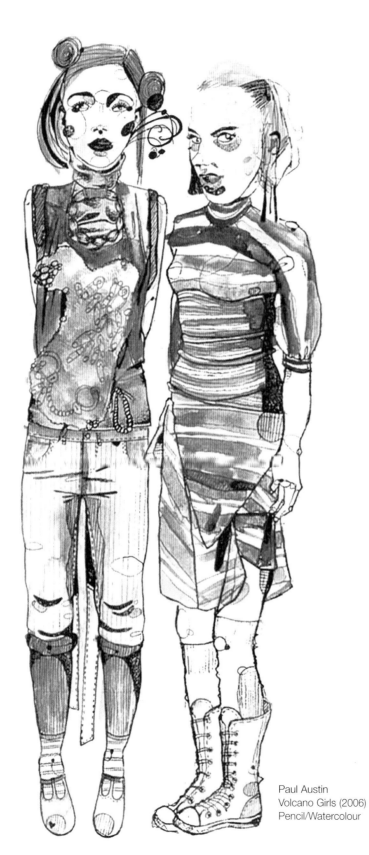

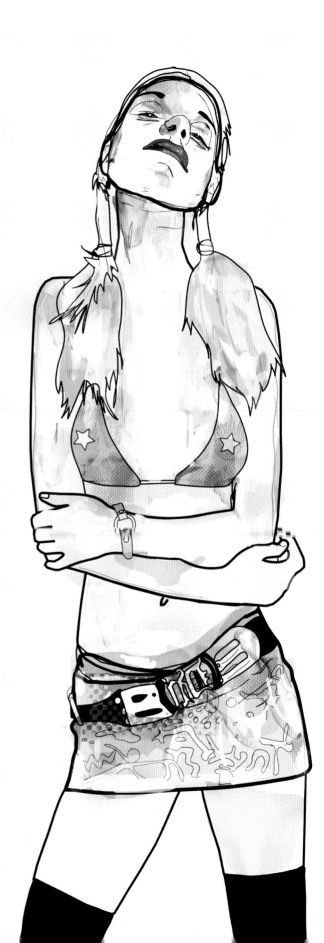

Paul Austin
Volcano Girls (2006)
Pencil/Watercolour

Cecilia Carlstedt
Untitled, *Habit* Magazine (2005)
Pencil/Adobe Illustrator/Adobe Photoshop

Jan Feindt
Personal (2005)
Pen/Ink/Adobe Photoshop

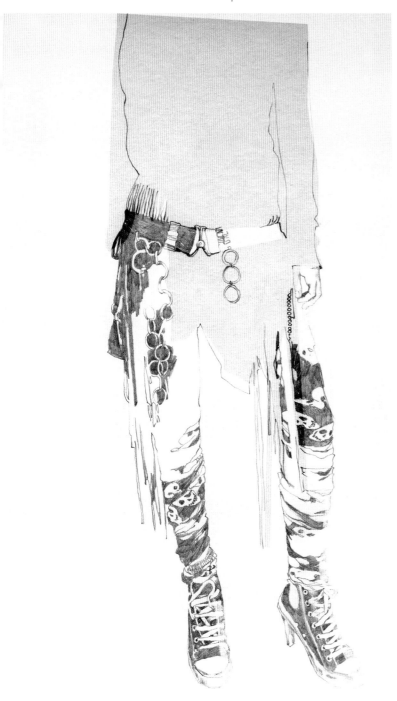

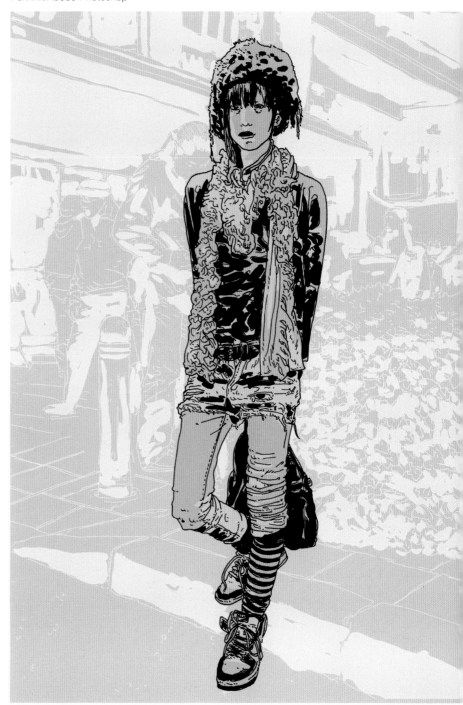

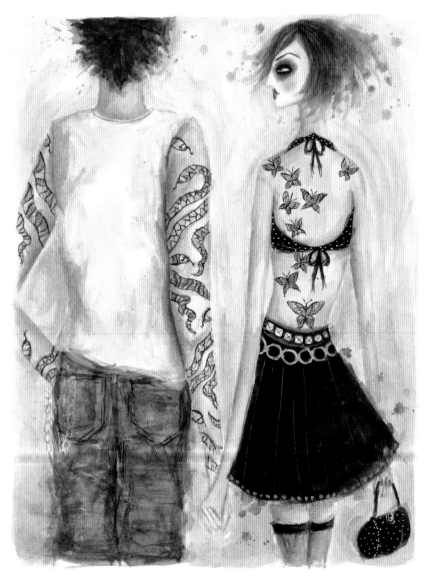

Bella Pilar
Snakes and Butterflies (2005)
Gouache

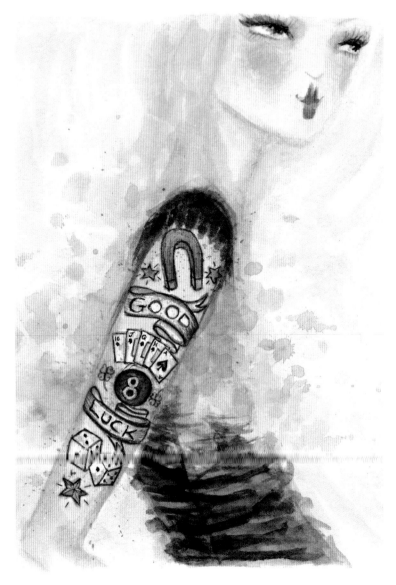

Bella Pilar
Good Luck Tat (2004)
Gouache

Mayrhosby Yeoshen
Yaoi Boy (2006)
Adobe Photoshop/Corel Painter

Paul Watmough
We Know (2006)
Pen/Ink/Adobe Photoshop

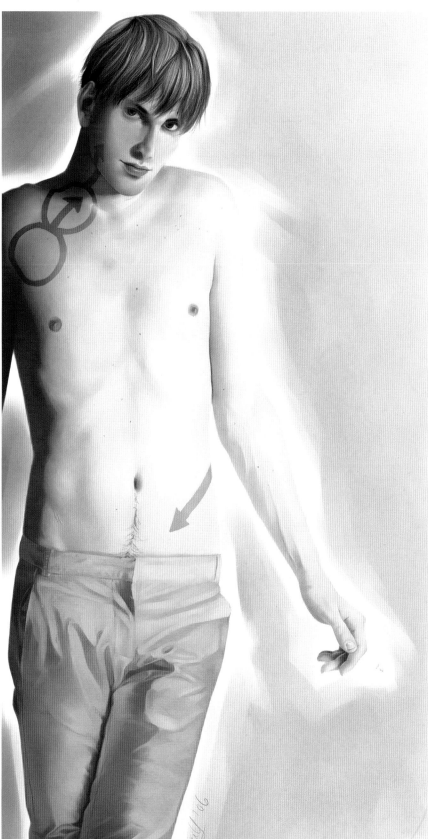

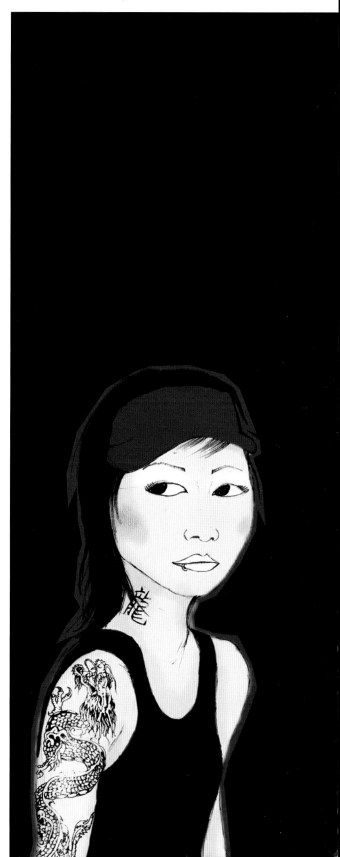

Naomi Devil
Hip-Hop Girl (2006)
Oil on canvas

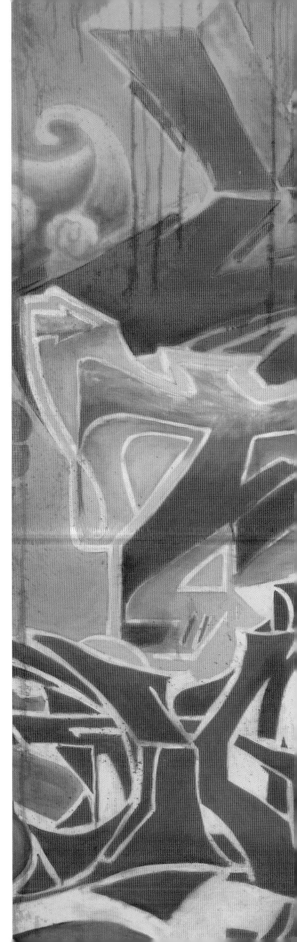

Joseph S Arruda
Kyraa (2003)
Adobe Photoshop/GNU Image
Manipulation Program

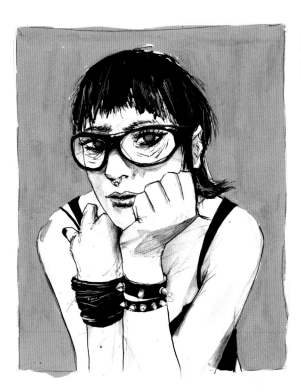

Joseph S Arruda
Coffee Stain (2004)
Adobe Photoshop/GNU Image
Manipulation Program

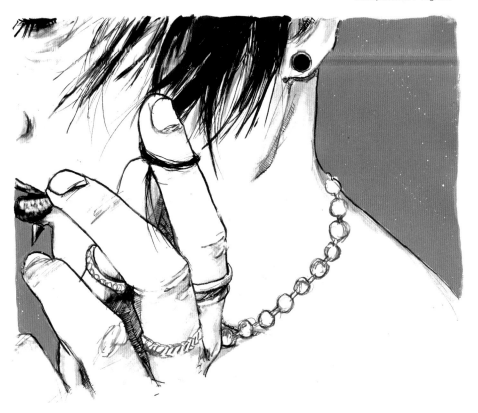

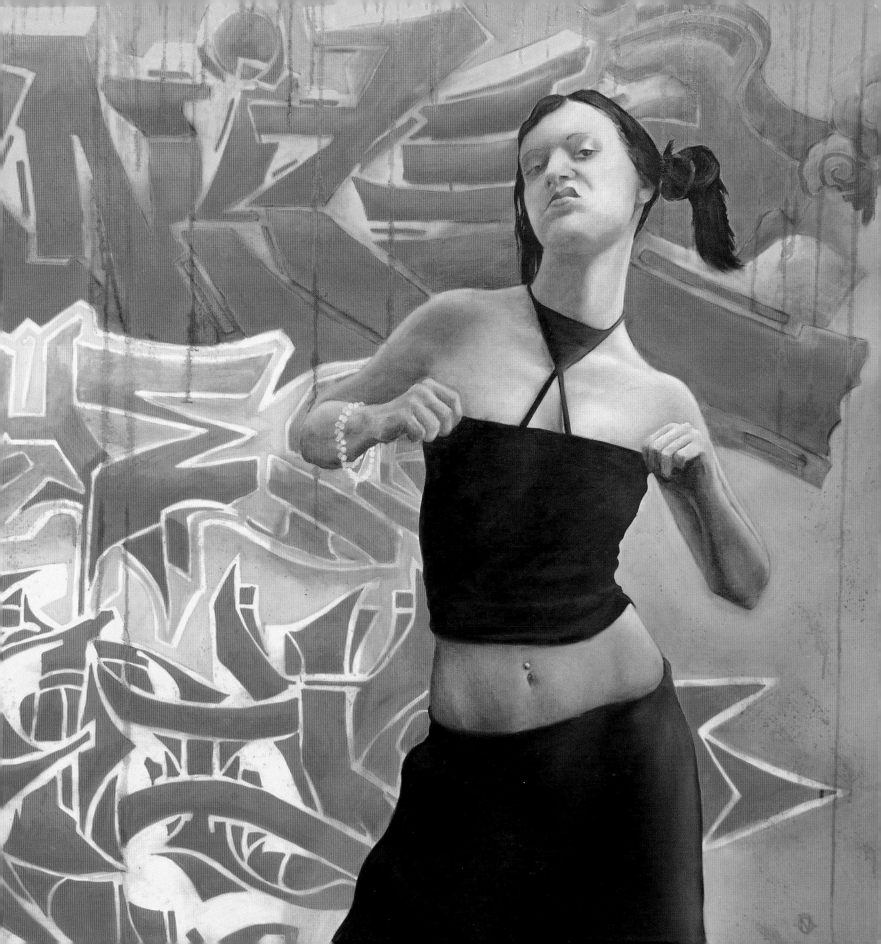

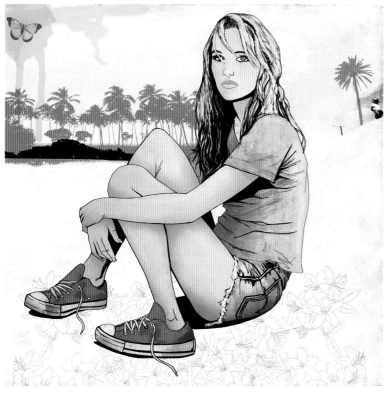

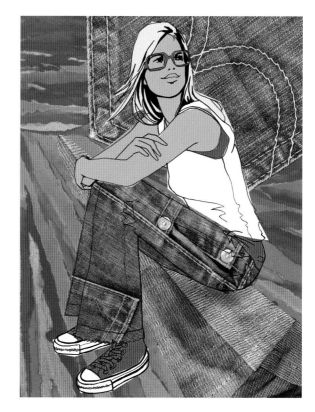

Amparo Losana
Untitled (2005)
Adobe Photoshop

Christopher King
Last Summer (2006)
Pen/Ink/Adobe Photoshop

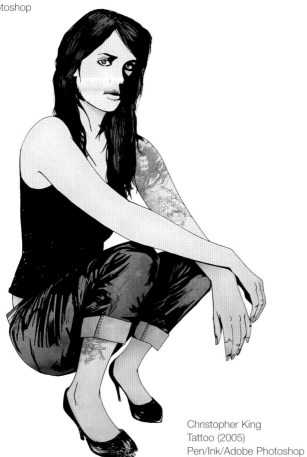

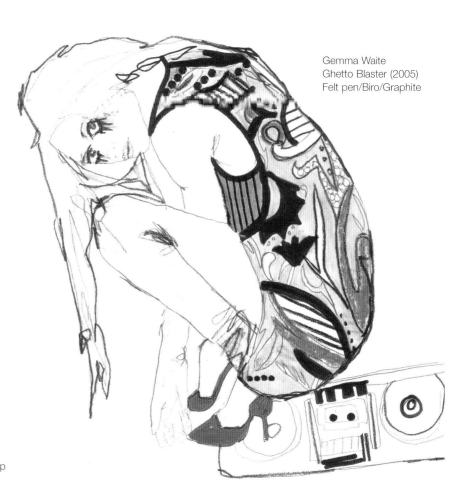

Gemma Waite
Ghetto Blaster (2005)
Felt pen/Biro/Graphite

Christopher King
Tattoo (2005)
Pen/Ink/Adobe Photoshop

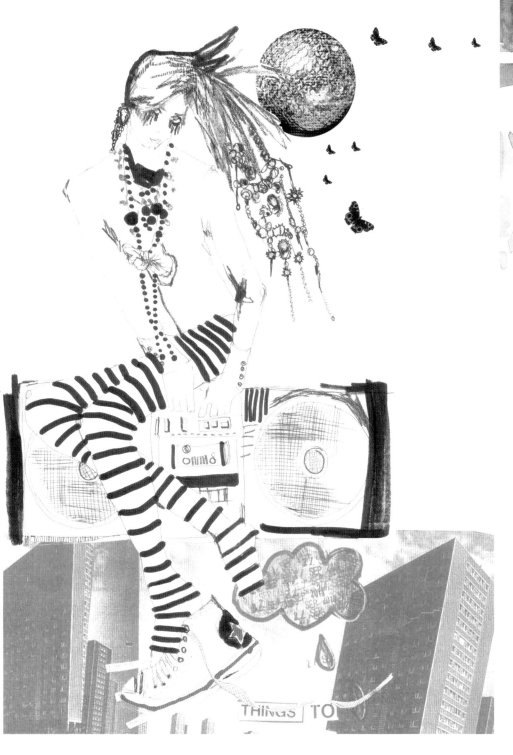

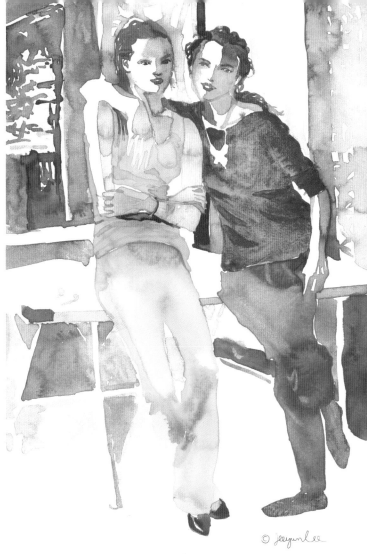

Jeeyun Lee
bf4ever (2005)
Watercolour

Gemma Waite
One World (2006)
Felt pen/Biro/Graphite/
Collage/Adobe Photoshop

147

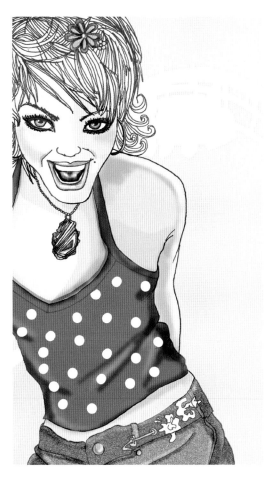

Helen Turner
Rollercoaster (2003)
Ink/Adobe Photoshop

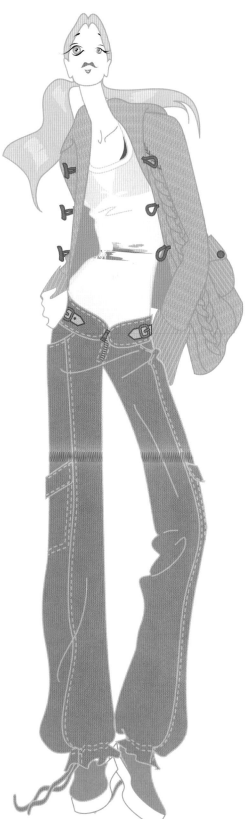

Susie Tsan-Ching Yang
Surfer Girl in Crochet Sweater (2004)
Adobe Illustrator

Kun-Sung Chung
Fashion Swap & Show, *Let's Party!*, Lobster Press (2004)
Adobe Illustrator

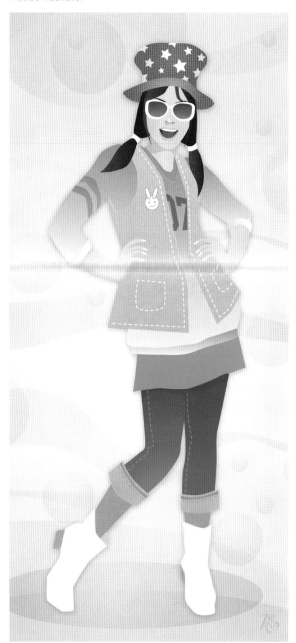

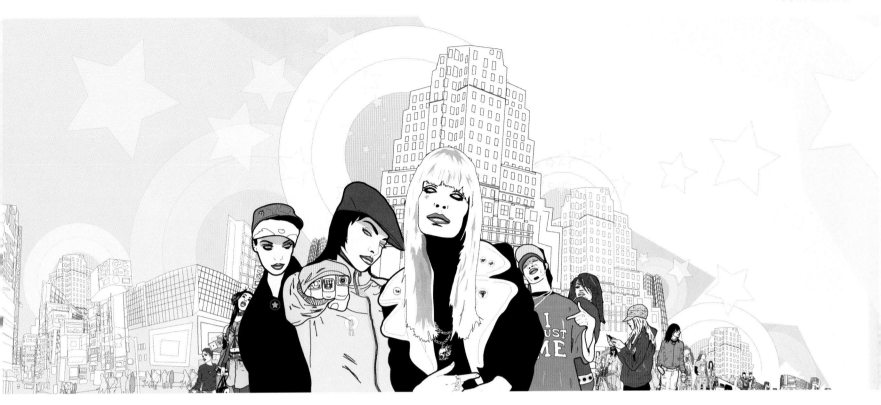

Giulio Iurissevich
Metropoli (2005)
Macromedia FreeHand/Adobe Illustrator

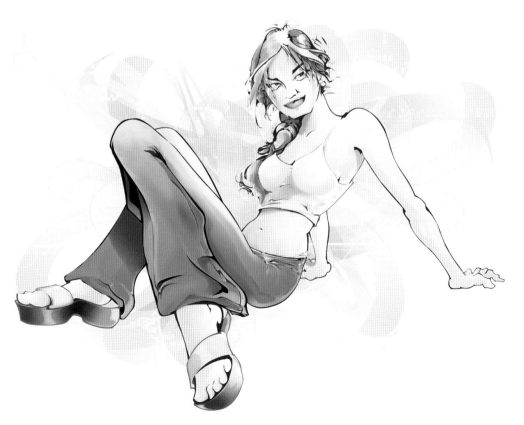

Varshesh Joshi
Untitled (2004)
Pencil/Ink/Macromedia FreeHand/
Adobe Flash/Adobe Photoshop

Stuart Holmes
Fashion Victim, *Computer Arts* (2004)
Adobe Illustrator

Anna Cangialosi
Louise Clements (2006)
Acrylic and tissue on wood

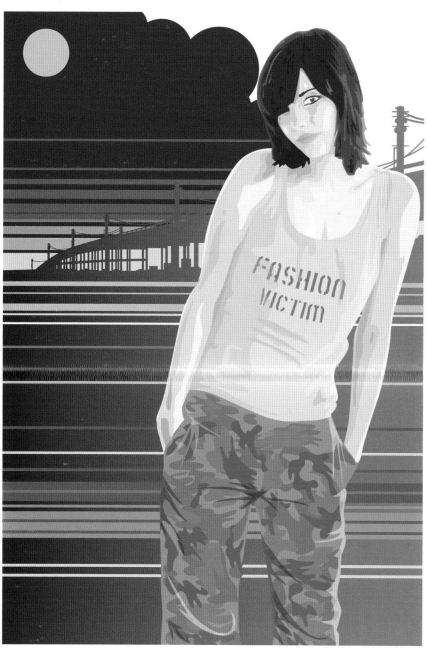

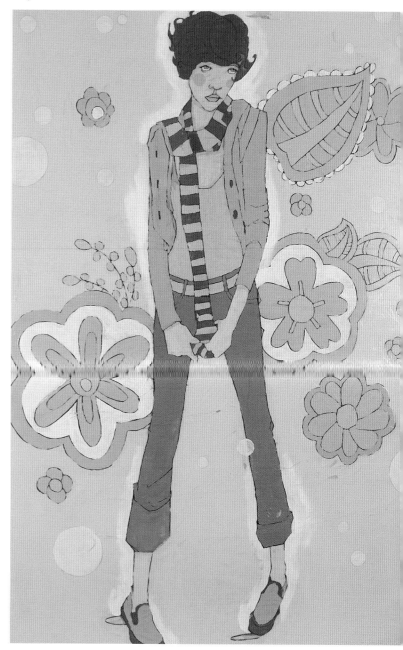

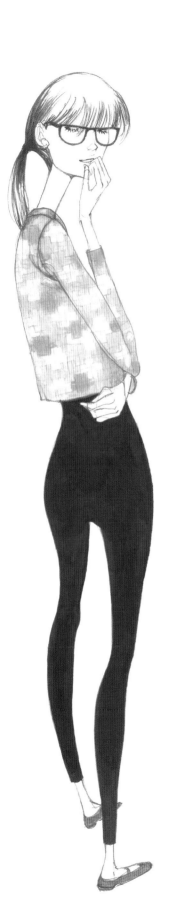

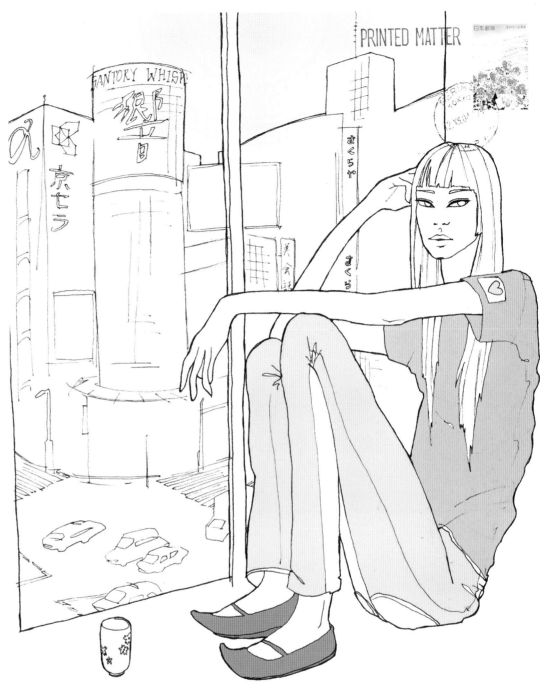

Laura Laine
Girl with Glasses (2006)
Pencil

Erica Sharp
Tokyo Tomboy (2005)
Adobe Photoshop

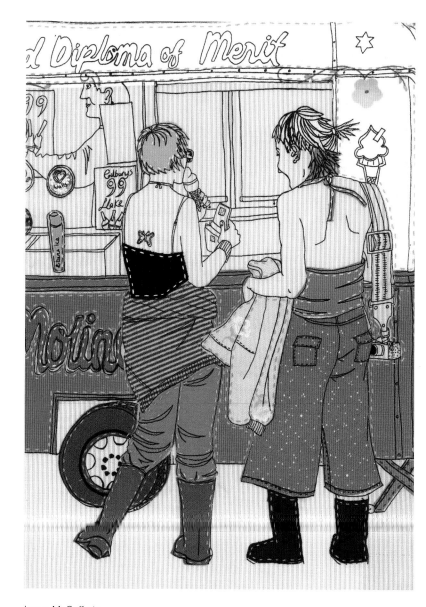

Laura McCafferty
Charlie and Heidi Buying Ice Cream (2006)
Textile/Print/Hand-stitching

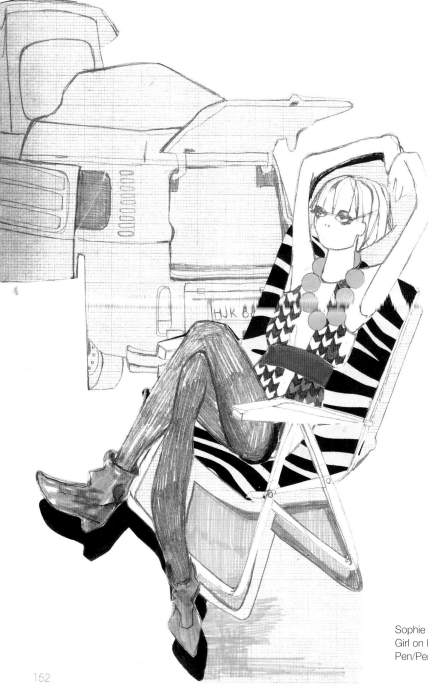

Sophie Wightman
Girl on Holiday (2006)
Pen/Pencil

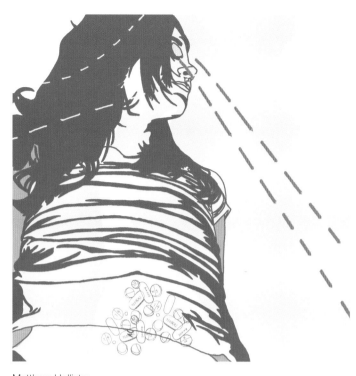

Matthew Hollister
Drugs (2005)
Ink on paper

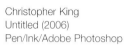

Christopher King
Untitled (2006)
Pen/Ink/Adobe Photoshop

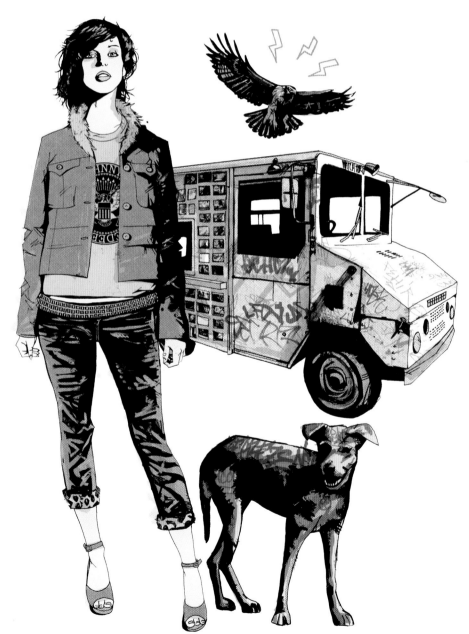

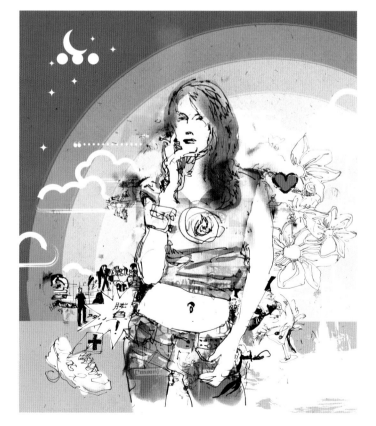

Christian Barthold
Streetgirl (2006)
India ink/Adobe Photoshop

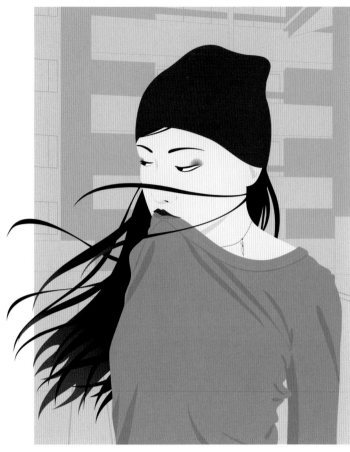

Cybèle
Girl in Pasadena (2001)
Adobe Illustrator

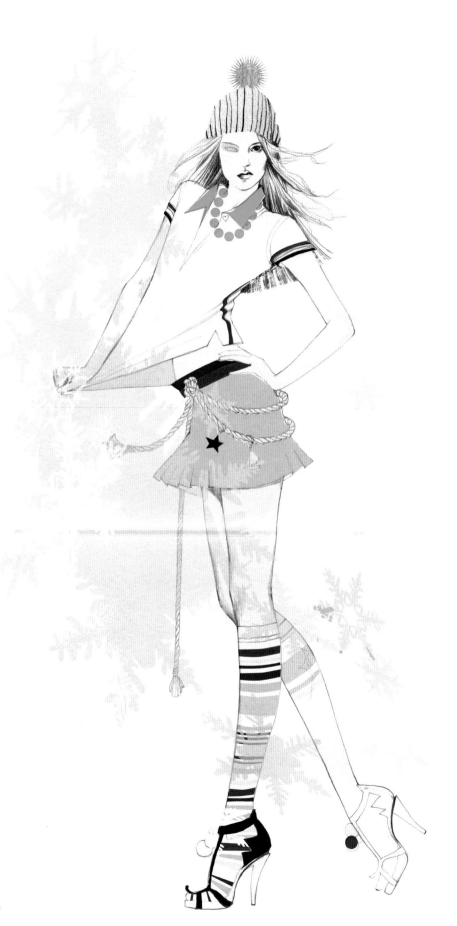

Cecilia Carlstedt
Untitled, for *Damernas Värld* (2005)
Pencil/Adobe Photoshop

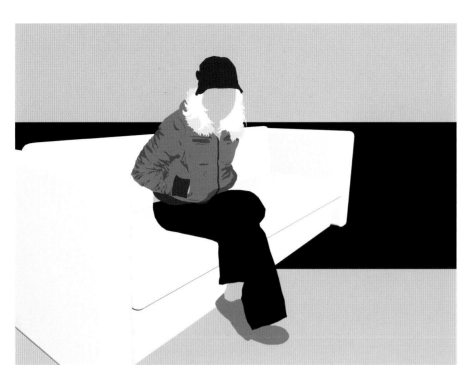

Marco Amitrano
Tina is Waiting (2005)
Adobe Photoshop/Discreet 3D Studio Max

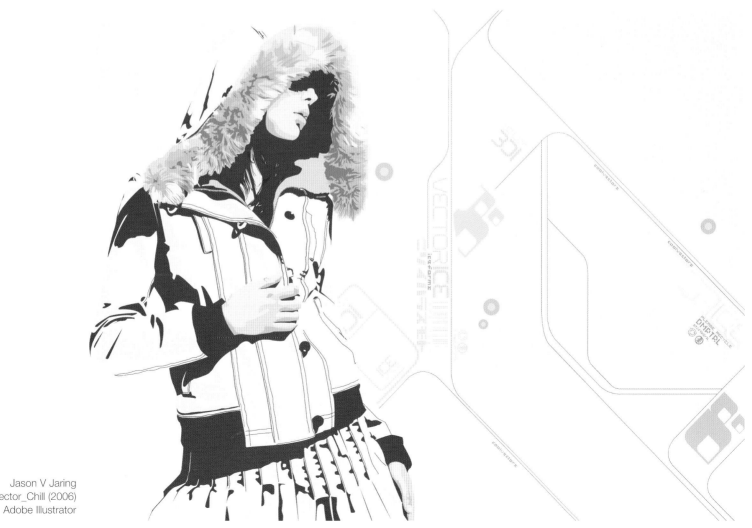

Jason V Jaring
Vector_Chill (2006)
Adobe Illustrator

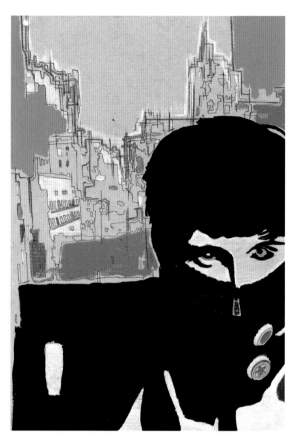

Jasper Sinchai Chadprajong
Johnny on Acid (2006)
Acrylic on corrugated card/Coloured pencil/Ink

Nicholas Billiris
Streets Are Watching (2005)
Adobe Photoshop/Adobe Illustrator

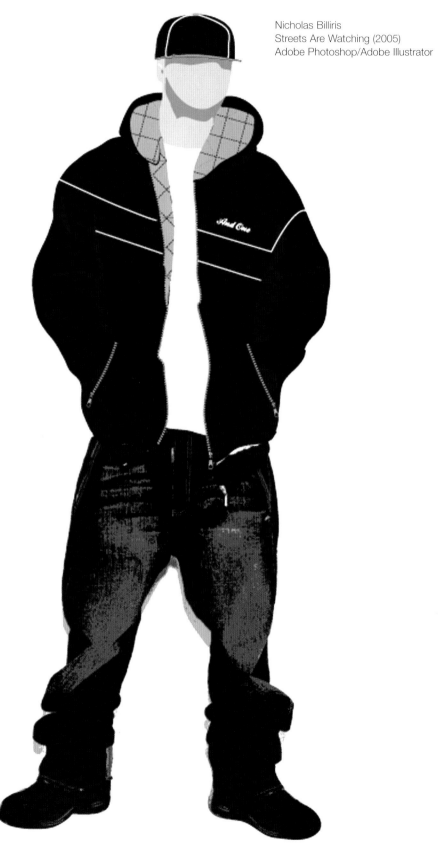

Helen Turner
Too Cool (2005)
Ink/Adobe Photoshop

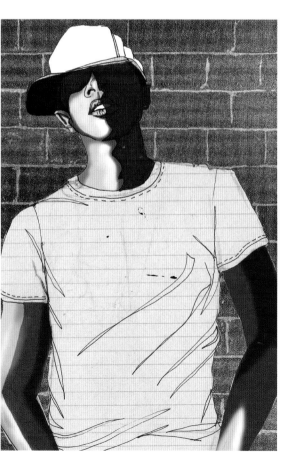

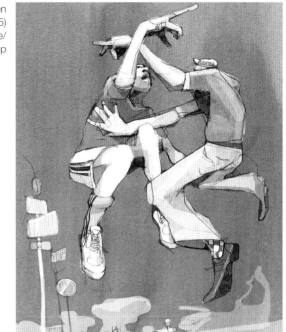

Alex Green
Greeting (2005)
Pencil/Pen/Paint/Collage/
Adobe Photoshop

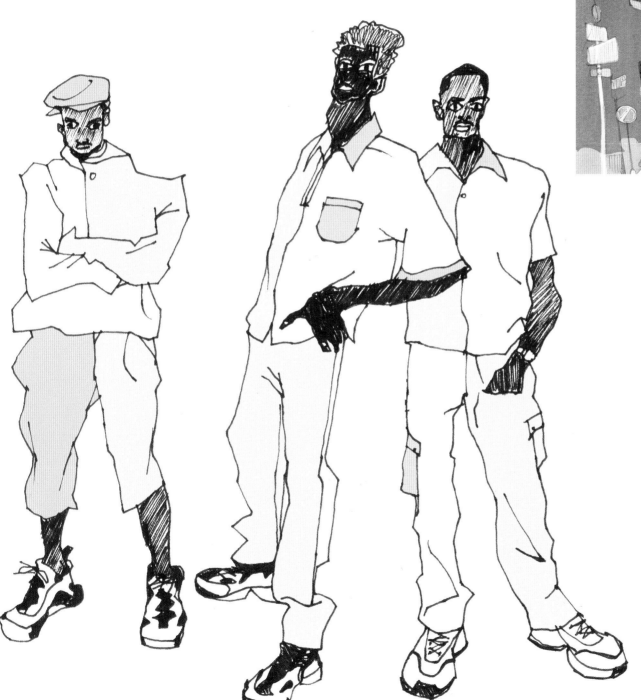

Lopetz:BD
3guys (2003)
Adobe Photoshop

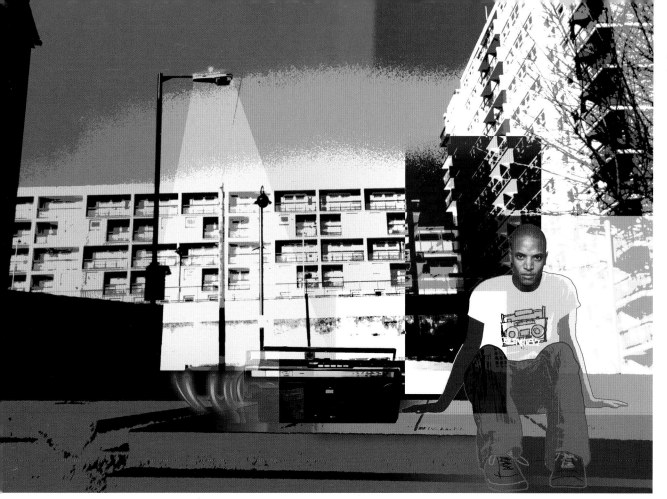

Jacqui Paull and Carl Melegari
Aaron (2004)
Adobe Photoshop

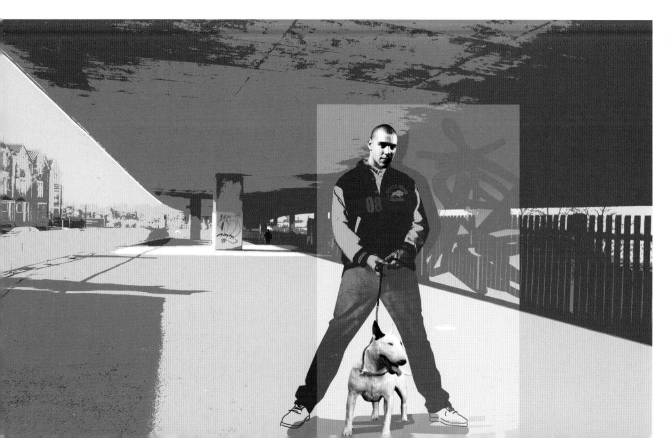

Jacqui Paull and Carl Melegari
Marc and Miu (2004)
Adobe Photoshop

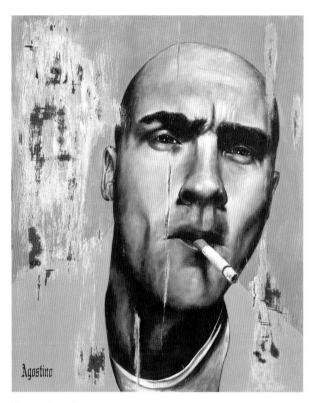

Vincent Agostino
Smoking Skin (2006)
Acrylic

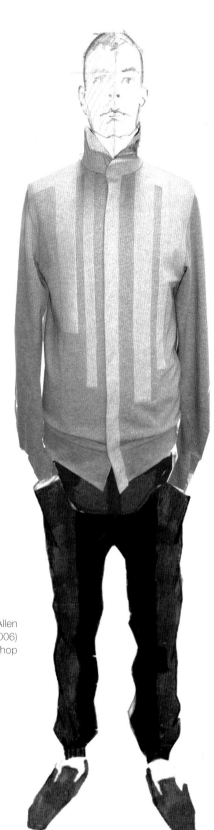

Emily Allen
Old Boy (2006)
Adobe Photoshop

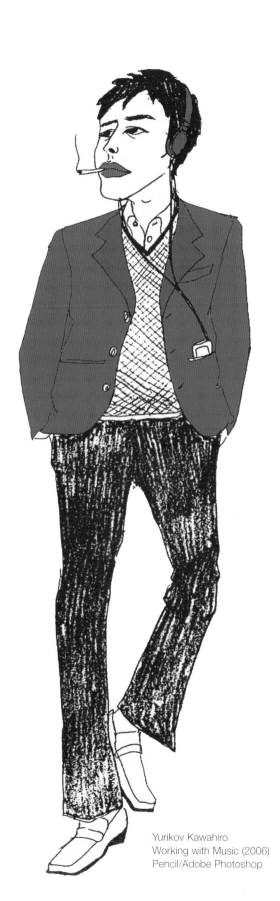

Yurikov Kawahiro
Working with Music (2006)
Pencil/Adobe Photoshop

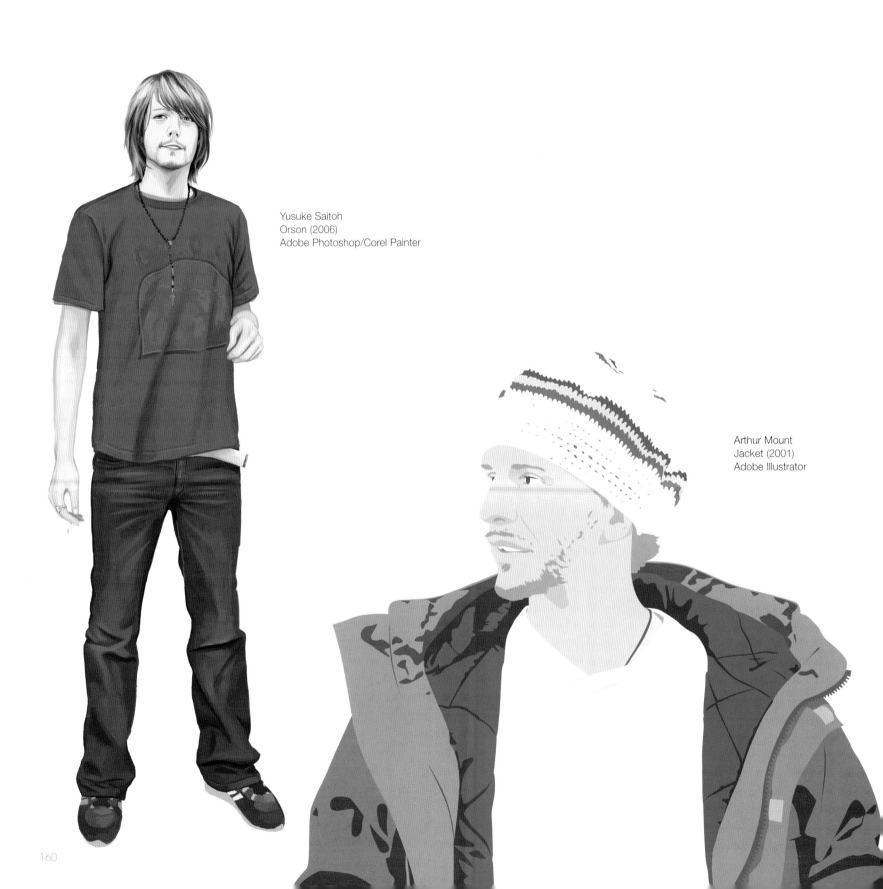

Yusuke Saitoh
Orson (2006)
Adobe Photoshop/Corel Painter

Arthur Mount
Jacket (2001)
Adobe Illustrator

Elena Lavdovskaya Konstantinovna
TSUM Menswear Campaign (2005)
Aquarelle/Ink/Adobe Photoshop

Jan Feindt
R.E.M. (2004)
Pen/Ink/Adobe Photoshop

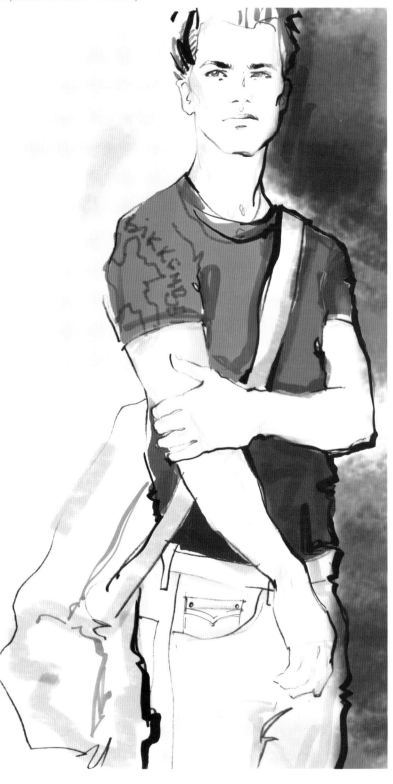

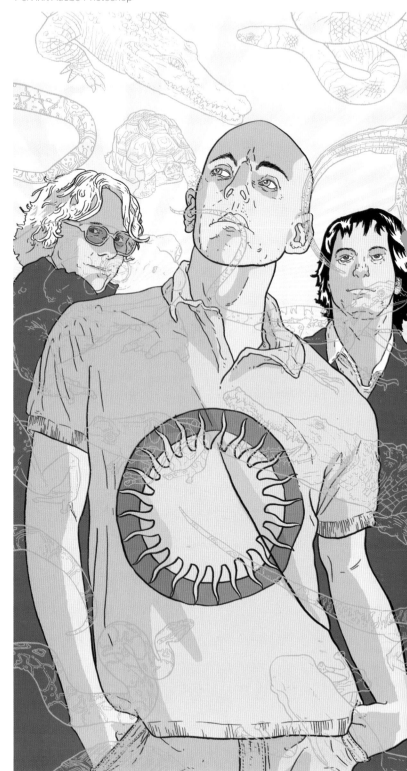

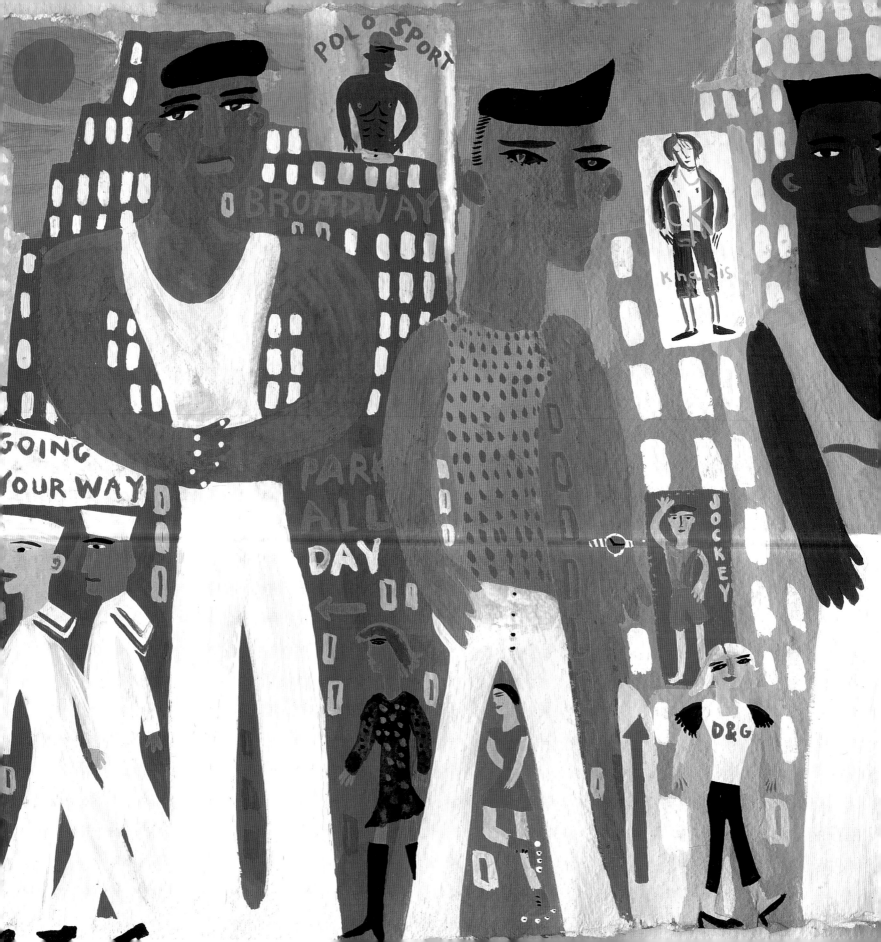

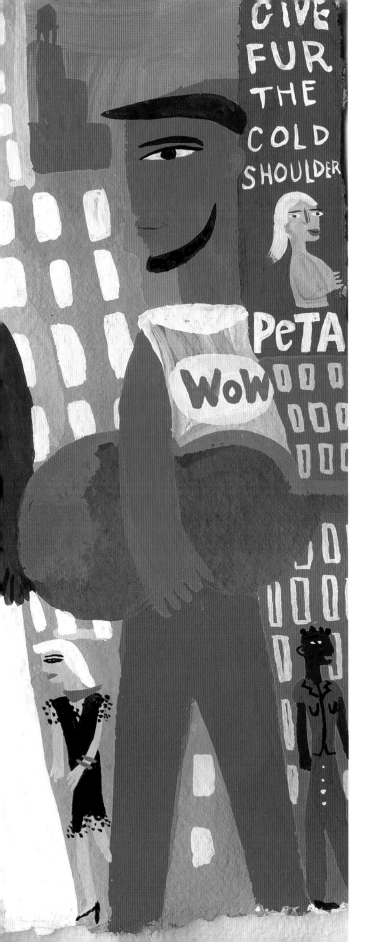

Christopher Corr
Broadway NYC (2002)
Gouache

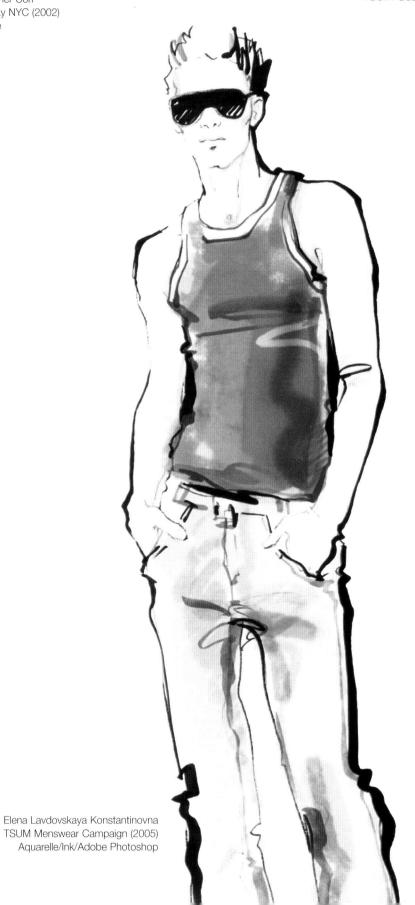

Elena Lavdovskaya Konstantinovna
TSUM Menswear Campaign (2005)
Aquarelle/Ink/Adobe Photoshop

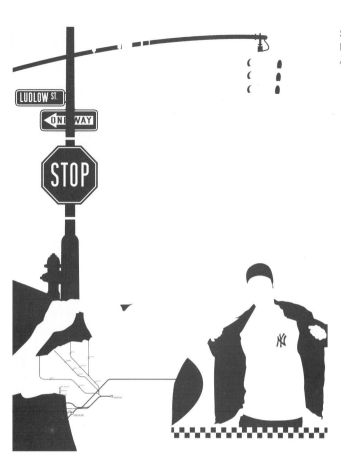

Stuart Holmes
NY: Brooklyn (2005)
Adobe Illustrator

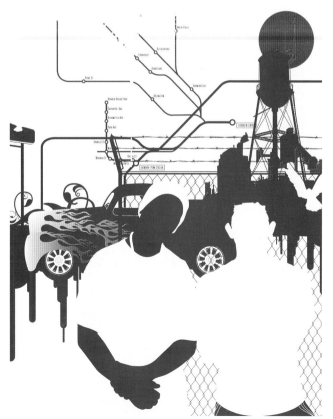

Stuart Holmes
NY: Queens (2005)
Adobe Illustrator

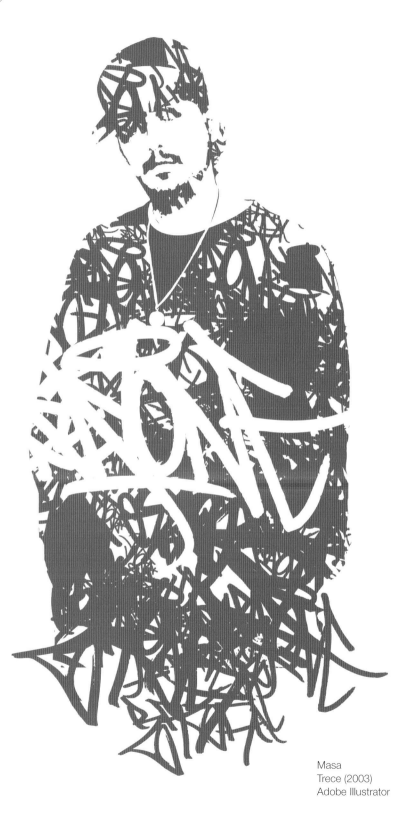

Masa
Trece (2003)
Adobe Illustrator

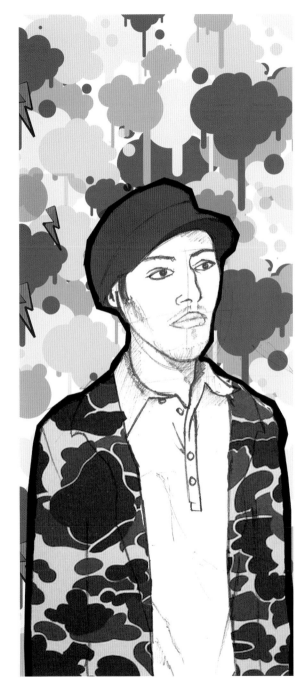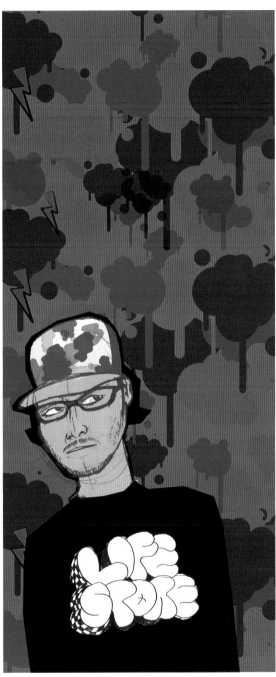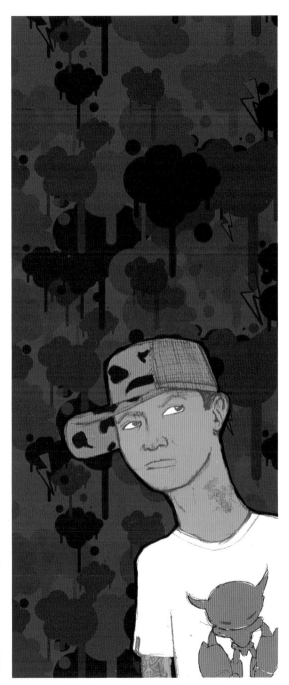

Paul Watmough
We Know (2006)
Pen/Ink/Adobe Photoshop

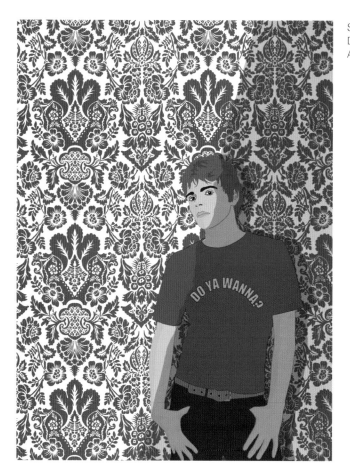

Stuart Holmes
Do ya' Wanna? (2001)
Adobe Illustrator

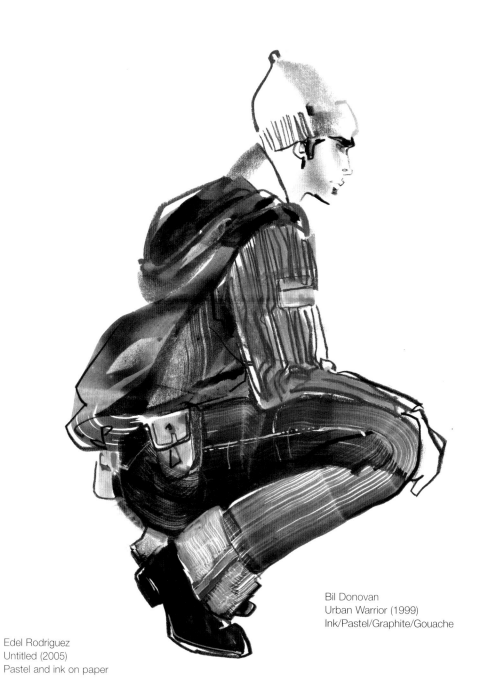

Bil Donovan
Urban Warrior (1999)
Ink/Pastel/Graphite/Gouache

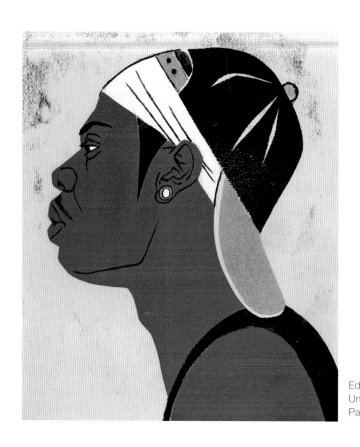

Edel Rodriguez
Untitled (2005)
Pastel and ink on paper

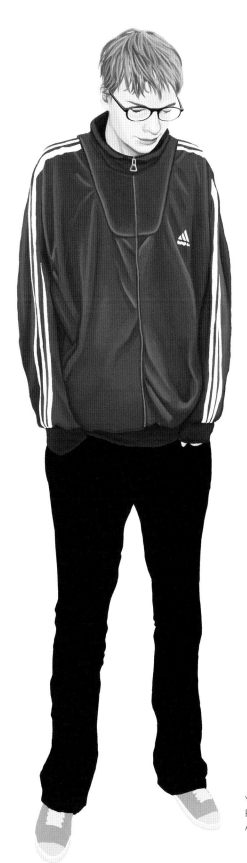

Yusuke Saitoh
Positivity (2004)
Adobe Photoshop/Corel Painter

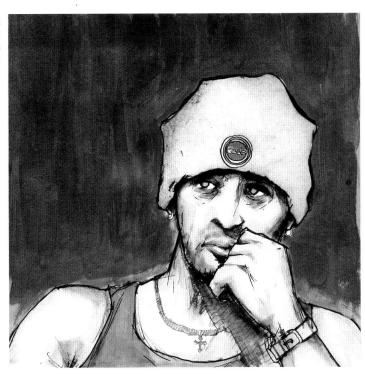

Joseph S Arruda
The Weez (2005)
Adobe Photoshop/GNU Image
Manipulation Program

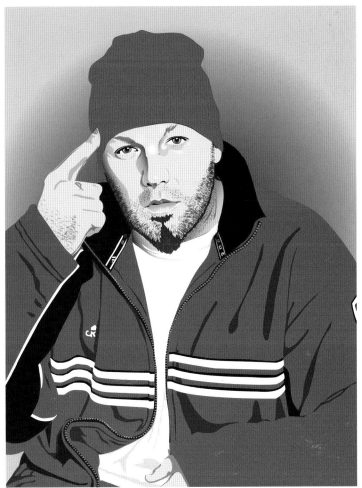

Zed
Freddy Durst,
Playboy Magazine (2002)
Adobe Illustrator

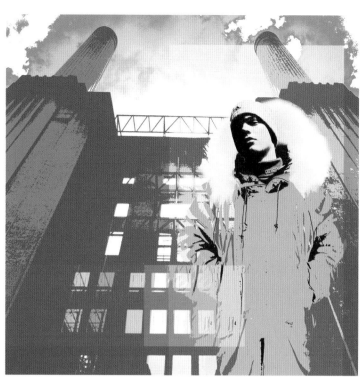

Jacqui Paull and Carl Melegari
Battersea Boy (2004)
Adobe Photoshop

Bil Donovan
Urban Guy (1998)
Graphite/Pastel/Gouache

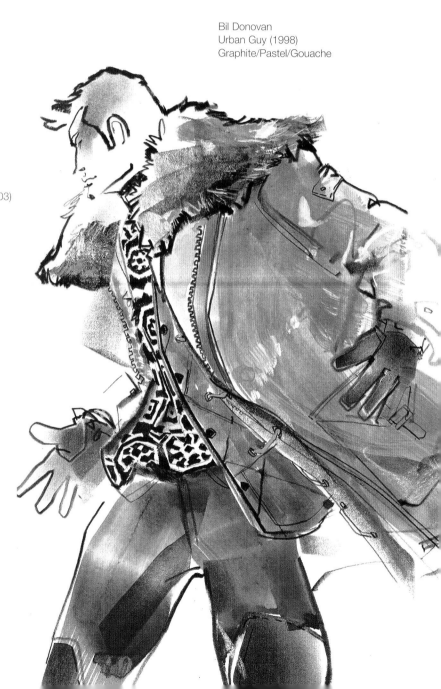

Stuart Holmes
Sunset & Boulevard (2003)
Adobe Illustrator

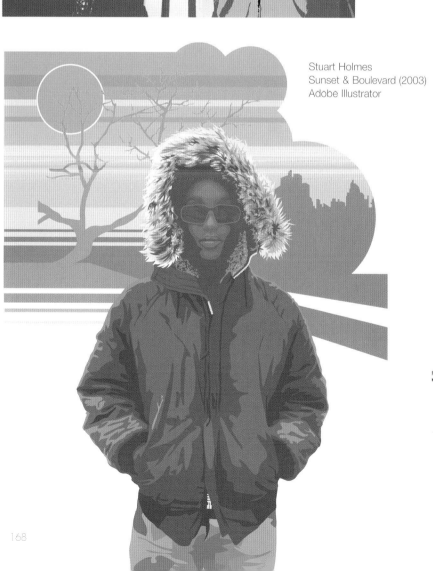

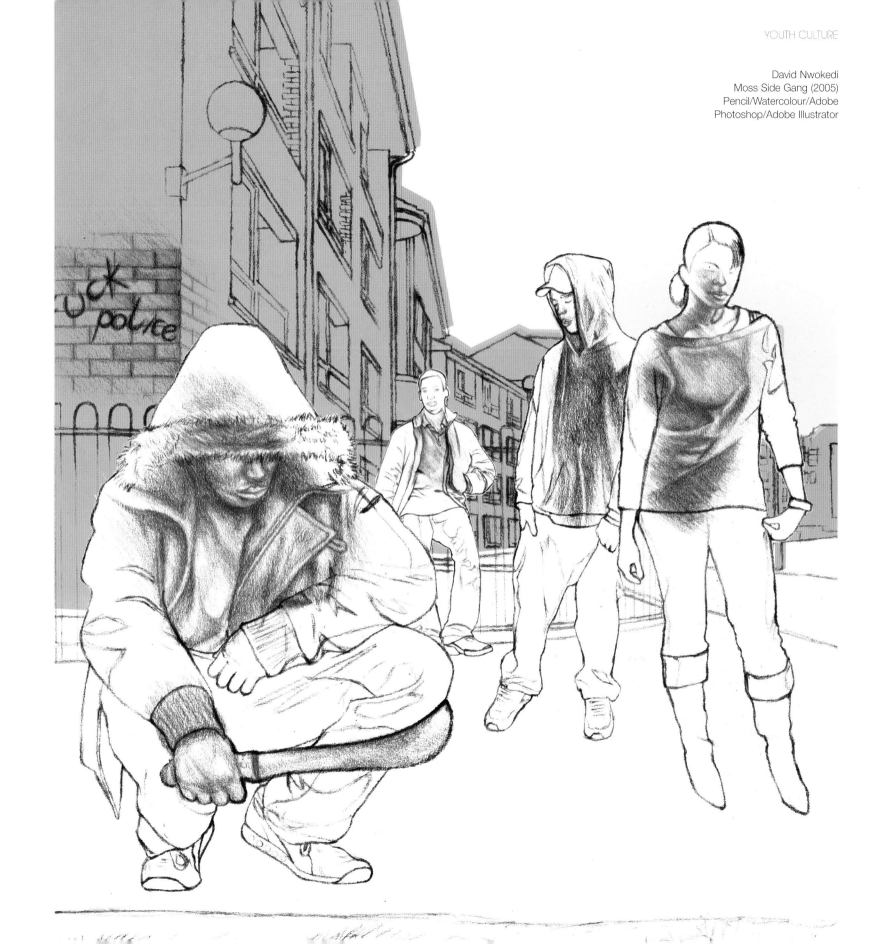

David Nwokedi
Moss Side Gang (2005)
Pencil/Watercolour/Adobe
Photoshop/Adobe Illustrator

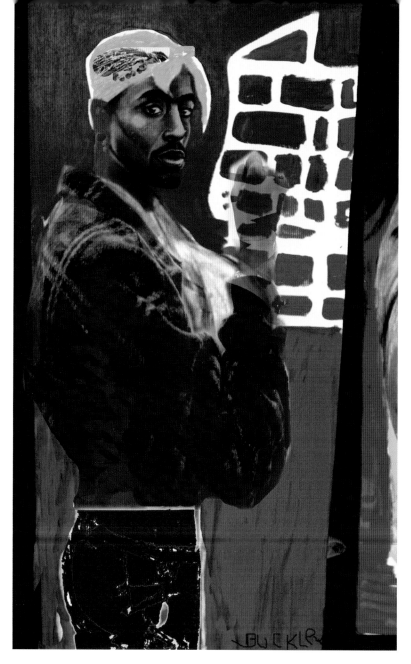

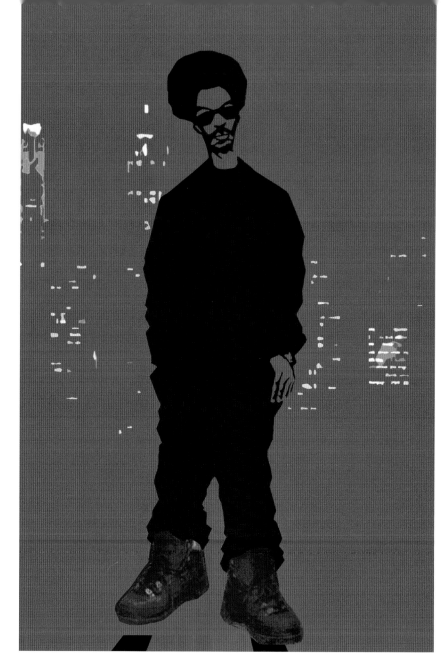

Omar Buckley
Gettofab (2006)
Oil/Charcoal/Coloured pencil/Acrylic/
Adobe Photoshop/Adobe Illustrator

Oscar Gimenez
Inner City (2001)
Ink/Adobe Photoshop

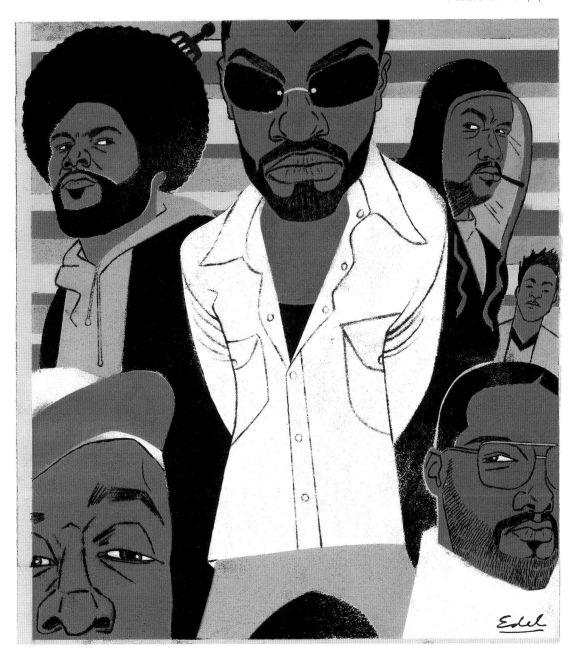

Edel Rodriguez
The Roots (2005)
Pastel and ink on paper

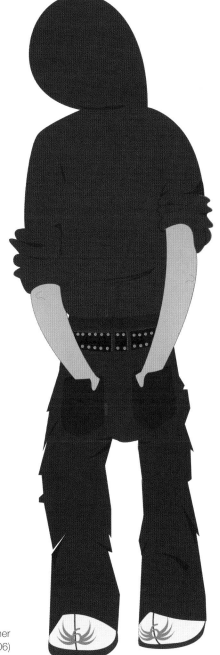

Sarah Turner
Alternative Music Fan (2006)
Adobe Illustrator

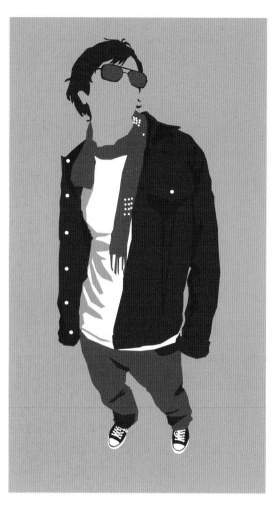

Marco Amitrano
Standing at the Door (2004)
Adobe Photoshop

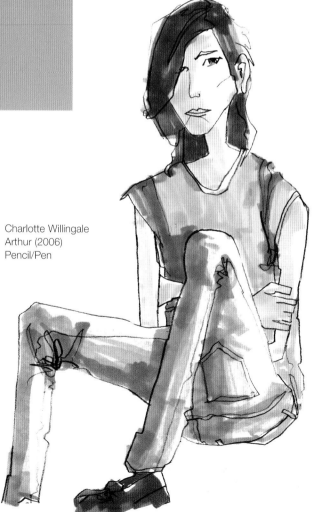

Charlotte Willingale
Arthur (2006)
Pencil/Pen

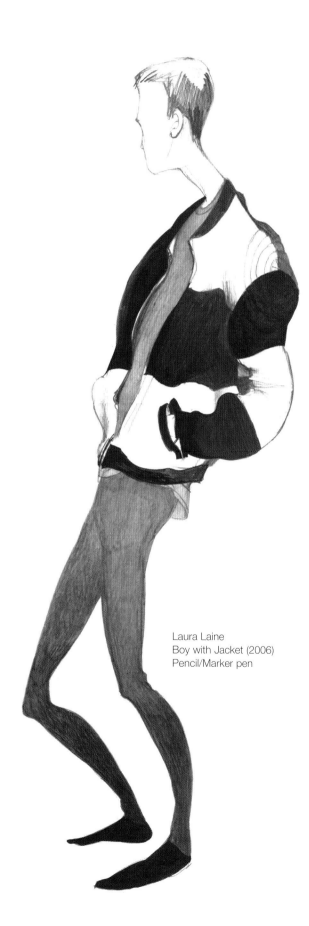

Laura Laine
Boy with Jacket (2006)
Pencil/Marker pen

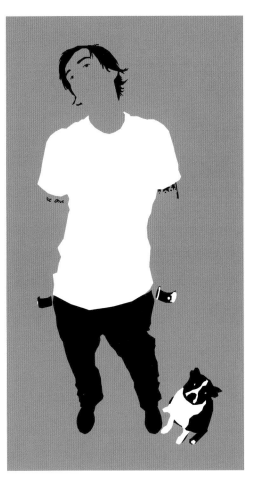

Marco Amitrano
Duke Duke (2004)
Adobe Photoshop

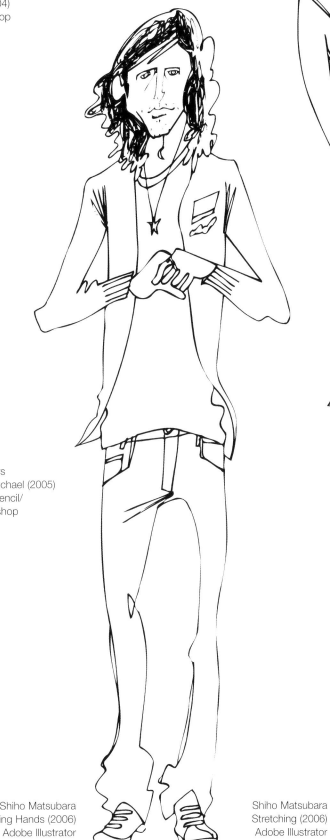

Anna Saunders
Dance with Michael (2005)
Watercolour pencil/
Adobe Photoshop

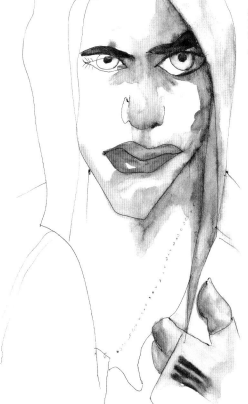

Shiho Matsubara
Rubbing Hands (2006)
Adobe Illustrator

Shiho Matsubara
Stretching (2006)
Adobe Illustrator

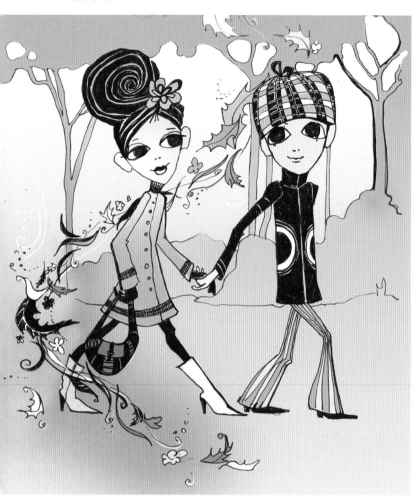

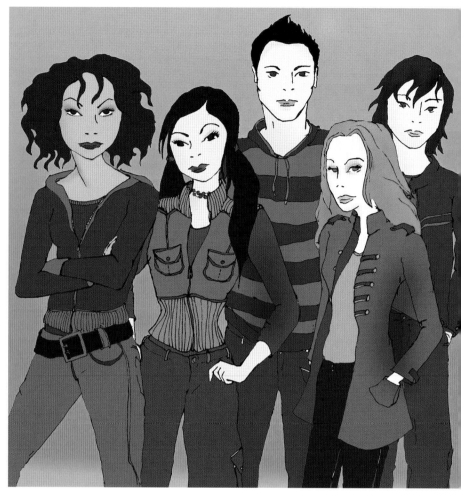

Elena Ambotaite
FALL, in Love (2006)
Pen/Adobe Photoshop

Madeleine Egremont
Young London (2006)
Pencil/Pen/Ink/Adobe Photoshop

Stuart Holmes
East LDN – Millennium Generation (2001)
Adobe Illustrator

Wayne Murray
Young Love? (2004)
Pencil/Adobe Illustrator

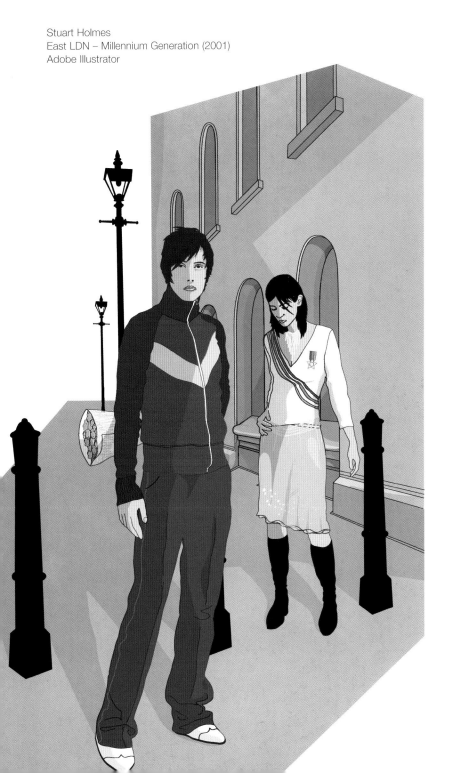

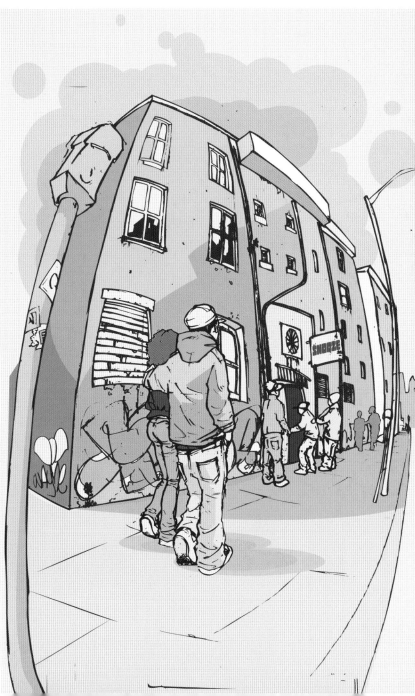

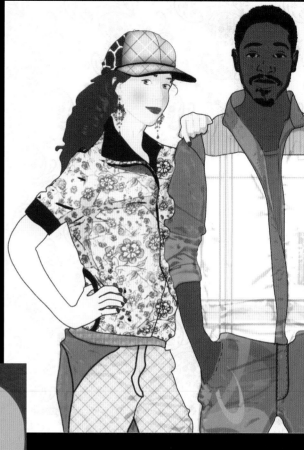

Lior Yefet Tabib
Young Couple (2005)
Adobe Photoshop/Macromedia FreeHand

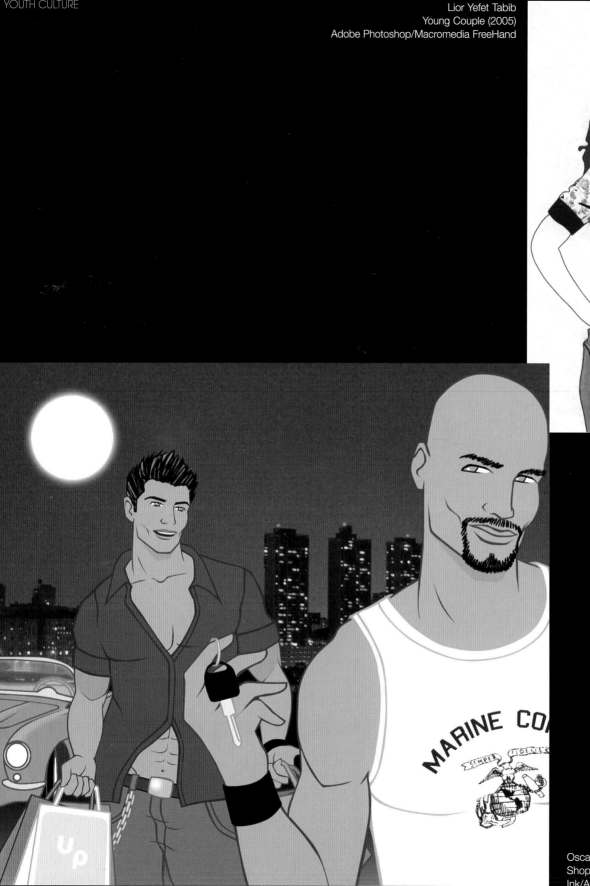

Oscar Gimenez
Shopping (2004)
Ink/Adobe Photoshop

Yumiko Kayukawa
Mii Ando Mai Beibi
(Me and My Baby) (2003)
Acrylic and ink on illustration board

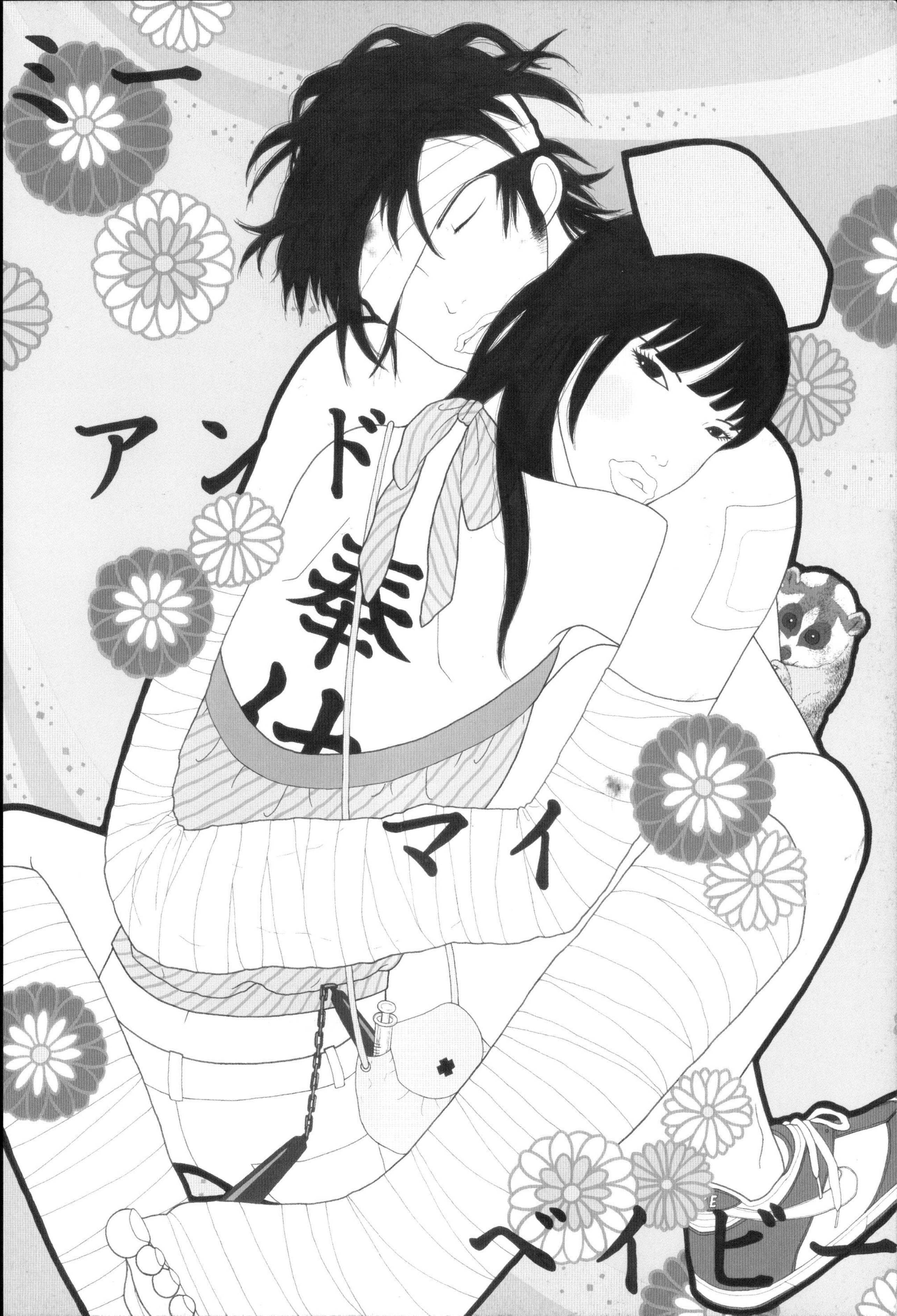

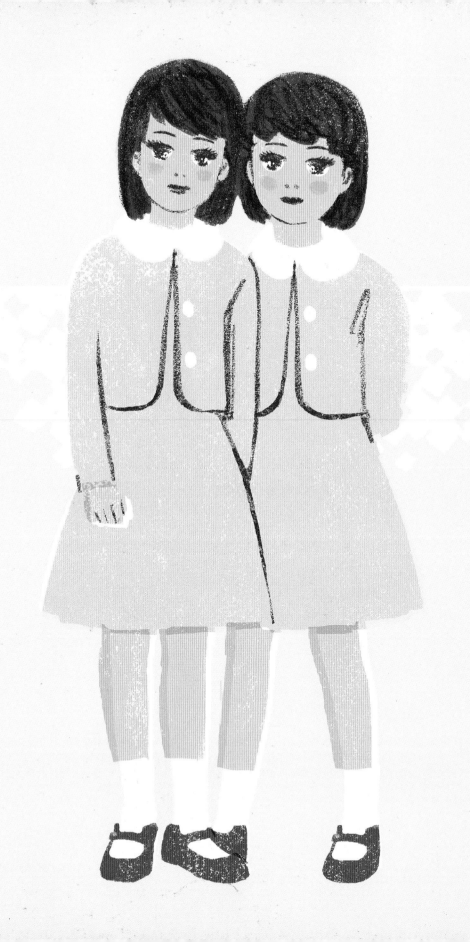

Children

babies   toddlers & tots   juniors   tweenies   teens

Tatsuro Kiuchi
Red Shoes (2004)
Adobe Photoshop

Annabelle J Verhoye
Diary of a Father (2003)
Chine collé/Adobe Photoshop

Wai
Juggling (2004)
Adobe Illustrator/Adobe Photoshop

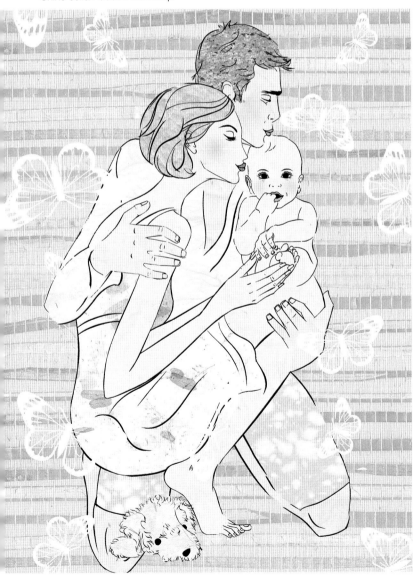

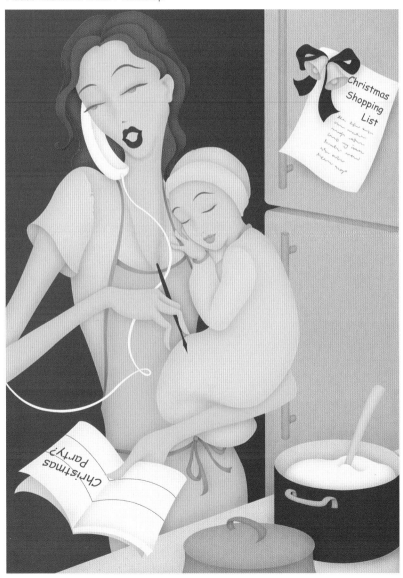

Nancy Davis
Mother and Child (2002)
Macromedia FreeHand

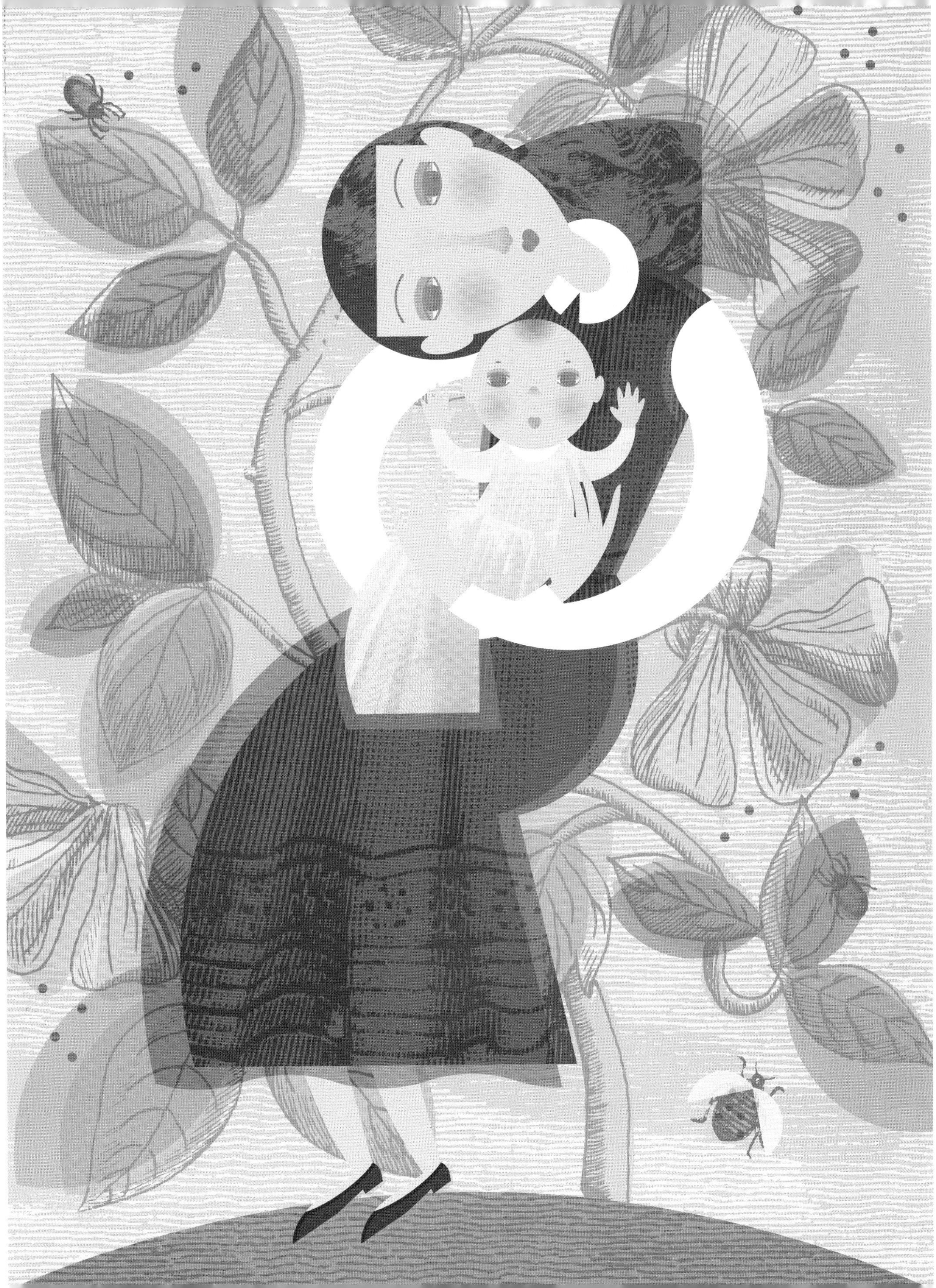

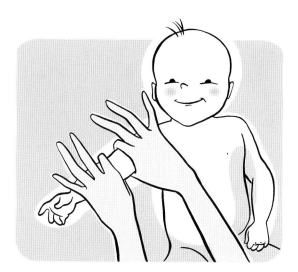
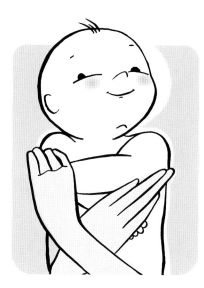

Dorothea Renault
Baby Spa (2004)
Adobe Illustrator

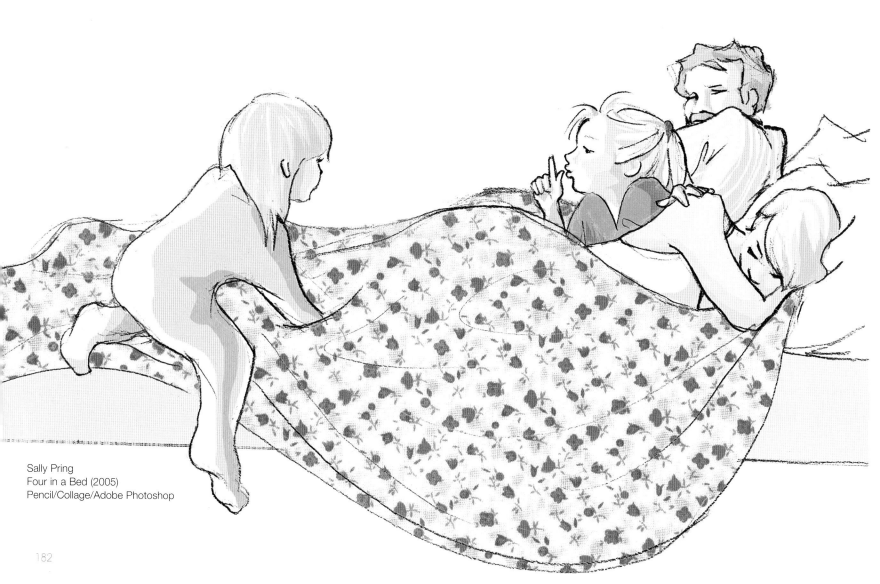

Sally Pring
Four in a Bed (2005)
Pencil/Collage/Adobe Photoshop

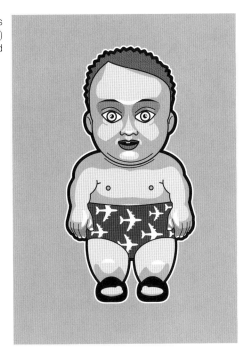

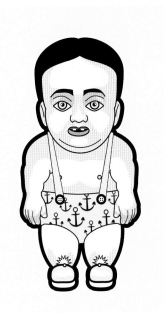

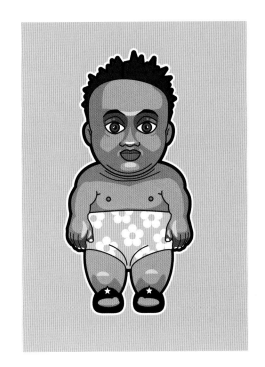

Tobias Wandres
Untitled (2003)
Macromedia FreeHand

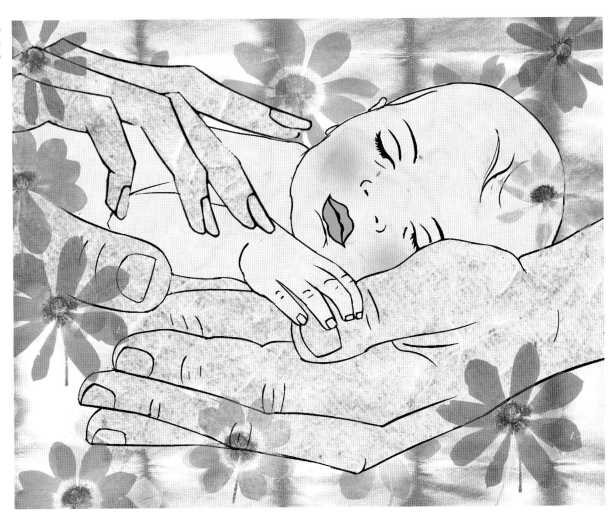

Annabelle J Verhoye
The Beginning (2005)
Chine collé/Adobe Photoshop

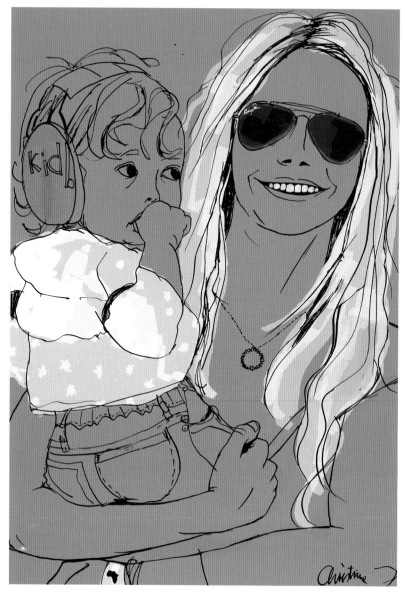

Christiane Engel
Gwyneth (2006)
Pen/Ink/Collage

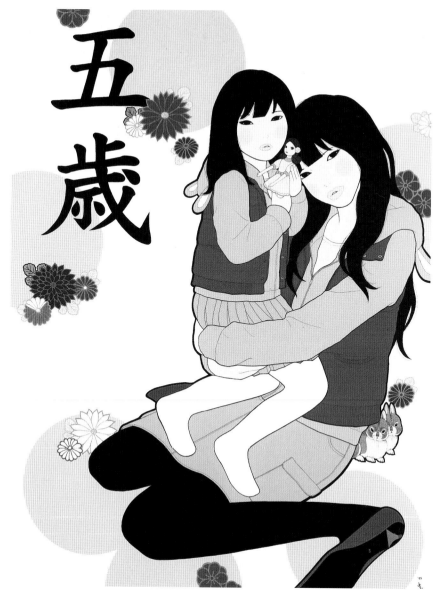

Yumiko Kayukawa
Gosai (Five Years Old) (2005)
Acrylic and ink on canvas

Christiane Engel
Baby on Futon (2005)
Oil pastel/Collage

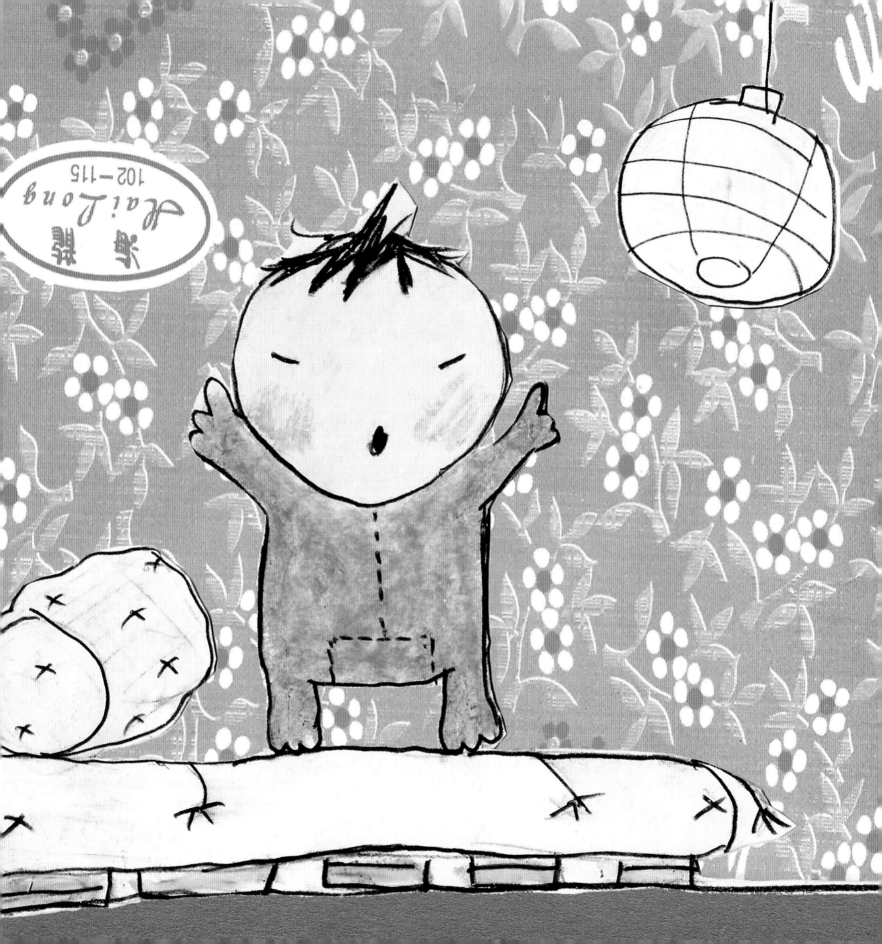

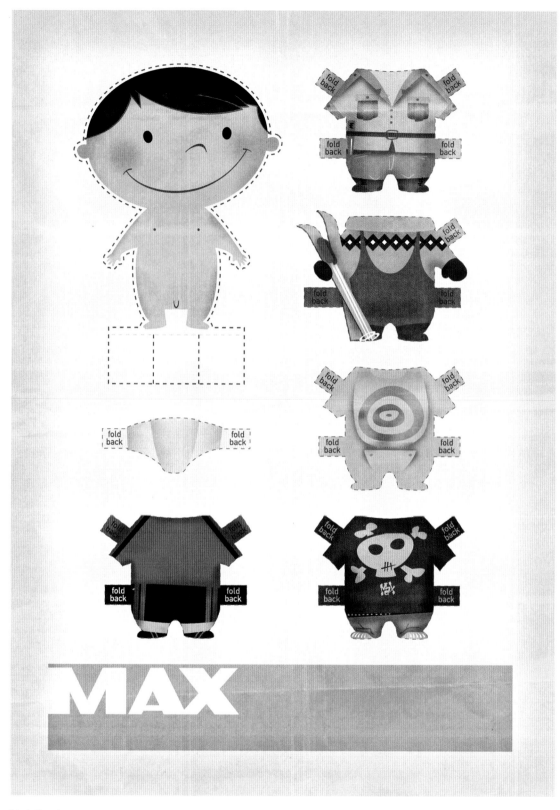

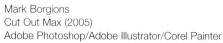
Mark Borgions
Cut Out Max (2005)
Adobe Photoshop/Adobe Illustrator/Corel Painter

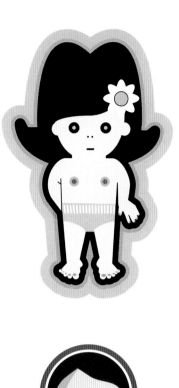

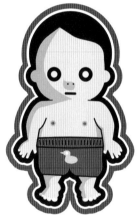

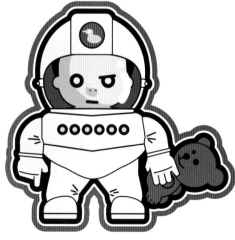

Tobias Wandres
Untitled (2004)
Macromedia FreeHand

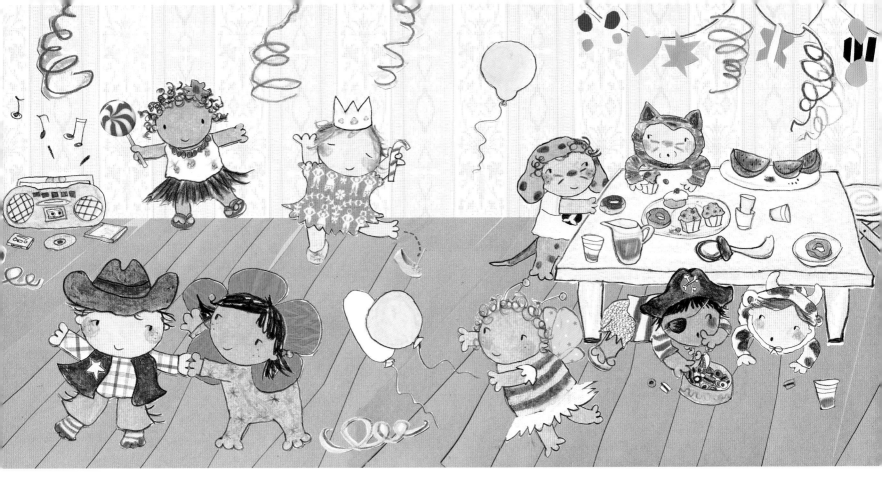

Christiane Engel
Fancy Dress Party (2005)
Oil pastel/Pencil/Collage

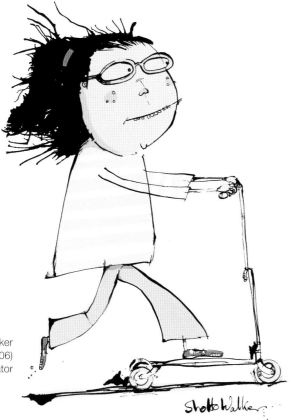

Sholto Walker
Scooter Girl (2006)
Ink on paper/Adobe Illustrator

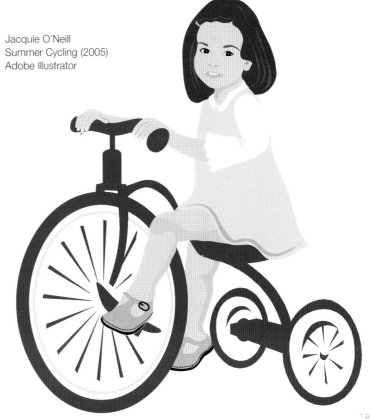

Jacquie O'Neill
Summer Cycling (2005)
Adobe Illustrator

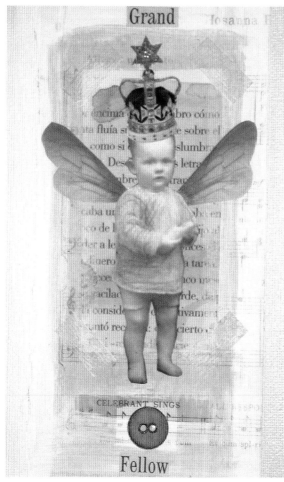

Claire Ann Baker
Grand Fellow (2003)
Vintage photo collage/Gouache/Found objects

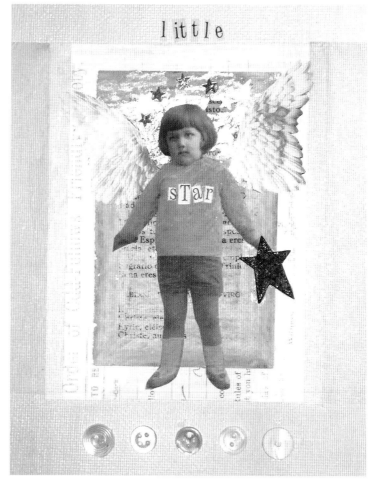

Claire Ann Baker
Little Star (2005)
Vintage photo collage/Gouache/Found objects

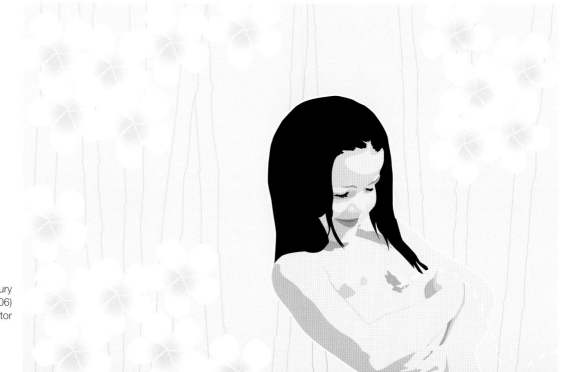

Kristie Jarita Lathbury
Sweet Bamboo (2006)
Adobe Illustrator

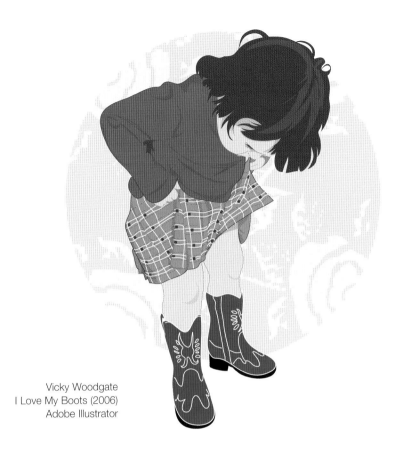

Vicky Woodgate
I Love My Boots (2006)
Adobe Illustrator

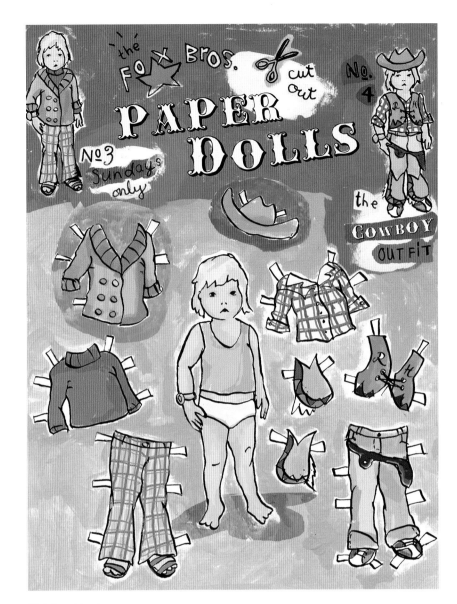

Christiane Engel
Fox Bros Paperdolls (2005)
Pen/Ink/Collage

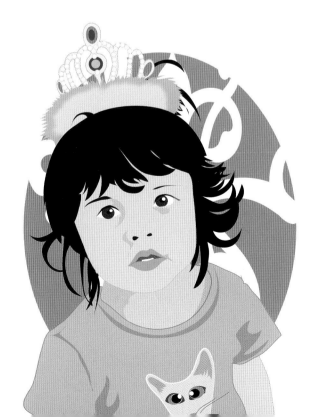

Vicky Woodgate
Princess for a Day (2006)
Adobe Illustrator

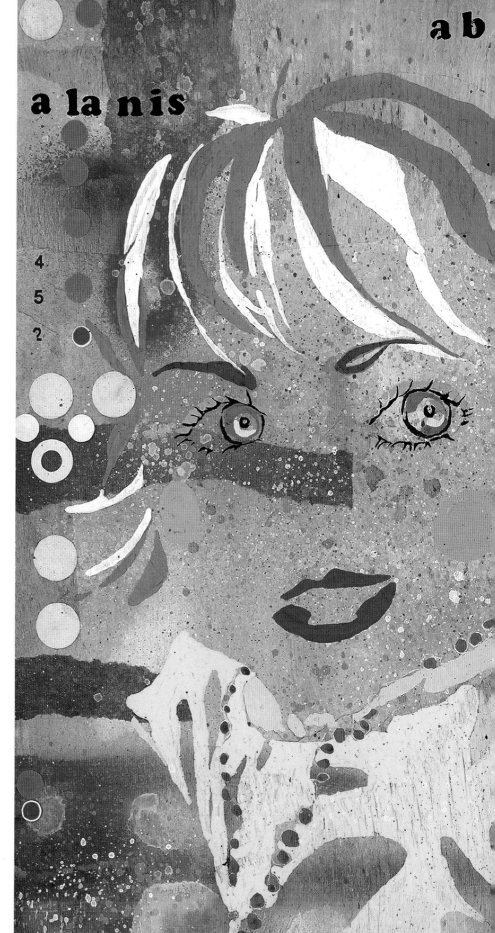

Sarah Beetson
Dress Up Like Mummy: Alanis, Abbie, Alice (2002)
Mixed media on wood

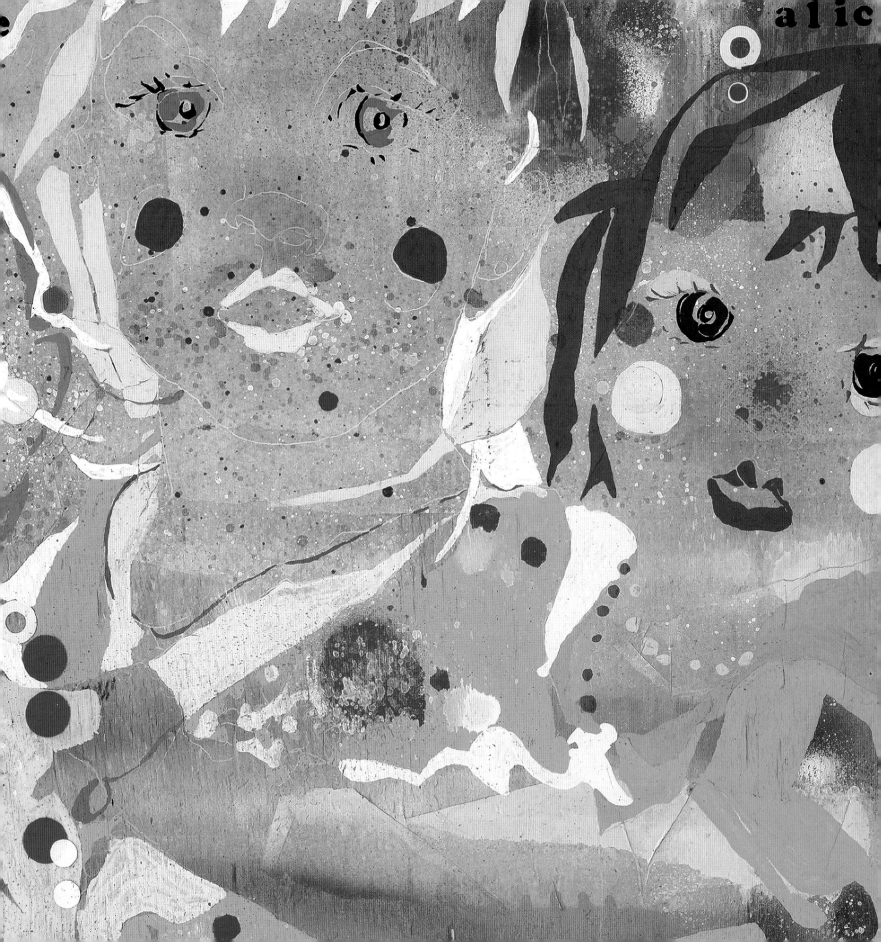

alic

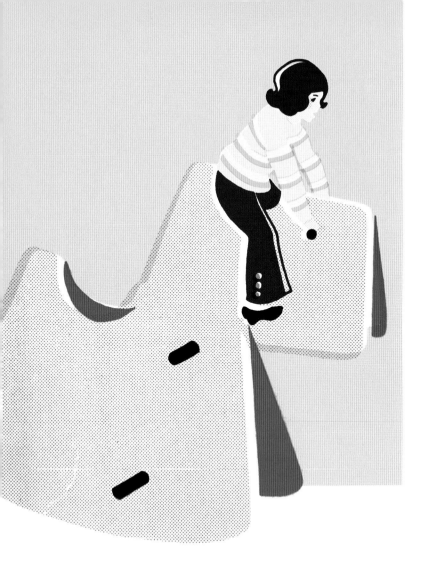

Asako Masunouchi
Fun Fun (2005)
Adobe Photoshop

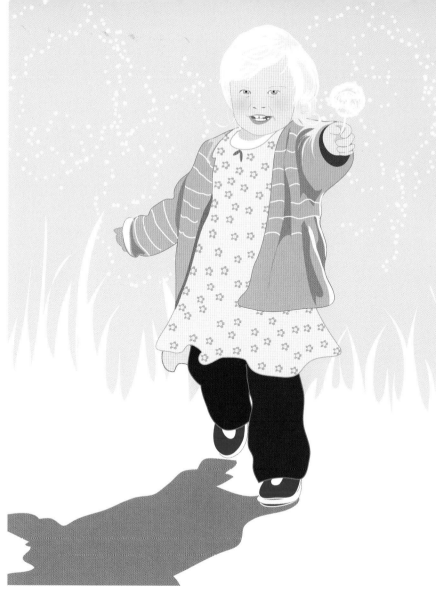

Vicky Woodgate
Untitled (2006)
Adobe Illustrator

Michael Frith
Frieda (1997)
Watercolour

192

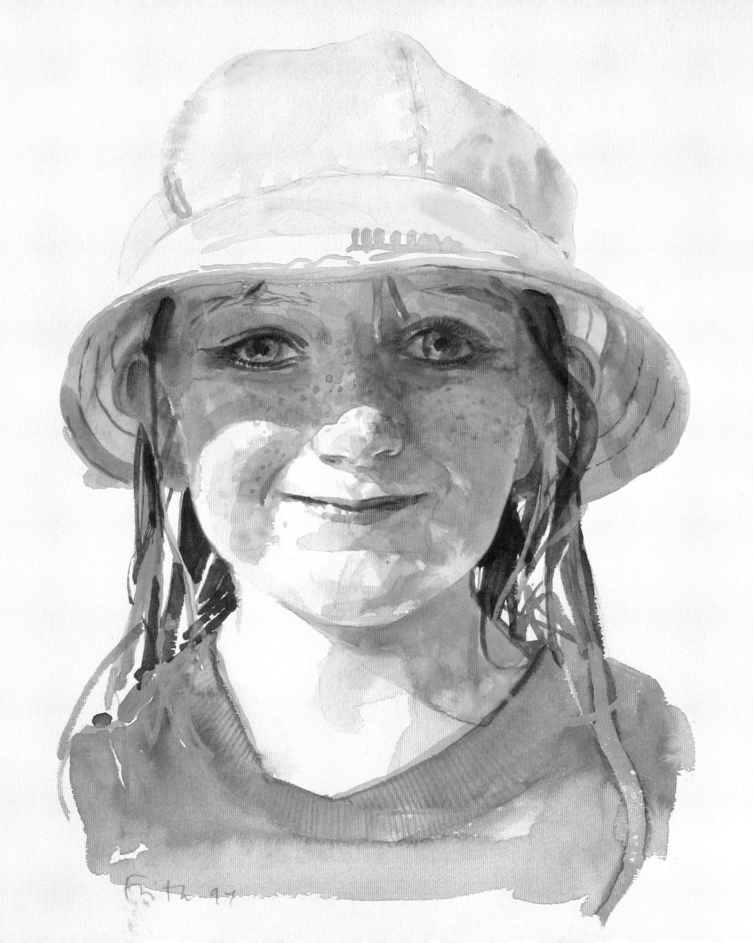

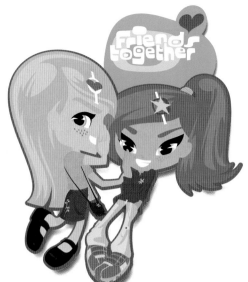

Rian Hughes
Friends Together (2004)
Adobe Illustrator/Adobe Photoshop

Kim Longhurst
I Dream of Pretty, Happy Things (2001)
Macromedia FreeHand/Adobe Photoshop

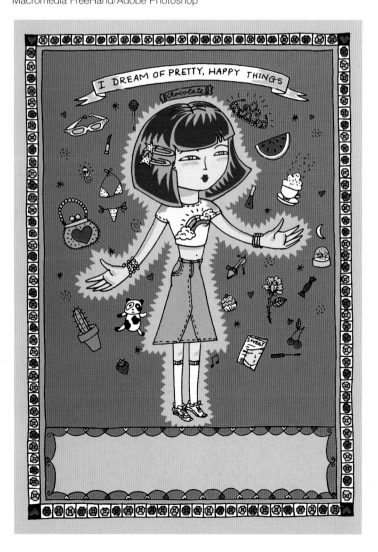

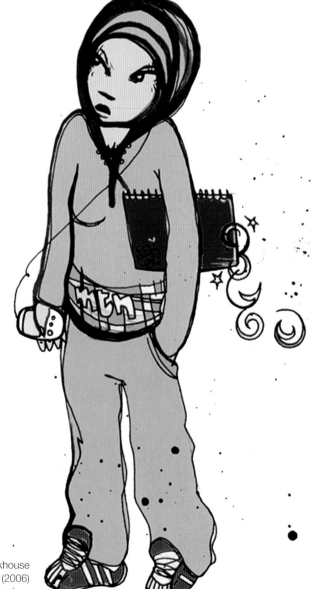

Charlotte Backhouse
Black Book (2006)
Ink/Spray paint/Adobe Photoshop

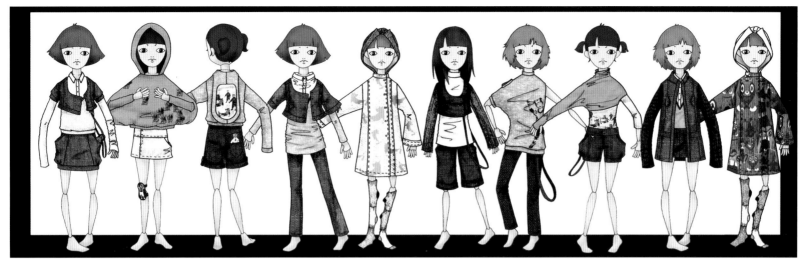

Yejin Yoon
Joy Box (2005)
Adobe Photoshop

Christiane Engel
Rude Beaver (2005)
Acrylic/Pen/Ink/Collage

Christiane Engel
Cheeky Fish (2005)
Acrylic/Pen/Ink/Collage

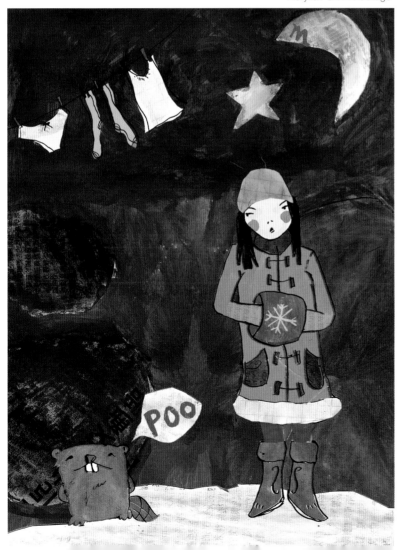

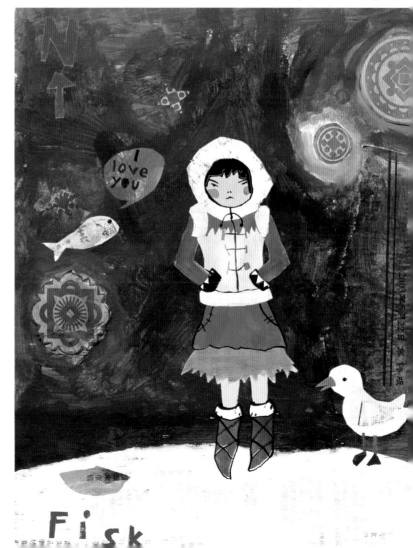

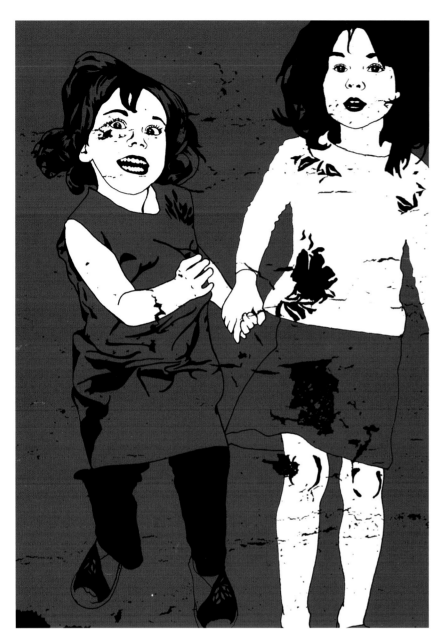

Lucy Allen
Woo Hoo! (2005)
Ink pen/Adobe Photoshop

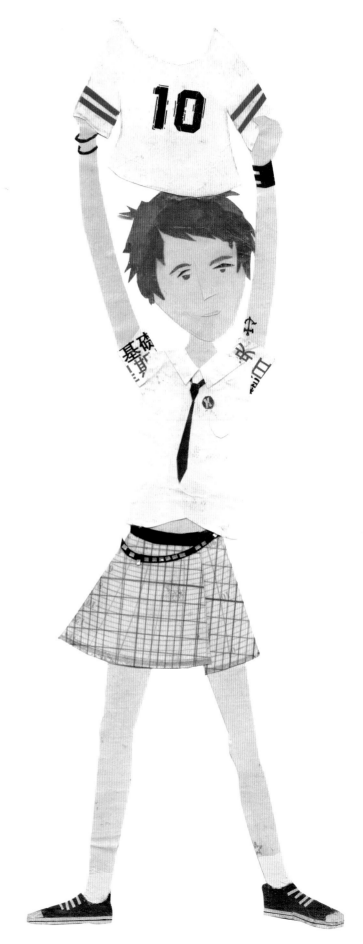

Christy McCaffrey
Punk Rock Girl (2003)
Cut paper

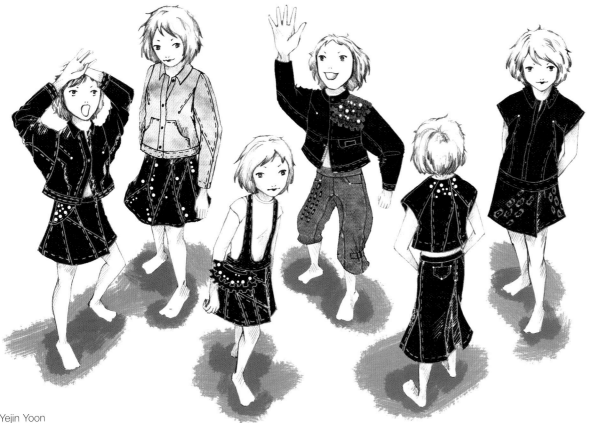

Yejin Yoon
Hallo! (2005)
Adobe Photoshop

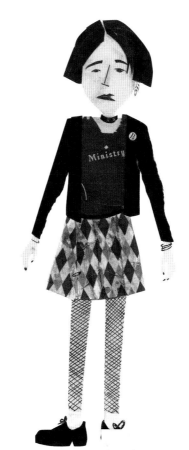

Christy McCaffrey
Seniors (2003)
Cut paper

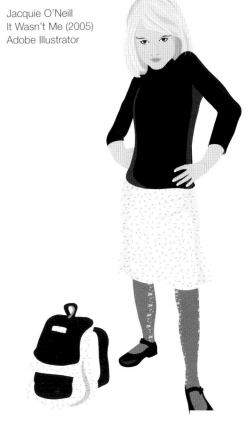

Jacquie O'Neill
It Wasn't Me (2005)
Adobe Illustrator

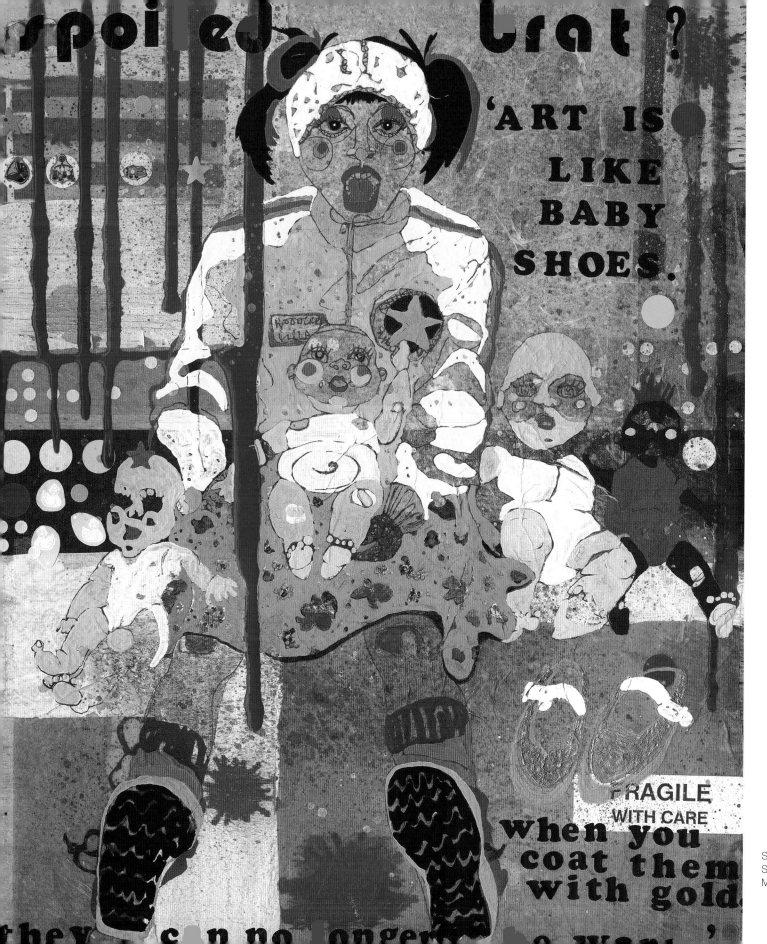

Sarah Beetson
Spoiled Brat (2004)
Mixed media on wood

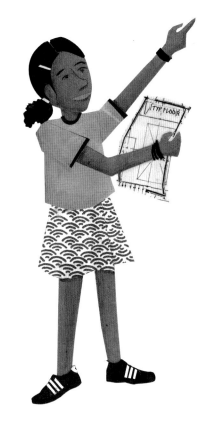

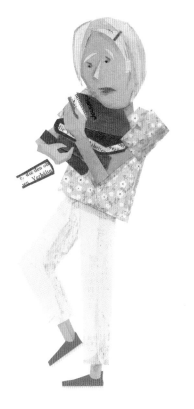

Christy McCaffrey
Frosh (2001)
Cut paper

Christy McCaffrey
Big, Big Plans (2001)
Cut paper

Christy McCaffrey
Indie Links (2001)
Cut paper

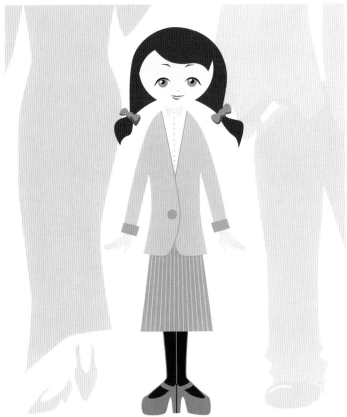

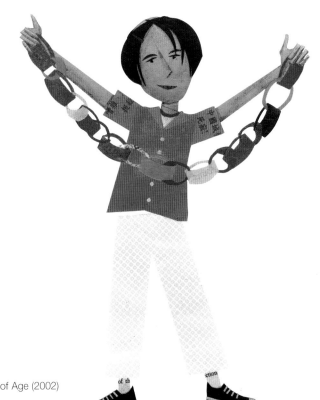

Karen Wegehenkel
Confirmation – Coming of Age (2002)
Adobe Illustrator

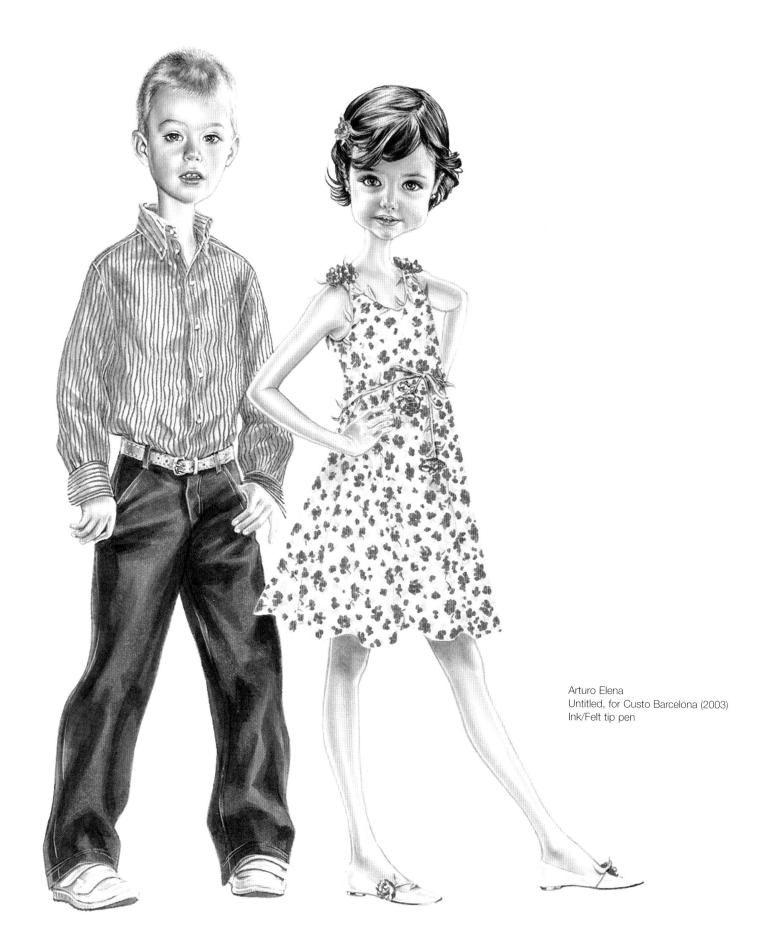

Arturo Elena
Untitled, for Custo Barcelona (2003)
Ink/Felt tip pen

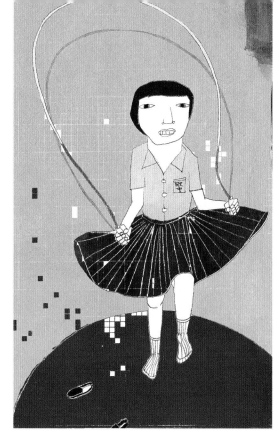

Yihsin Wu
An Odd Moment 2 (2005)
Pencil/Collage/Acrylic/Adobe Photoshop

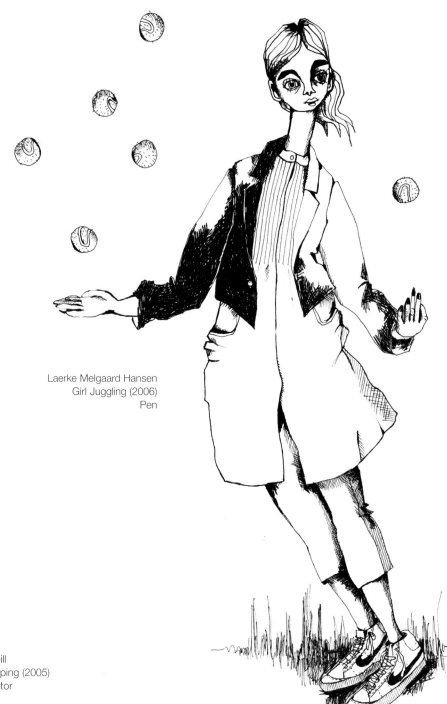

Laerke Melgaard Hansen
Girl Juggling (2006)
Pen

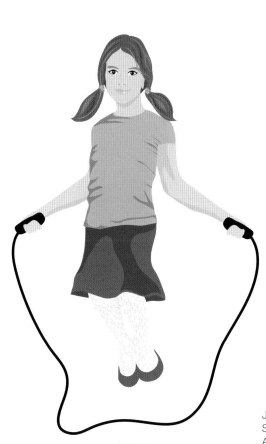

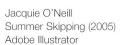

Jacquie O'Neill
Summer Skipping (2005)
Adobe Illustrator

Christy McCaffrey
@#*$ Prom (2004)
Cut paper

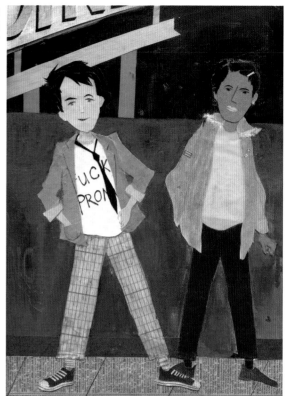

Marina A Townsend
Paperboy (2002)
Charcoal

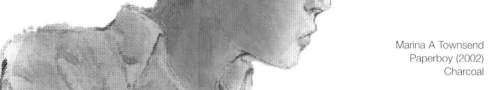

Hayato Jome
Kei (2004)
Acrylic/Adobe Photoshop

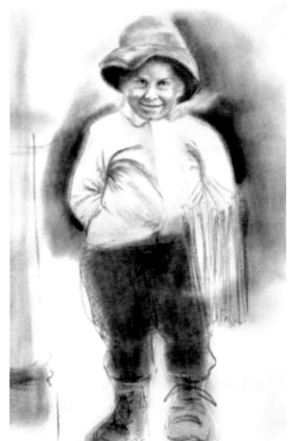

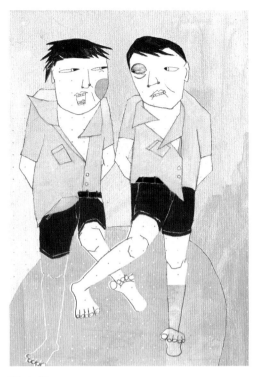

Yihsin Wu
Fighting (2006)
Pencil/Collage/Acrylic/Adobe Photoshop

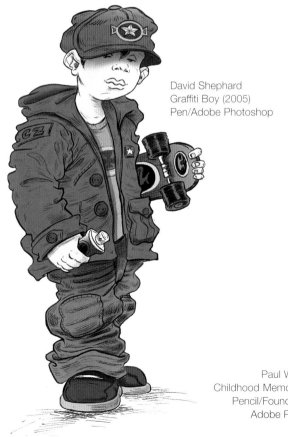

David Shephard
Graffiti Boy (2005)
Pen/Adobe Photoshop

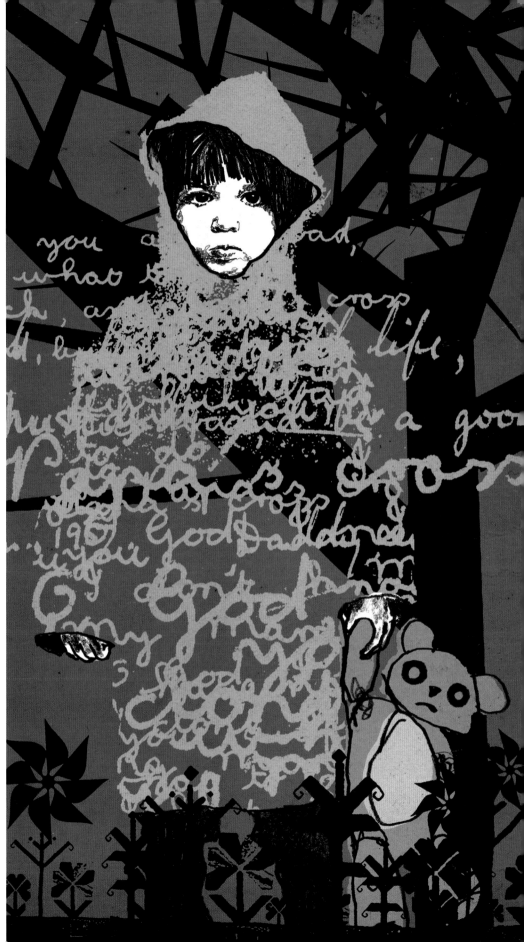

Paul Willoughby
Childhood Memoirs (2005)
Pencil/Found imagery/
Adobe Photoshop

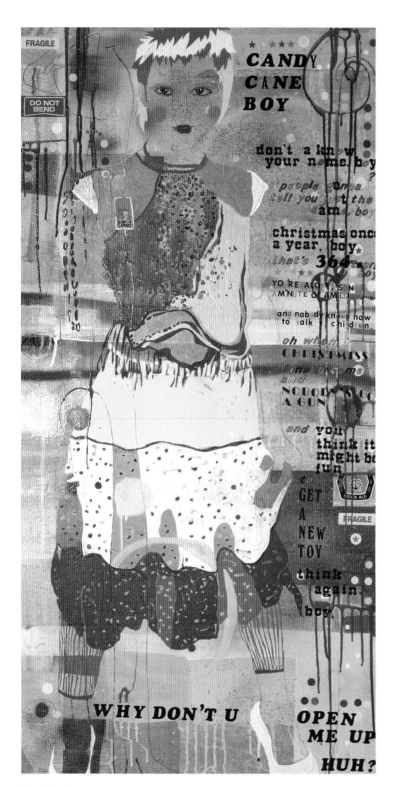

Sarah Beetson
Mail Order Boys – Candy Cane Boy (2004)
Mixed media on wood

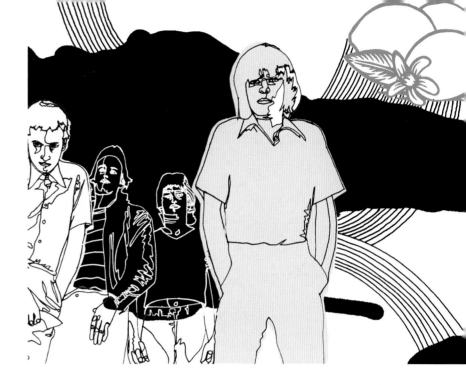

Matthew Hollister
Portrait of XTC (2004)
Ink on paper

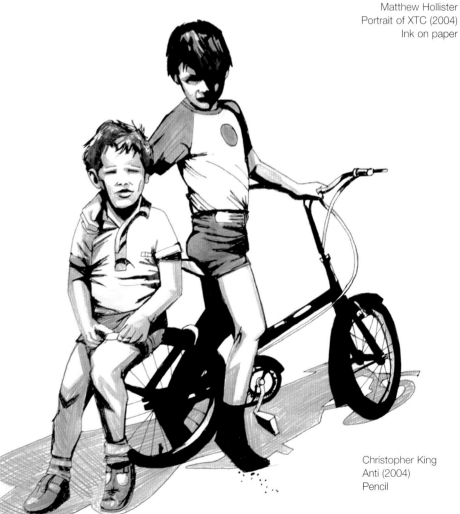

Christopher King
Anti (2004)
Pencil

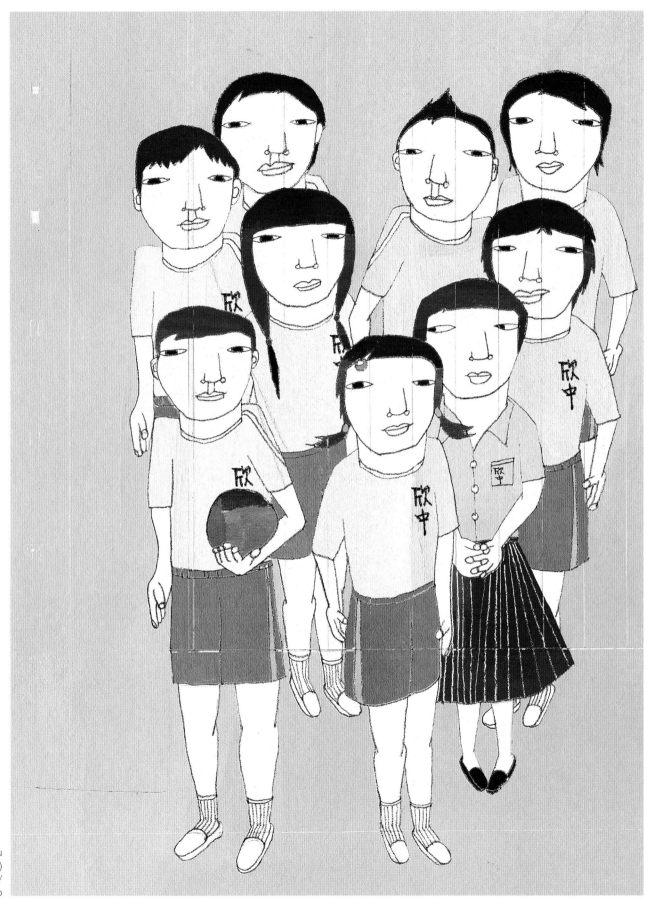

Yihsin Wu
An Odd Moment 1 (2005)
Pencil/Collage/Acrylic/
Adobe Photoshop

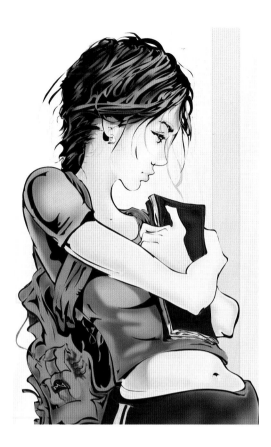

Varshesh Joshi
Untitled (2004)
Pencil/Ink/Macromedia FreeHand/
Adobe Flash/Adobe Photoshop

Wayne Murray
Smiler (2005)
Pencil/Adobe Illustrator

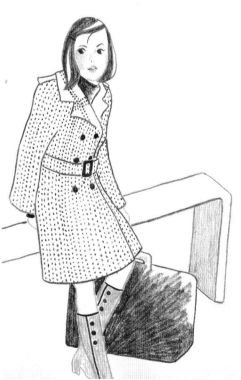

Asako Masunouchi
I'll Write to you Soon (2005)
Coloured pencil

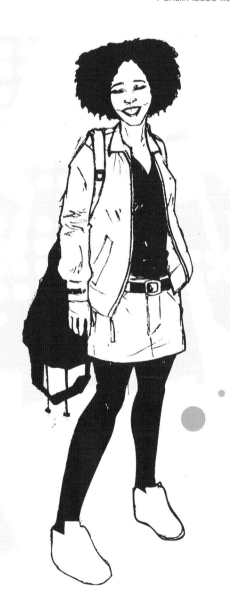

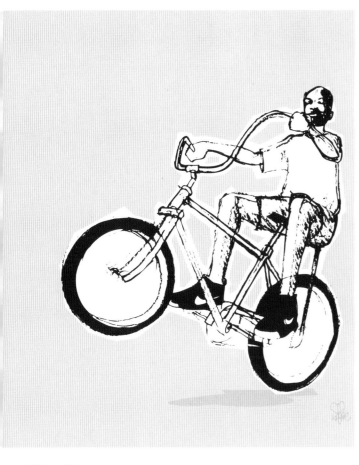

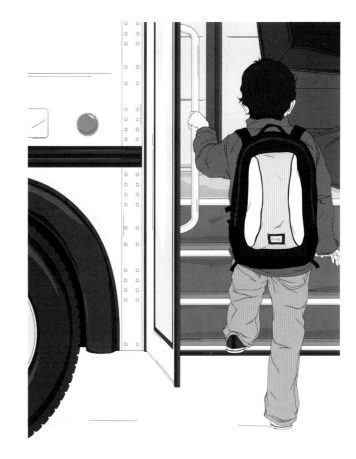

Wayne Murray
Wheelie (2005)
Pencil/Adobe Illustrator

Daniel Chen
First Day (2005)
Macromedia FreeHand/Adobe Photoshop

Christy McCaffrey
Professional What? (2004)
Cut paper

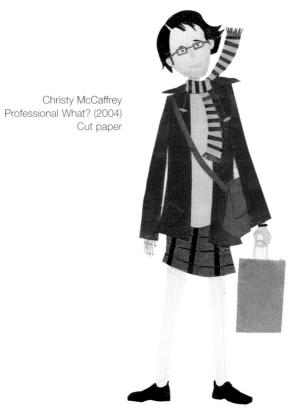

Christy McCaffrey
Sophomores (2004)
Cut paper

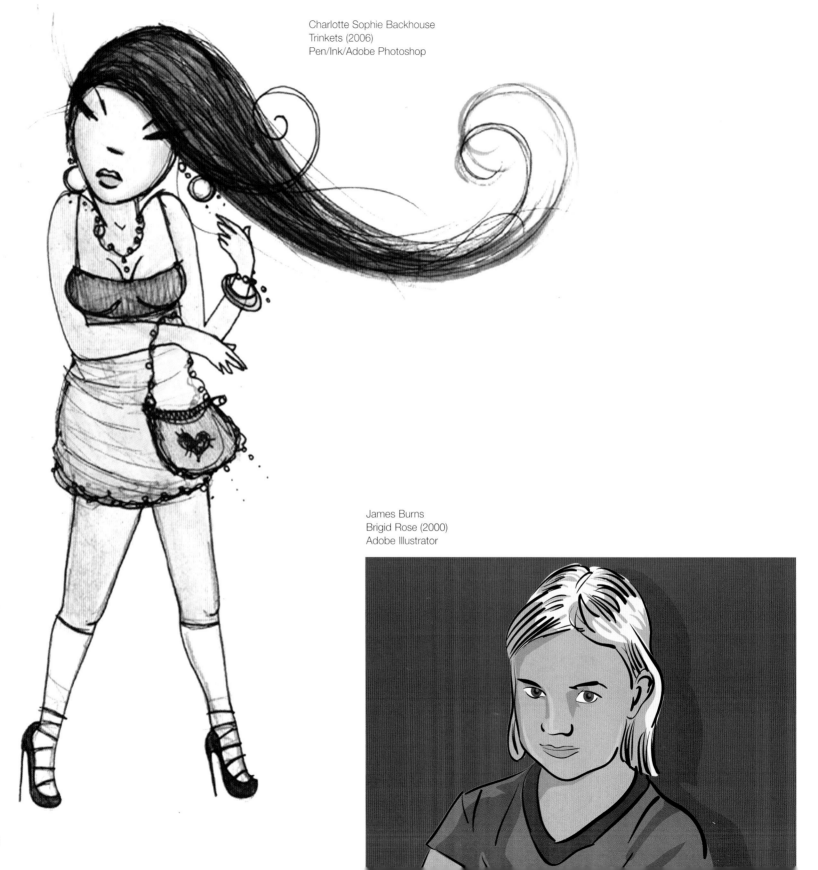

Charlotte Sophie Backhouse
Trinkets (2006)
Pen/Ink/Adobe Photoshop

James Burns
Brigid Rose (2000)
Adobe Illustrator

Margat Aurélie
Adonescance n*1 (2005)
Collage/Ink/Oil pastel

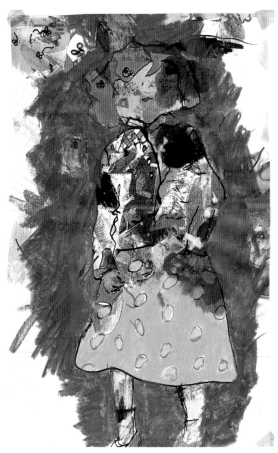

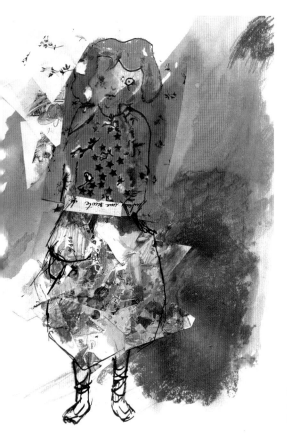

Claudio Parentela
Untitled (2005)
Ink and pen on paper

Margat Aurélie
Adonescance n*2 (2005)
Collage/Ink/Oil pastel

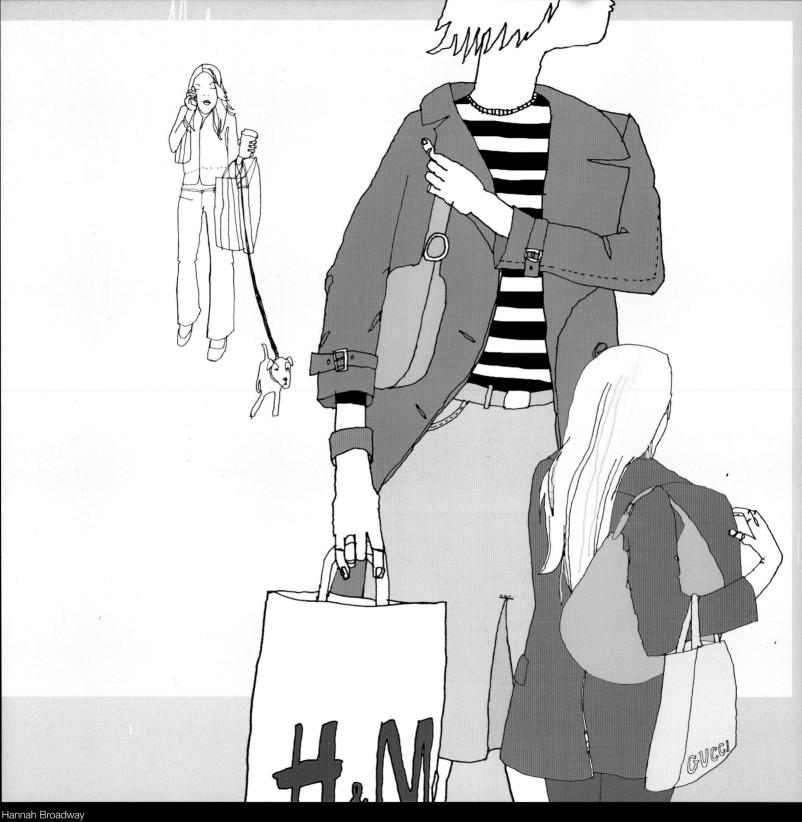

Hannah Broadway
Shopping (2006)
Fine liner/Adobe Photoshop

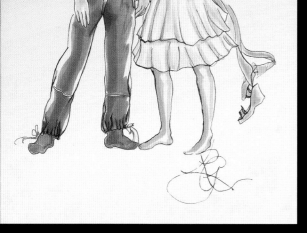

Raissa Gabriel
Buddy Up (2006)
Ink/Marker pen

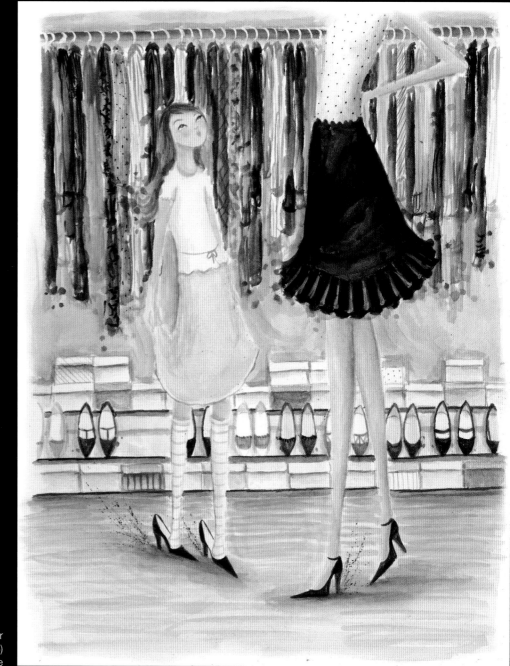

Bella Pilar
Mom's Closet (2005)
Gouache

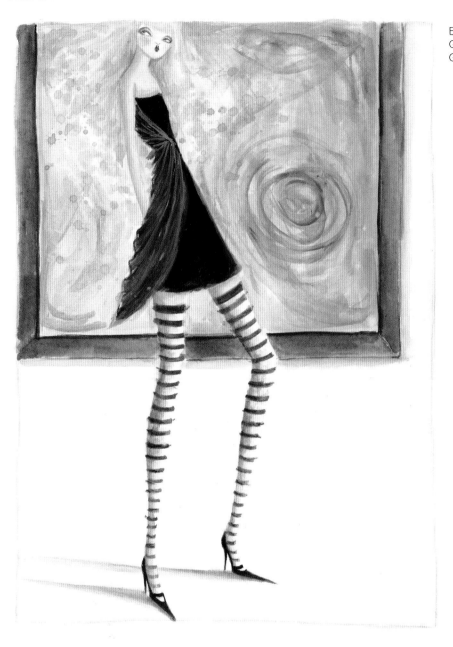

Bella Pilar
Grey Art (2005)
Gouache

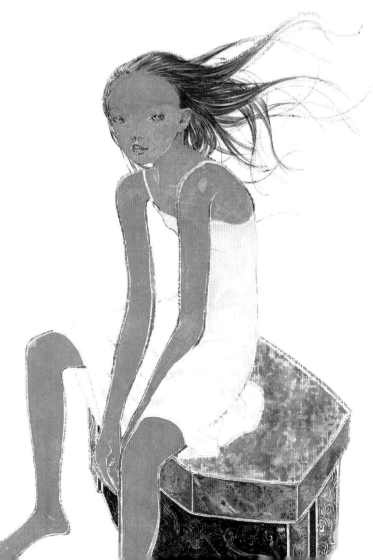

Hayato Jome
Zushiban Guard of Feretory (2003)
Acrylic on paper

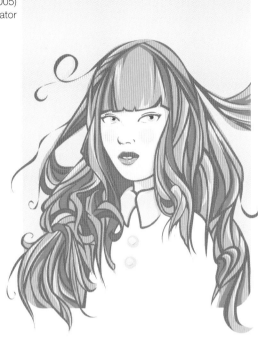

Rhiannon Cunag
Rapunzel (2005)
Adobe Illustrator

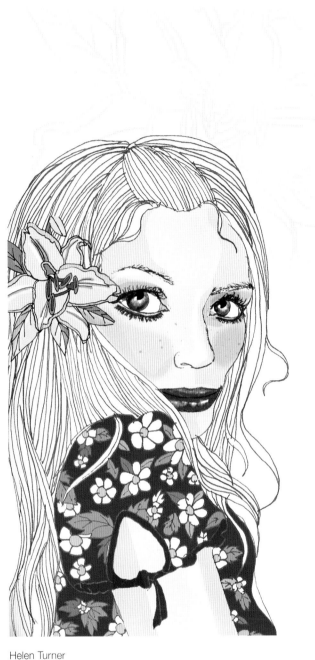

Helen Turner
Lily (2003)
Ink/Adobe Photoshop

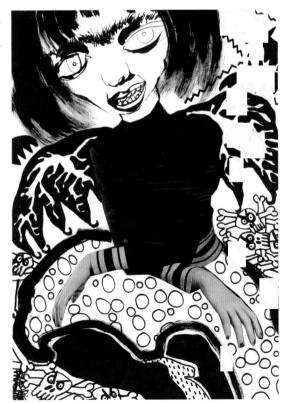

Claudio Parentela
Untitled (2005)
Ink and pen on paper

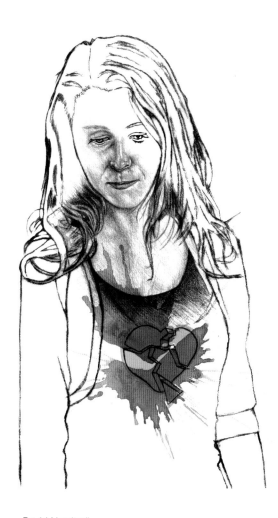

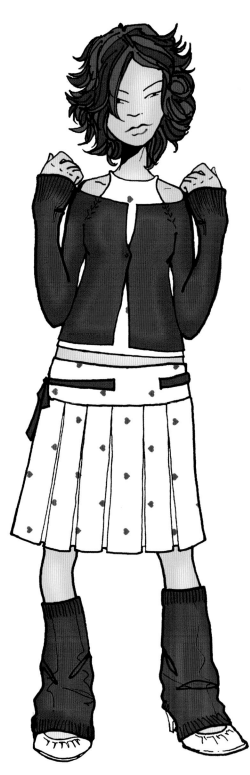

Jeeyun Lee
Girl in Red (2005)
Watercolour

David Nwokedi
What Does Your Soul Look Like? (2006)
Pencil/Watercolour/Adobe Photoshop/Adobe Illustrator

Ekua Doduwa Akumanyi
Hattie (2003)
Ink pen/Adobe Photoshop

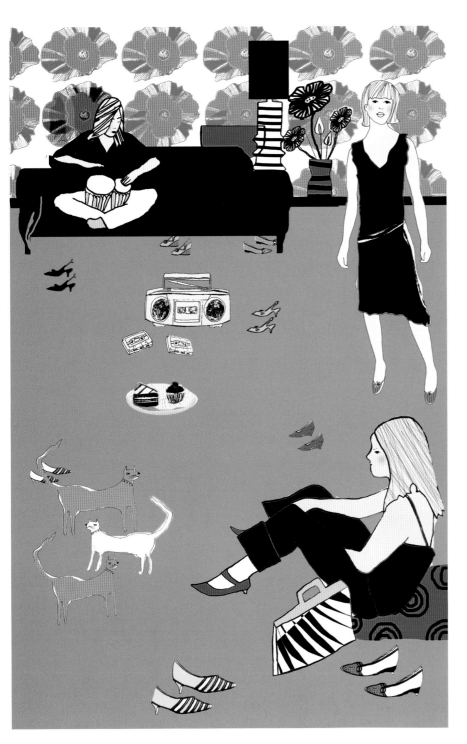

Tiffany Lynch
Interior Birds (2005)
Pen/Ink/Adobe Photoshop

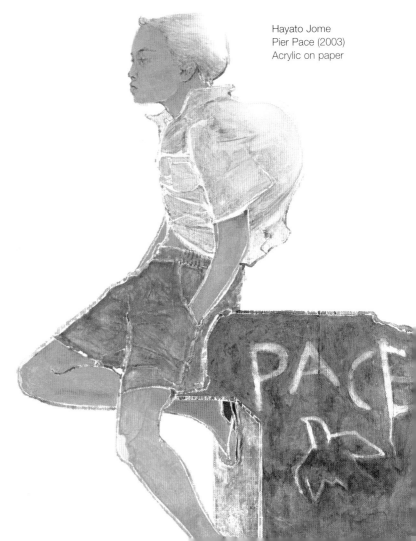

Hayato Jome
Pier Pace (2003)
Acrylic on paper

Marguerite Sauvage
University Coming Soon, What Choice... (2005)
Pencil/Adobe Photoshop

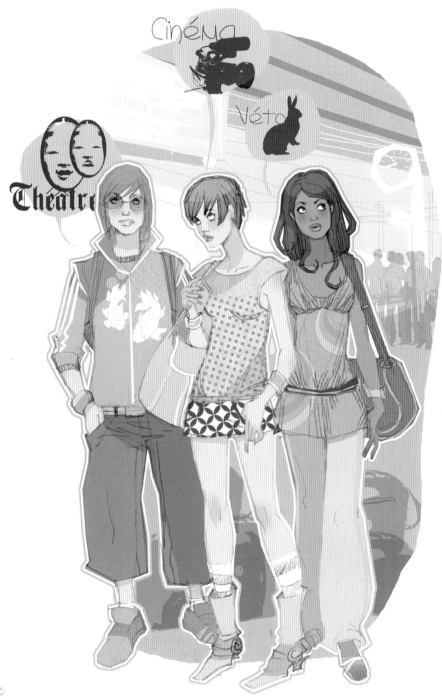

Rhiannon Cunag
Love at First Sight (2005)
Adobe Illustrator

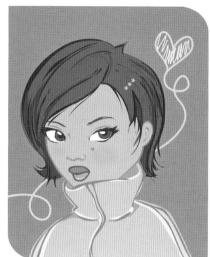

Jens Rotzsche
Vintage of '88 (2005)
Adobe Illustrator

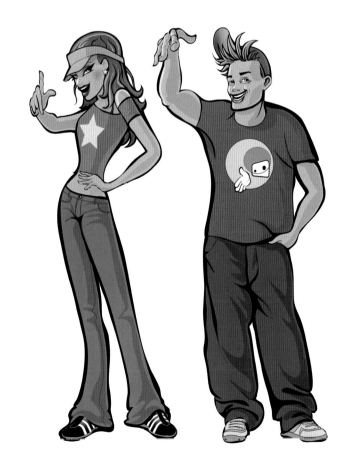

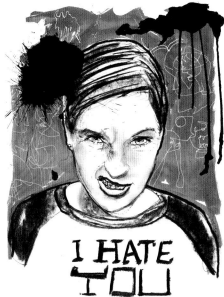

Christian Barthold
I Hate You! (2004)
India ink/Adobe Photoshop

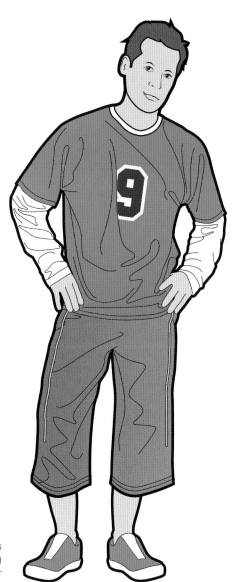
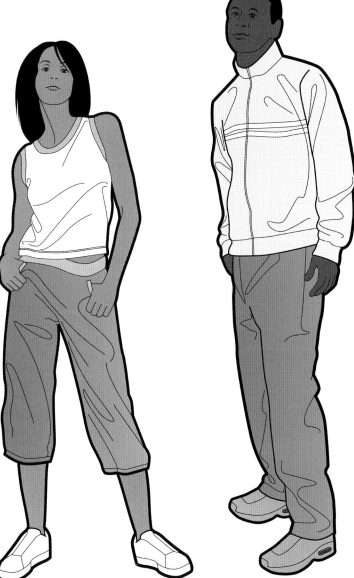

Stuart Holmes
Teens, MET Police website (2006)
Adobe Illustrator

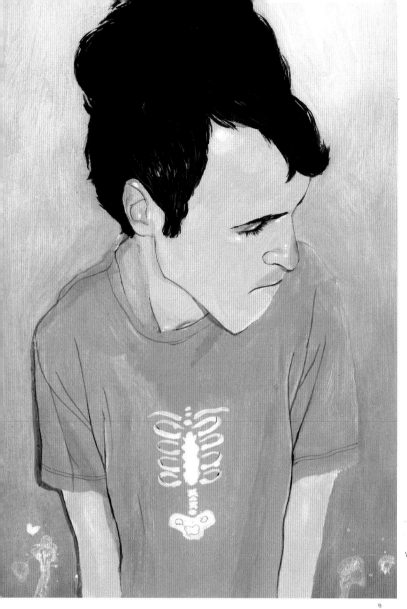

Meirav Shaul
Alon in Blue (2006)
Acrylic on paper

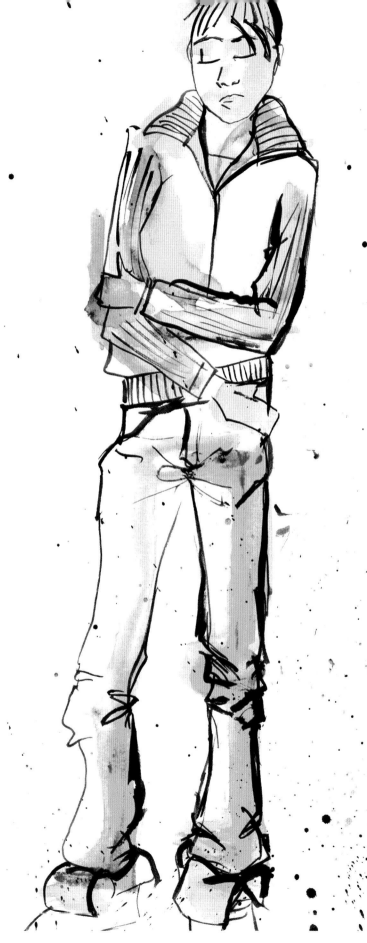

Claire Townsend
Casual Attitude (2006)
Watercolour/Ink

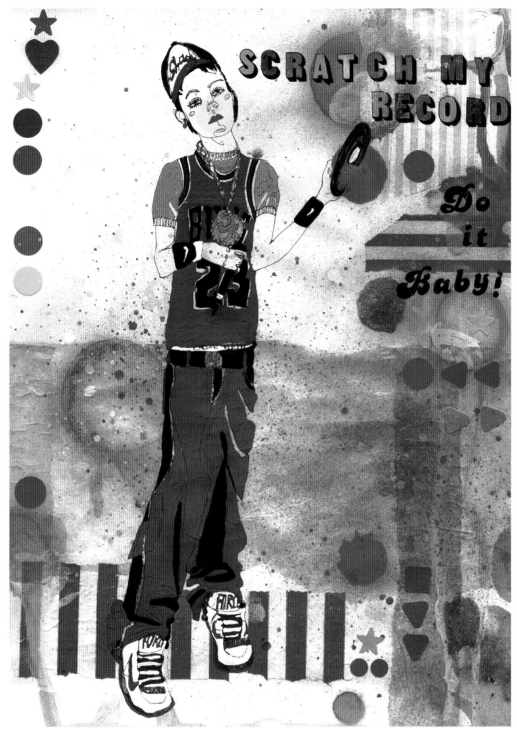

Sarah Beetson
The New Music Revolution – Scratch My Record (2005)
Mixed media on wood

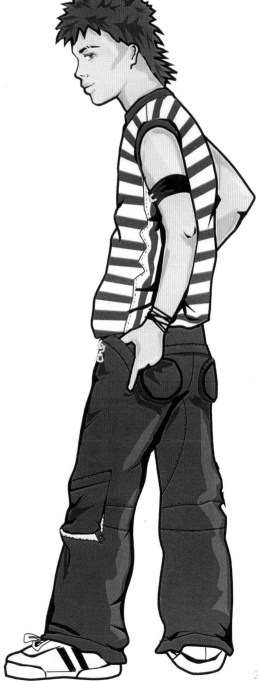

Naomi Austin
Playin' It Cool (2004)
Adobe Illustrator

219

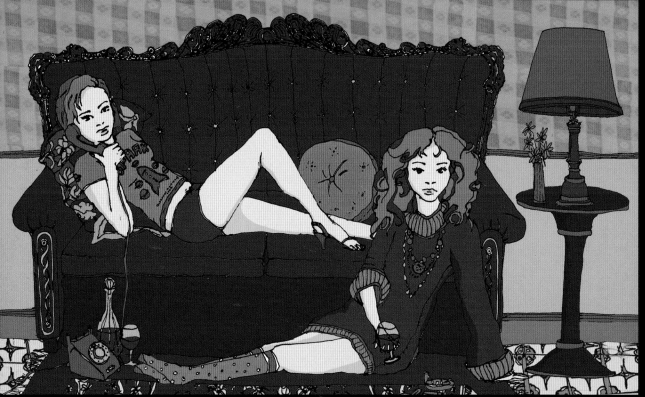

Medeleine Egremont
Relax (2005)
Pencil/Pen/Ink/Adobe Photoshop

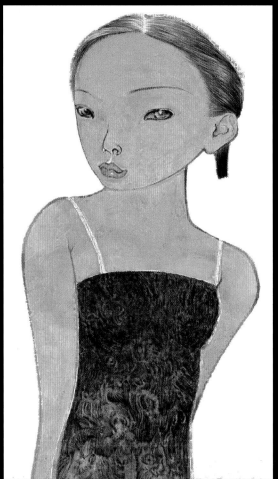

Hayato Jome
Etude of Field Rose (2001)
Acrylic on paper

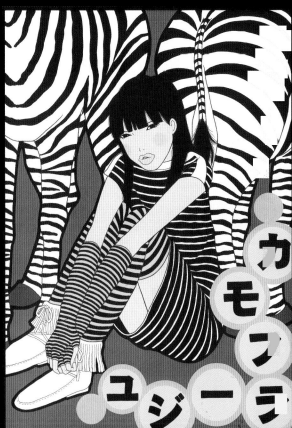

Yumiko Kayukawa
Kamofuraaju (Camouflage) (2003)
Acrylic and ink on illustration board

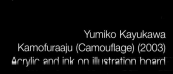

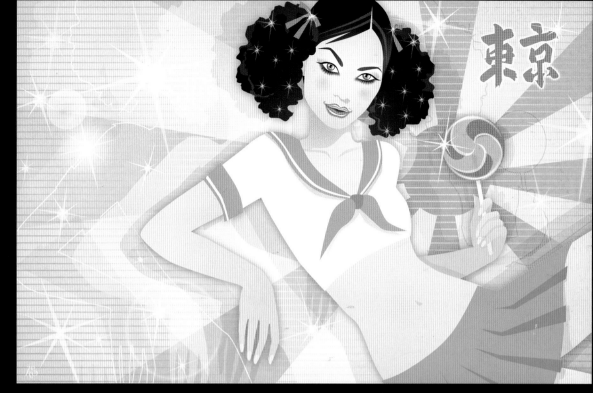

Kun-Sung Chung
Tokyo Girl (2006)
Adobe Illustrator

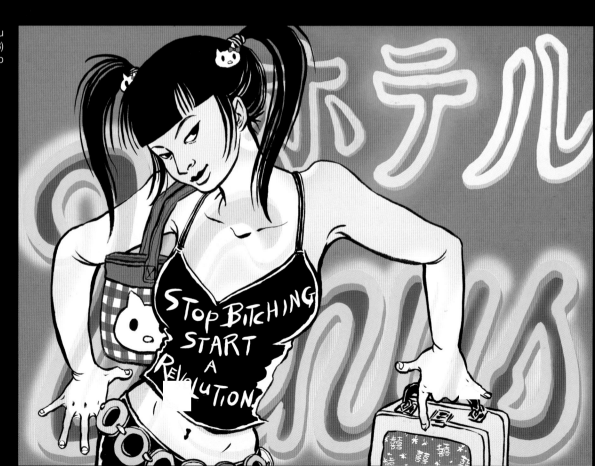

Yuko Shimizu
Untitled, *The Village Voice* (2003)
Ink/Adobe Photoshop

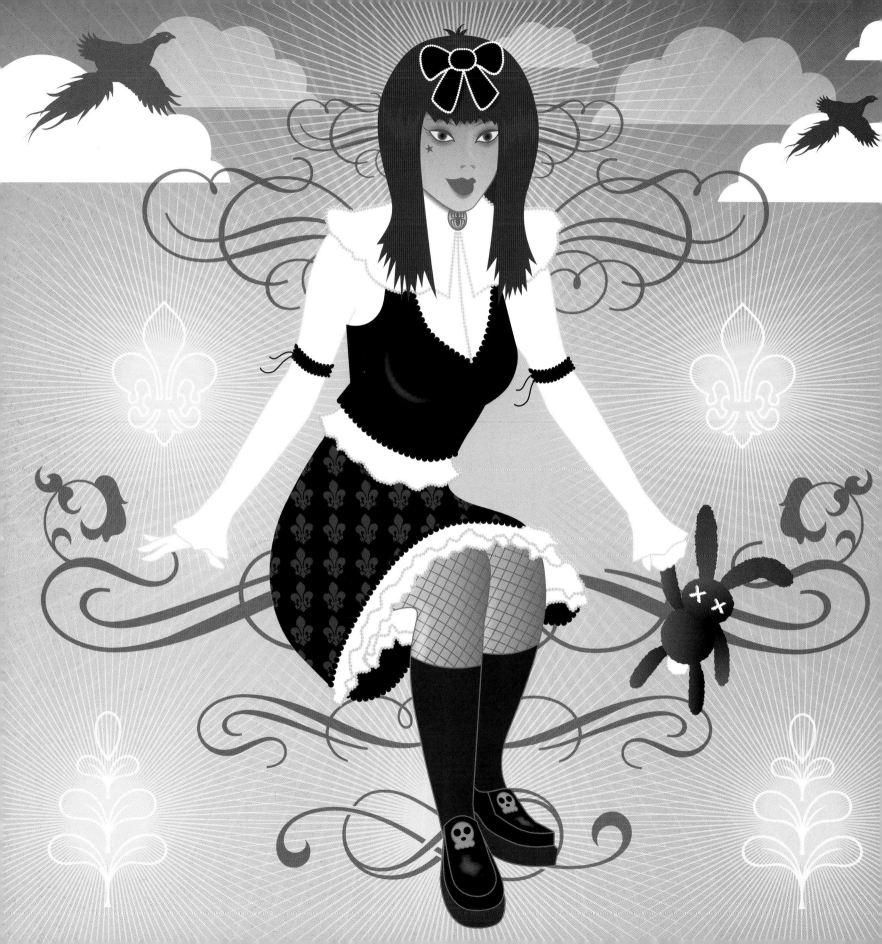

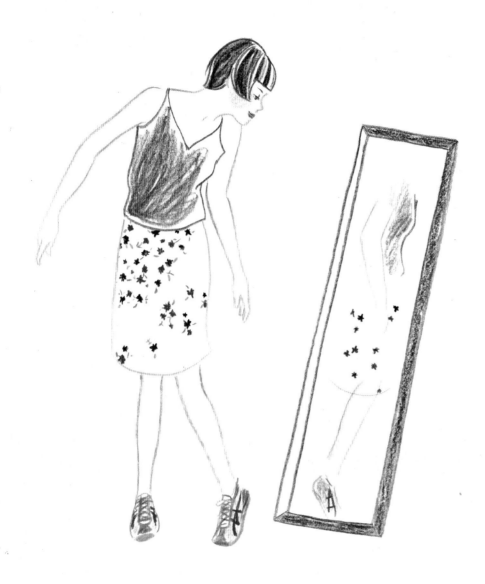

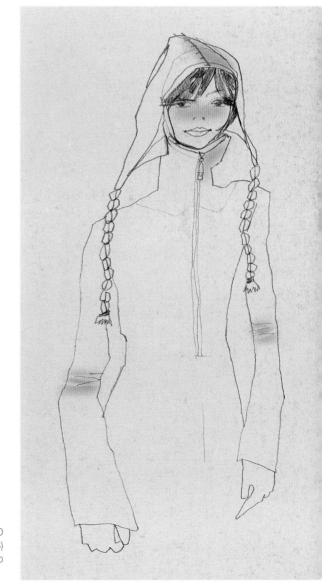

Asako Masunouchi
Make Her Envy (2005)
Coloured pencil

Robert Weiss
Gothic Lolita (2006)
Adobe Illustrator

Lopetz:BD
Raincoat (2003)
Adobe Photoshop

Christy McCaffrey
Radio, Radio (2005)
Cut paper

Daniel Chen
My Time (2005)
Macromedia FreeHand/Adobe Photoshop

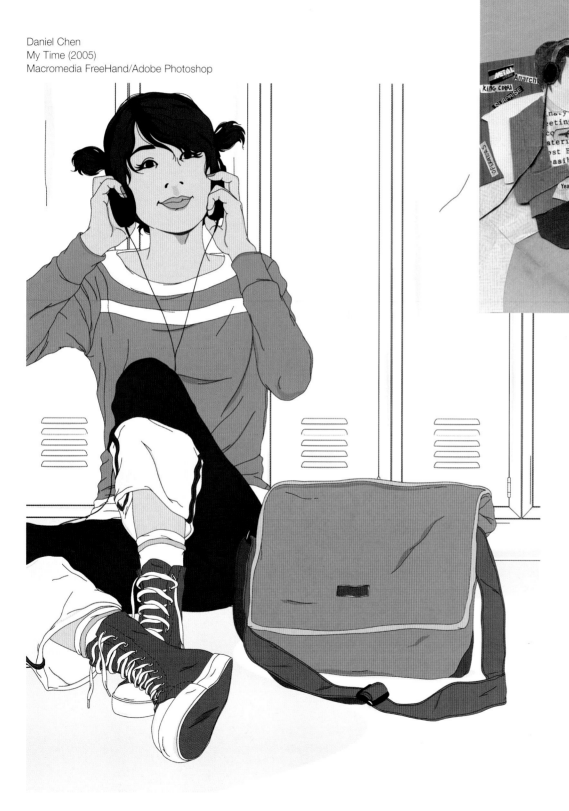

Rian Hughes
Bootleg (2005)
Adobe Illustrator/Adobe Photoshop

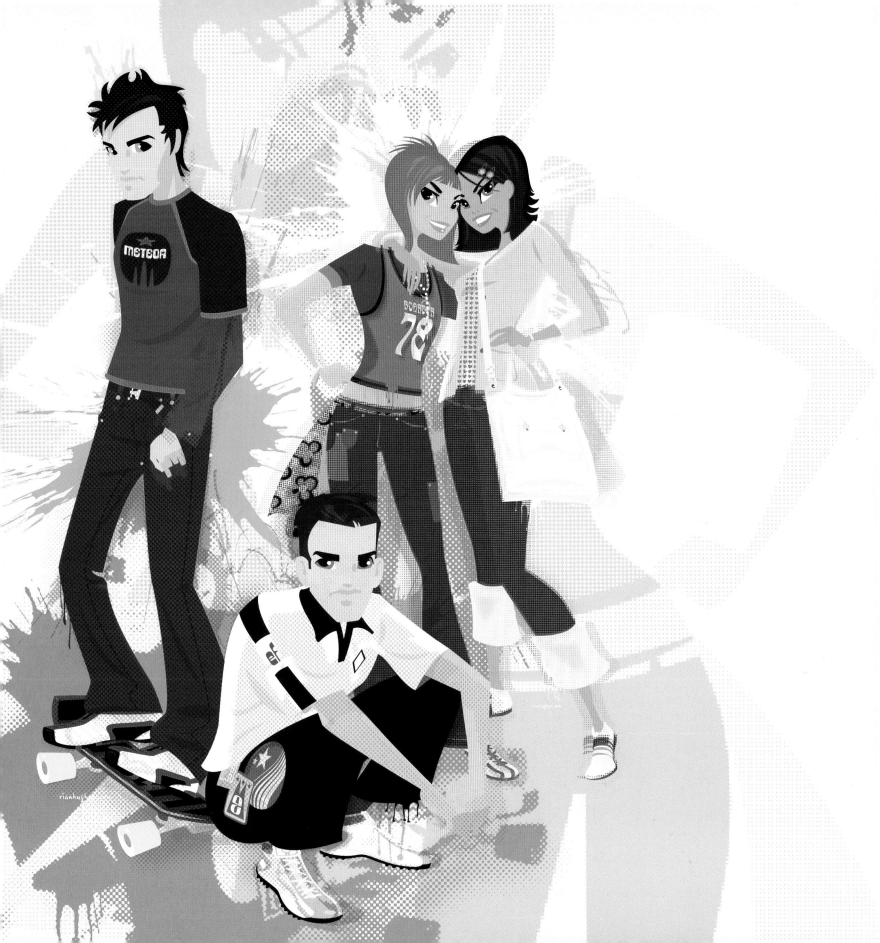

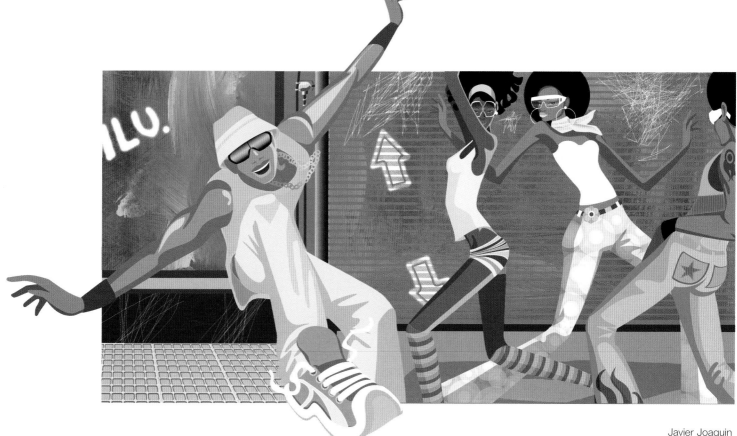

Javier Joaquin
Dancing in the Street (2005)
Adobe Illustrator

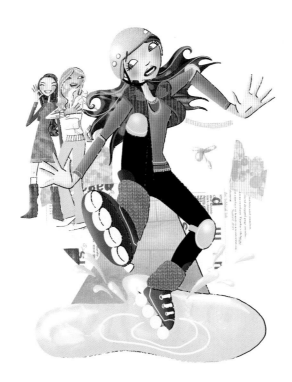

Katie Wood
Embarrassing Moment: Rollerblades (2005)
Adobe Photoshop

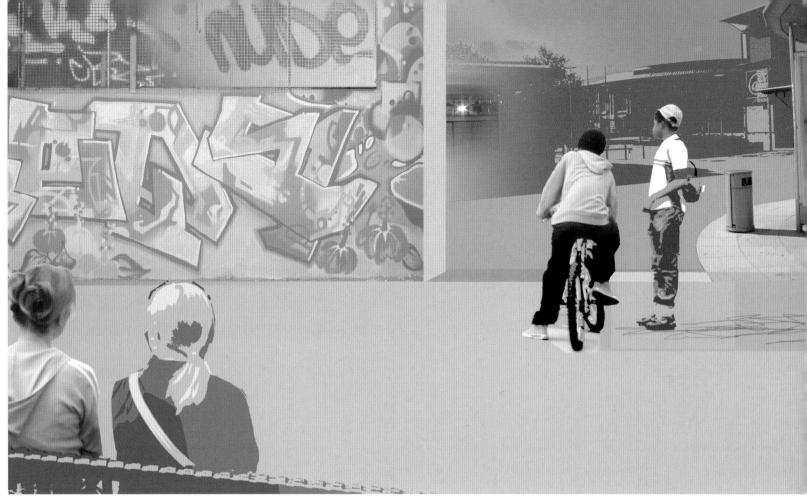

Jacqui Paull and Carl Melegari
Looking-out (2003)
Adobe Photoshop

Madeleine Egremont
Skate Park (2006)
Pencil/Pen/Ink/Adobe Photoshop

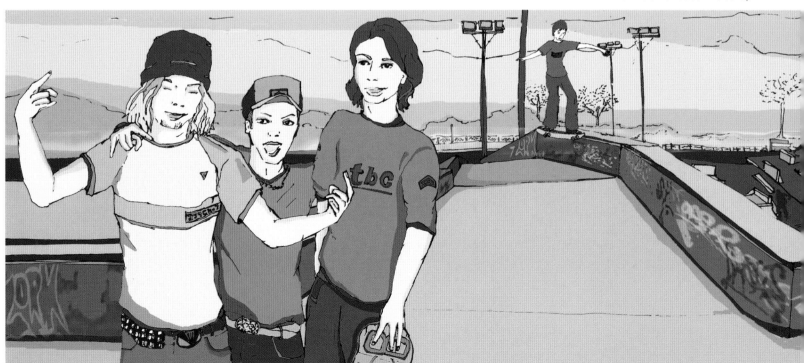

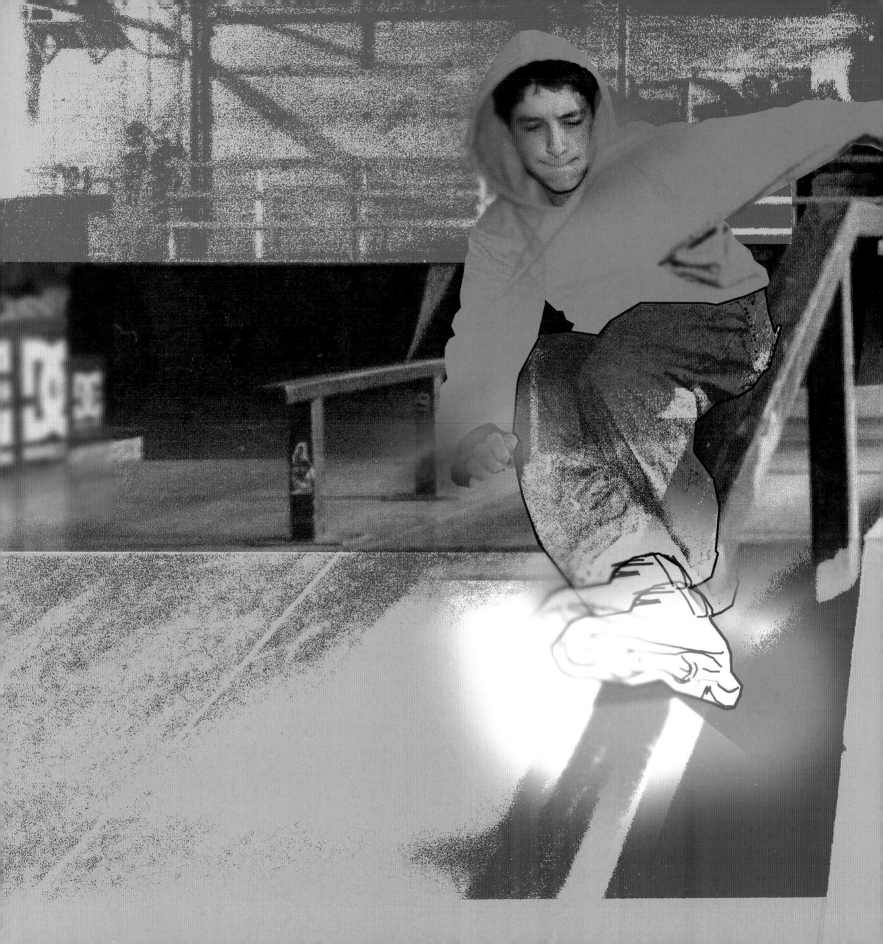

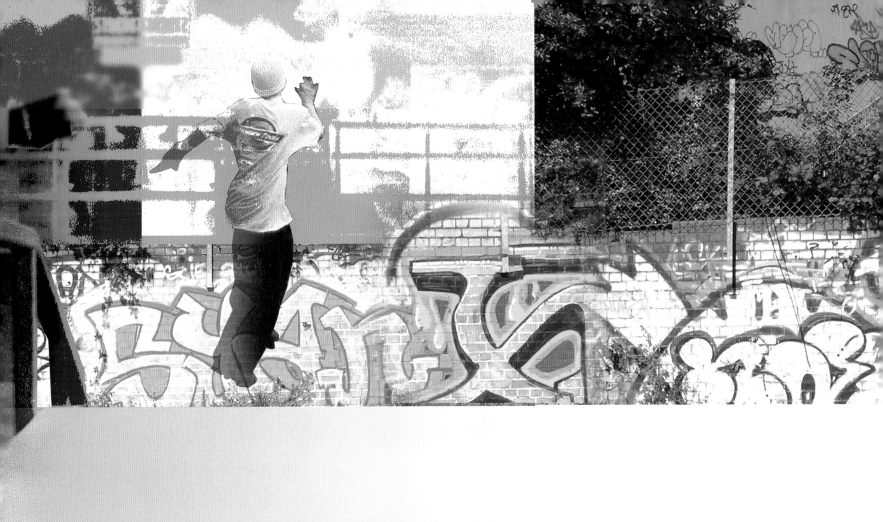

Jacqui Paull and Carl Melegari
The Grind (2003)
Adobe Photoshop

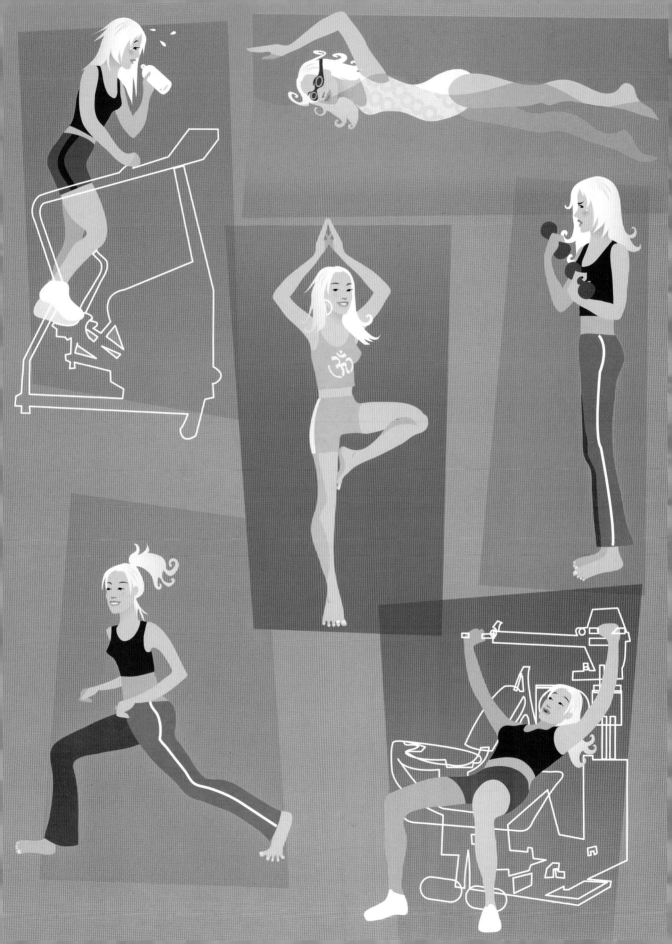

Sport and Leisure

gym   track   ball games   snow & ice

blades & boards   biking   aquatics

Martina Farrow
Express (2003)
Adobe Illustrator

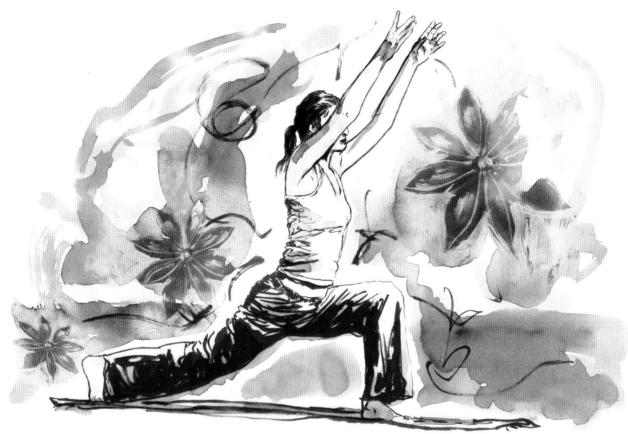

Christian Barthold
Fitness (2005)
India ink/Gouache/Adobe Photoshop

James Burns
Yoga (2004)
Adobe Illustrator

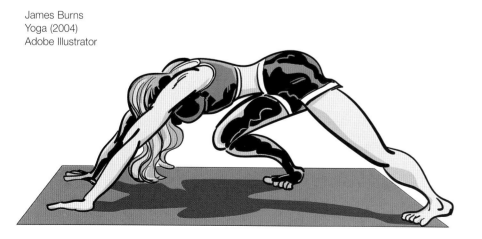

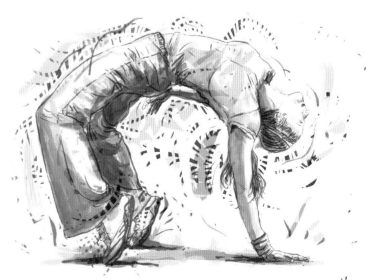

Christian Barthold
Sports (2005)
India ink/Gouache/Adobe Photoshop

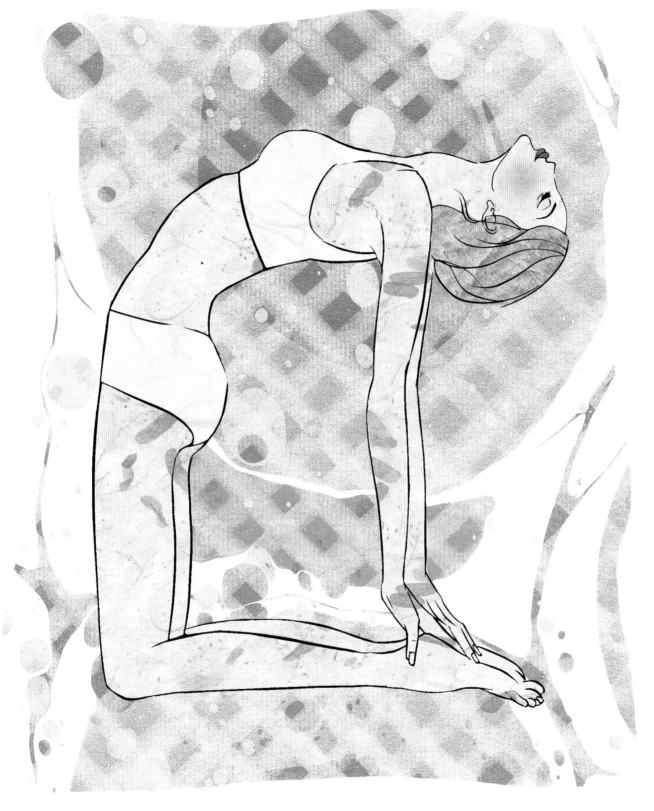

Annabelle J Verhoye
Indulge Yourself (2003)
Chine collé/Adobe Photoshop

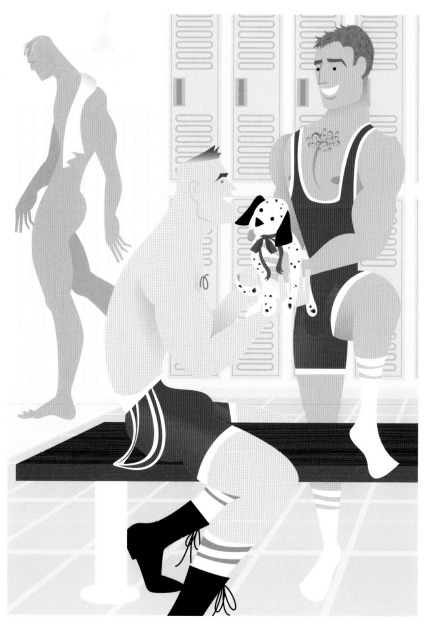

Jason O'Malley
Locker Room (2006)
Adobe Illustrator

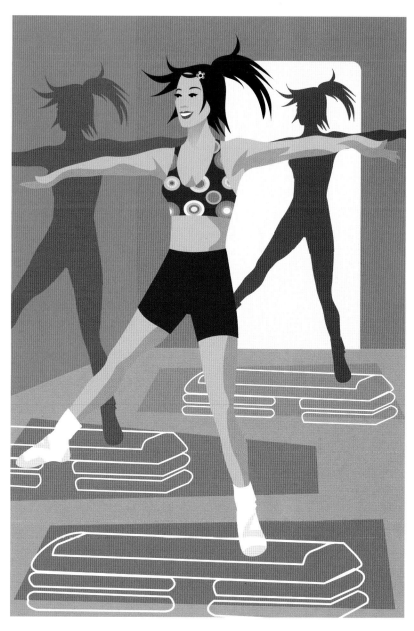

Martina Farrow
Ban Cellulite (2004)
Adobe Illustrator

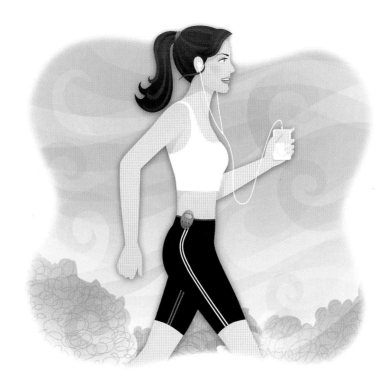

Kun-Sung Chung
Jogging Girl (2005)
Adobe Illustrator

Hayato Jome
Shujinko – Hero in You (2001)
Acrylic on paper

Tanya Unger
Ballerina (2006)
Adobe Illustrator

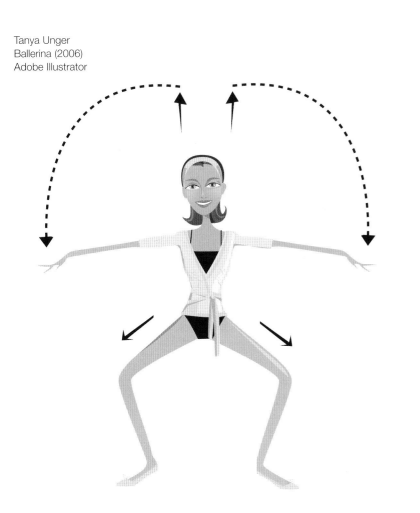

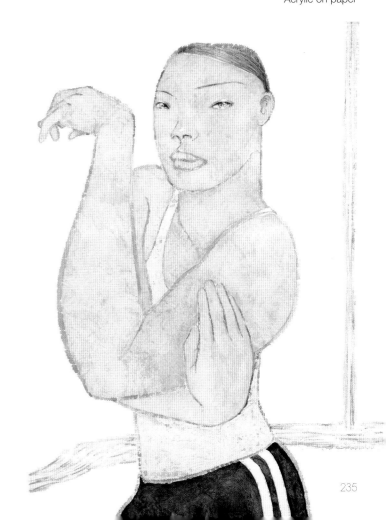

235

Daniel Mackie
Get Down and Give Me 10 (2004)
Pencil/Adobe Photoshop

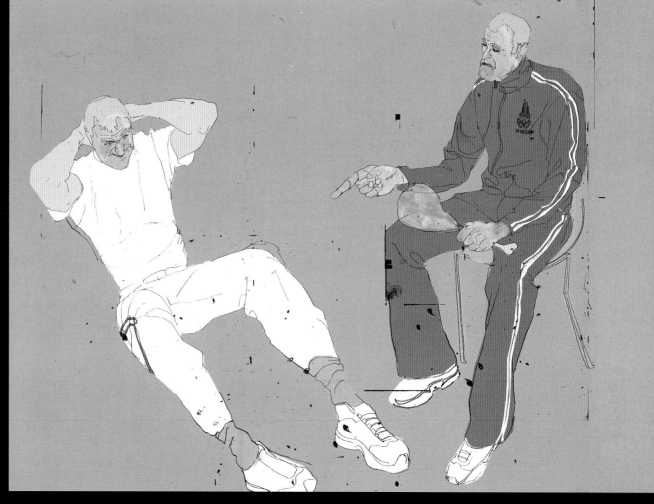

Jason O'Malley
Sexy Massage (2006)
Adobe Illustrator

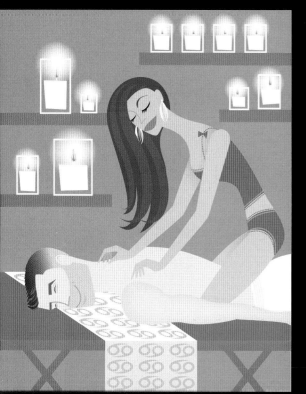

Vincent Agostino
Weight Training Series (2004)
Clockwise from top left:
Squats; Press Ups; Dumb
Bell Lifts; Dumb Bell Curls
Acrylic

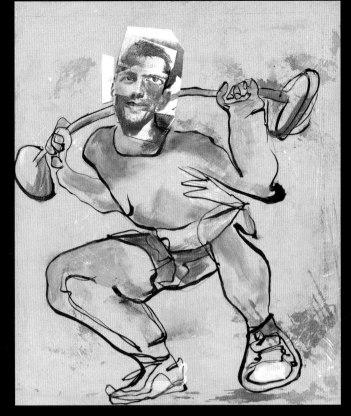

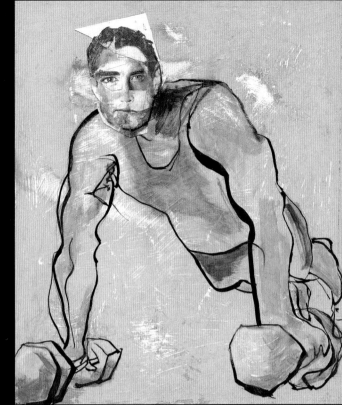

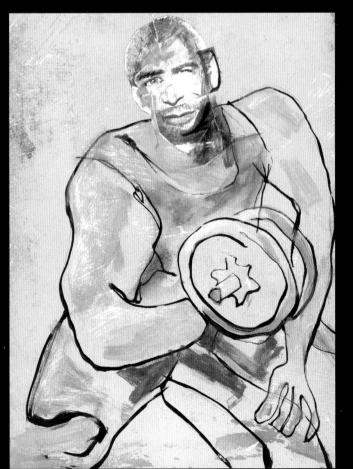

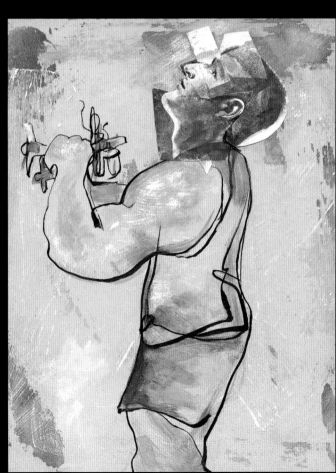

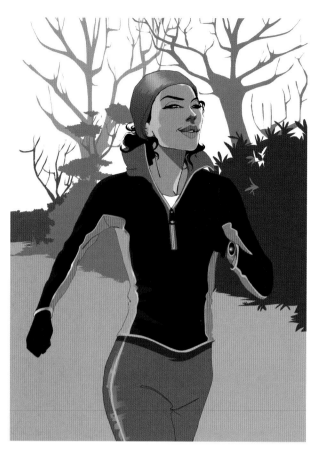

Gavin Reece
Morning Run (2004)
Adobe Photoshop

Öscar Gimenez
Needing a Massage? (2004)
Pencil/Adobe Photoshop

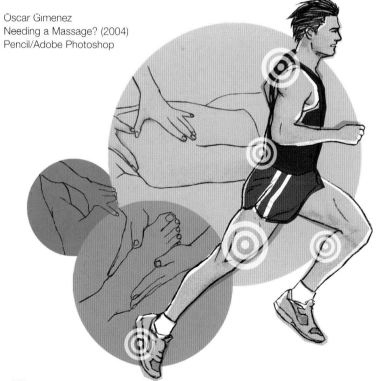

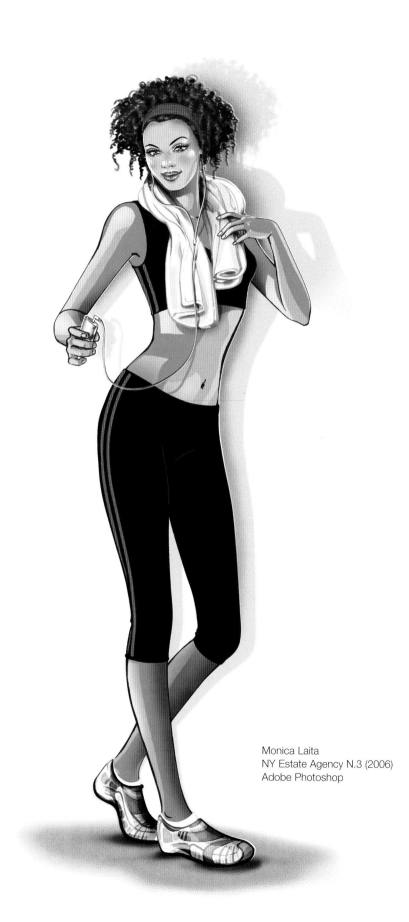

Monica Laita
NY Estate Agency N.3 (2006)
Adobe Photoshop

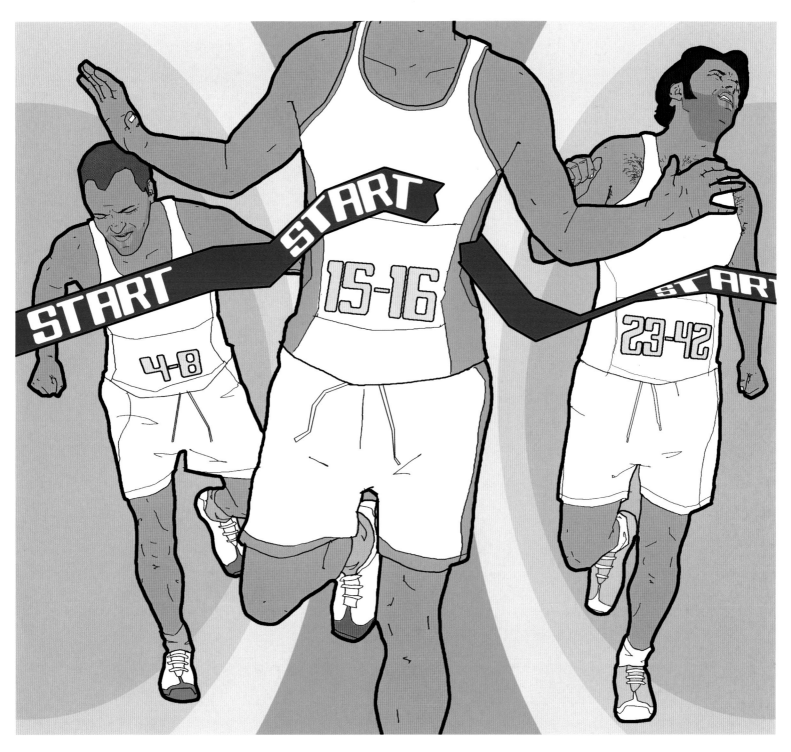

Lee Woodgate
How to ... Finish (2005)
Adobe Photoshop

Jonathan Williams
50/50 Ball (2005)
Pencil/Adobe Photoshop

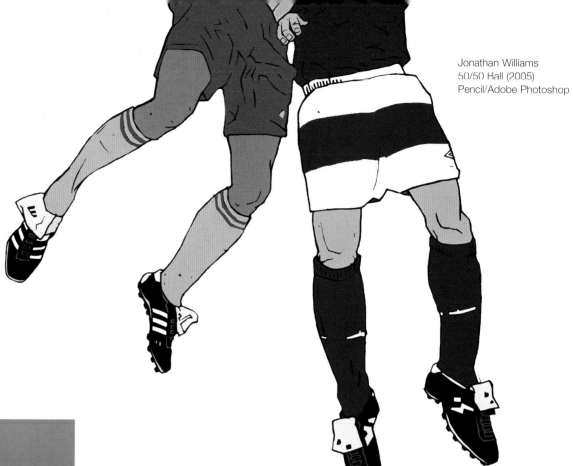

Naomi Austin
Heading for Glory (2006)
Adobe Illustrator

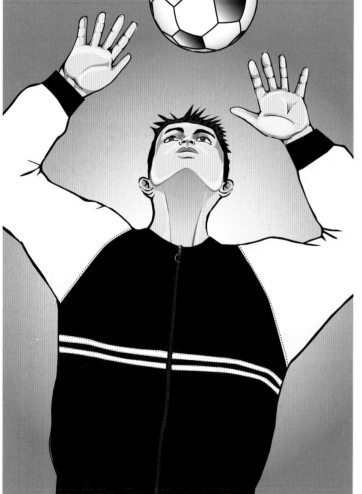

Iván Solbes Canales
Football Day! (2004)
Ink/Paper/Macromedia FreeHand/Adobe Photoshop

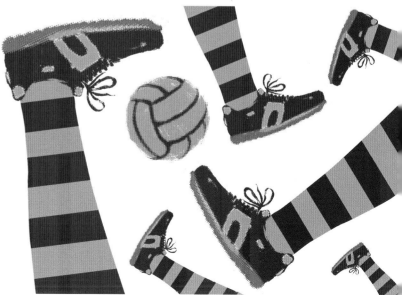

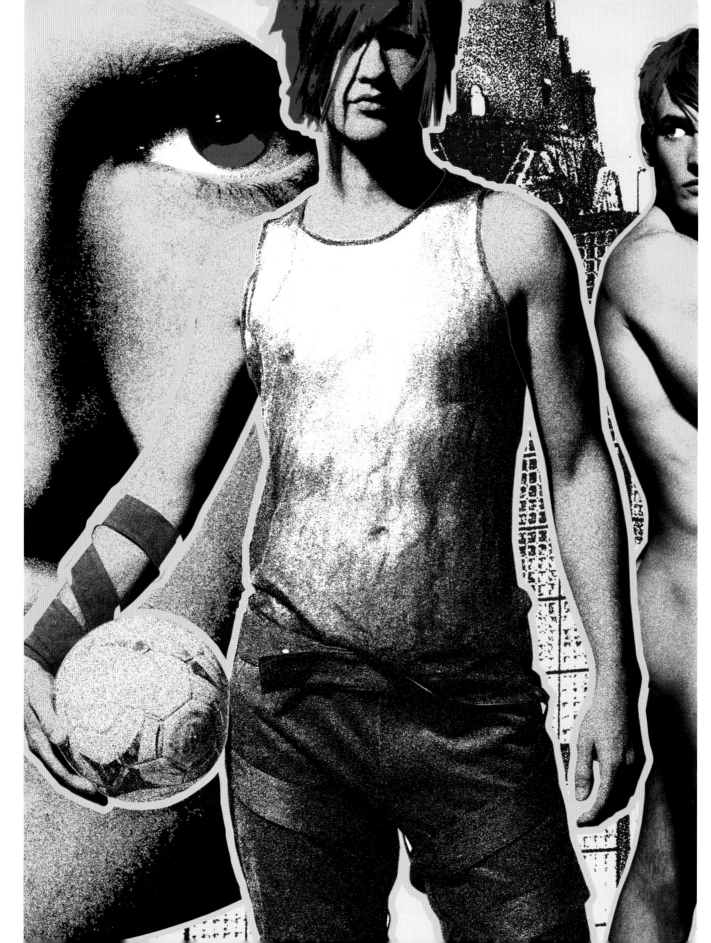

Nick Larrett
Jack, Waiting (2003)
Adobe Photoshop

Nicholas Billiris
Rebirth of Slick (2006)
Adobe Photoshop/Adobe Illustrator

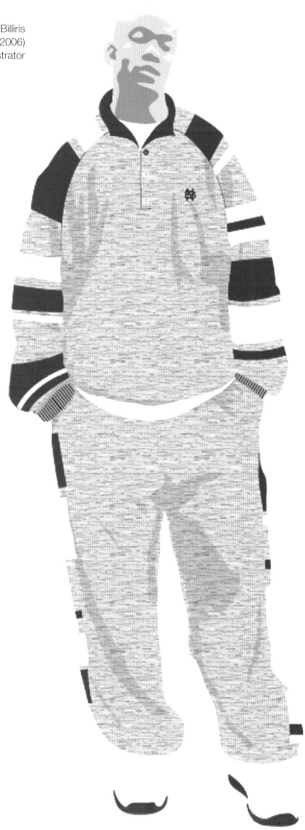

Borja Uriarte
Rugby Player (2005)
Fabric

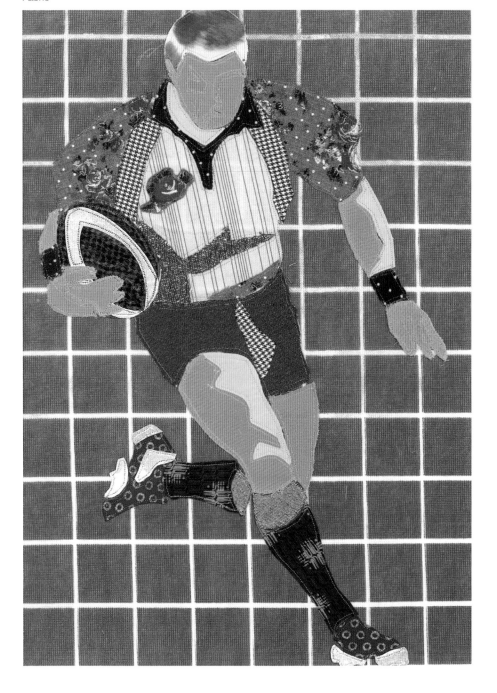

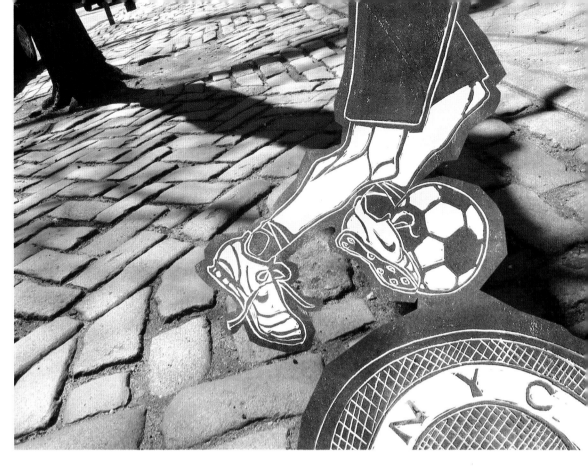

Marco Gallotta
Urban Play (2006)
Linocut/Photography/Adobe Photoshop

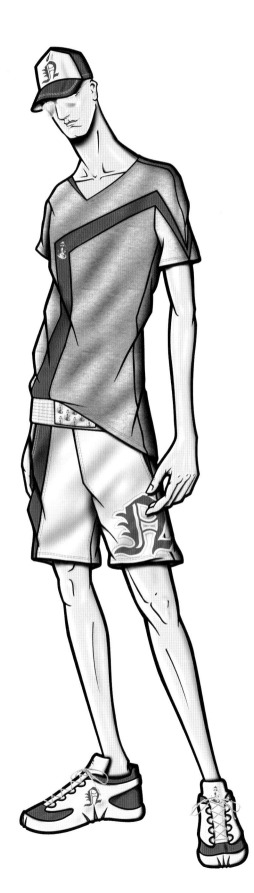

Julian Kloster
Court Practice Gear (2005)
Adobe Photoshop/Adobe Illustrator

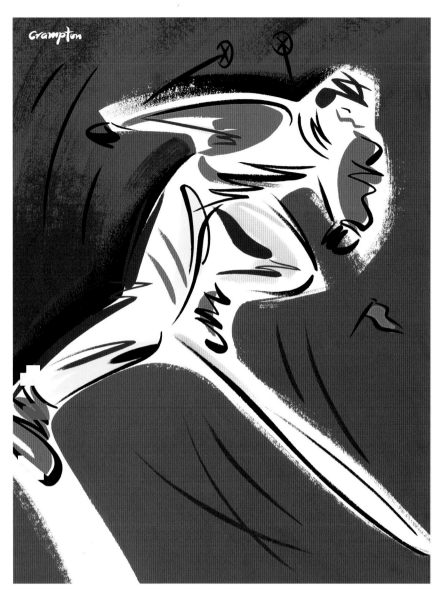

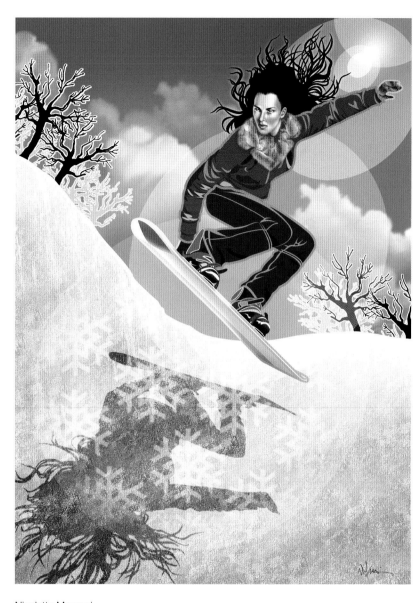

Michael Crampton
Ski Poster (2003)
Gouache

Nicoletta Mazzesi
Skier (2004)
Adobe Photoshop/Adobe Illustrator

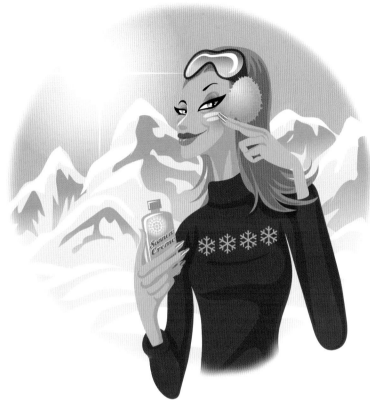

Jens Rotzsche
Glacial Suntan (2005)
Adobe Illustrator

Jens Rotzsche
The Alpinator (2005)
Adobe Illustrator

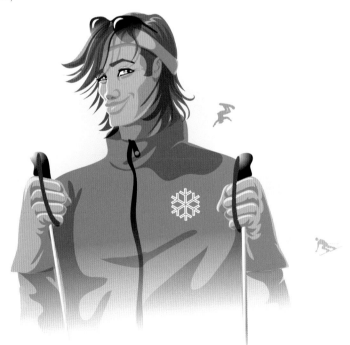

Arthur Mount
Jeremy Bloom (2005)
Adobe Illustrator

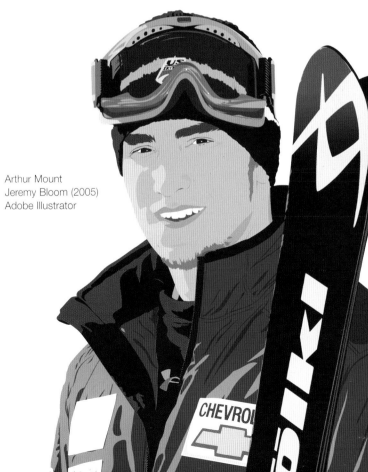

Megan Davidson
Powder Love (2006)
Adobe Illustrator/Adobe Photoshop

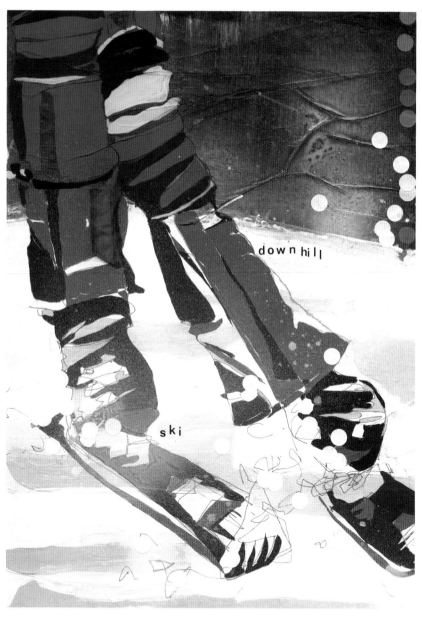

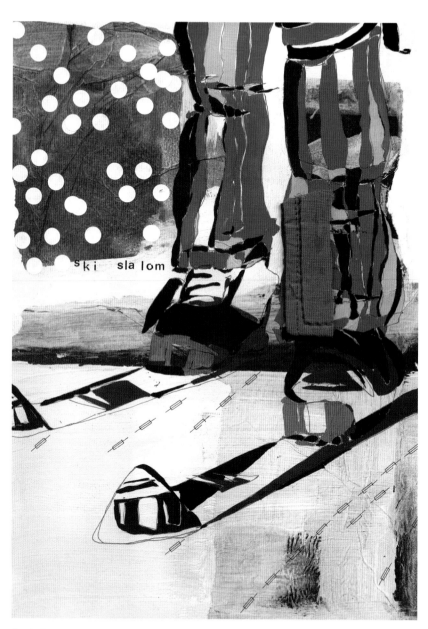

Sarah Beetson
Ellesse – Downhill Skiing (2002)
Acrylic and gouache on paper

Sarah Beetson
Ellesse – Slalom Skiing (2002)
Acrylic and gouache on paper

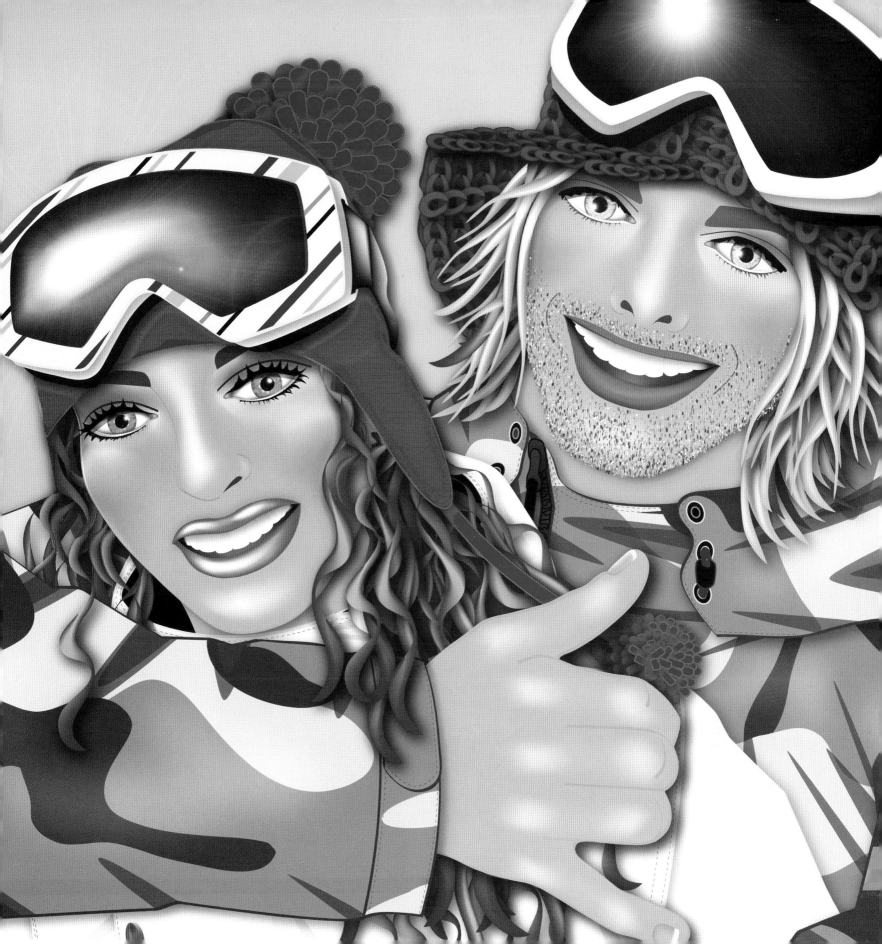

Pinglet
Aspen (2002)
Adobe Illustrator

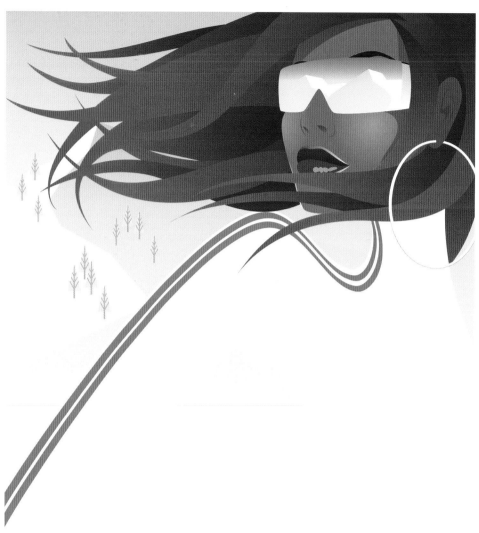

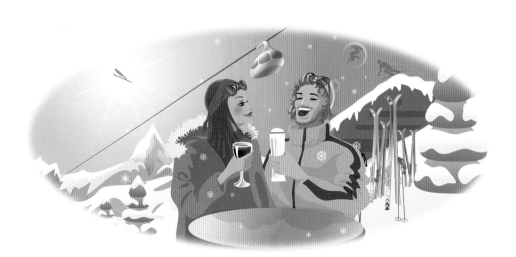

Jens Rotzsche
Aprés Ski Scheme (2005)
Adobe Illustrator

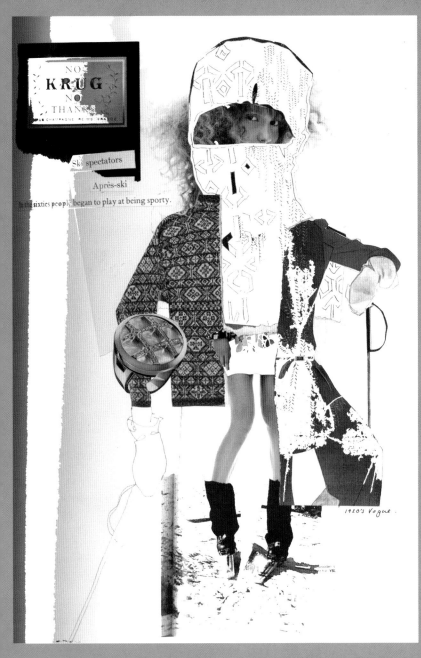

Nina Jensen-Collman
Après Ski (2006)
Collage

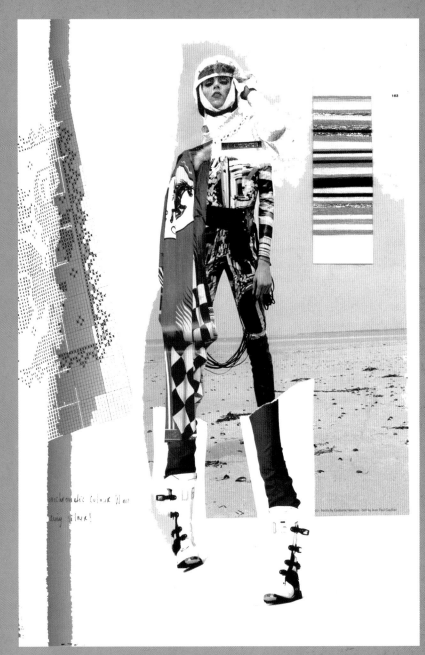

Nina Jensen-Collman
Monochrome (2006)
Collage

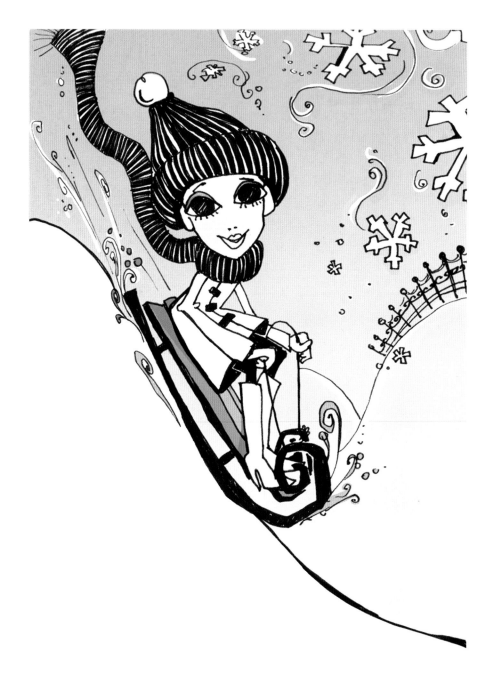

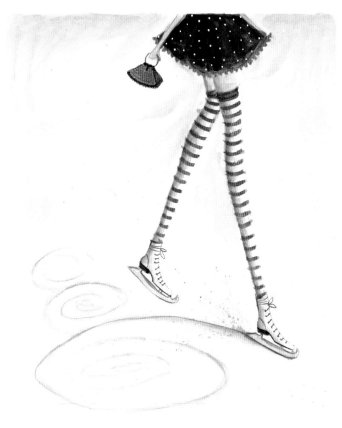

Bella Pilar
Ice Skating (2005)
Gouache

Elena Ambotaite
Catch Me if you Can (2006)
Pen/Adobe Photoshop

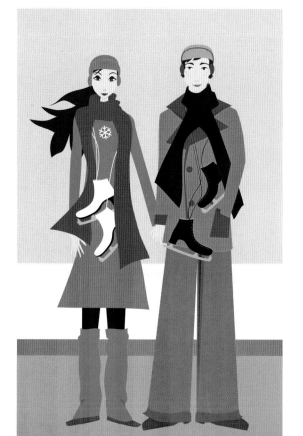

Lulu
Somerset House Ice Rink, London (2002)
Adobe Illustrator

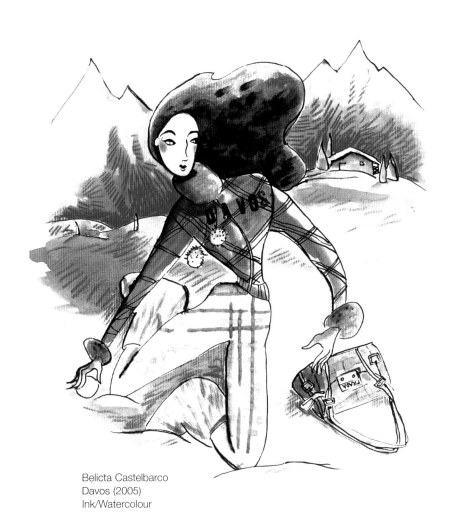

Belicta Castelbarco
Davos (2005)
Ink/Watercolour

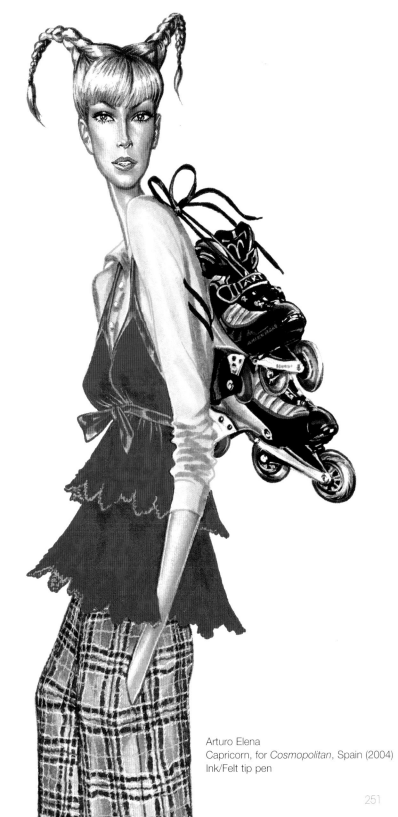

Arturo Elena
Capricorn, for *Cosmopolitan*, Spain (2004)
Ink/Felt tip pen

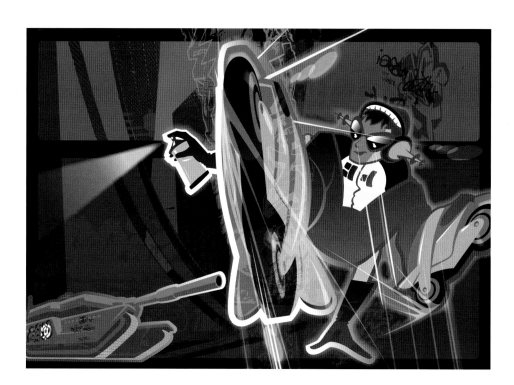

Rian Hughes
Jet Set Radio Future (2002)
Adobe Illustrator/Adobe Photoshop

Jacqui Paull and Carl Melegari
Erik (2005)
Adobe Photoshop

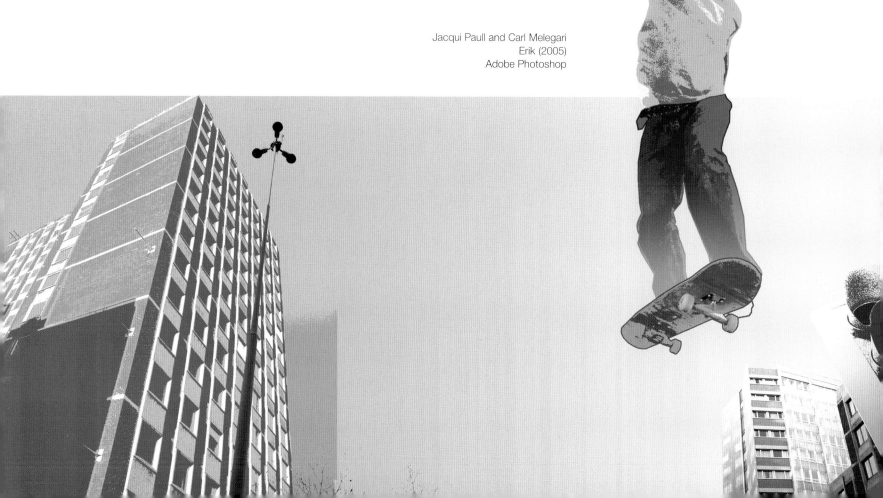

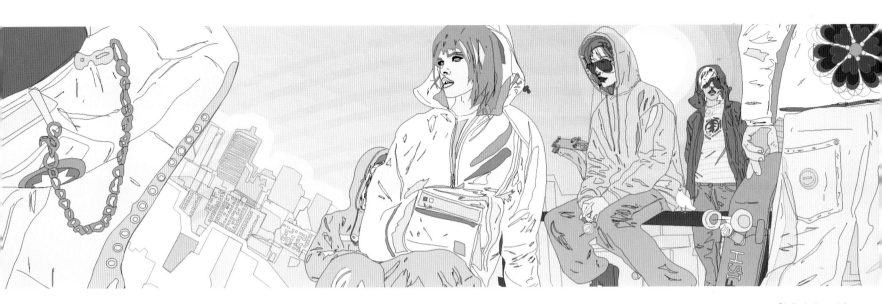

Giulio Iurissevich
Skates (2005)
Adobe Illustrator

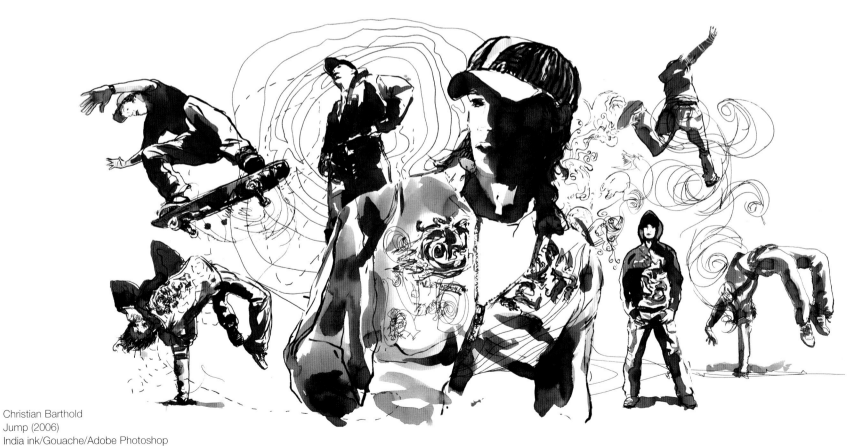

Christian Barthold
Jump (2006)
India ink/Gouache/Adobe Photoshop

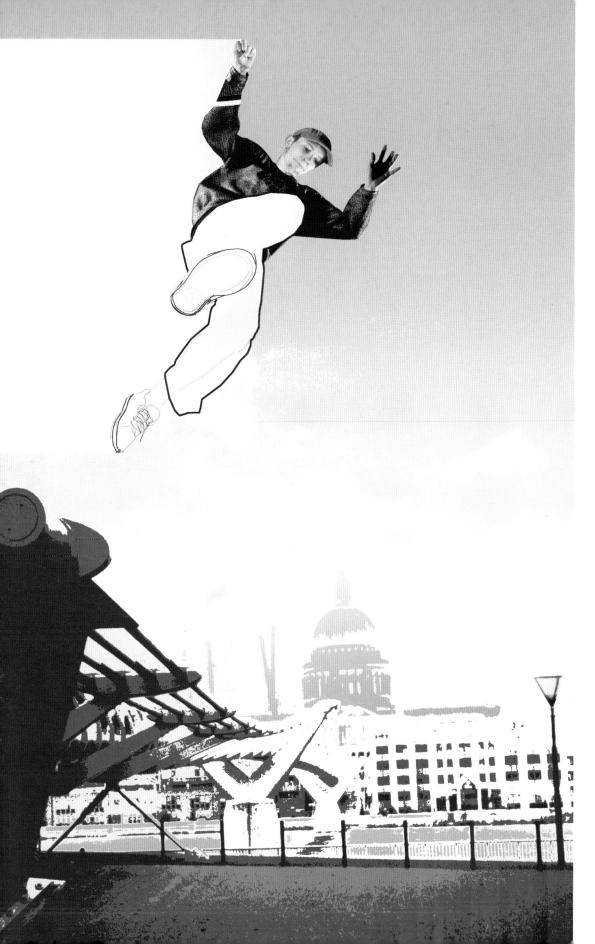

Jacqui Paull and Carl Melegari
Free Runner (2003)
Adobe Photoshop

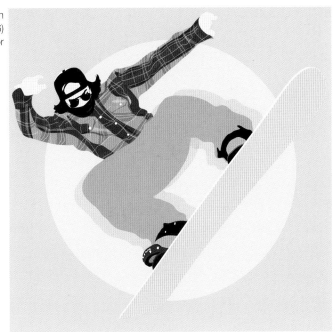

Coburn
Snowboarder (2006)
Adobe Illustrator

Christian Barthold
Skater (2006)
India ink/Gouache/Adobe Photoshop

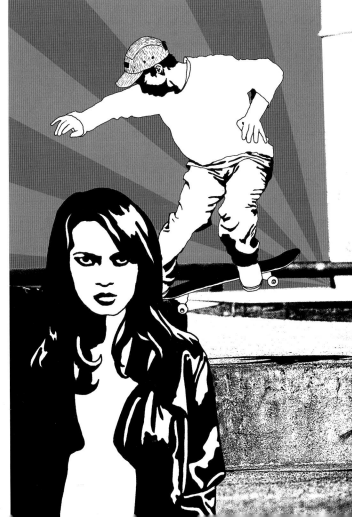

Lucy Allen
Skateboard Widow (2005)
Ink pen/Adobe Photoshop

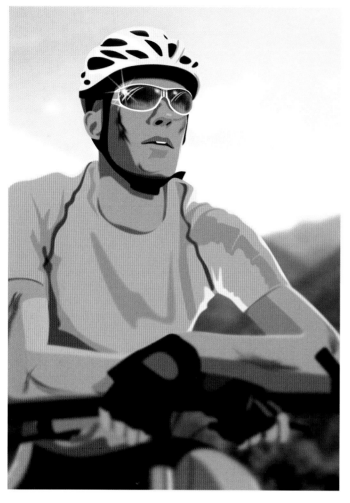

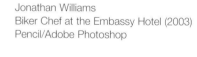

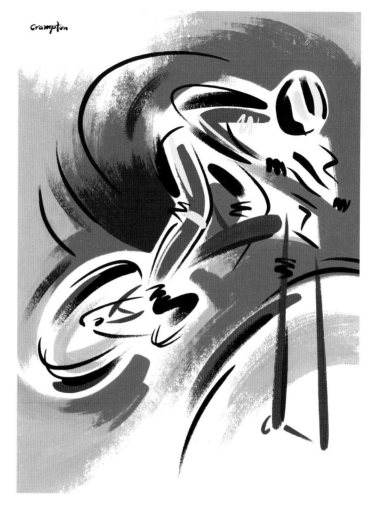

Michael Crampton
BMX Cyclist (2005)
Gouache

Herman Yap
Action Guy for Nivea Men, Singapore (2005)
Macromedia FreeHand/Adobe Photoshop

Jonathan Williams
Biker Chef at the Embassy Hotel (2003)
Pencil/Adobe Photoshop

Amy De Wolfe
Bike Ride (2005)
Adobe Illustrator

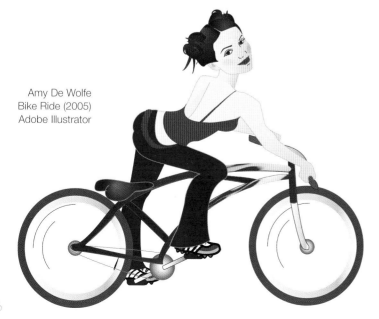

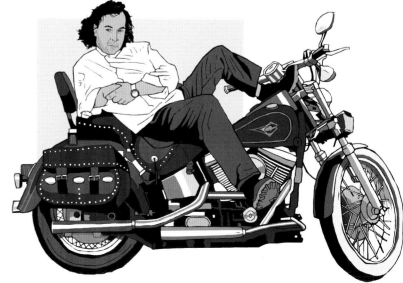

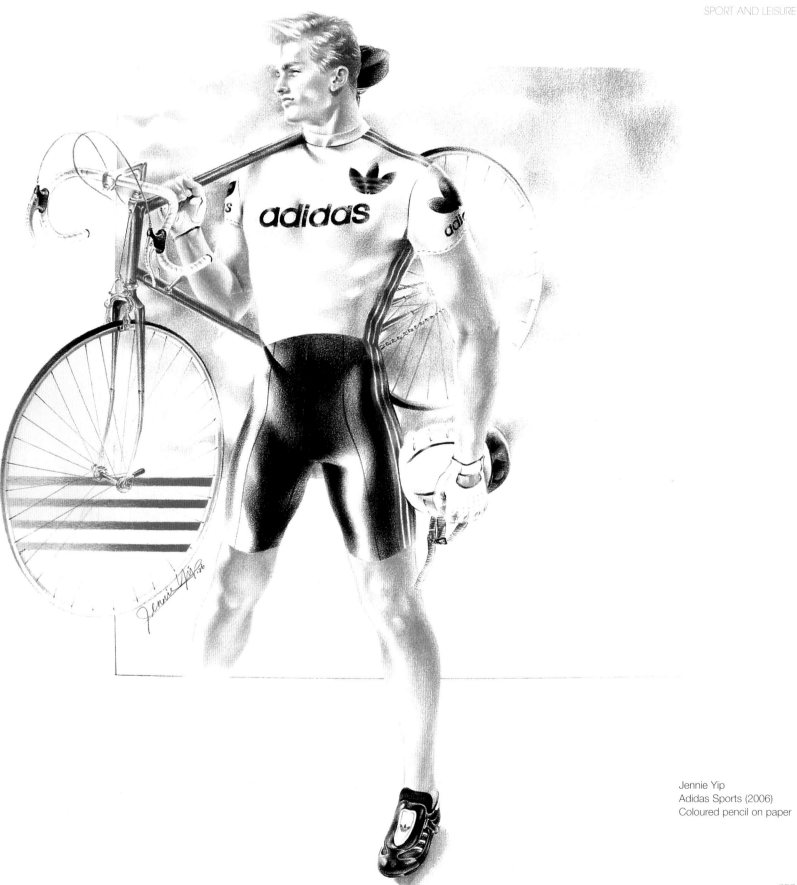

Jennie Yip
Adidas Sports (2006)
Coloured pencil on paper

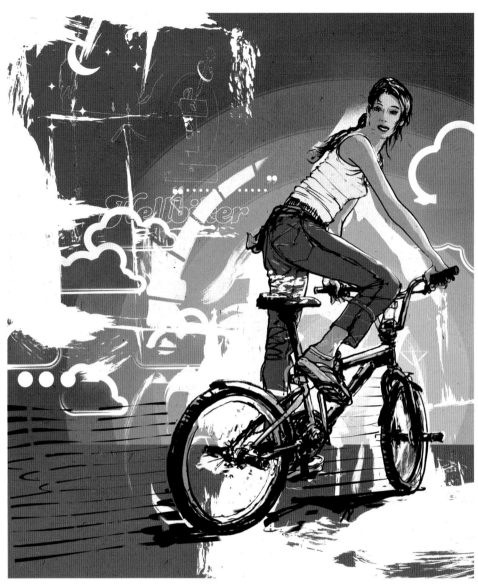

Christian Barthold
Hellbiker (2006)
India ink/Adobe Photoshop/Adobe Illustrator

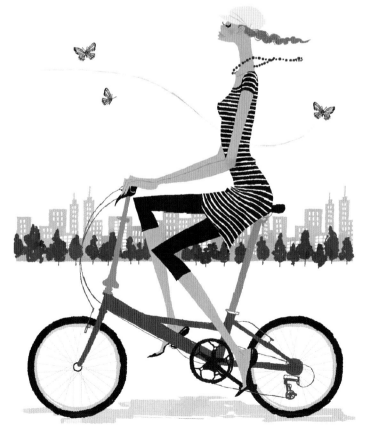

Yuko Yoshioka
Aller Contre le Vent (2006)
Adobe Photoshop

Dilek Peker
Weekend in Capri (2005)
Adobe Photoshop

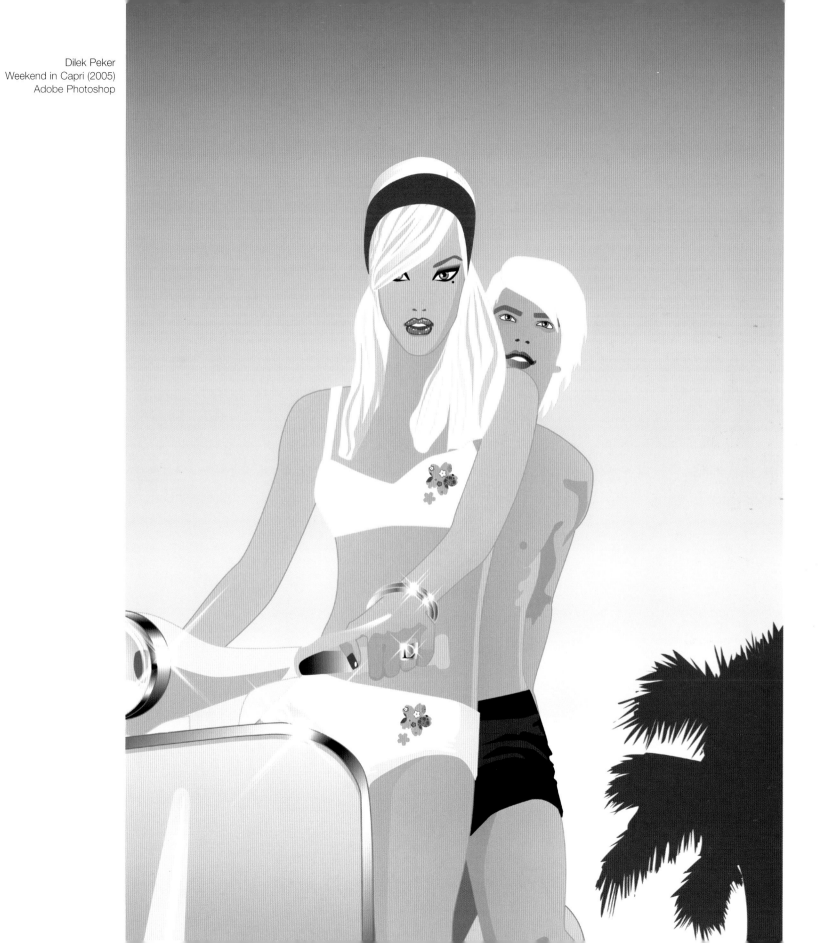

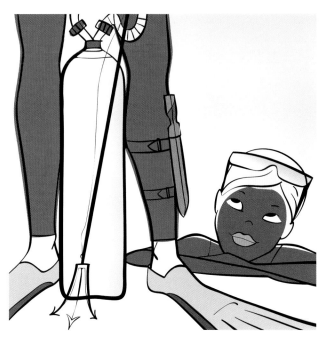

Dorothea Renault
Summer 2005 (2005)
Adobe Illustrator

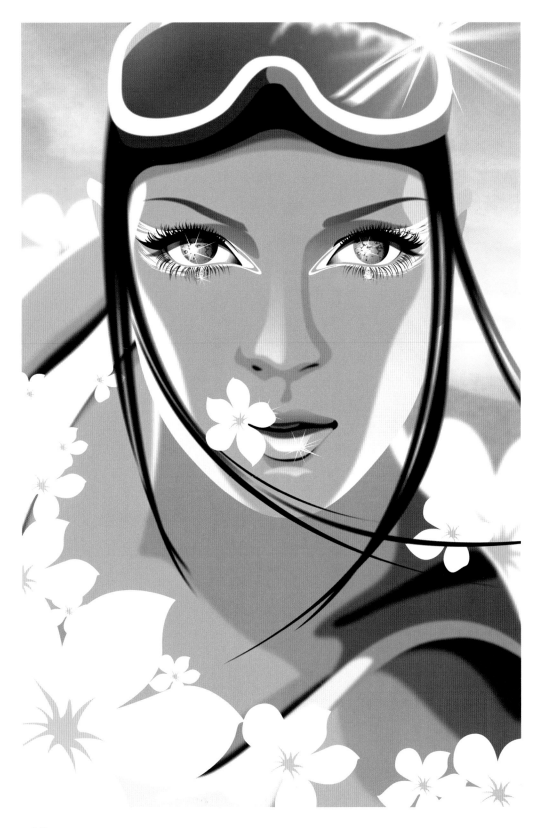

Herman Yap
Beach Girl (2005)
Macromedia FreeHand/Adobe Photoshop

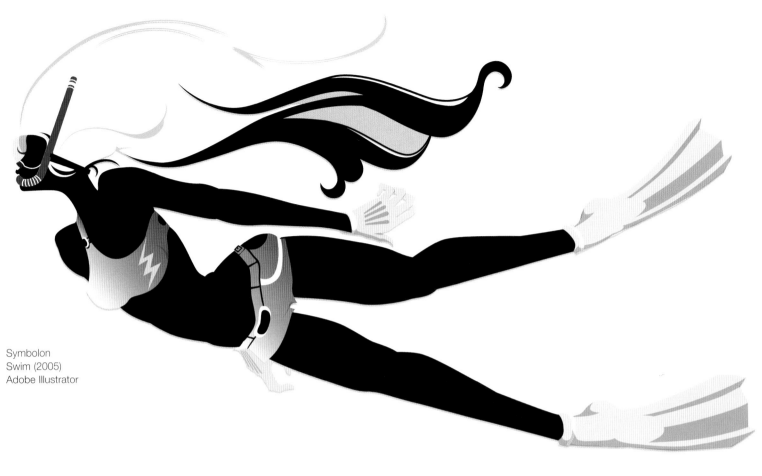

Symbolon
Swim (2005)
Adobe Illustrator

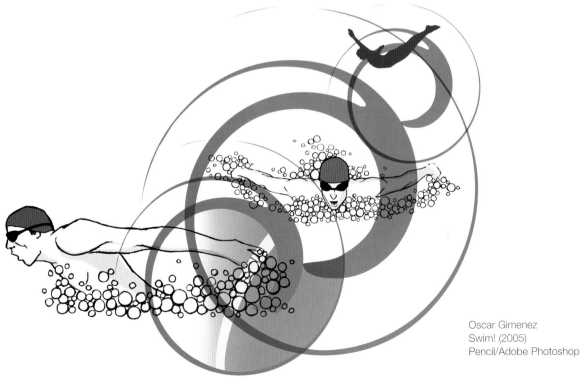

Oscar Gimenez
Swim! (2005)
Pencil/Adobe Photoshop

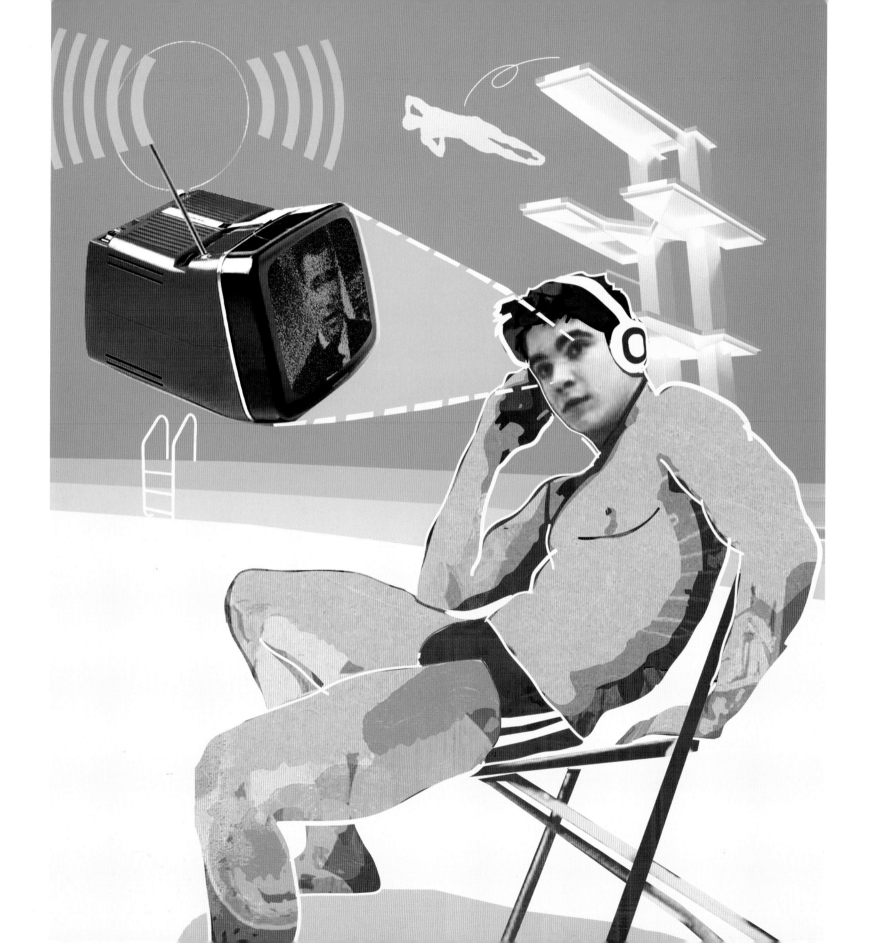

Andy Potts
Alexandre Despatie (2005)
Pencil/Paint/Adobe
Photoshop/Adobe Illustrator

Jason O'Malley
Beach Boy (2005)
Adobe Illustrator

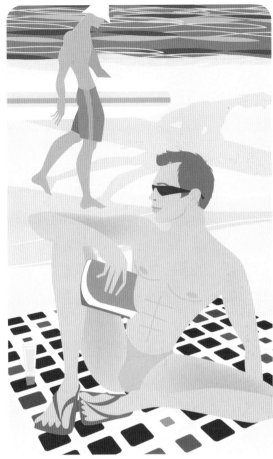

Leonid Gurevich
Surfer (2006)
Pen/Ink/Marker pen

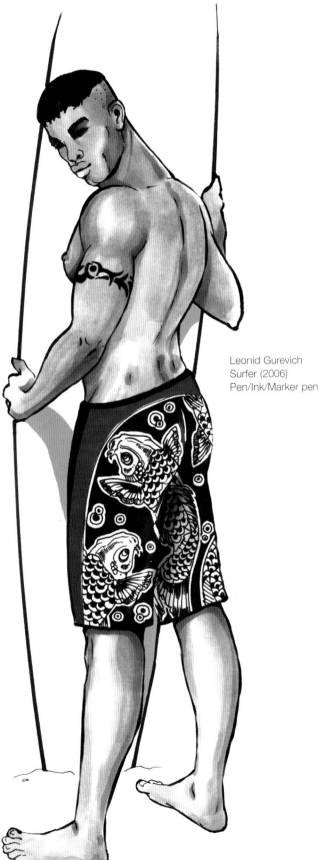

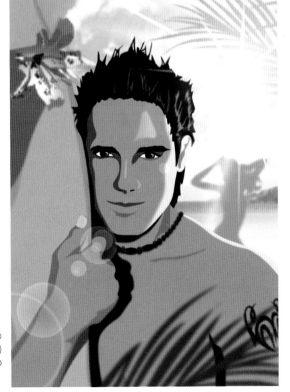

Herman Yap
Sunseeker for Nivea Men, Singapore (2005)
Macromedia FreeHand/Adobe Photoshop

Monsieur Z
Swiss Girls (2005)
Adobe Illustrator

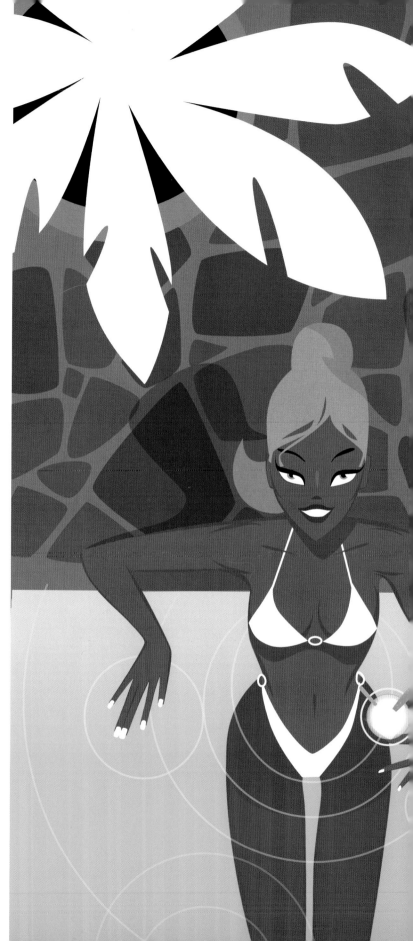

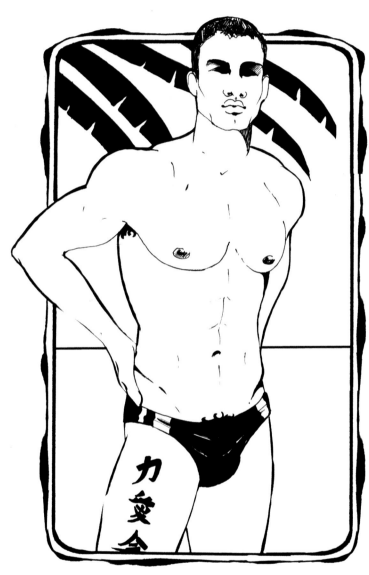

Leonid Gurevich
Lucas (2006)
Pen/Ink/Marker pen

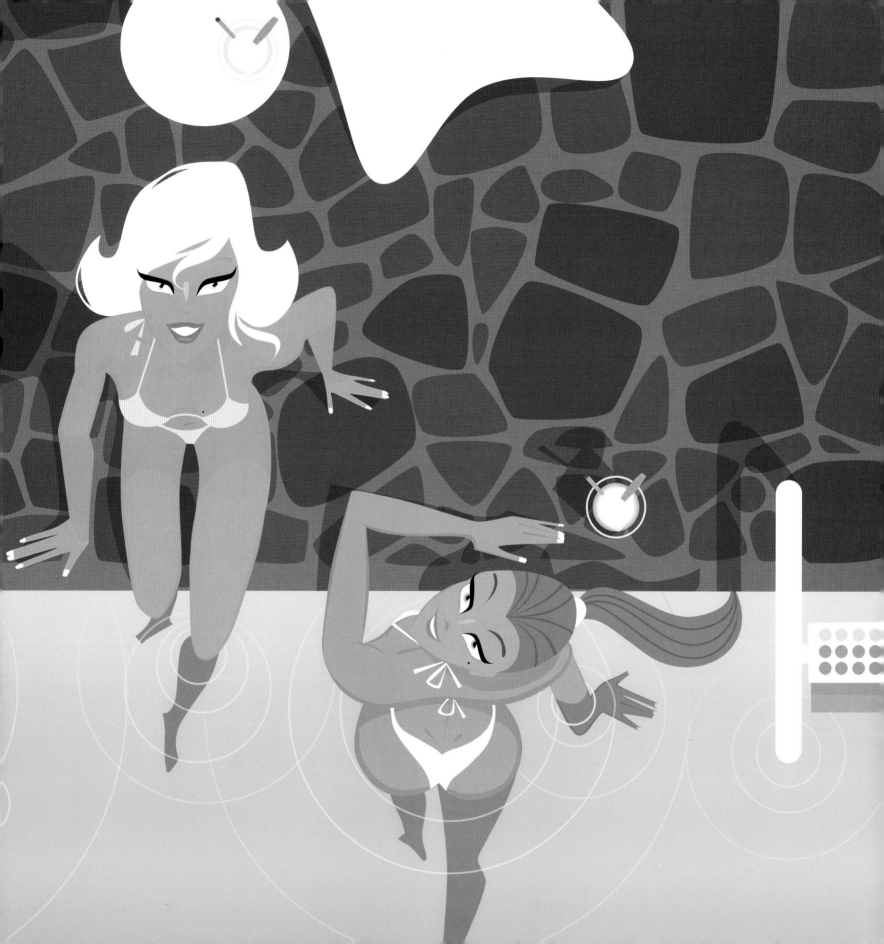

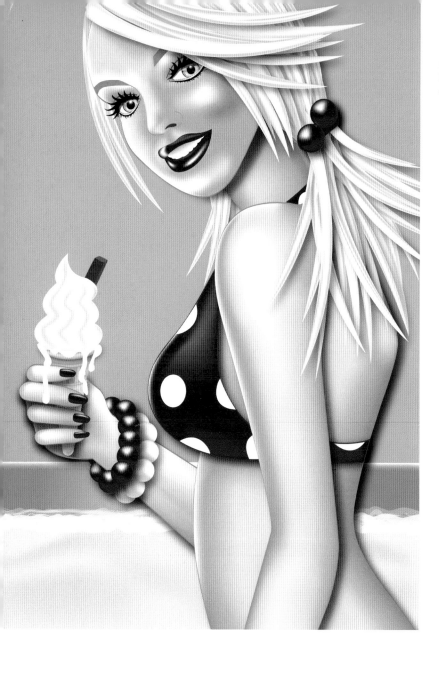

Megan Davidson
Polka-dot Bikini (2005)
Adobe Illustrator/Adobe Photoshop

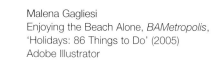

Malena Gagliesi
Enjoying the Beach Alone, *BAMetropolis*,
'Holidays: 86 Things to Do' (2005)
Adobe Illustrator

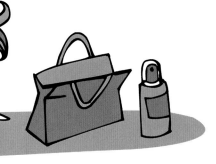

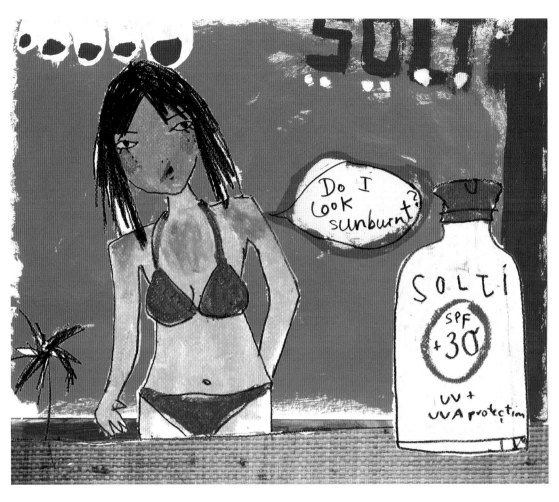

Christiane Engel
Sunburn (2005)
Oil pastel/Pencil/Collage

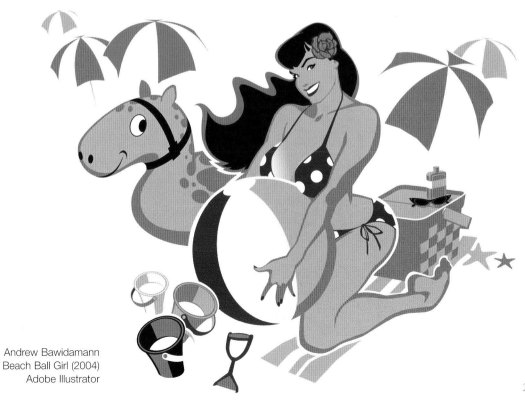

Andrew Bawidamann
Beach Ball Girl (2004)
Adobe Illustrator

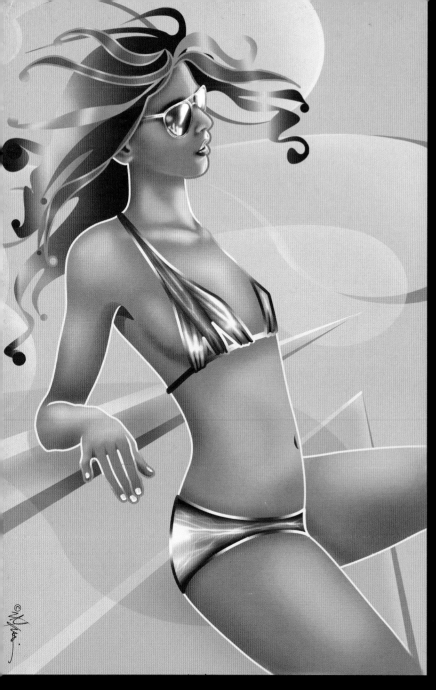

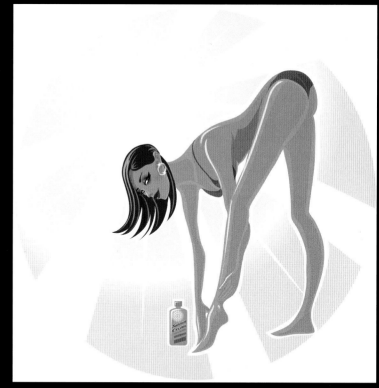

Jens Rotzsche
Siren of Suntan (2006)
Adobe Illustrator

Nicoletta Mazzesi
Summertime (2004)
Adobe Photoshop/Adobe Illustrator

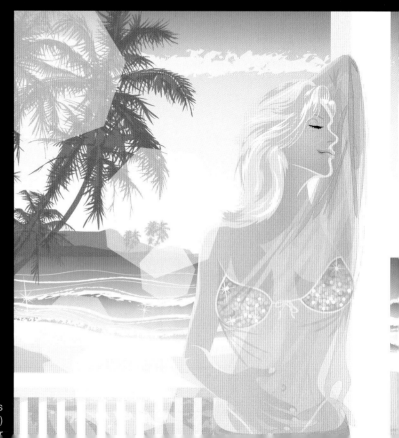

Stuart Holmes
Beach Veranda (2002)
Adobe Illustrator

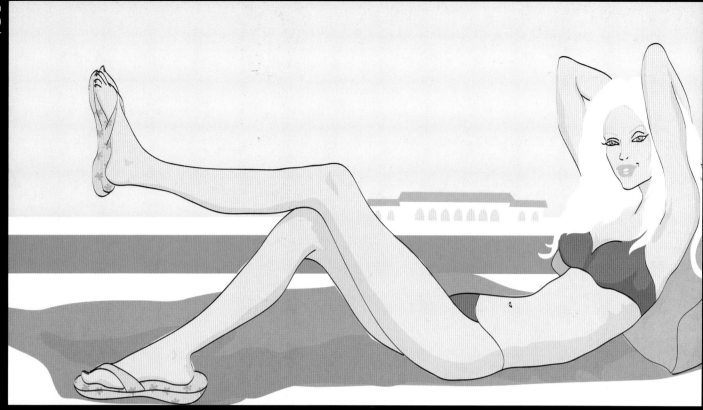

Fiona Maclean
Bondi Bikini Babe (2005)
Adobe Illustrator

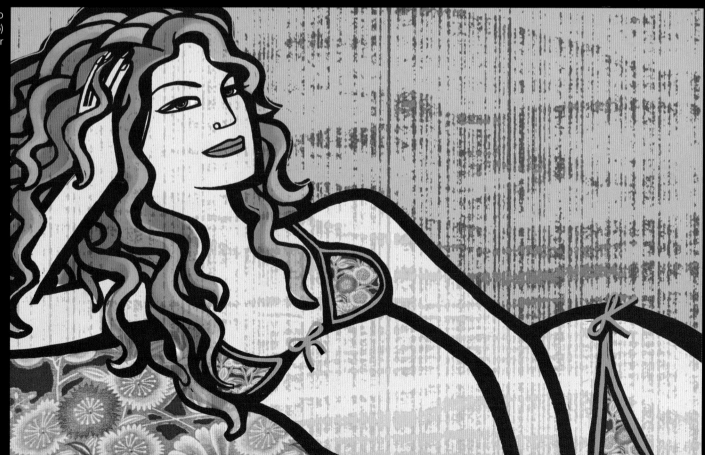

Marcella Peluffo
Flower Bikini (2006)
Corel Painter

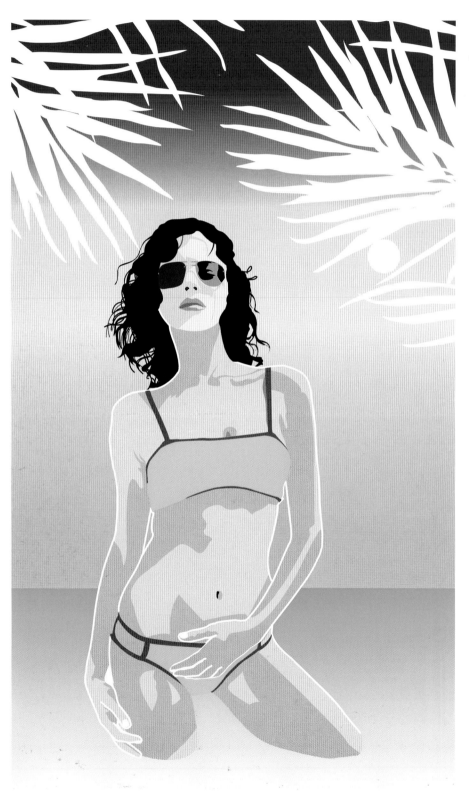

Kristie Jarita Lathbury
Hot Beach (2006)
Adobe Illustrator

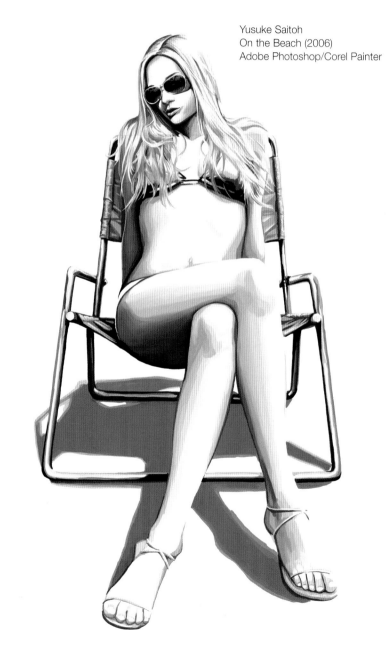

Yusuke Saitoh
On the Beach (2006)
Adobe Photoshop/Corel Painter

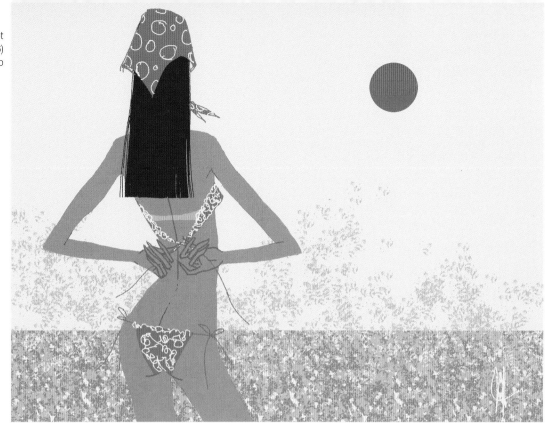

Christophe Lardot
Dans Les Champs (2006)
Adobe Photoshop

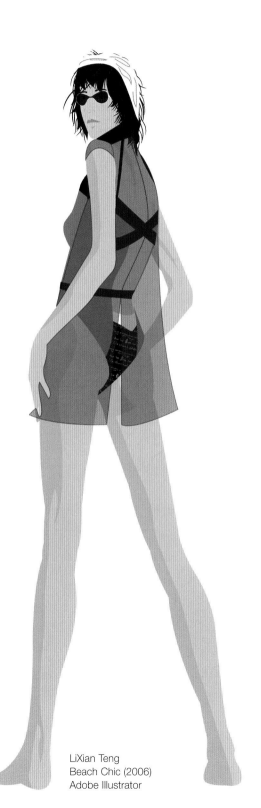

LiXian Teng
Beach Chic (2006)
Adobe Illustrator

Ekaterina Matveeva
Summer Cocktail (2006)
Wacom Cintiq/Adobe Photoshop/Adobe Illustrator

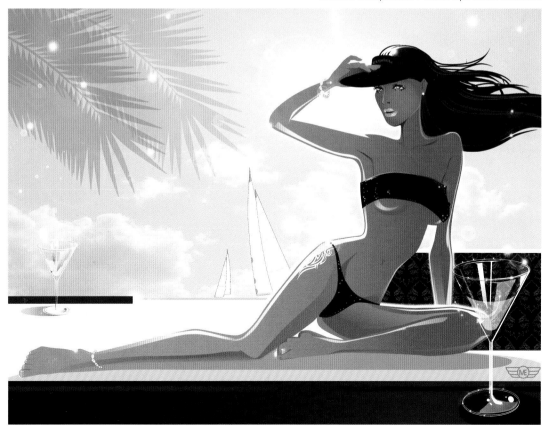

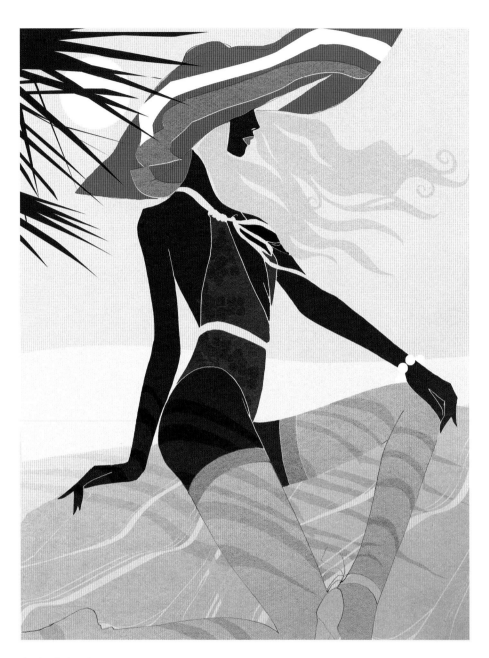

Cecilia Carlstedt
Untitled, *Mall* Magazine (2006)
Pencil/Adobe Photoshop

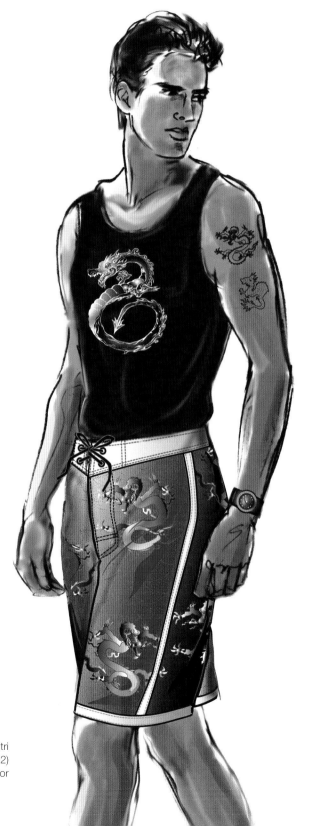

Marsha Silvestri
Surf Tank and Trunk with Dragons (2002)
Charcoal/Adobe Photoshop/Adobe Illustrator

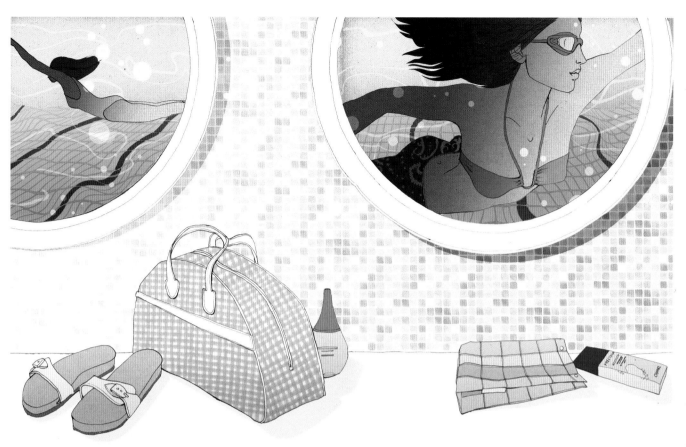

Tina Berning
Über wasser (2002)
Ball pen/Vector Graphic/
OCD paper/Adobe Photoshop

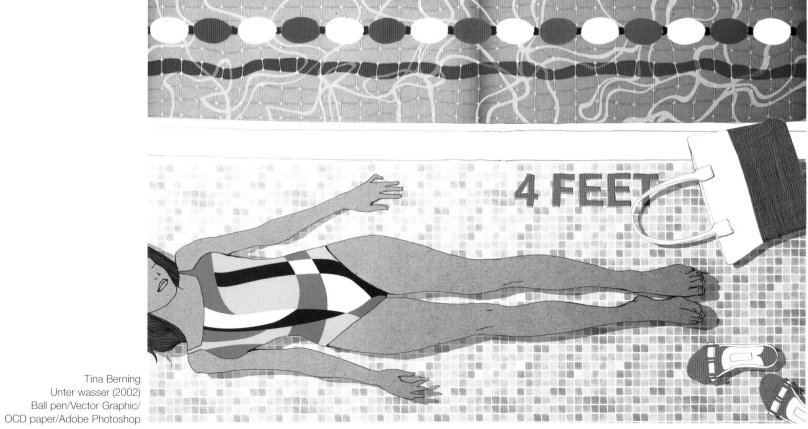

Tina Berning
Unter wasser (2002)
Ball pen/Vector Graphic/
OCD paper/Adobe Photoshop

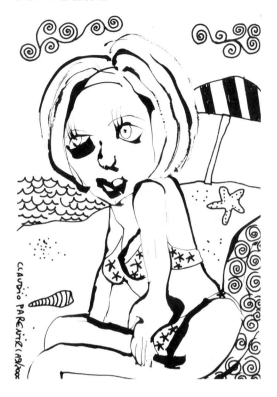

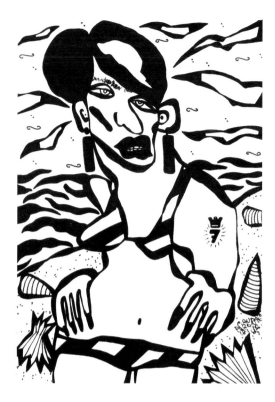

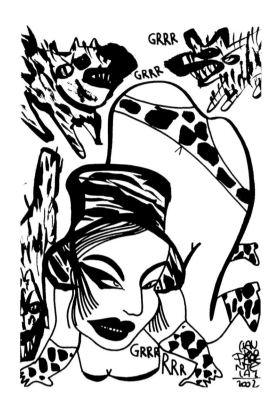

Claudio Parentela
Untitled (2005)
Ink and pen on paper

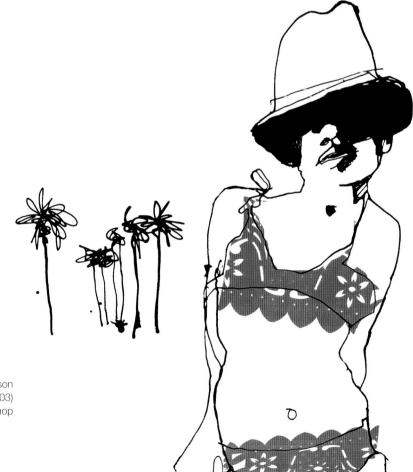

Stina Persson
Tourist (2003)
Ink/Mexican cut papers/Adobe photoshop

Zed
C&A Swimwear (2002)
Adobe Illustrator

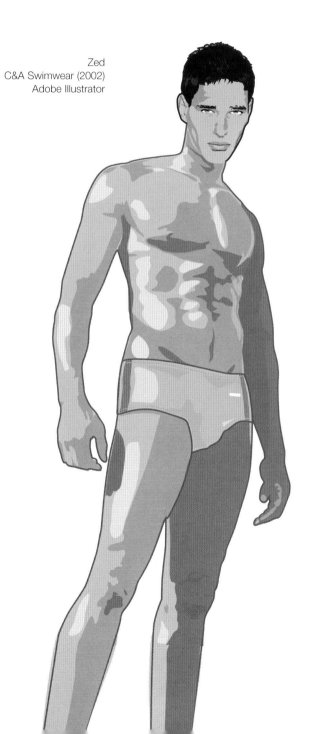

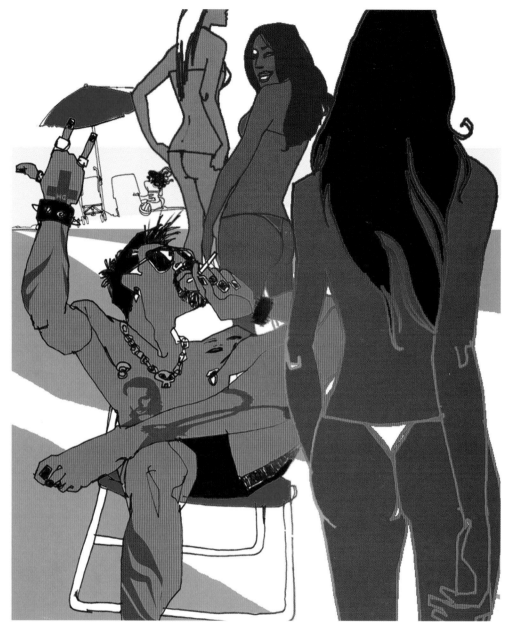

John Jay Cabuay
Thongs in the Sun (2006)
Pen/Ink/Adobe Photoshop

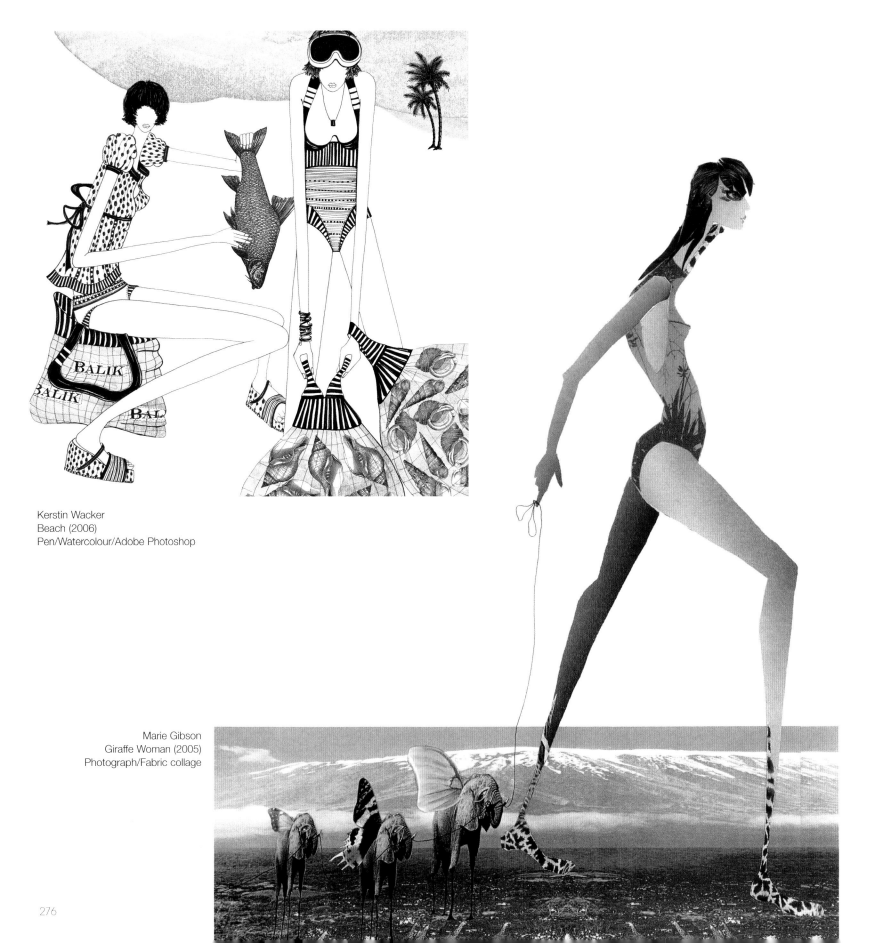

Kerstin Wacker
Beach (2006)
Pen/Watercolour/Adobe Photoshop

Marie Gibson
Giraffe Woman (2005)
Photograph/Fabric collage

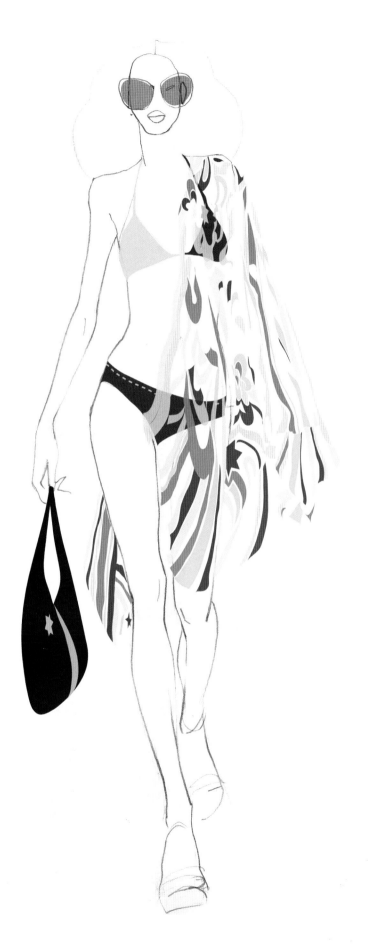

Cecilia Carlstedt
Damernas Värld (2004)
Pencil/Adobe Illustrator

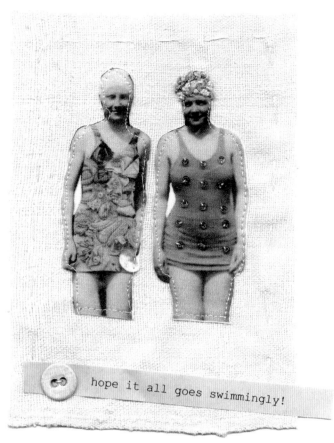

hope it all goes swimmingly!

Claire Ann Baker
2 Swimmers (2006)
Mixed media/Vintage fabrics/Paper/Photo transfer/Hand stitch

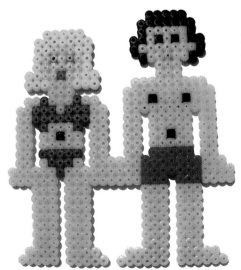

Katherine Prange
Untitled (2005)
Plastic beads

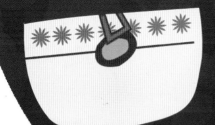

Accessories

footwear   bags   headwear   eyewear

jewellery   techno   umbrellas

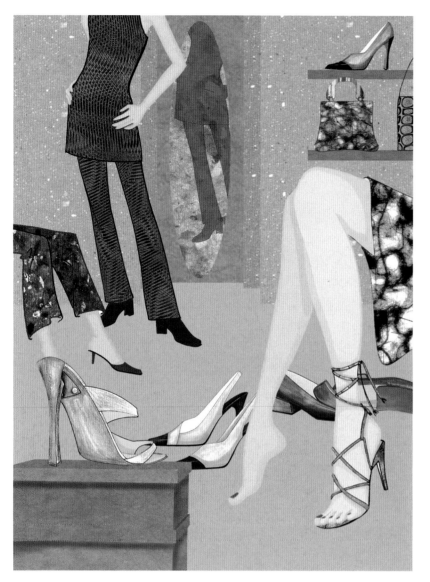

Maria Cardelli
Shoe Shopping (2000)
Adobe Photoshop

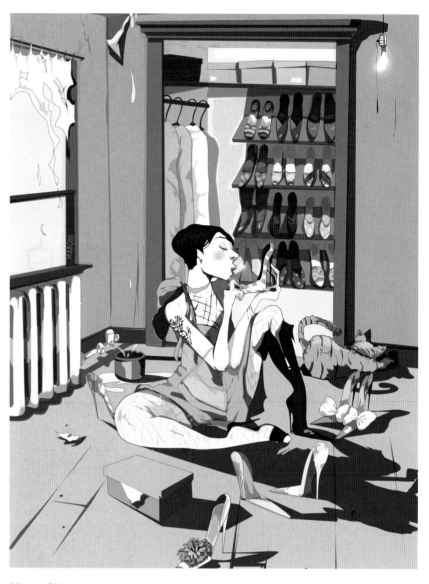

Marcos Chin
The Cost of a Fab Life (2004)
Adobe Illustrator

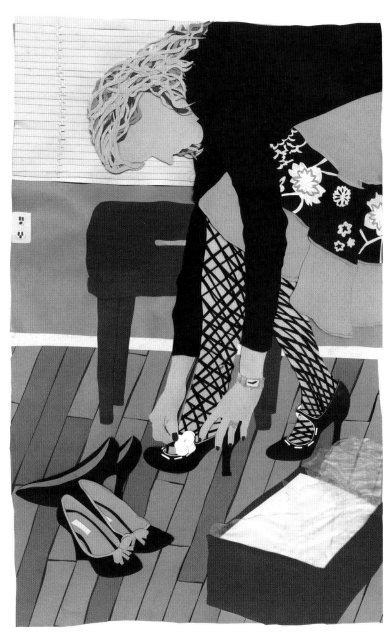

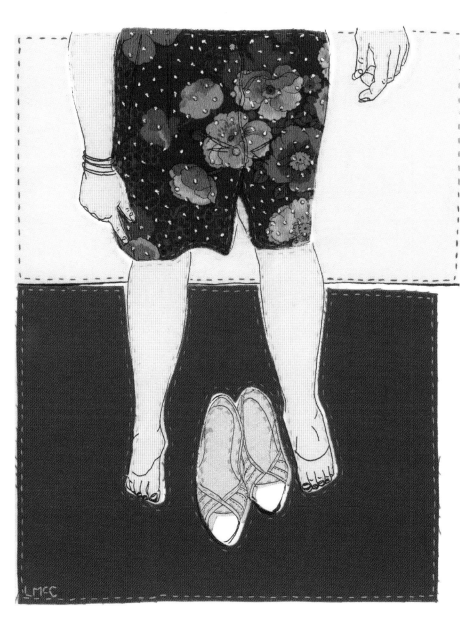

Sherill Gross
Beauty Ritual #10 (2006)
Paper

Laura McCafferty
Mel on the Dancefloor at 2am (2005)
Textile/Print/Hand-stitching

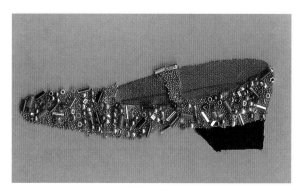

Lys Wilcox
Mary Jane (2003)
Beads/Fabric/Collage

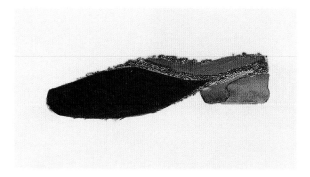

Lys Wilcox
Slipper (2003)
Collage/Taffeta fabric paper

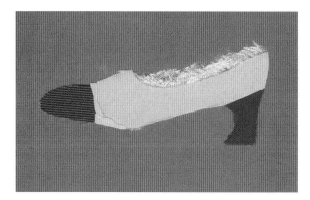

Lys Wilcox
Spectator Pump (2003)
Collage/Fabric paper

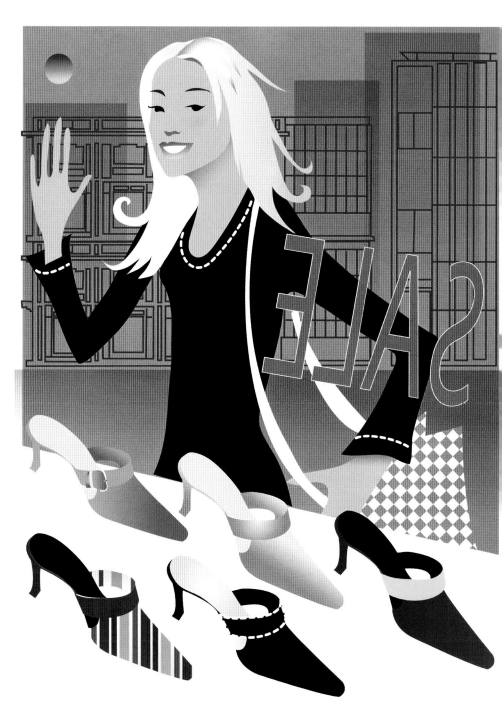

Martina Farrow
Shoe Shop (2003)
Adobe Illustrator

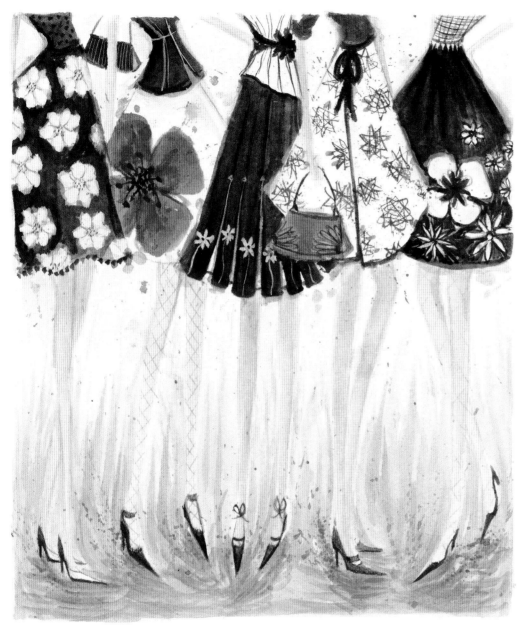

Bella Pilar
Floral Skirt (2004)
Gouache

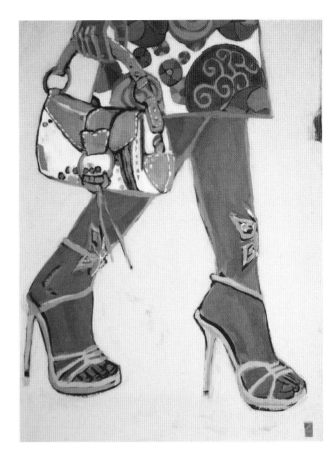

Zachariah O'Hora
Float Like a Butterfly (2005)
Acrylic on board

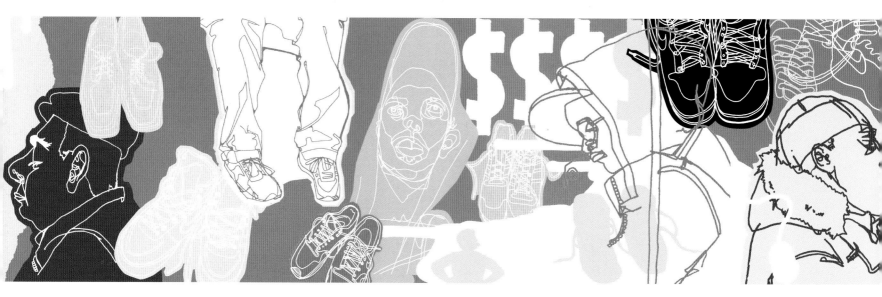

Matthew Hollister
Spoils (2004)
Ink on paper

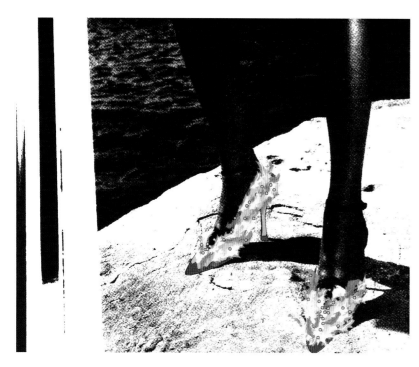

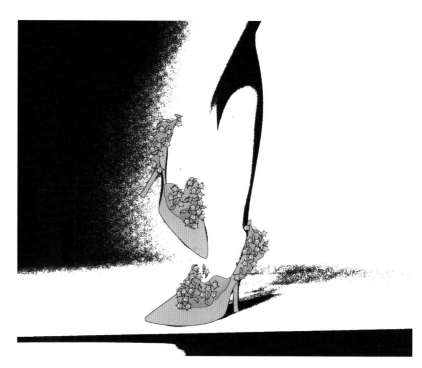

Janet Pui Kee Lui
My Fairytale Collection: Phoenix (2005)
Photocopy/Adobe Photoshop/Adobe Illustrator

Janet Pui Kee Lui
My Fairytale Collection: Forest (2005)
Photocopy/Adobe Photoshop/Adobe Illustrator

Laura McCafferty
Cowgirl Boots (2006)
Textile/Print/
Hand-stitching

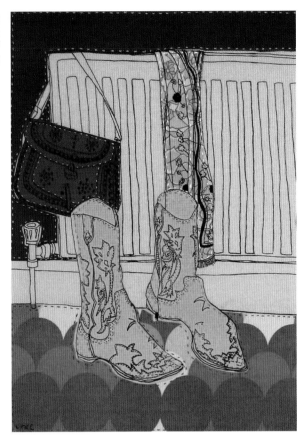

Erica Sharp
Green Boots (2005)
Adobe Photoshop

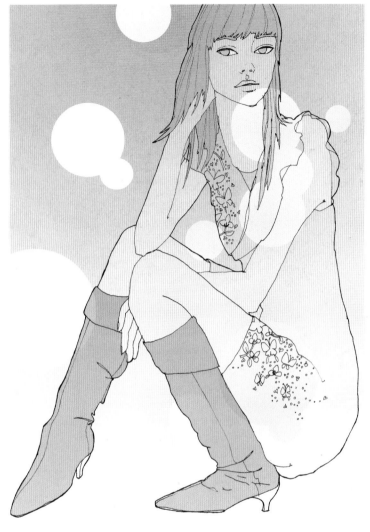

Kari Modén
Boots (2005)
Adobe Illustrator

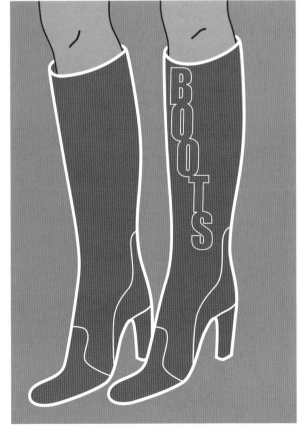

Christiane Engel
Sushi Boots (2005)
Pen/Ink/Acrylic

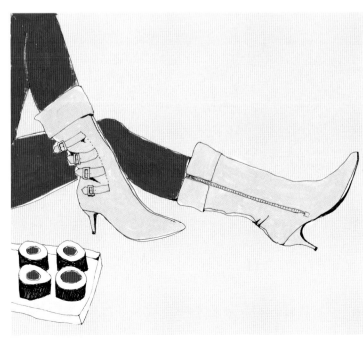

285

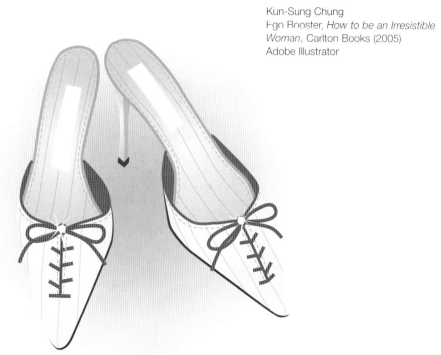

Kun-Sung Chung
Ego Booster, *How to be an Irresistible Woman*, Carlton Books (2005)
Adobe Illustrator

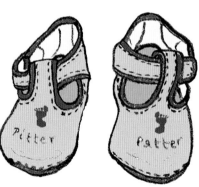

Louise Alexander
Pitter Patter (2005)
Pencil/Adobe Photoshop

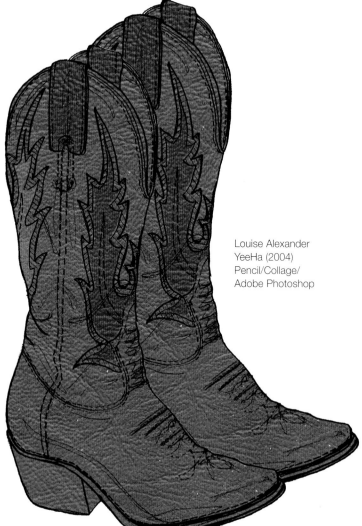

Louise Alexander
YeeHa (2004)
Pencil/Collage/
Adobe Photoshop

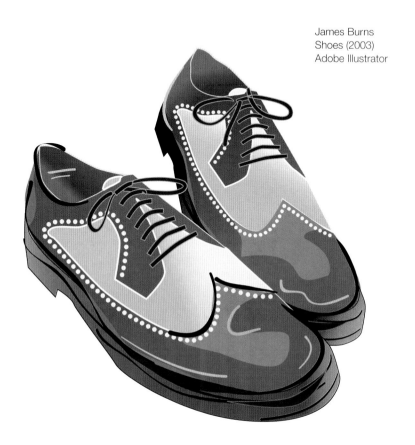

James Burns
Shoes (2003)
Adobe Illustrator

Kat Devine
Put Your Shoes On (2005)
Acrylic/Ink/Embroidery on cotton

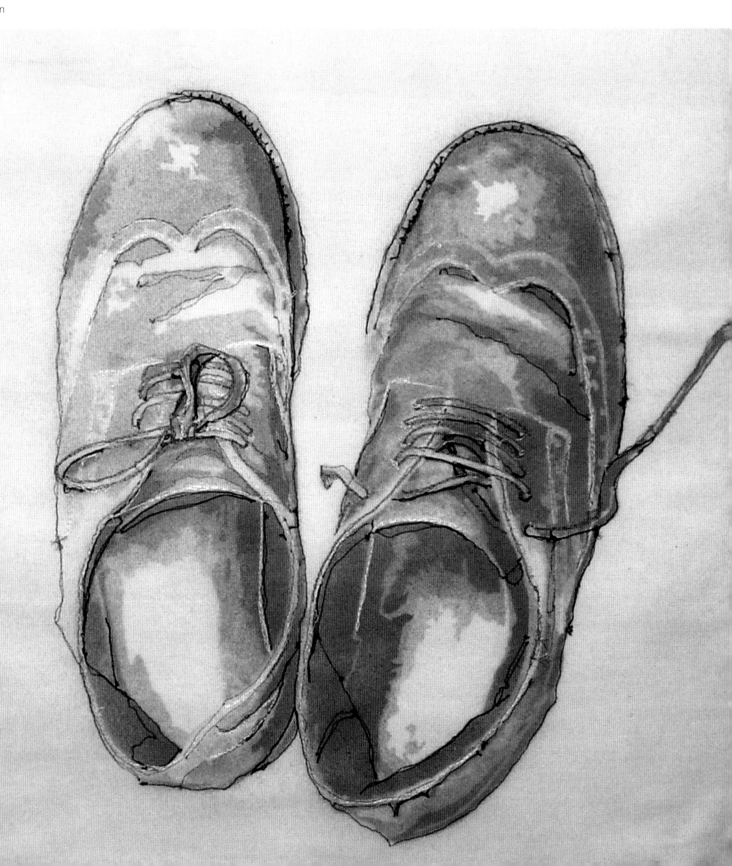

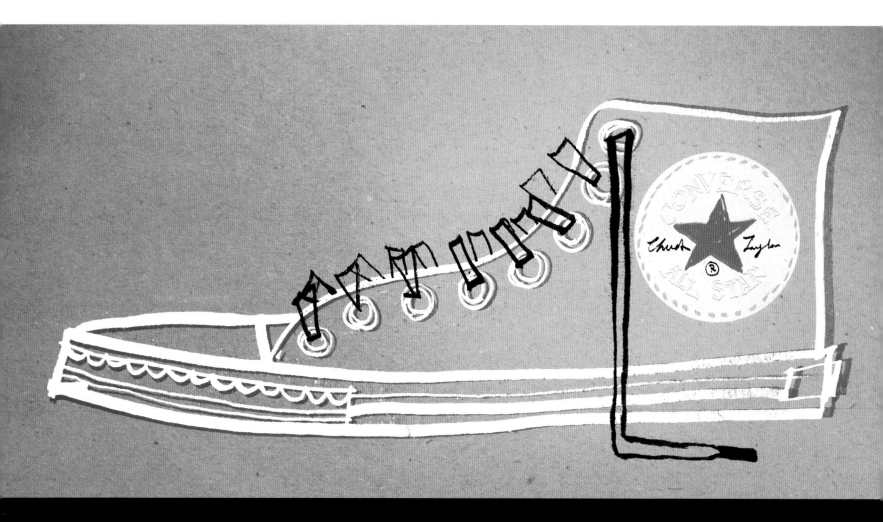

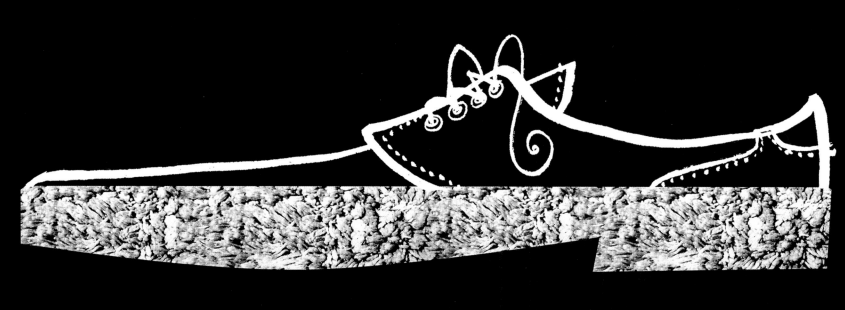

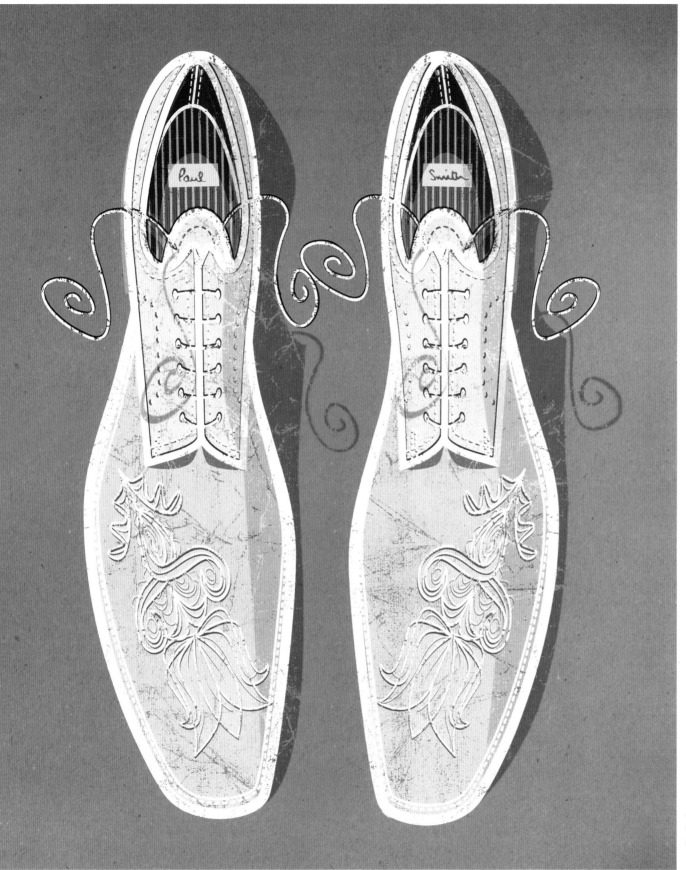

Jonas Bergstrand
Shoes (2005)
Adobe Illustrator/Adobe Photoshop

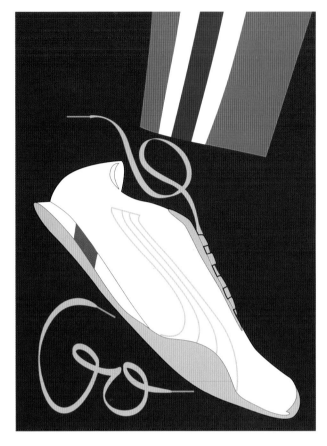

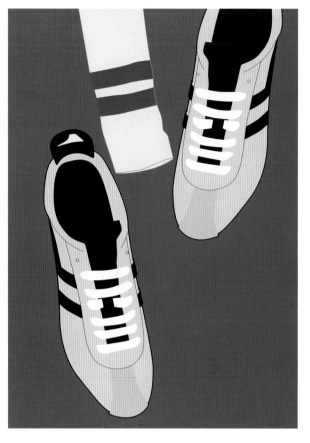

Kari Modén
Sneakers, *Jack* magazine (2004)
Adobe Illustrator

Kari Modén
Sneakers, *Jack* magazine (2004)
Adobe Illustrator

Jonathan Williams
Trainers (2002)
Pencil/Adobe Photoshop

Scott Wills
Denim Boot (2003)
Adobe Photoshop

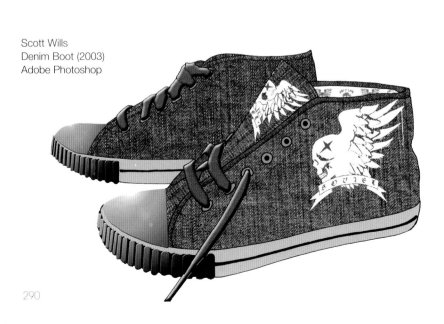

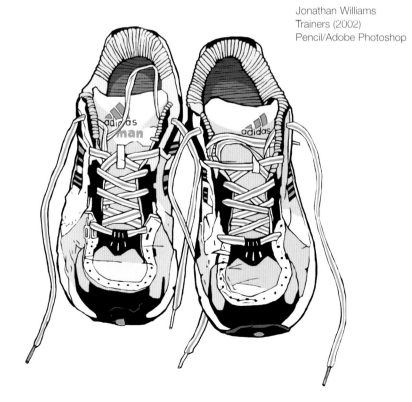

Fhiona Galloway
Bees (2006)
Macromedia FreeHand

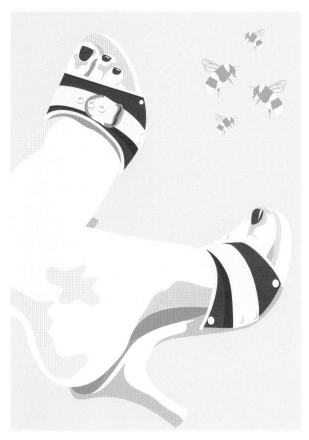

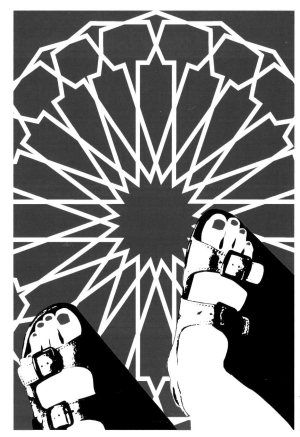

Iván Solbes Canales
Turismo de Suelos (2004)
Ink/Paper/Macromedia
FreeHand/Adobe Photoshop

Iván Solbes Canales
Sol Solero (2004)
Ink/Paper/Macromedia
FreeHand/Adobe Photoshop

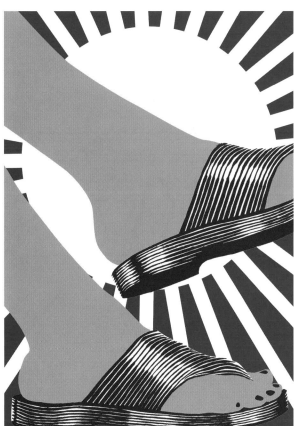

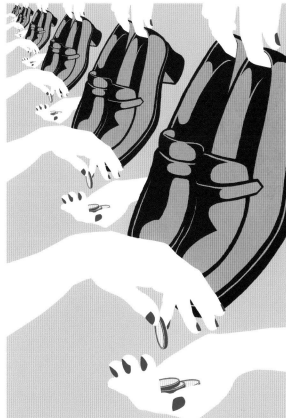

Iván Solbes Canales
Sales (2004)
Ink/Paper/Macromedia
FreeHand/Adobe
Photoshop

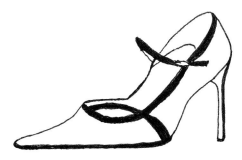

Malena Gagliesi
Buenos Aires Street Fashion: Golden
Leaves Bag, *BAMetropolis* (2006)
Adobe Illustrator

Lucy Truman
Shopaholic (2004)
Corel Painter/Corel Draw

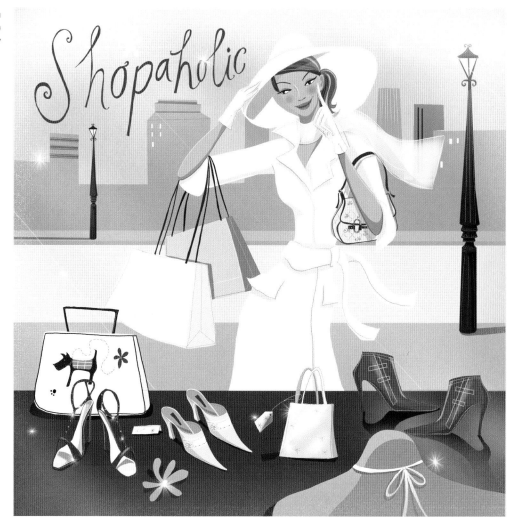

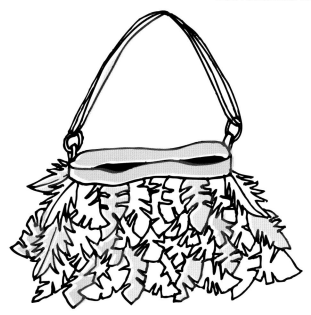

Tania Howells
Heel Boy (2004)
Ink

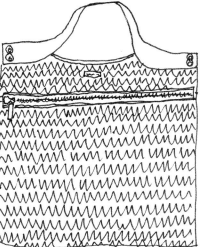

Tania Howells
Tweed (2004)
Ink

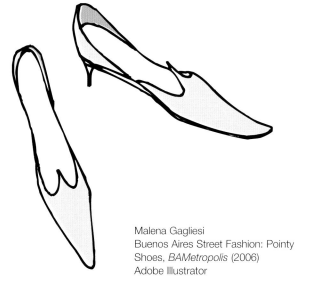

Malena Gagliesi
Buenos Aires Street Fashion: Pointy
Shoes, *BAMetropolis* (2006)
Adobe Illustrator

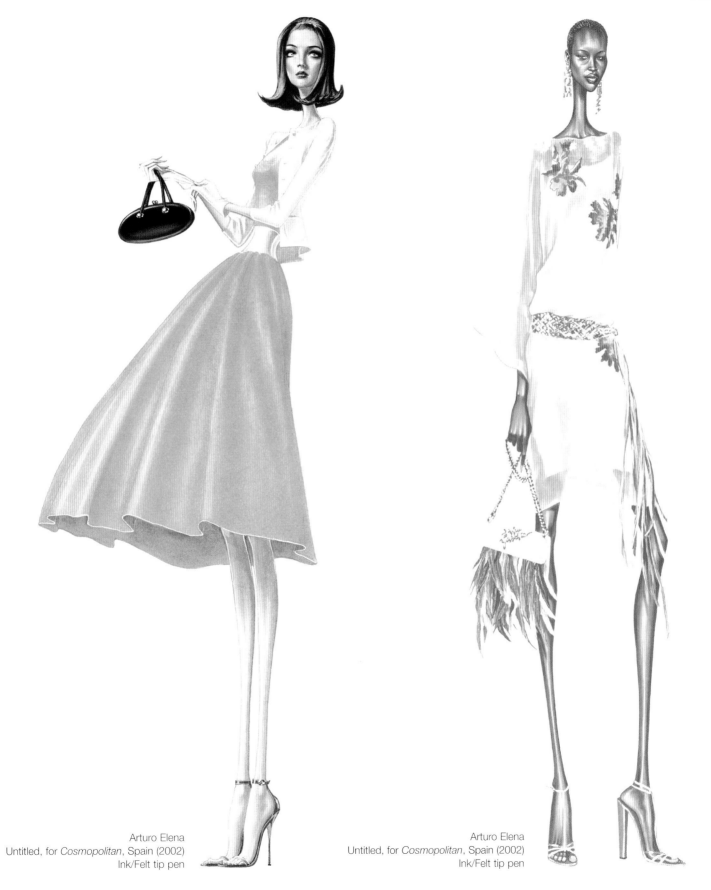

Arturo Elena
Untitled, for *Cosmopolitan*, Spain (2002)
Ink/Felt tip pen

Arturo Elena
Untitled, for *Cosmopolitan*, Spain (2002)
Ink/Felt tip pen

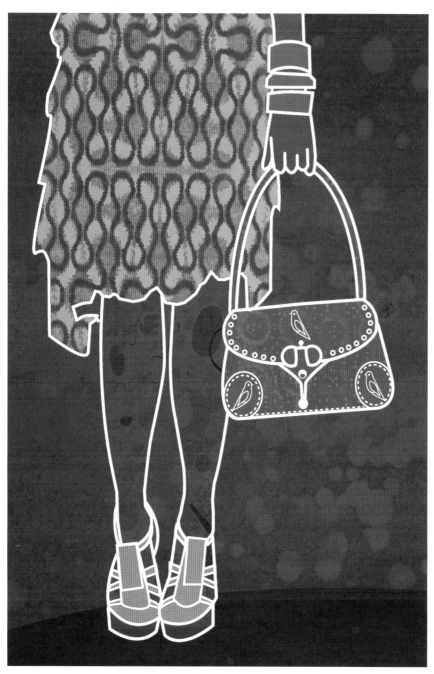

Gillian Cook
Handbag and Shoes (2006)
Adobe Photoshop

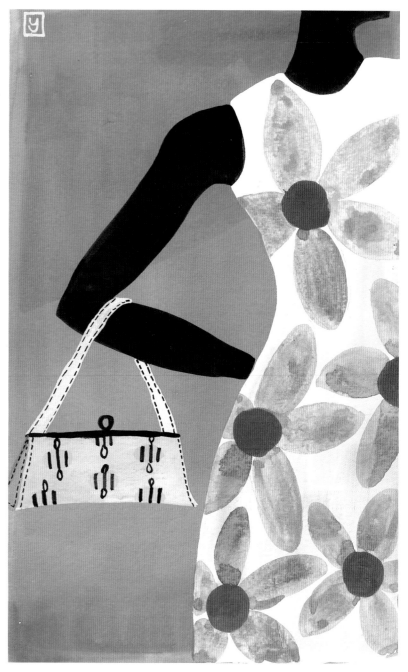

Yolanda Gonzalez
Flower Dress (2005)
Gouache on paper

Alessandra Scandella
Lady in Blue (2005)
Corel Painter/Adobe Photoshop

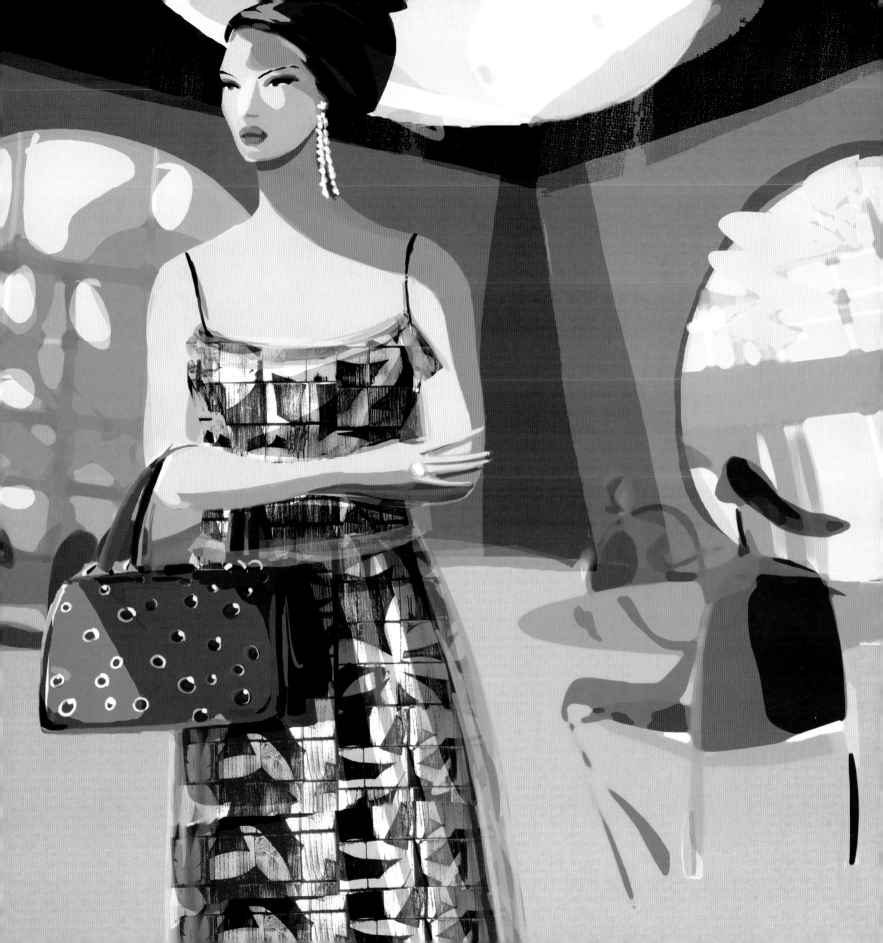

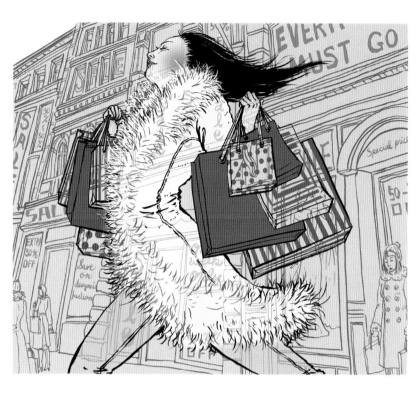

Yuko Shimizu
Untitled, *The Village Voice* (2002)
Ink/Adobe Photoshop

Sam Wilson
I Love Shopping (2006)
Paint/Crayon/Ink/Collage/Adobe Photoshop

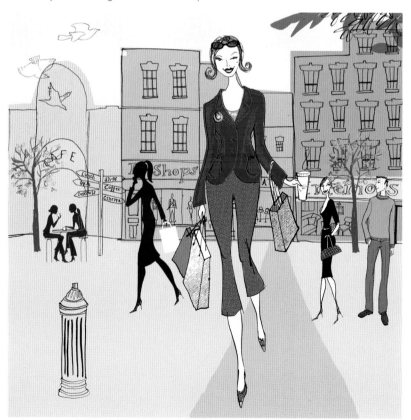

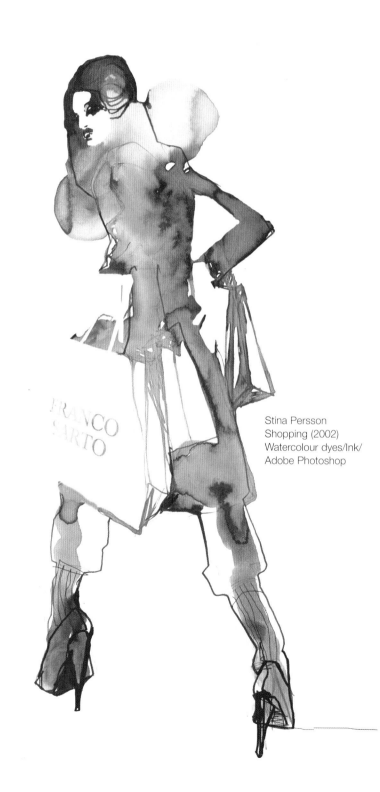

Stina Persson
Shopping (2002)
Watercolour dyes/Ink/
Adobe Photoshop

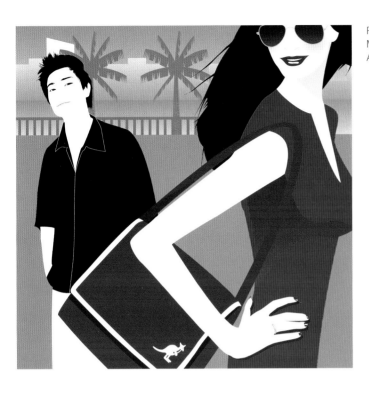

Pinglet
Messenger (2002)
Adobe Illustrator

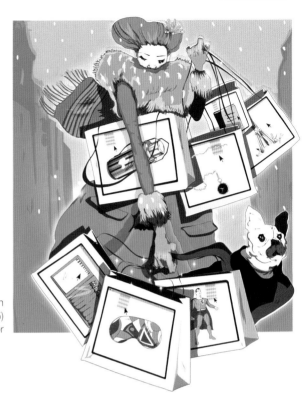

Marcos Chin
Cool Gifts (2005)
Adobe Illustrator

Gavin Reece
Trolley Chic (2005)
Adobe Photoshop

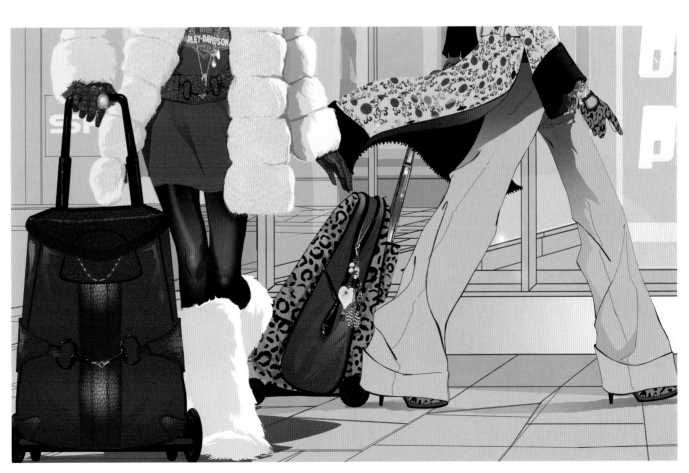

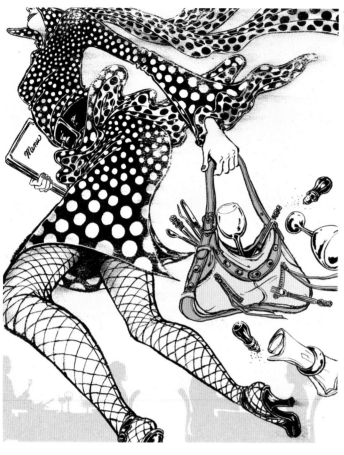

Yuko Shimizu
Untitled, *Chow* Magazine (2005)
Ink/Adobe Photoshop

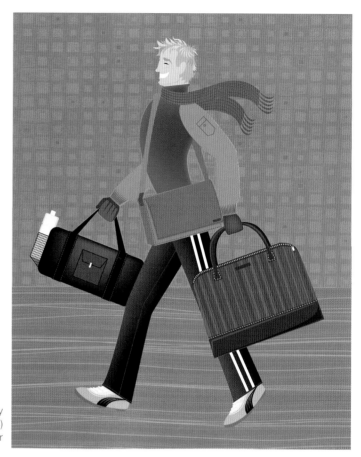

Jason O'Malley
Bags for Men (2004)
Adobe Illustrator

Carlo Stanga
NY Run (2004)
Adobe Photoshop

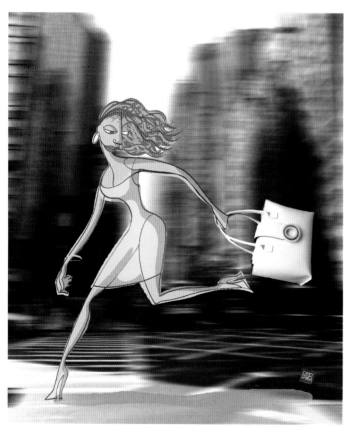

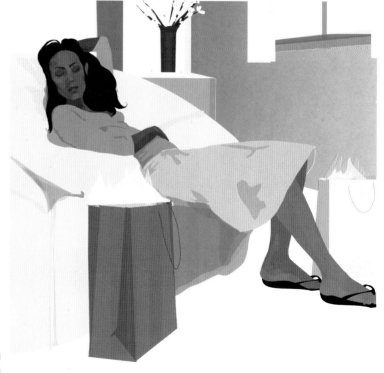

Kyra Kendall
Nap (2006)
Adobe Illustrator

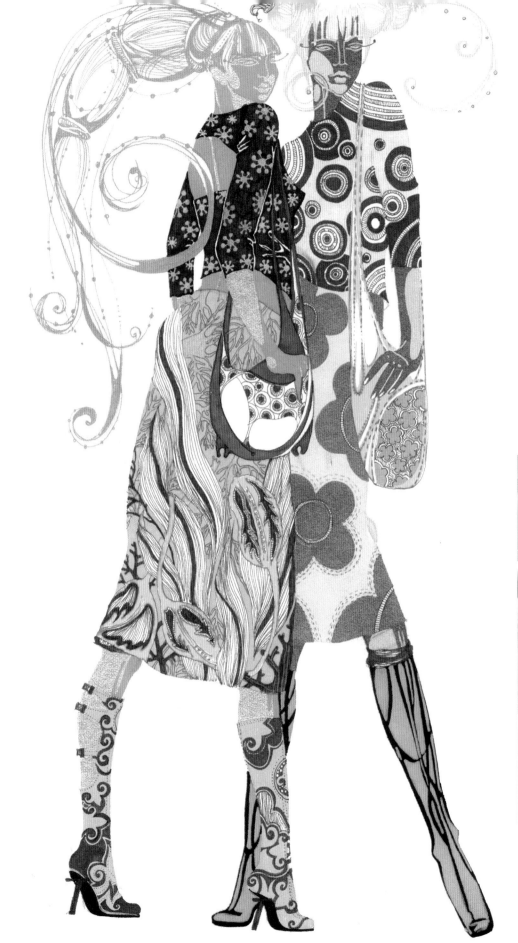

Sonya Suhariyan
Florescence (2005)
Gouache/Acrylic/Felt tip pen

Pinglet
Gatehold (2002)
Adobe Illustrator

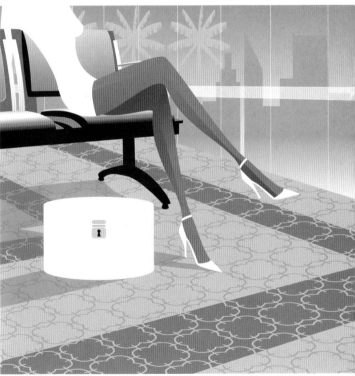

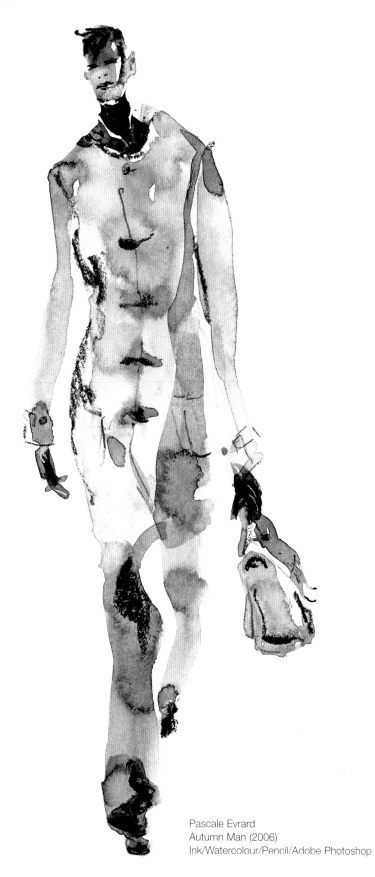

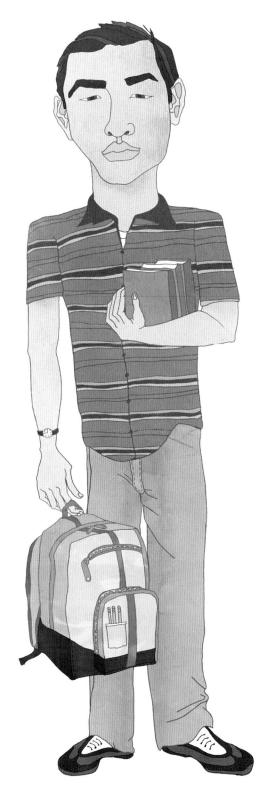

Pascale Evrard
Autumn Man (2006)
Ink/Watercolour/Pencil/Adobe Photoshop

Kim Rosen
The Academic (2004)
Ink/Acrylic/Adobe Photoshop

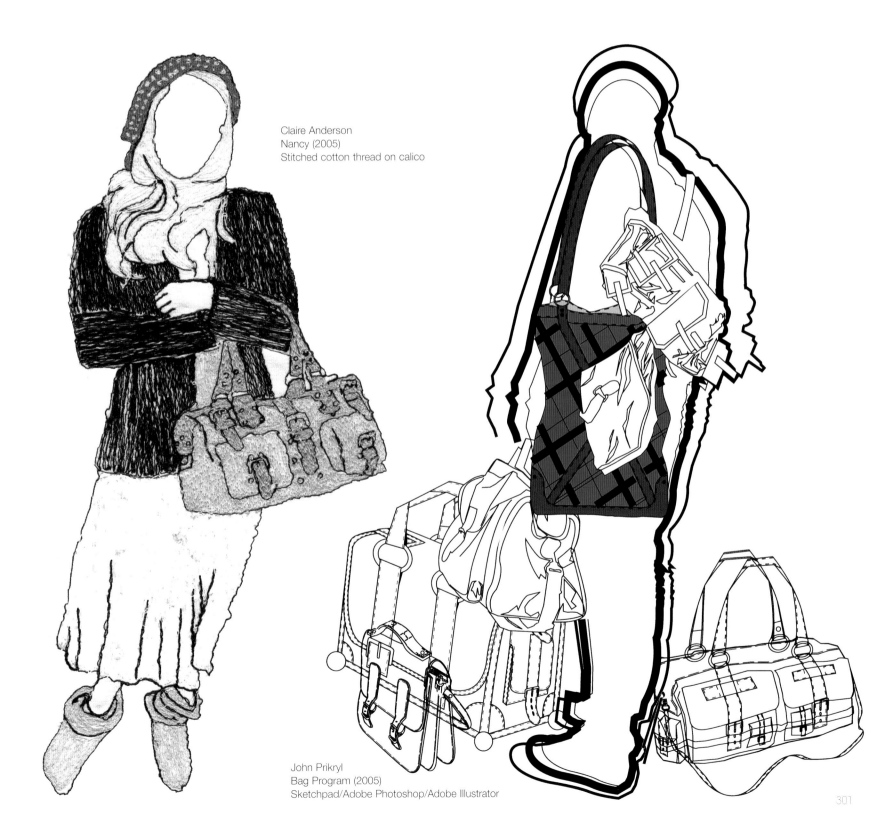

Claire Anderson
Nancy (2005)
Stitched cotton thread on calico

John Prikryl
Bag Program (2005)
Sketchpad/Adobe Photoshop/Adobe Illustrator

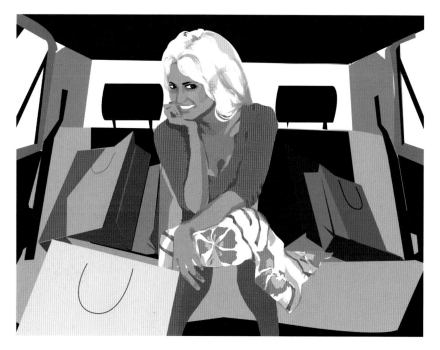

Kyra Kendall
Spender (2006)
Adobe Illustrator

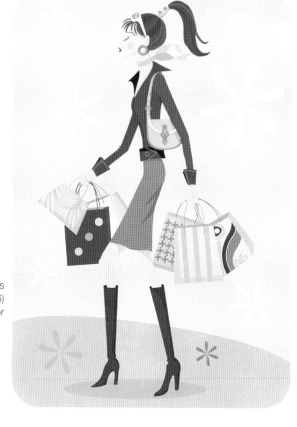

Nina Edwards
Shop Girl (2006)
Adobe Illustrator

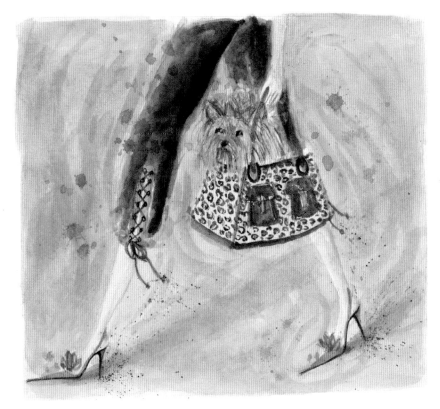

Bella Pilar
Yorkie (2004)
Gouache

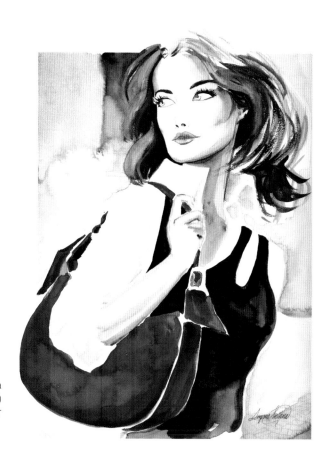

Amparo Losana
Longchamp for *Elle* magazine (2004)
Watercolour

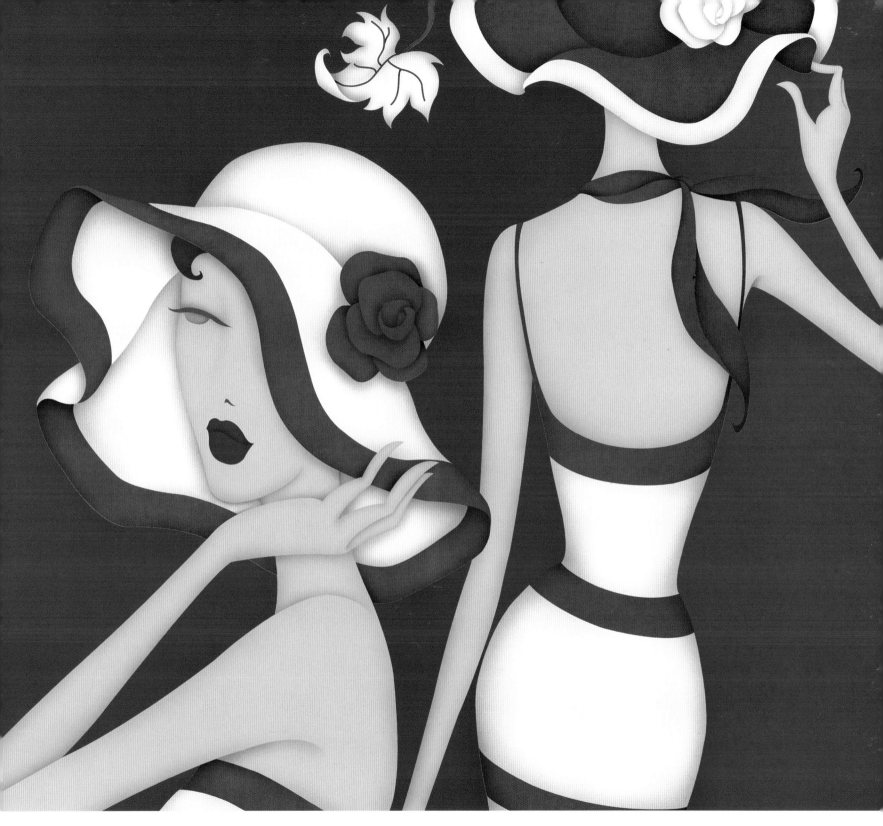

Wai
Windy (2006)
Adobe Illustrator/Adobe Photoshop

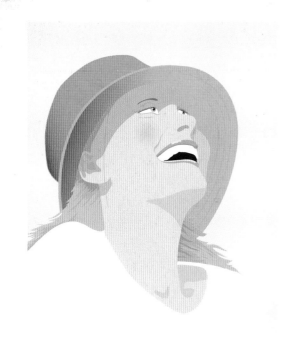

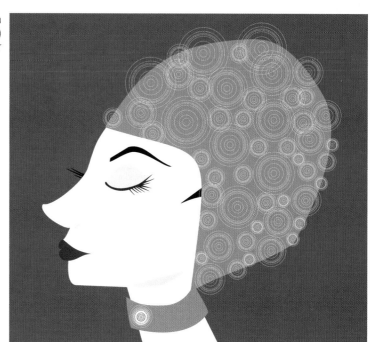

Lulu
Summertime (2003)
Adobe Illustrator

Stuart Holmes
Spring Has Sprung (2002)
Adobe Illustrator

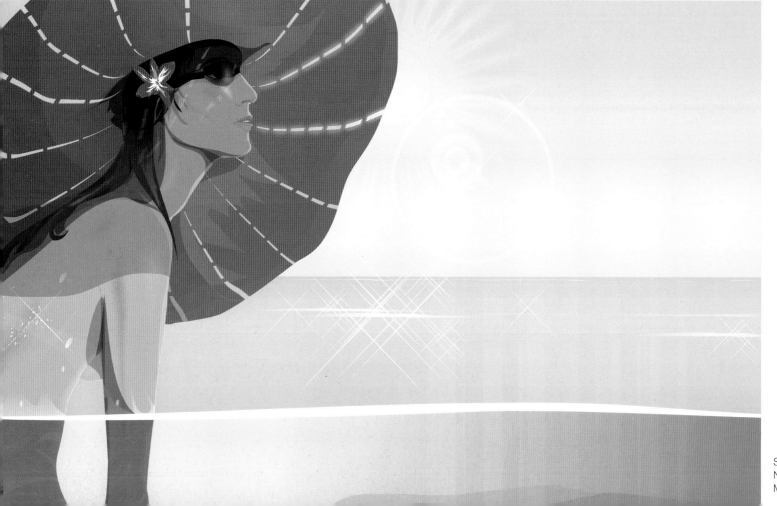

Sofia Dias
Nudity (2005)
Macromedia FreeHand

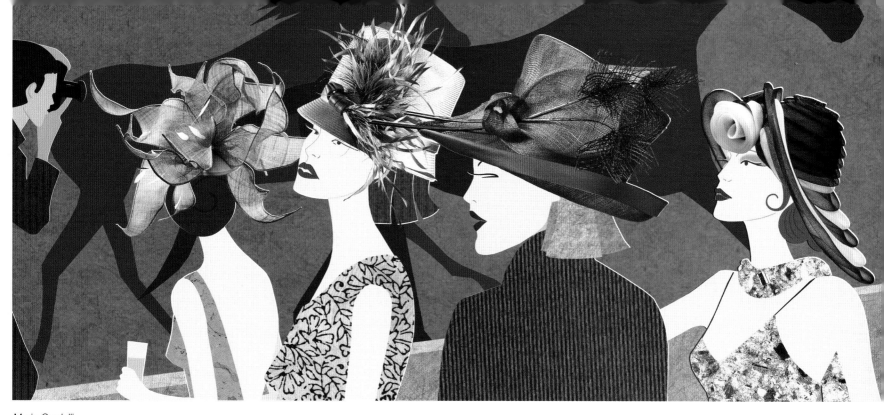

Maria Cardelli
Horse Race, *The Times* (2002)
Adobe Photoshop

Henry Obasi
Kangol Autumn/Winter, Snow Lovers (2006)
Adobe Photoshop/Adobe Illustrator/Paint/Ink

Giulio Iurissevich
Paris Lounge (2003)
Macromedia FreeHand/Adobe Illustrator

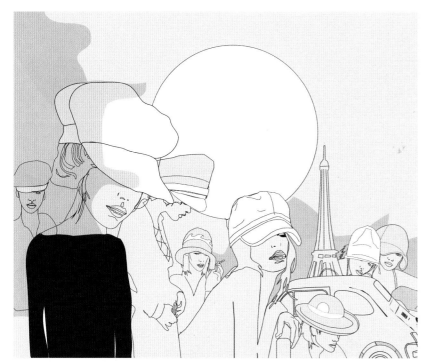

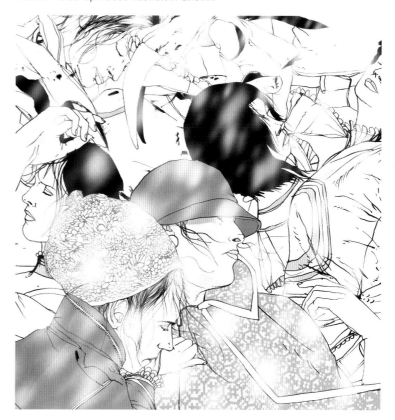

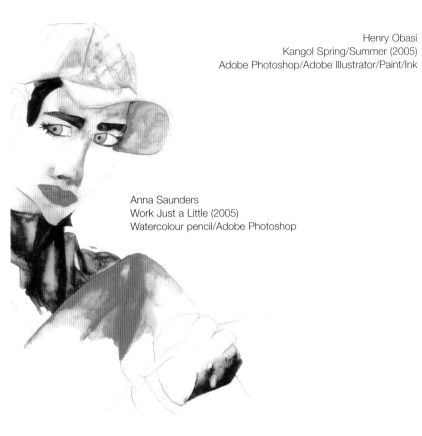

Anna Saunders
Work Just a Little (2005)
Watercolour pencil/Adobe Photoshop

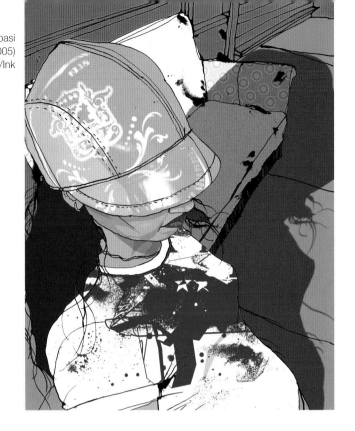

Henry Obasi
Kangol Spring/Summer (2005)
Adobe Photoshop/Adobe Illustrator/Paint/Ink

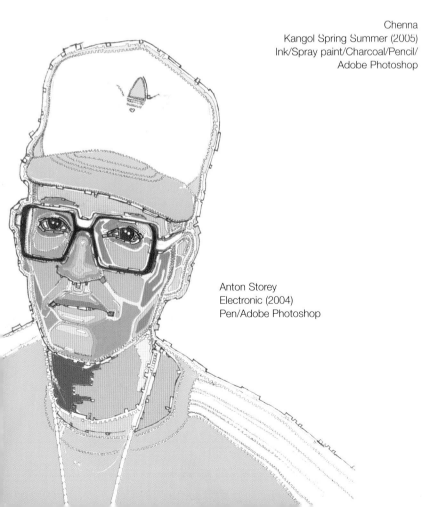

Anton Storey
Electronic (2004)
Pen/Adobe Photoshop

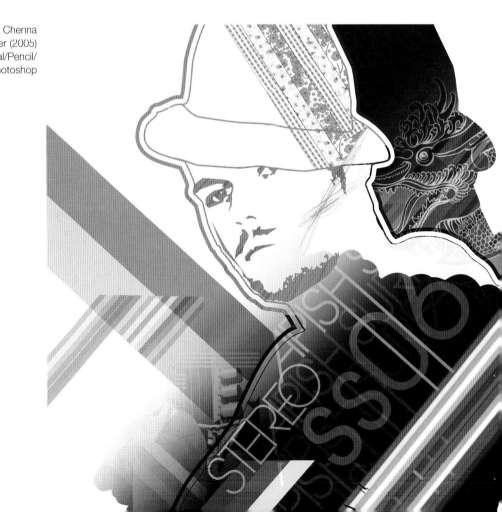

Chenna
Kangol Spring Summer (2005)
Ink/Spray paint/Charcoal/Pencil/
Adobe Photoshop

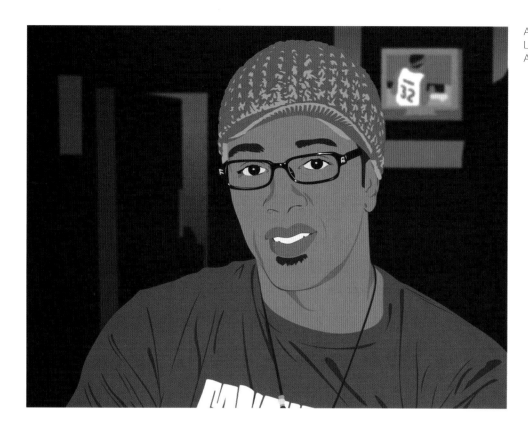

Arthur Mount
Larry (2005)
Adobe Illustrator

Henry Obasi
Kangol Autumn/Winter, Snow Hunter (2006)
Adobe Photoshop/Adobe Illustrator/Paint/Ink

Jonathan Williams
Things You Shouldn't Do Over the Age
of 30: Wear a Kangol Hat (2003)
Pencil/Adobe Photoshop

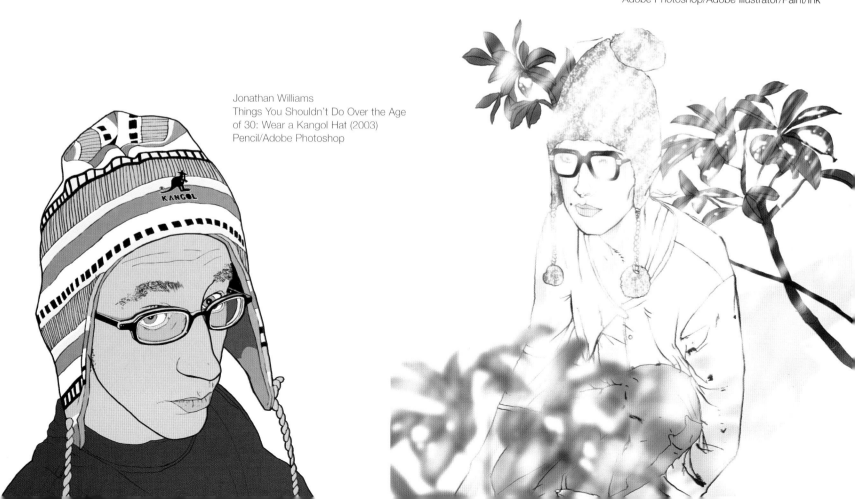

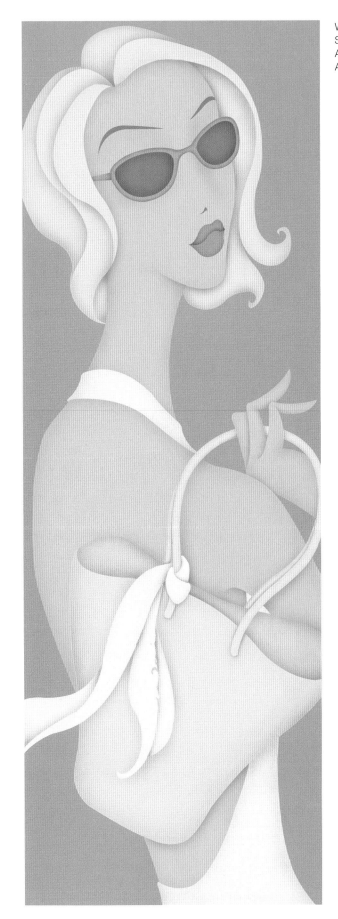

Wai
Spring (2005)
Adobe Illustrator/
Adobe Photoshop

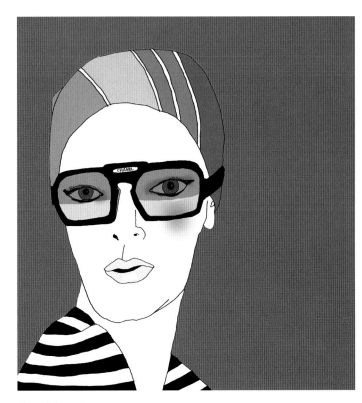

Hannah Broadway
Chanel Sunglasses (2006)
Fine liner/Adobe Photoshop

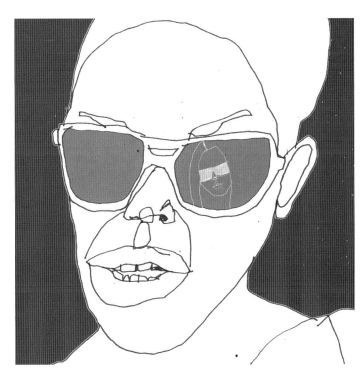

Hannah Broadway
Looking Pretty Cool (2006)
Fine liner/Adobe Photoshop

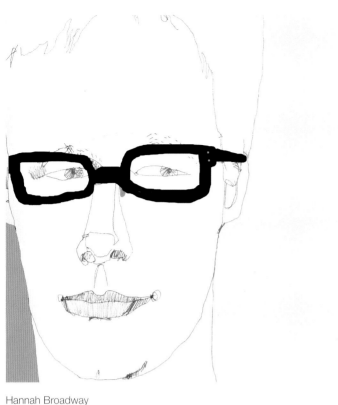

Hannah Broadway
Felix Wears Glasses (2006)
Biro/Adobe Photoshop

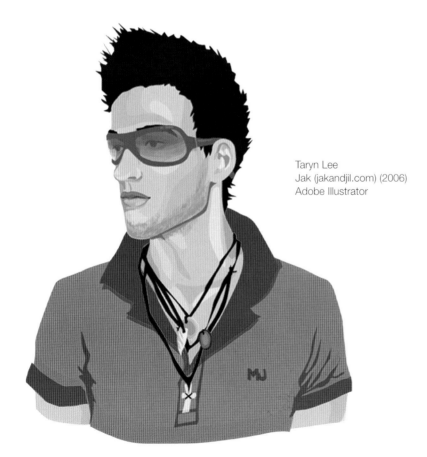

Taryn Lee
Jak (jakandjil.com) (2006)
Adobe Illustrator

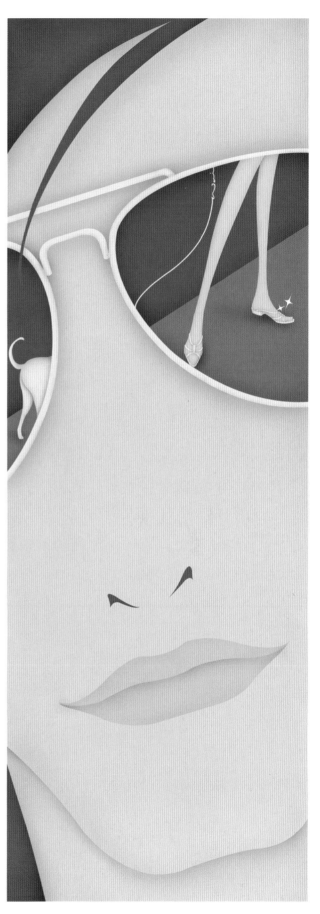

Wai
Reflection (2005)
Adobe Illustrator/
Adobe Photoshop

Maria Cardelli
Taurus, *Vital*
Magazine (2000)
Adobe Photoshop

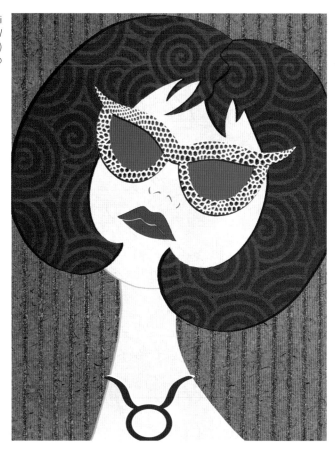

Aga Baranska
Drama (2006)
Collage/Paint/
Adobe Photoshop

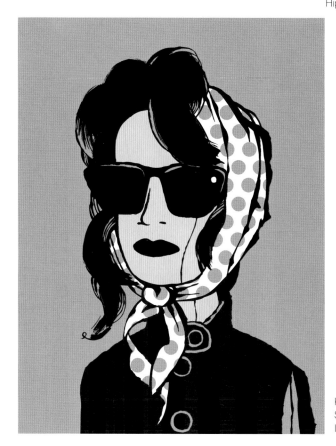

addictive,
don't start

Jason O'Malley
Hipster Eyewear (2006)
Adobe Illustrator

Maria Cardelli
Accessories,
Telecom (2001)
Adobe Photoshop

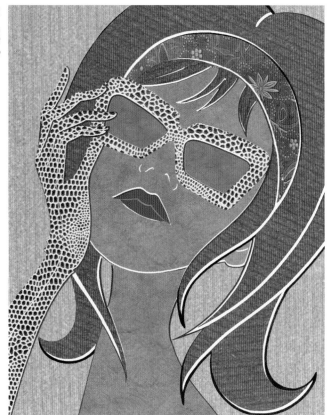

310

Kenneth Andersson
Shades (2005)
Ink/Adobe Illustrator

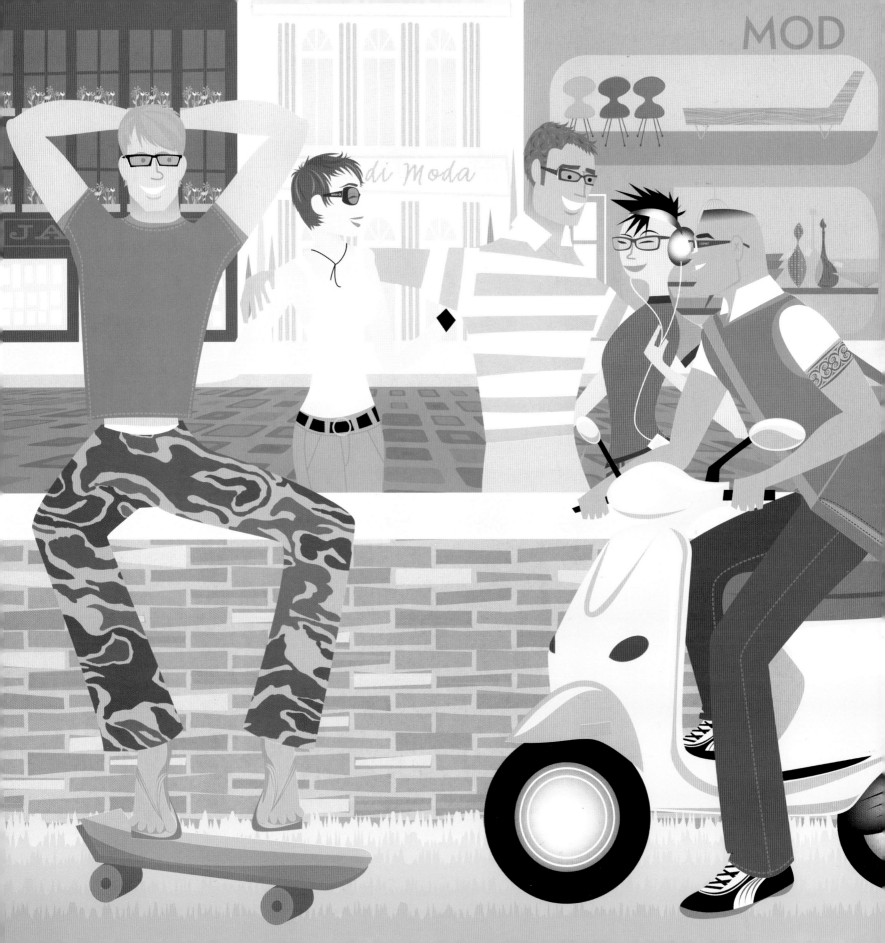

Margot Mace van Huijkelom
Lady with Glasses (2006)
Watercolour/Ink pen

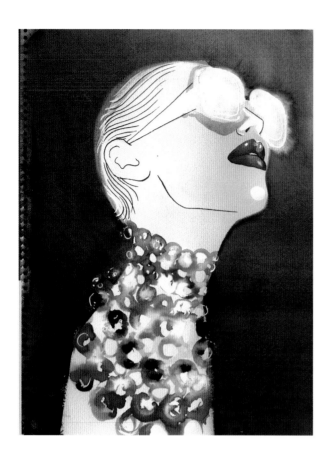

Pierre-Paul Pariseau
Waiting for Marcello (2005)
Adobe Photoshop

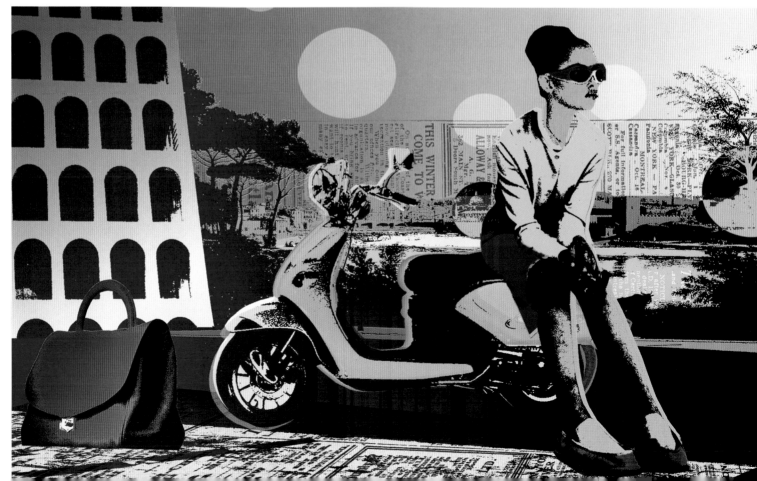

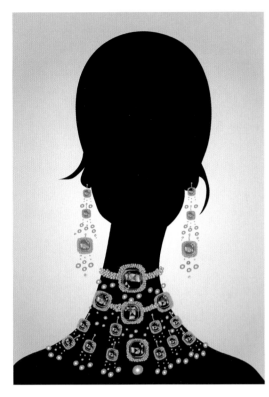

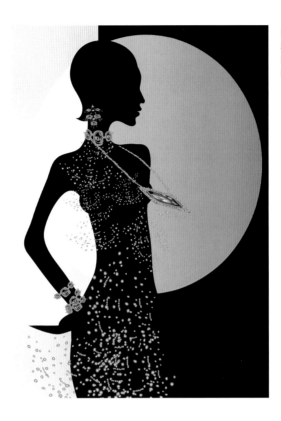

Natascha Engelmann
Silhouette II (2000)
Pencil/Watercolour/Adobe
Photoshop/Adobe Illustrator

Natascha Engelmann
Silhouette I (2000)
Pencil/Watercolour/Adobe
Photoshop/Adobe Illustrator

Erica Glasier
Valentine (2003)
Adobe Photoshop/Adobe Illustrator

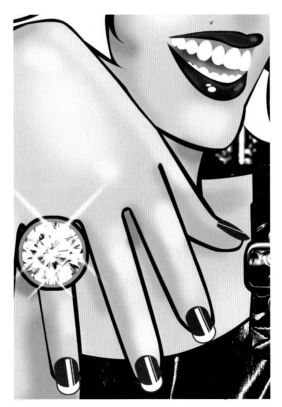

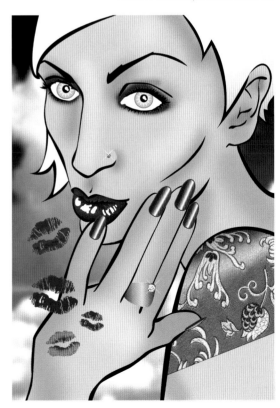

Erica Glasier
Engaged (2003)
Adobe Photoshop/Adobe Illustrator

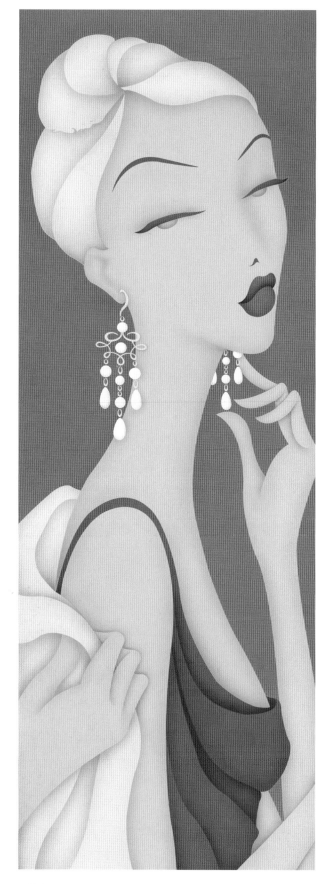

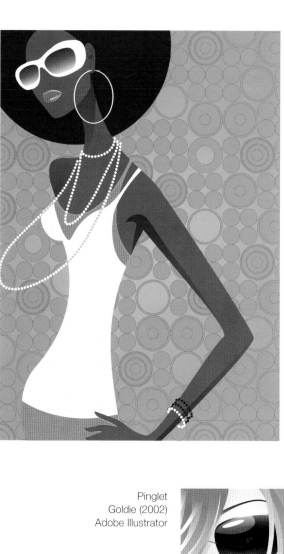

Pinglet
Jade (2002)
Adobe Illustrator

Pinglet
Goldie (2002)
Adobe Illustrator

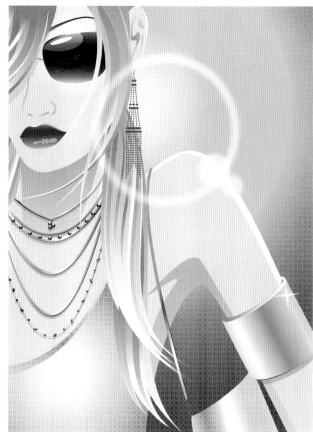

Wai
Drop (2005)
Adobe Illustrator/
Adobe Photoshop

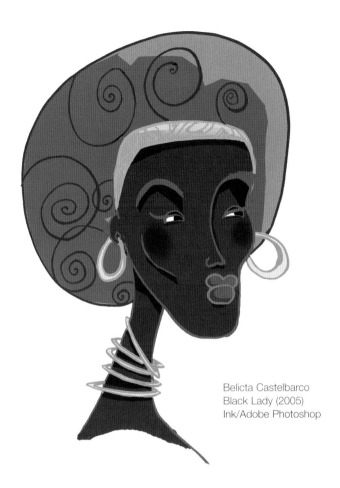

Belicta Castelbarco
Black Lady (2005)
Ink/Adobe Photoshop

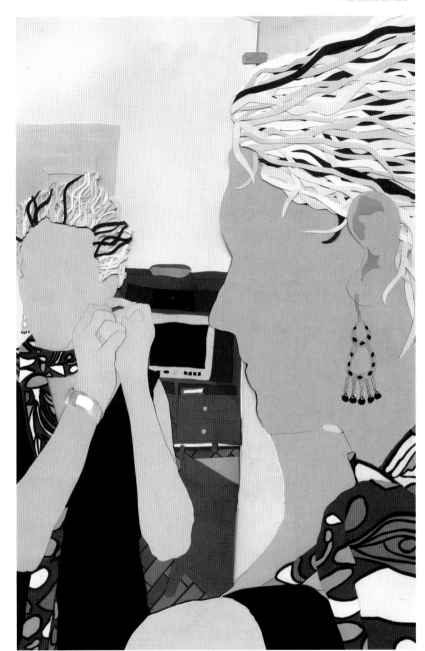

Sherill Gross
Beauty Ritual #11 (2006)
Paper

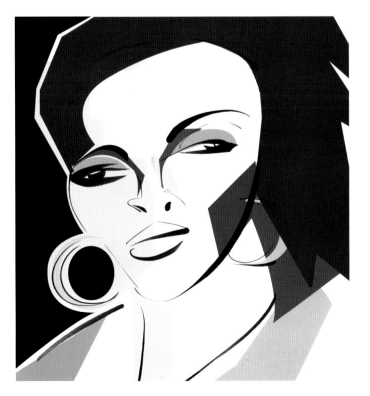

Rob Arnow
Untitled (1998)
Adobe Photoshop

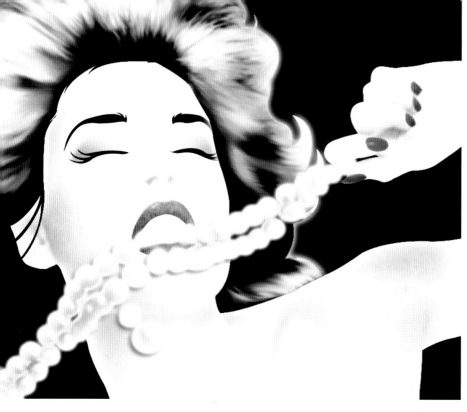

Ewa Brockway
Pink Pearls (2005)
Adobe Photoshop

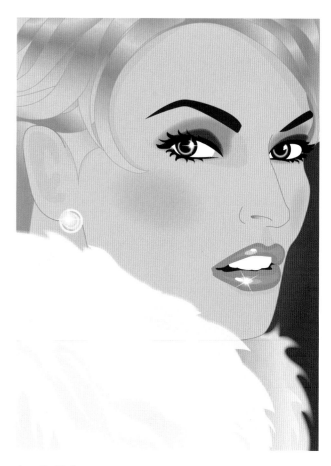

Amy De Wolfe
Spotted (2006)
Adobe Illustrator

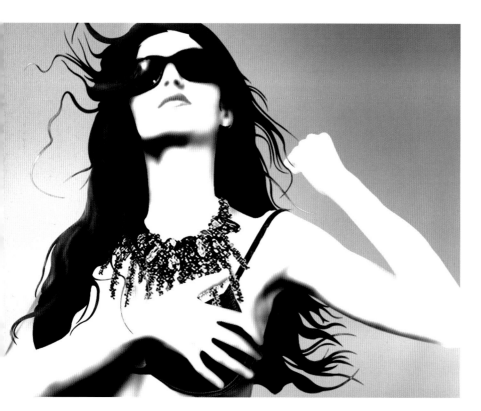

Ewa Brockway
Power of Beauty (2005)
Adobe Photoshop

Menisha
St Valentine (2006)
Adobe Photoshop

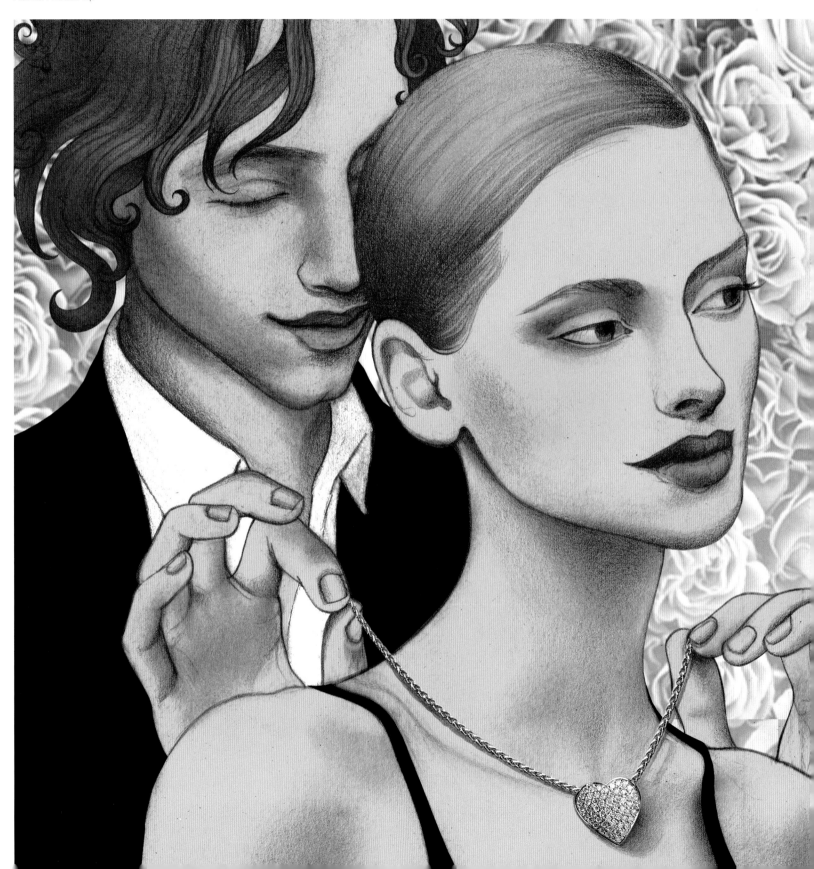

Anna Tuomaala and Natalie Eley
Kate (2005)
Pencil/Adobe Photoshop

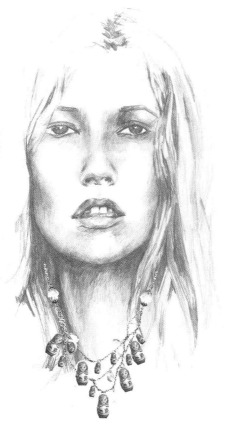

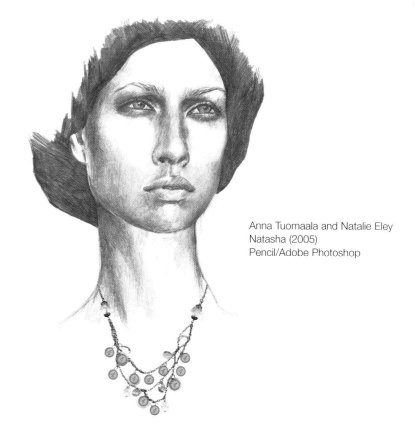

Anna Tuomaala and Natalie Eley
Natasha (2005)
Pencil/Adobe Photoshop

Steph Dix
Hazy Jane (2005)
Pencil/Adobe Photoshop

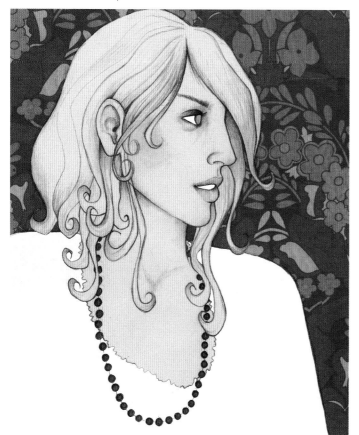

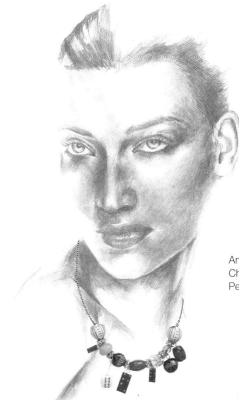

Anna Tuomaala and Natalie Eley
Christy (2005)
Pencil/Adobe Photoshop

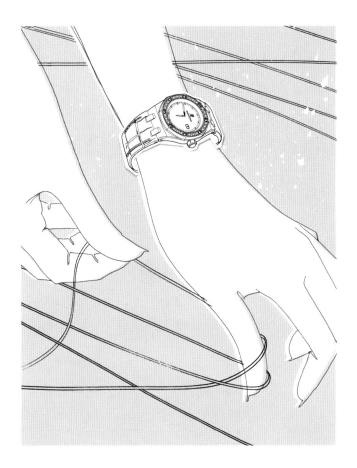

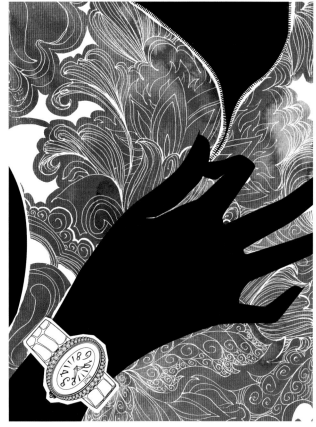

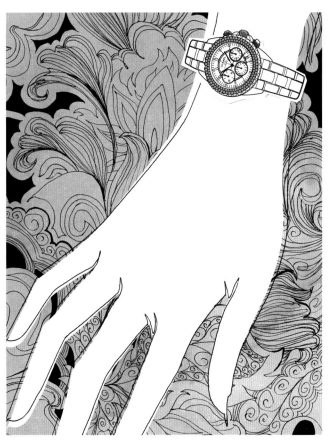

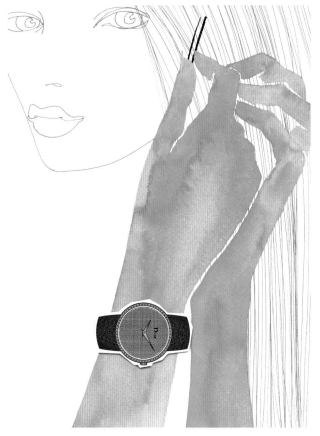

Tina Berning
Herzblut (2004)
Watercolour/Pen/
Adobe Photoshop

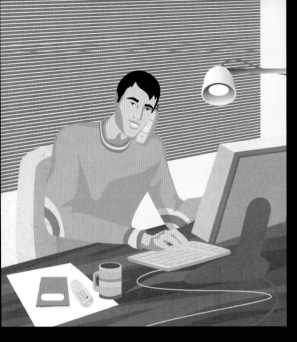

Javier Joaquin
My Desk (2004)
Adobe Illustrator

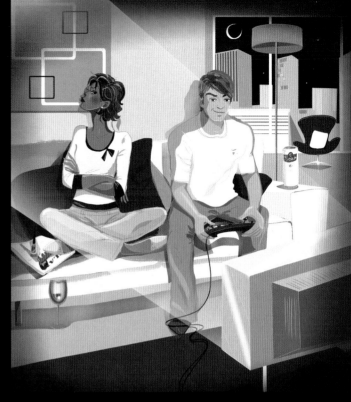

Lucy Truman
Oh Boy! (2005)
Corel Painter

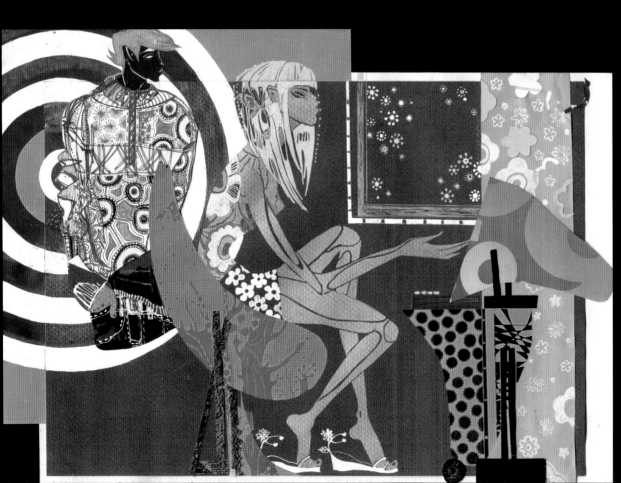

Sonya Suhariyan
Love in the Cover (2005)
Gouache/Acrylic/Felt tip pen

Alex Green
Playtime (2005)
Pencil/Paint/Pen/Collage/
Adobe Photoshop

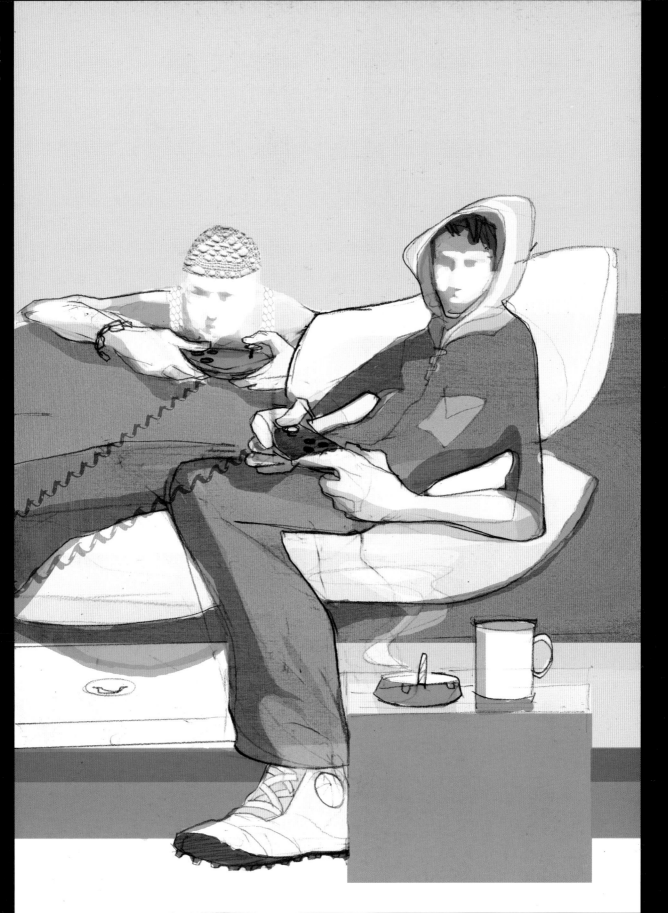

Cecilia Carlstedt
Untitled, *Bon* Magazine (2005)
Pencil/Adobe Illustrator/Adobe Photoshop

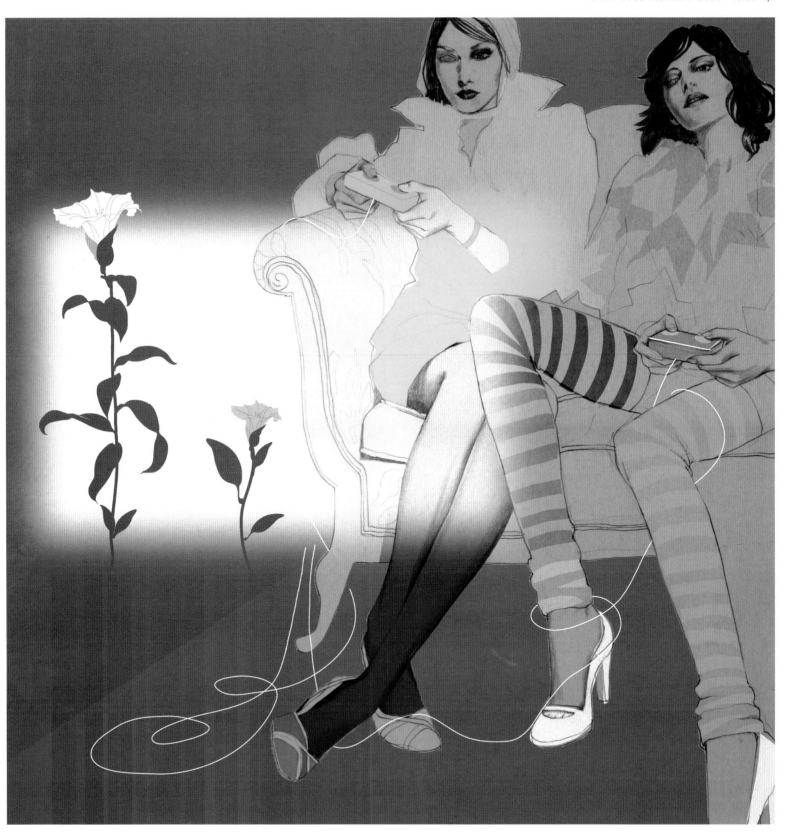

Sofia Dias
Digital Attitude (2004)
Macromedia FreeHand

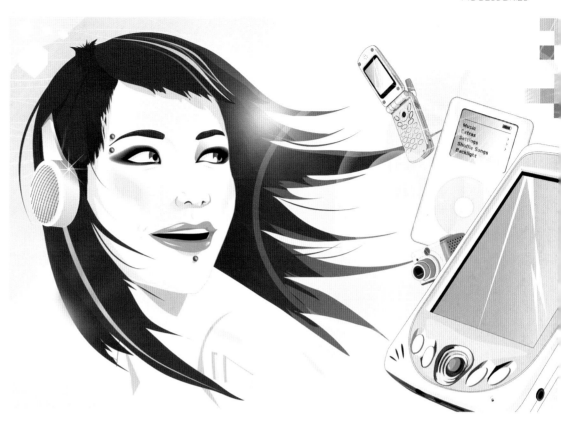

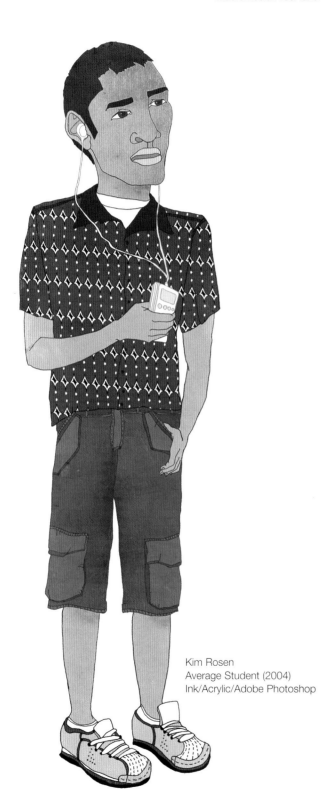

Herman Yap
Summer Headphones (2002)
Macromedia FreeHand/Adobe Photoshop

Kim Rosen
Average Student (2004)
Ink/Acrylic/Adobe Photoshop

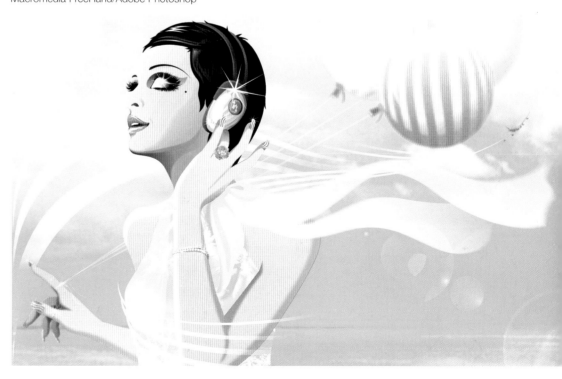

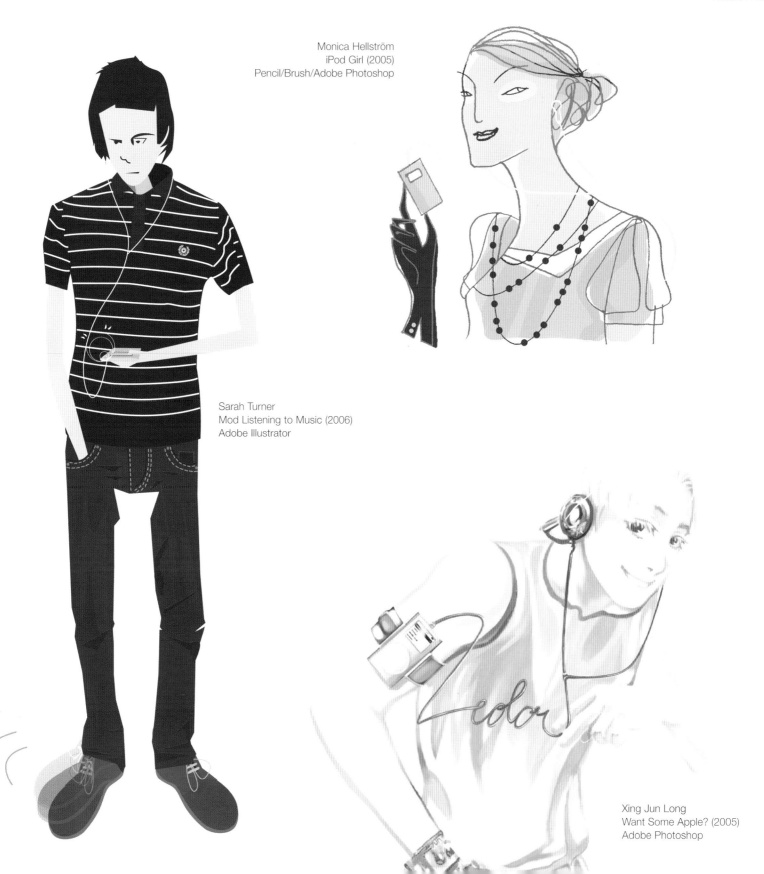

Monica Hellström
iPod Girl (2005)
Pencil/Brush/Adobe Photoshop

Sarah Turner
Mod Listening to Music (2006)
Adobe Illustrator

Xing Jun Long
Want Some Apple? (2005)
Adobe Photoshop

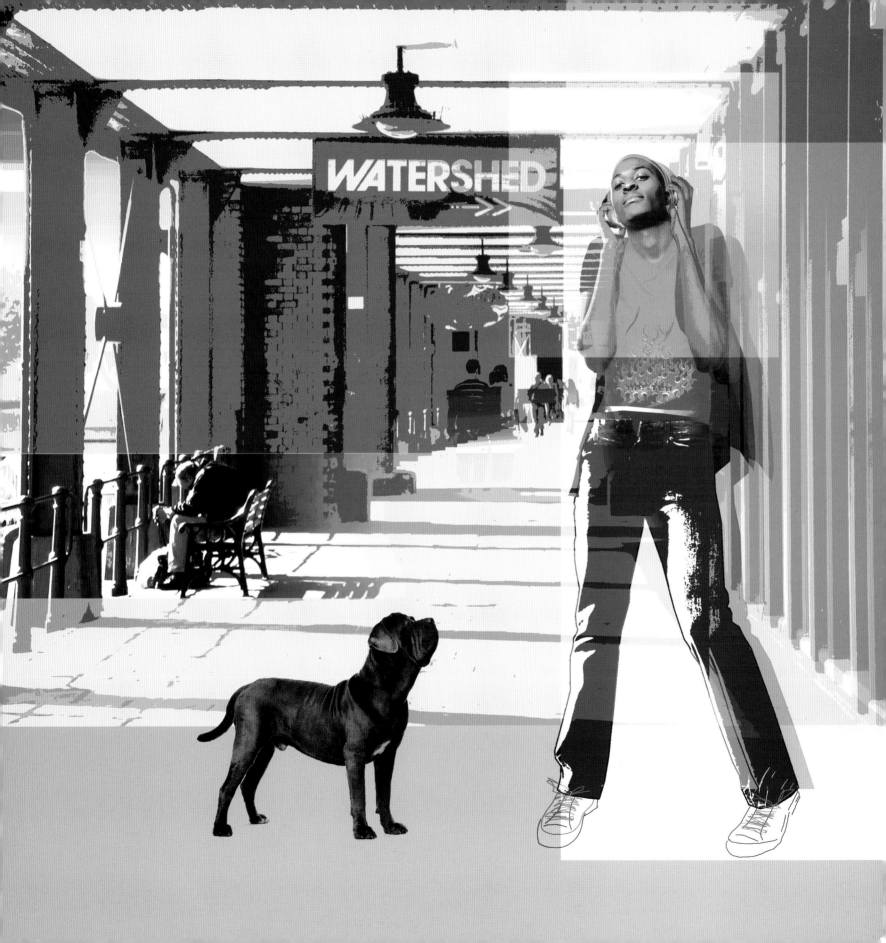

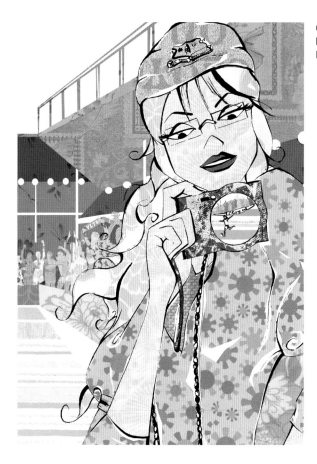

Georgina Fearns
Football Mum (2005)
Ink on paper/Adobe Photoshop

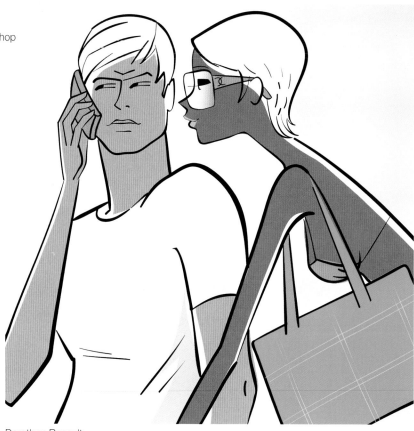

Dorothea Renault
Couple (2005)
Adobe Illustrator

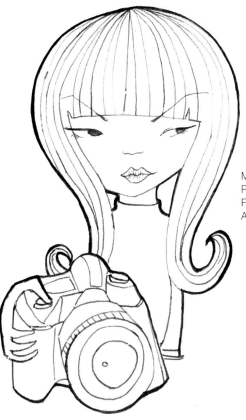

Malena Gagliesi
Personal Stationary Card: Malala
Fontan, Photographer (2004)
Adobe Illustrator

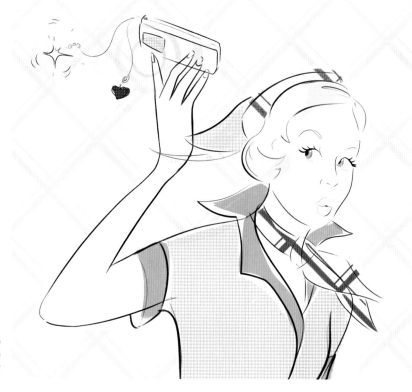

Astrid Mueller (Potatomammadesign)
Lucy (2006)
Corel Painter

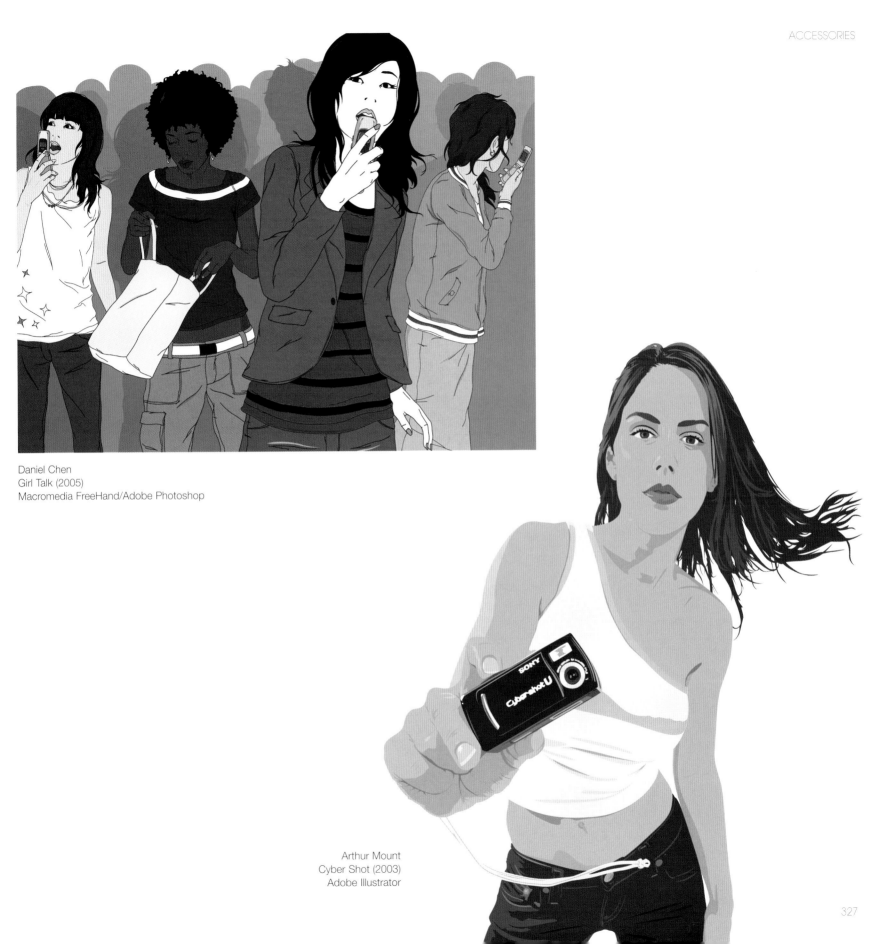

Daniel Chen
Girl Talk (2005)
Macromedia FreeHand/Adobe Photoshop

Arthur Mount
Cyber Shot (2003)
Adobe Illustrator

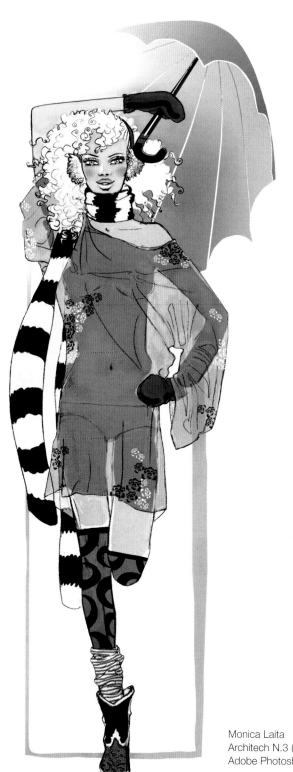

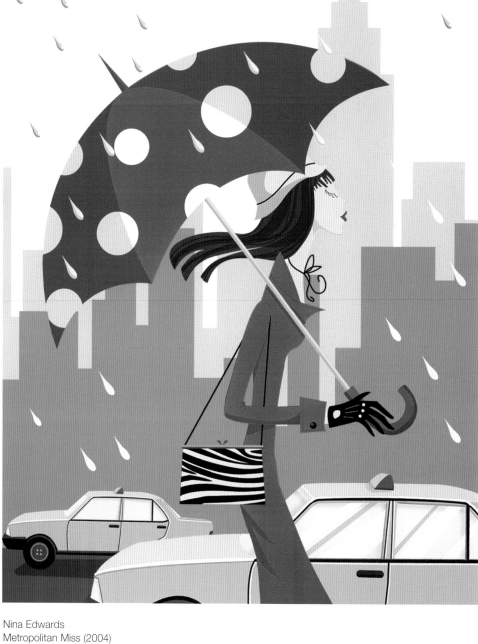

Monica Laita
Architech N.3 (2006)
Adobe Photoshop

Nina Edwards
Metropolitan Miss (2004)
Adobe Illustrator/Adobe Photoshop

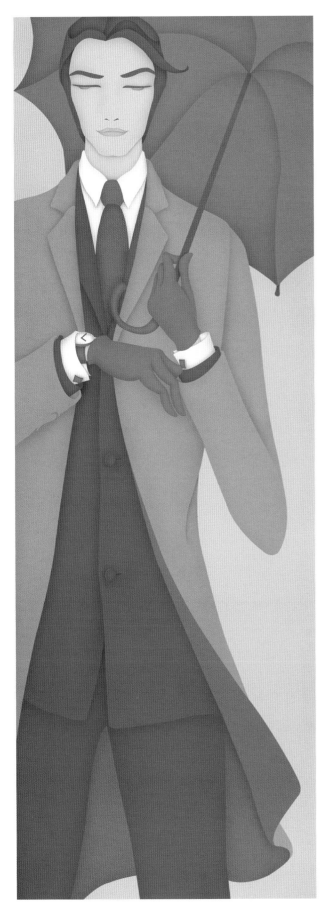

Wai
Late (2006)
Adobe Illustrator/
Adobe Photoshop

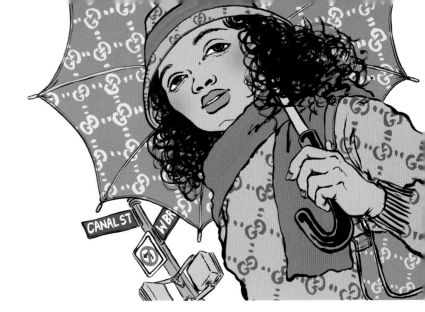

Yuko Shimizu
Untitled, *The Village Voice* (2003)
Ink/Adobe Photoshop

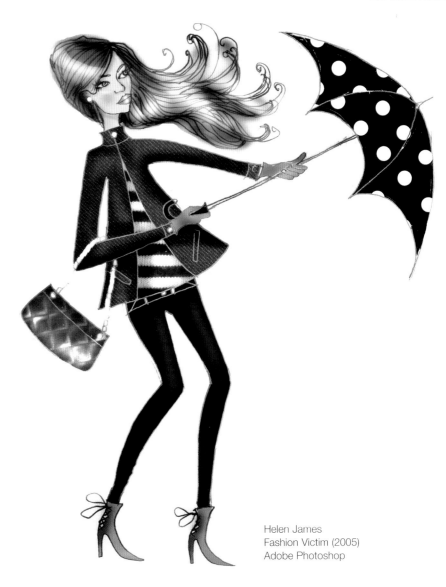

Helen James
Fashion Victim (2005)
Adobe Photoshop

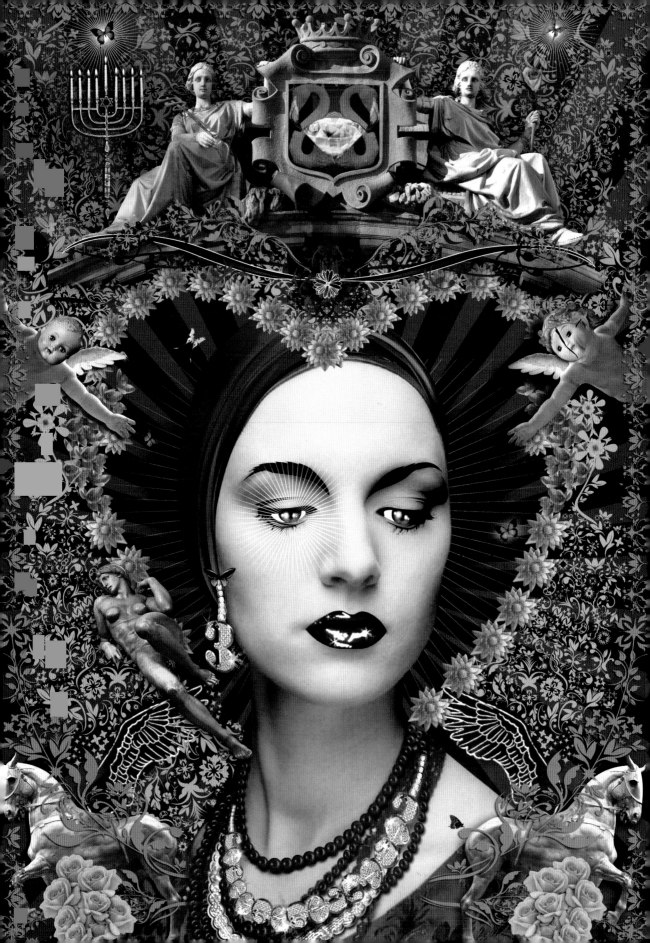

Beauty and Glamour

grooming   cosmetics   make-up   hair   eye candy   hunks

Jens Rotzsche
Early Risers (2006)
Adobe Illustrator

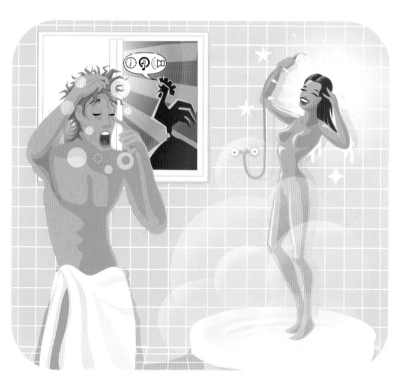

Christopher Corr
Clean Guy (2003)
Gouache

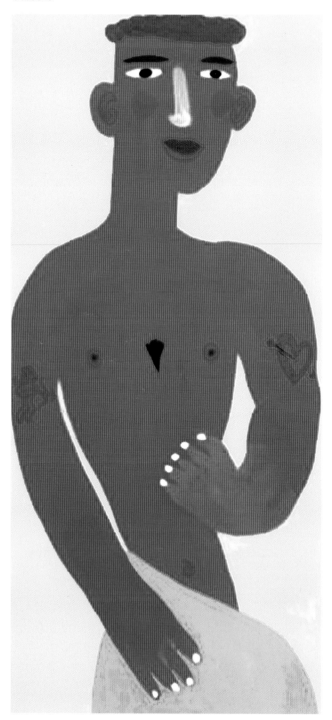

Wai
Aquarius (2006)
Adobe Illustrator/
Adobe Photoshop

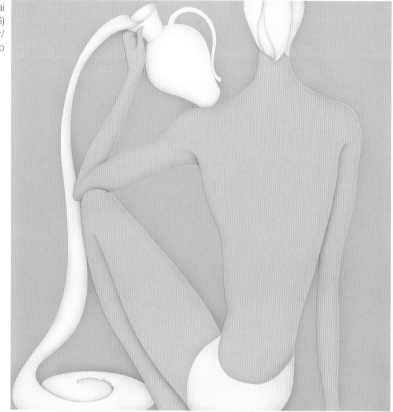

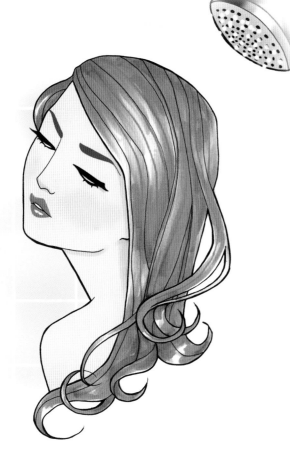

J David McKenney
Rinse (2005)
Ink/Adobe Photoshop

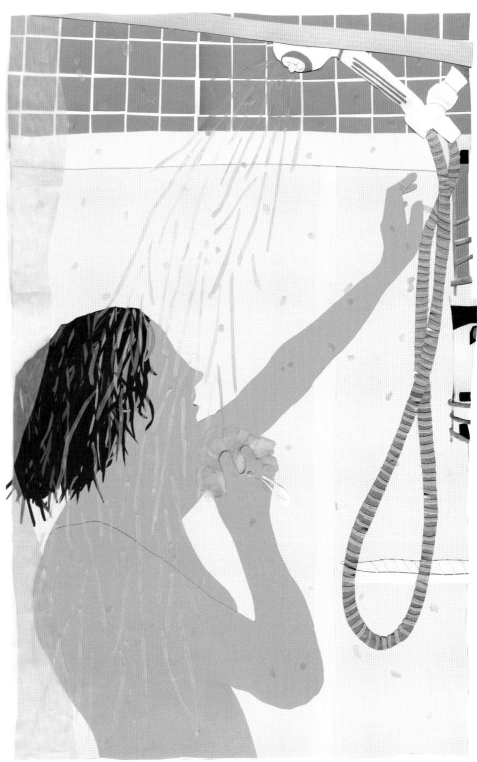

Sherill Gross
Beauty Ritual #4 (2005)
Paper

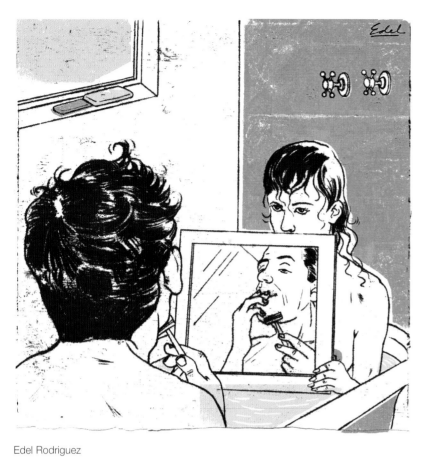

Edel Rodriguez
Nine Songs (2005)
Oil-based ink on paper/Adobe Photoshop

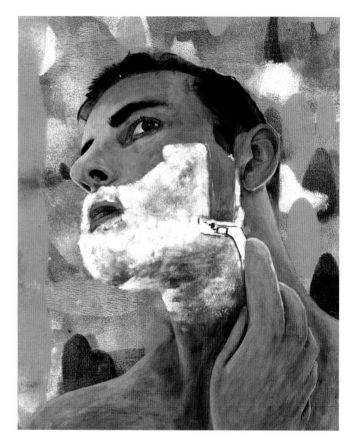

Vincent Agostino
Shaving Tips (2006)
Acrylic

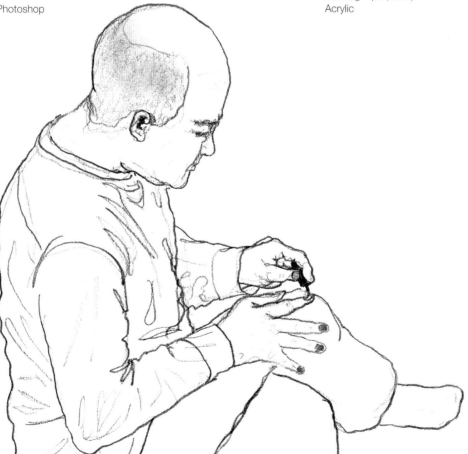

Louise Alexander
Nathan's Nails (2004)
Pencil

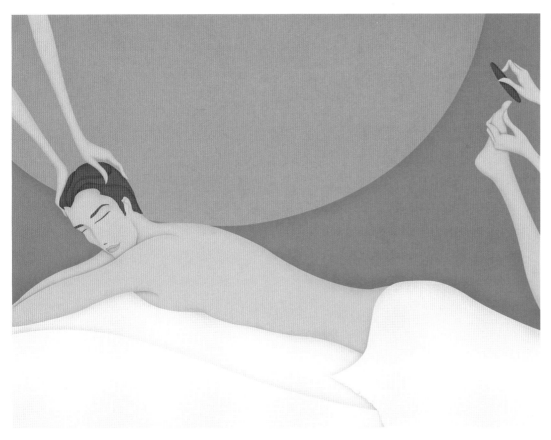

Wai
Beauty (2006)
Adobe Illustrator/
Adobe Photoshop

Christopher Corr
Clean Shave (2004)
Gouache

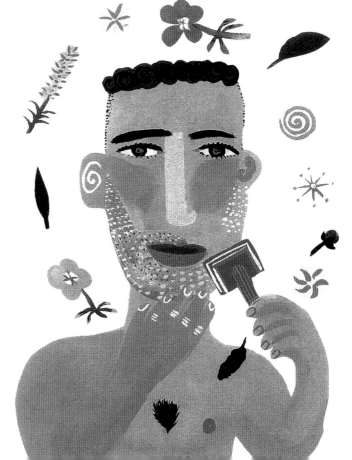

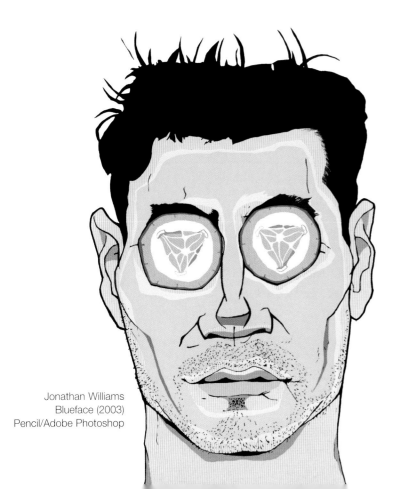

Jonathan Williams
Blueface (2003)
Pencil/Adobe Photoshop

335

Annika Wester
Make-up (2005)
Ink pen/Gouache

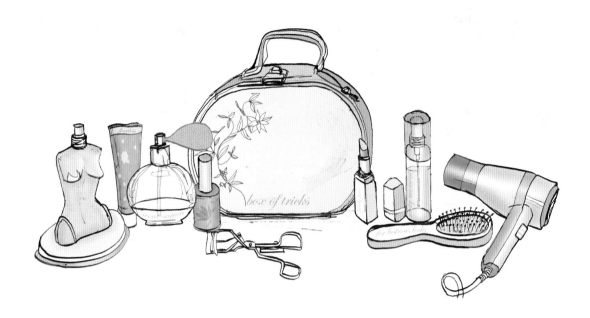

Helen Turner
Beauty Tools (2005)
Ink/Adobe Photoshop

Jens Rotzsche
A Sacrifice for Venus (2006)
Adobe Illustrator

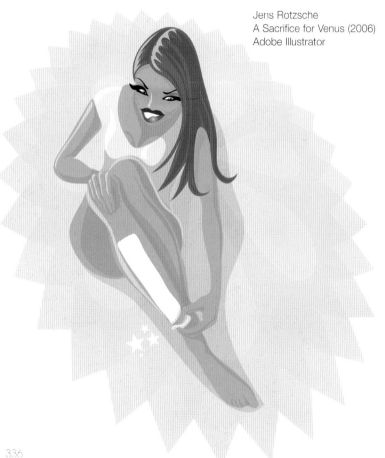

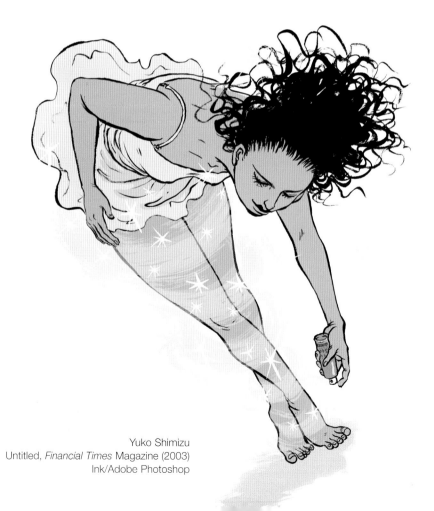

Yuko Shimizu
Untitled, *Financial Times* Magazine (2003)
Ink/Adobe Photoshop

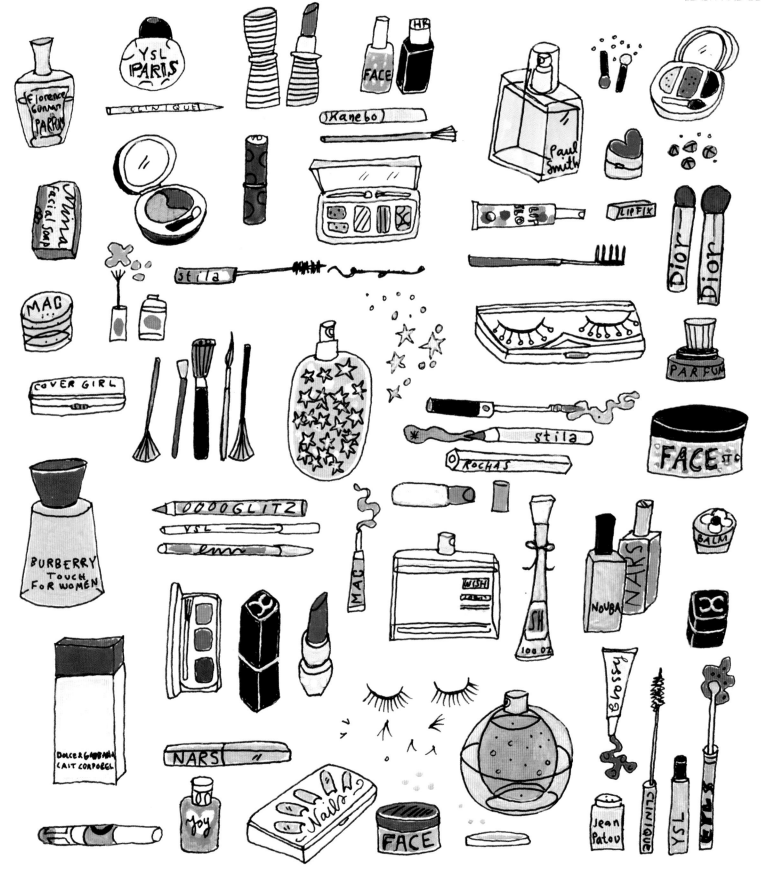

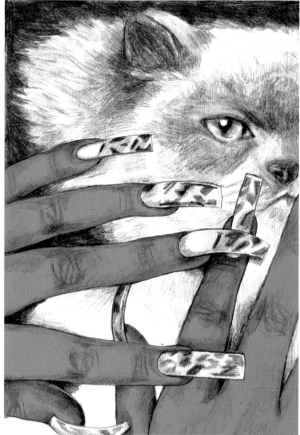

Jeanne Detallante
Freddie's Cat 1 (2005)
Adobe Photoshop

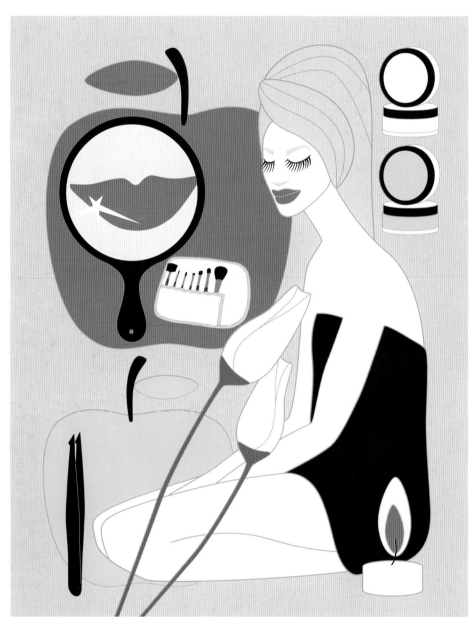

Kari Modén
Brand New Day, *VeroModa* magazine (2006)
Adobe Illustrator

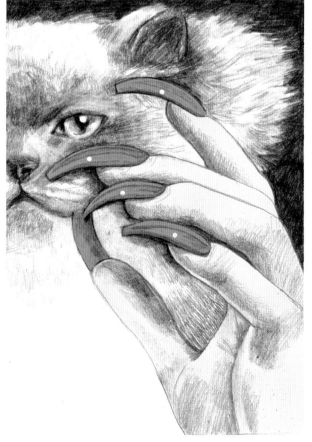

Jeanne Detallante
Freddie's Cat 2 (2005)
Adobe Photoshop

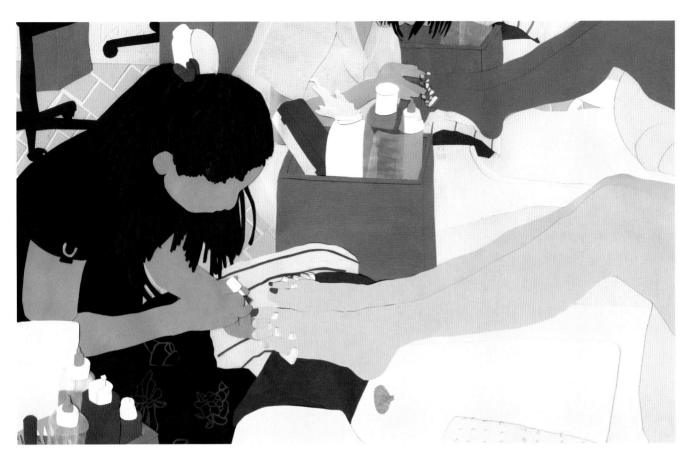

Sherill Gross
Beauty Ritual #7 (2005)
Paper

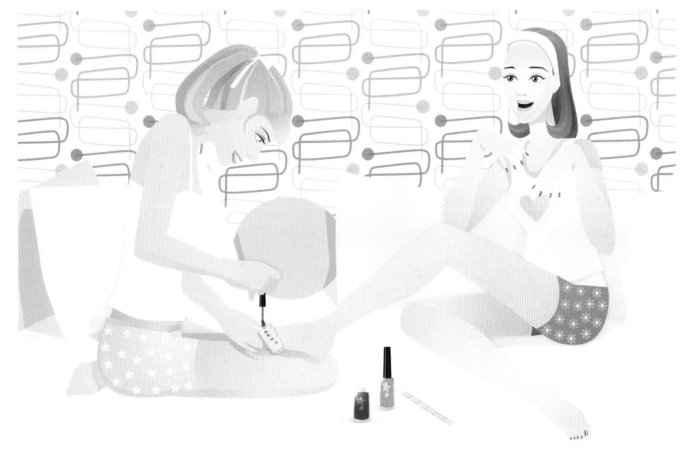

Kun-Sung Chung
Quick 'n' Easy, *Let's Party!*, Lobster
Press (2004)
Adobe Illustrator

339

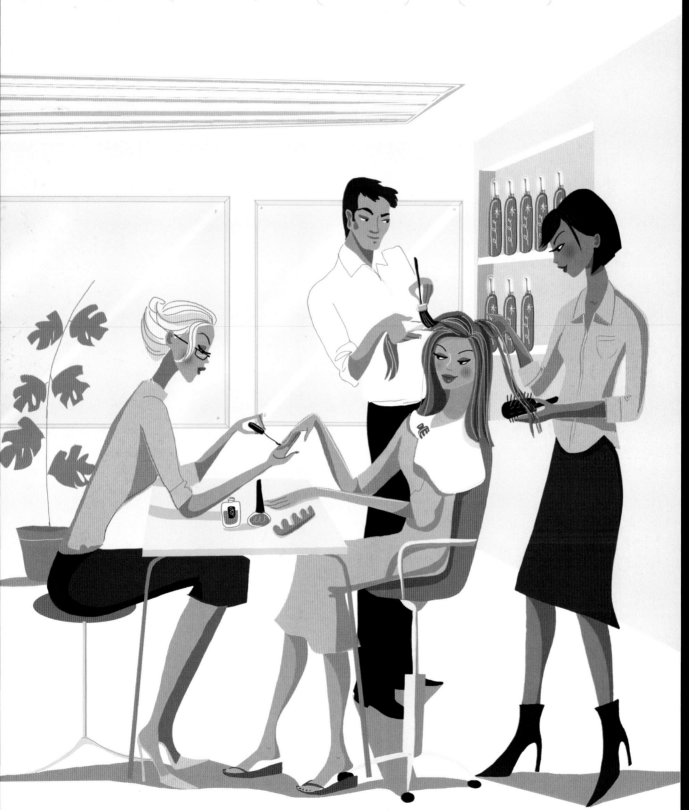

Lucy Truman
The Salon (2004
Corel Painter

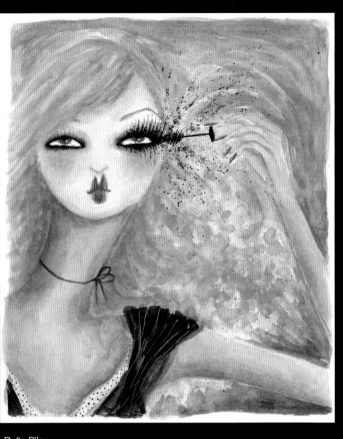

Bella Pilar
Applying Mascara (2004)
Gouache

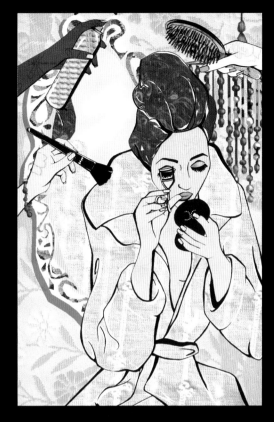

Georgina Fearns
Pampered (2005)
Ink on paper/Adobe Photoshop

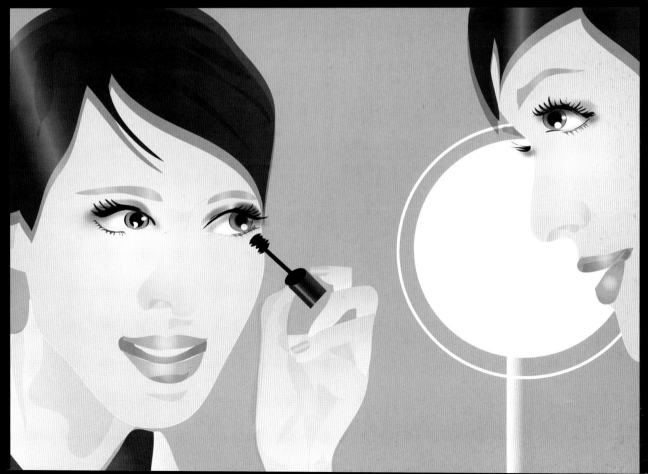

Natascha Engelmann
Lashes (2005)
Pencil/Adobe Photoshop

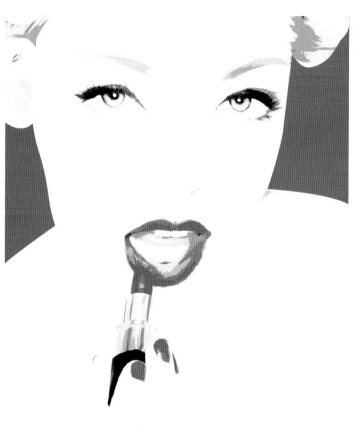

Eleanor Ferguson
Lips (2005)
Acrylic/Corel Painter/
Adobe Photoshop

Bella Pilar
Applying Lipstick (2004)
Gouache

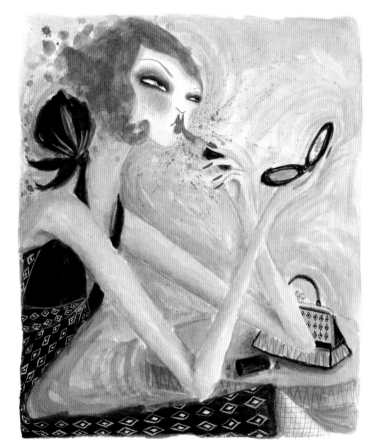

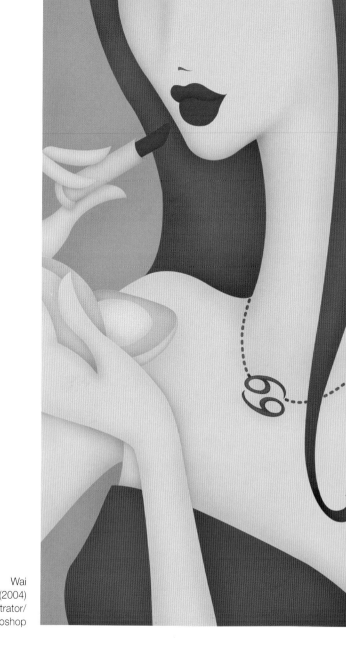

Wai
Lipstick (2004)
Adobe Illustrator/
Adobe Photoshop

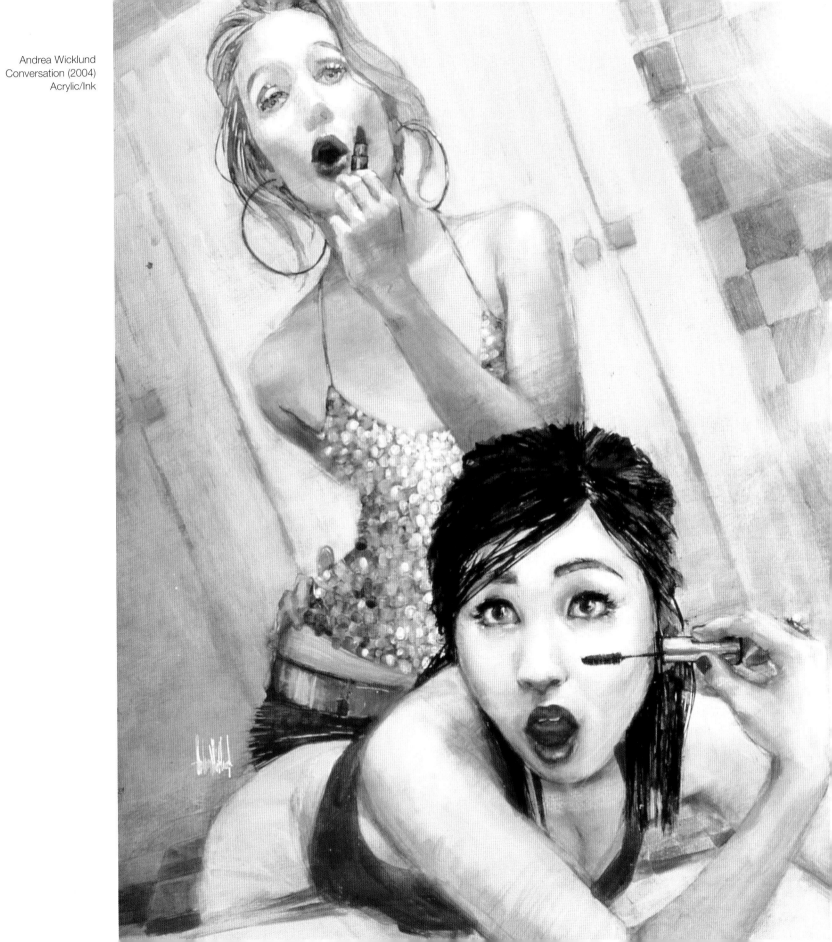

Andrea Wicklund
Conversation (2004)
Acrylic/Ink

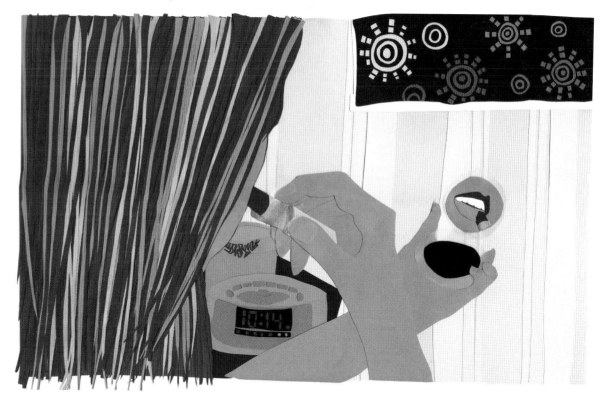

Sherill Gross
Beauty Ritual #8 (2005)
Paper

Diana Ponce
Jani Paris (2003)
Watercolour

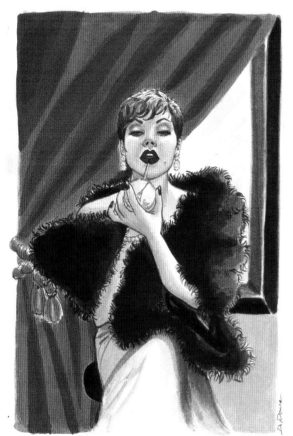

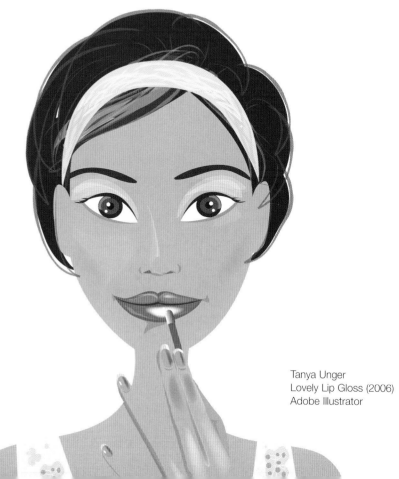

Tanya Unger
Lovely Lip Gloss (2006)
Adobe Illustrator

Lucy Truman
Maybe She's Born With It (2005)
Corel Painter

345

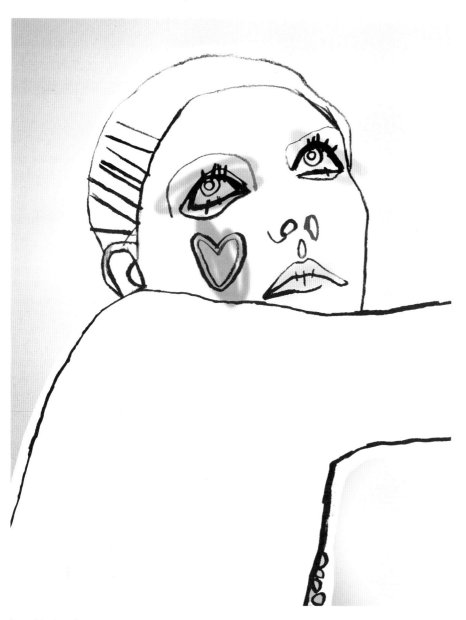

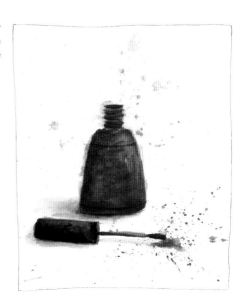

Bella Pilar
Nail Polish (2004)
Gouache

Lucy MacLeod
Thirties Girl (2006)
Charcoal/Adobe Photoshop

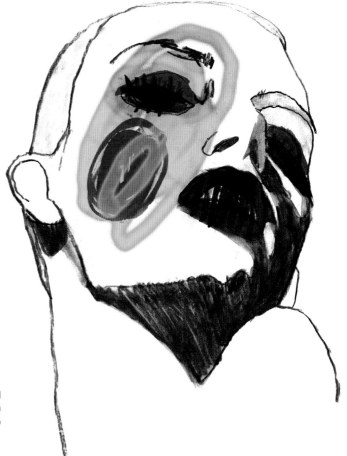

Lucy MacLeod
Rouge (2005)
Charcoal/Adobe Photoshop

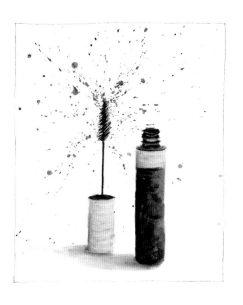

Bella Pilar
Mascara (2004)
Gouache

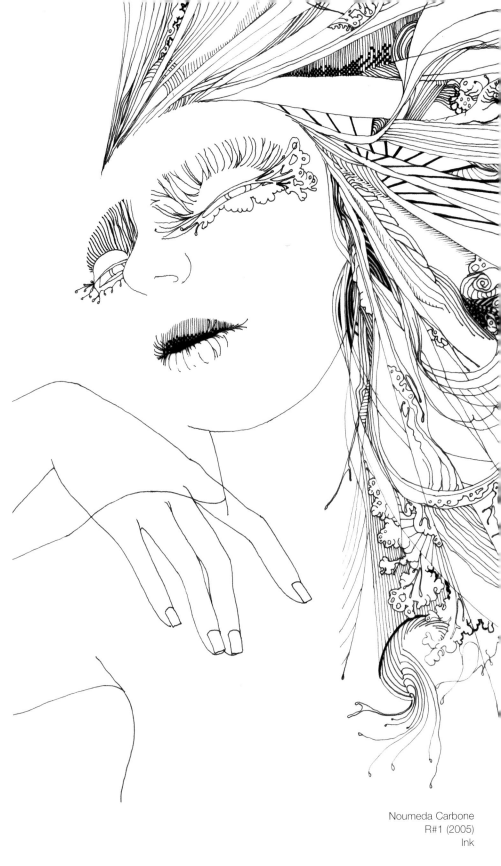

Noumeda Carbone
R#1 (2005)
Ink

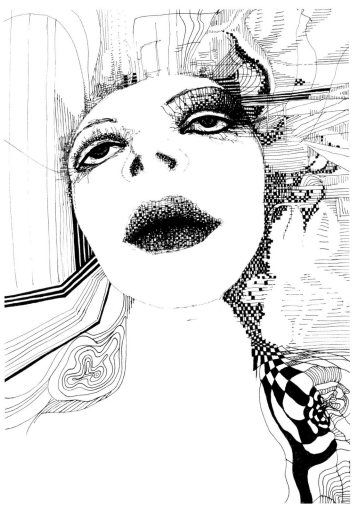

Noumeda Carbone
R#3 (2005)
Ink

347

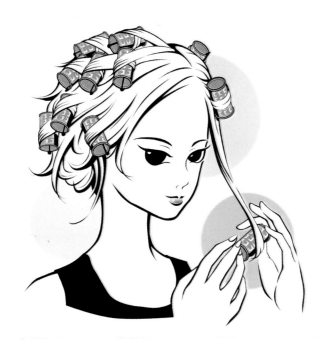

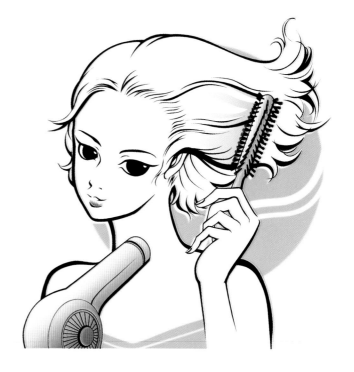

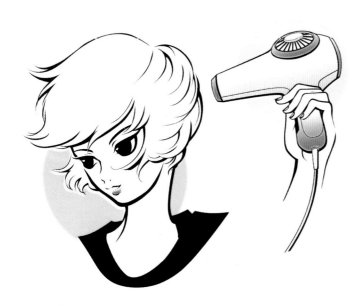

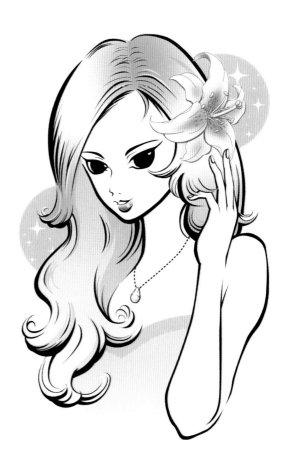

Symbolon
Hair Care (2004)
Adobe Illustrator

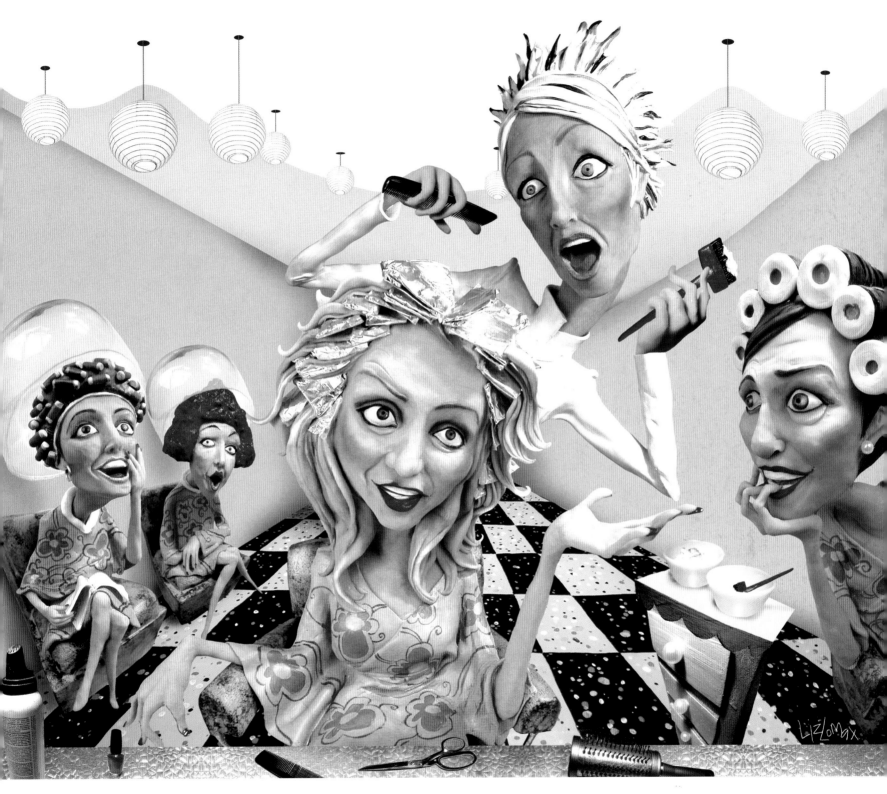

Liz Lomax
Beauty Secrets (2004)
Acrylic and oil paint on Super Sculpey/Insulation
foam/Foamcore/Aluminium Foil/Adobe Photoshop

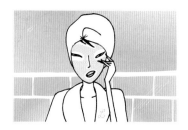

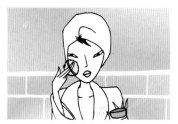

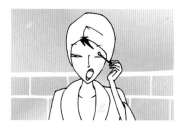

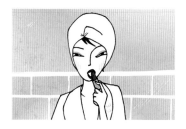

Malena Gagliesi
Beauty Steps, *Santo Buenos Aires Agency* (2006)
Adobe Illustrator

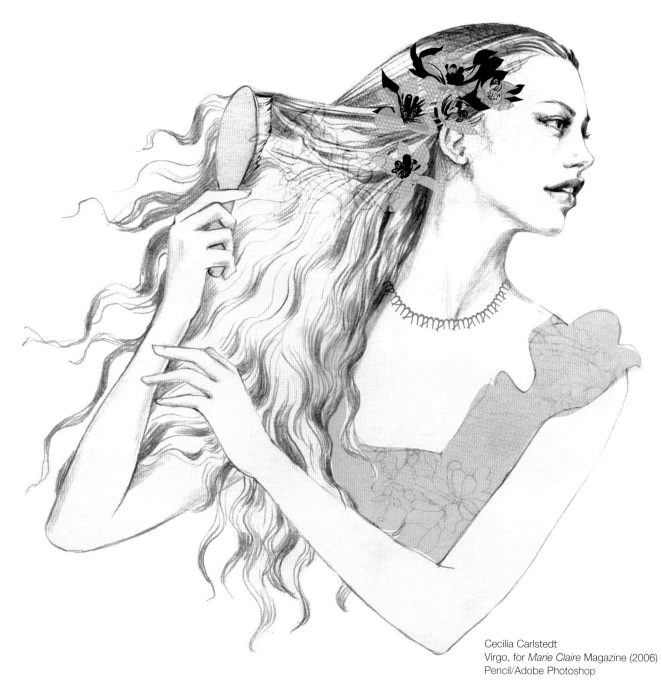

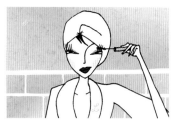

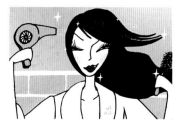

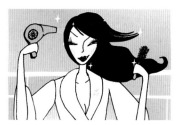

Cecilia Carlstedt
Virgo, for *Marie Claire* Magazine (2006)
Pencil/Adobe Photoshop

Yolanda Gonzales
Fro (1998)
Gouache on paper

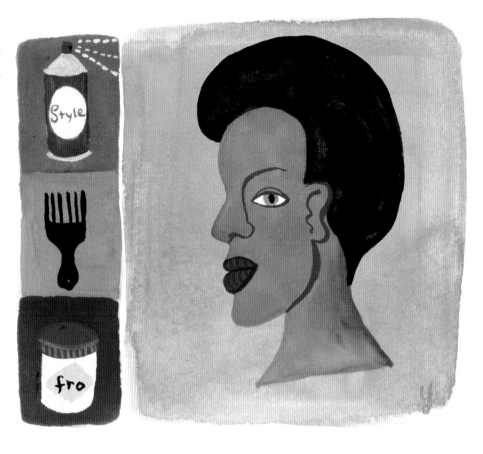

Sherill Gross
Beauty Ritual #9 (2005)
Paper

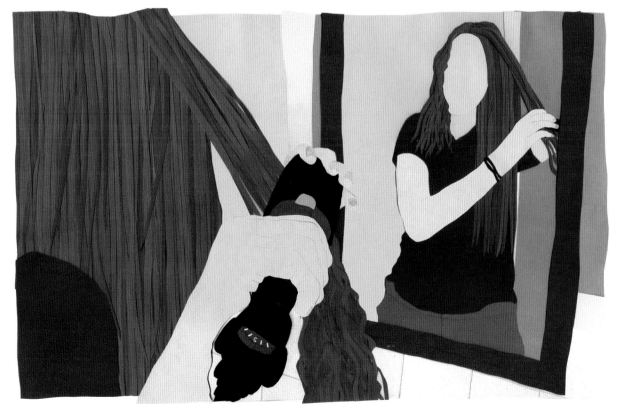

Natascha Engelmann
Cut (2006)
Pencil/Watercolour/Adobe
Photoshop/Adobe Illustrator

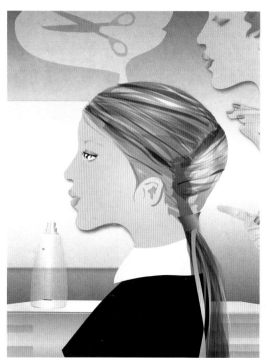

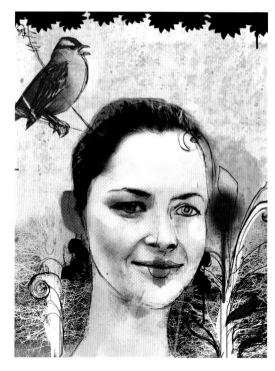

Genevieve Kelly
Woman and Song Bird (2005)
Wallpaper/Collage/Photograph/Adobe Photoshop

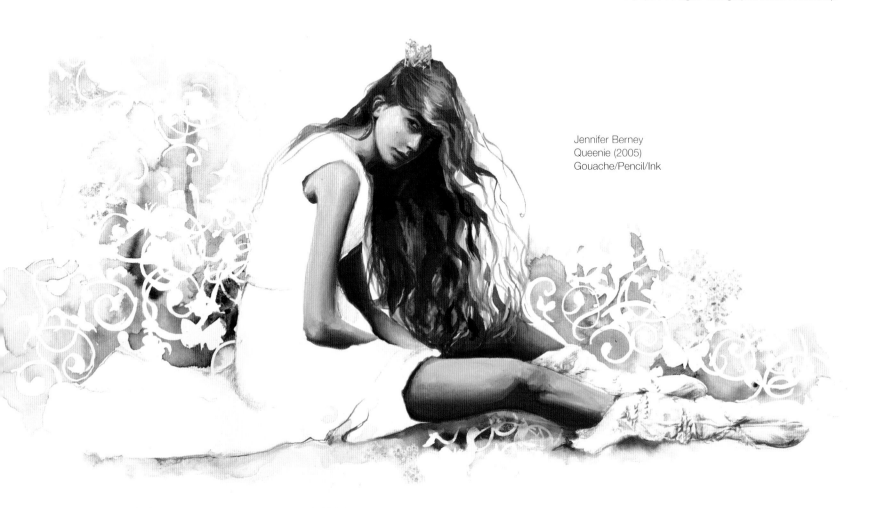

Jennifer Berney
Queenie (2005)
Gouache/Pencil/Ink

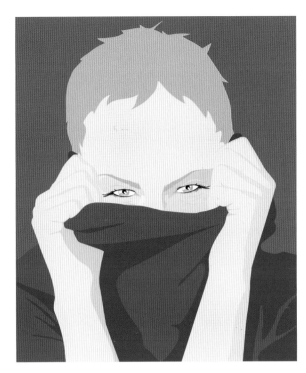

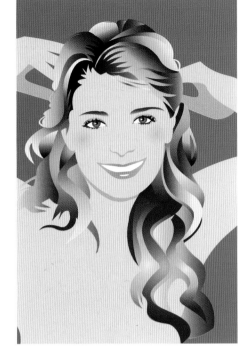

Martina Farrow
Mischa (2005)
Adobe Illustrator

Stuart Holmes
Peek-a-boo! (2000)
Adobe Illustrator

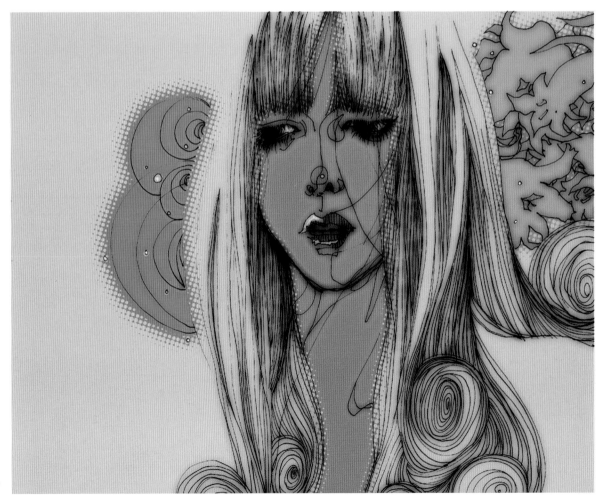

Woonyoung Chang
Mirror, Don't Want to See Myself (2006)
Micra pigma pen/Adobe Photoshop

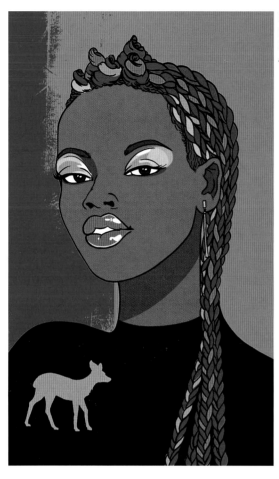

Kim Longhurst
Babylon (2005)
Macromedia FreeHand/
Adobe Photoshop

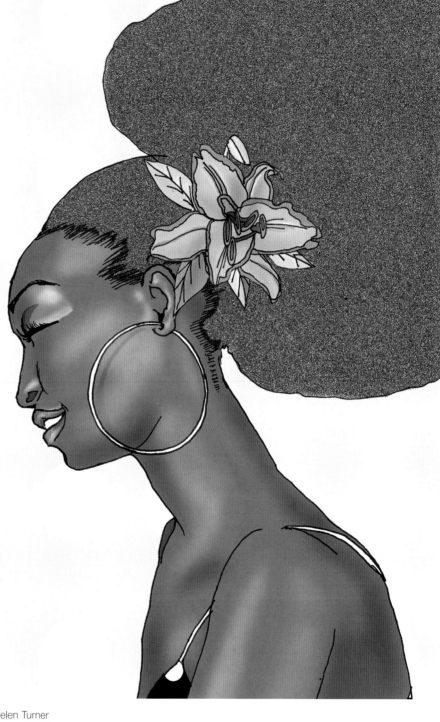

Helen Turner
Hoops (2005)
Ink/Adobe Photoshop

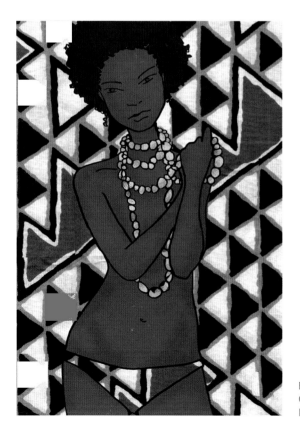

Ekua Doduwa Akumanyi
Gyia (2005)
Ink pen/Adobe Photoshop

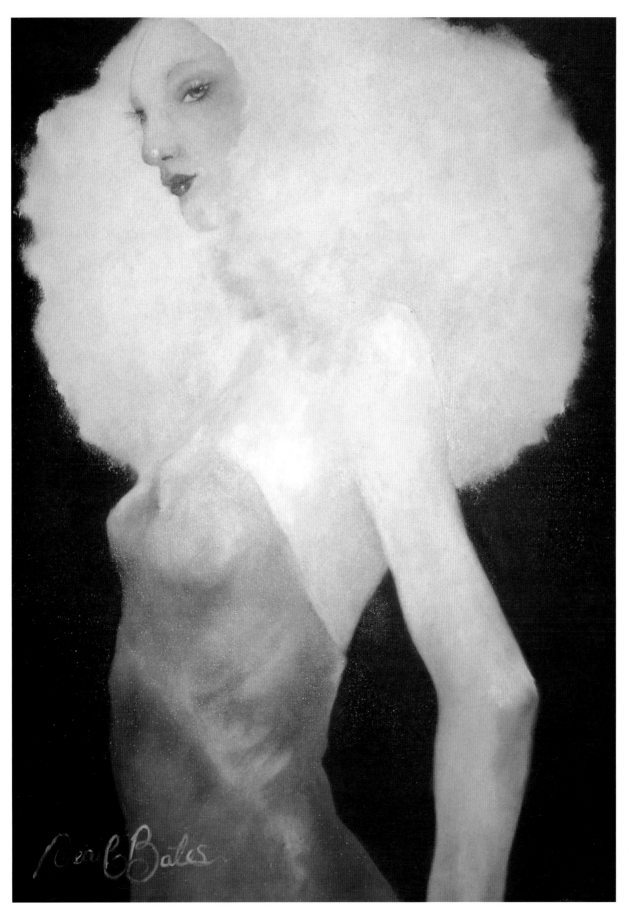

Pearl Bates
Winter Dreams (2005)
Oil on canvas

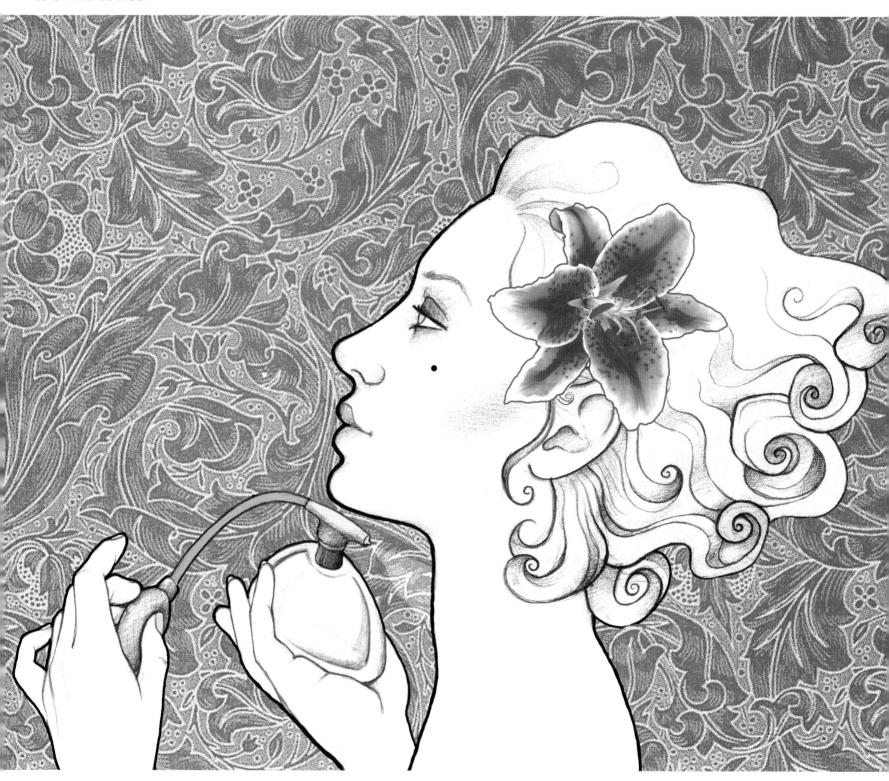

Steph Dix
Lily (2005)
Pencil/Adobe Photoshop

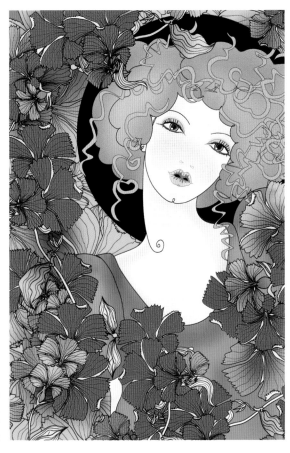

Ella Tjader
Madonna (2005)
Adobe Illustrator/
Adobe Photoshop

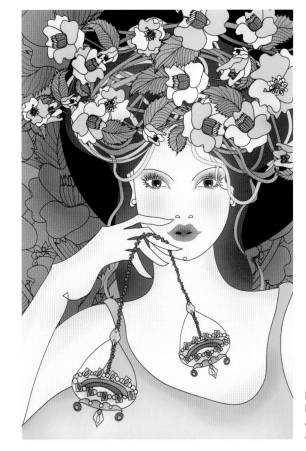

Ella Tjader
Libra (2005)
Adobe Illustrator/
Adobe Photoshop

Ella Tjader
Mexican Bride (2005)
Adobe Illustrator/
Adobe Photoshop

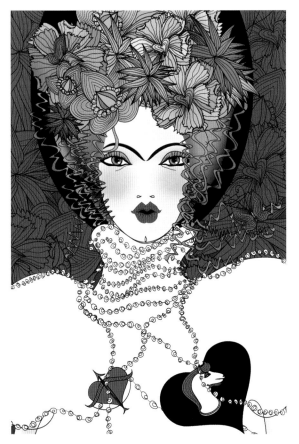

Ella Tjader
Scorpio (2005)
Adobe Illustrator/
Adobe Photoshop

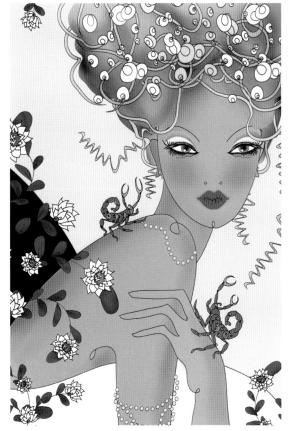

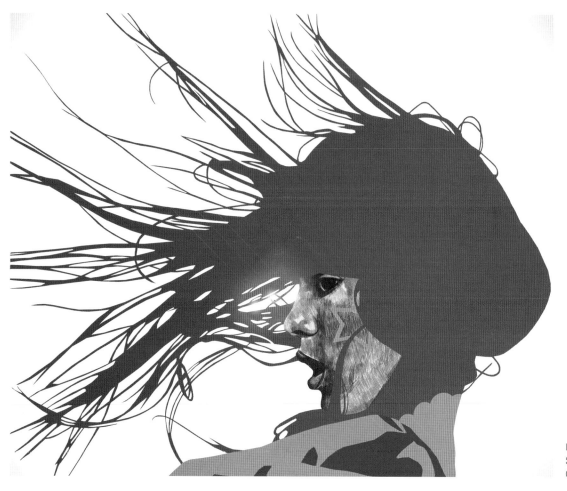

Claire McMahon
Perfume (2006)
Adobe Photoshop/Adobe Illustrator

Lucy MacLeod
Scarlet Fever (2005)
Charcoal/Adobe Photoshop

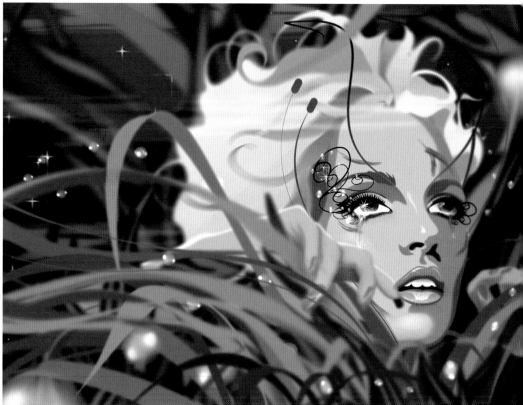

Herman Yap
Midnight Magic (2005)
Macromedia FreeHand/Adobe Photoshop

358

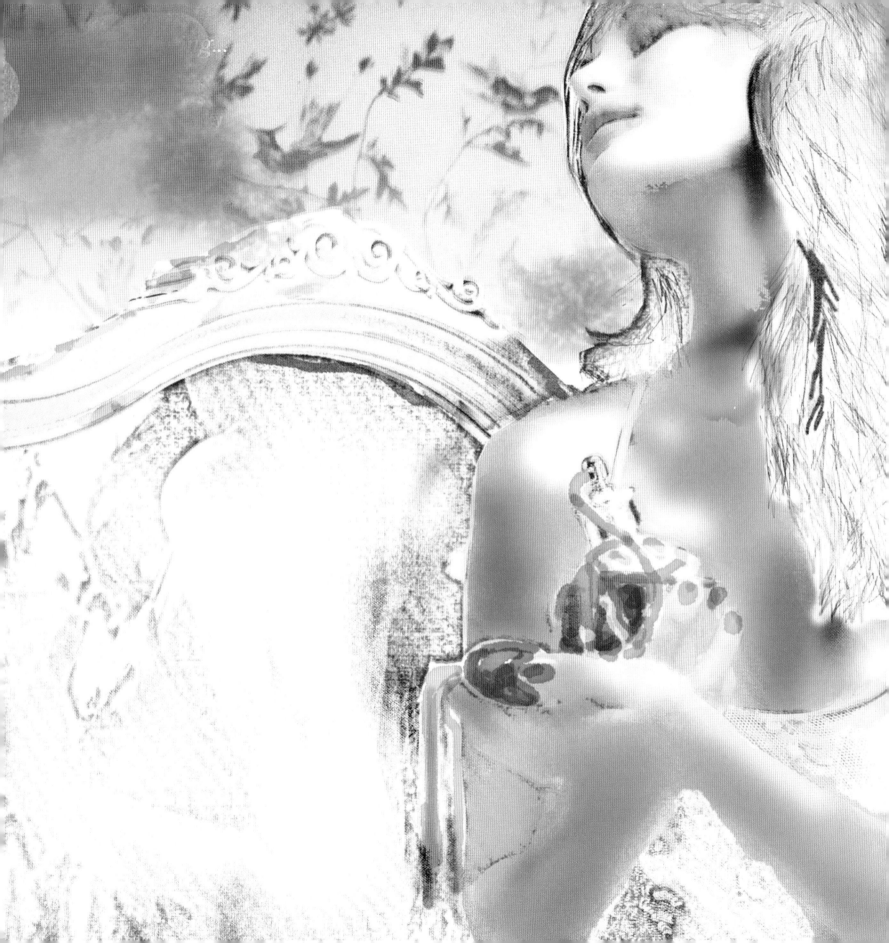

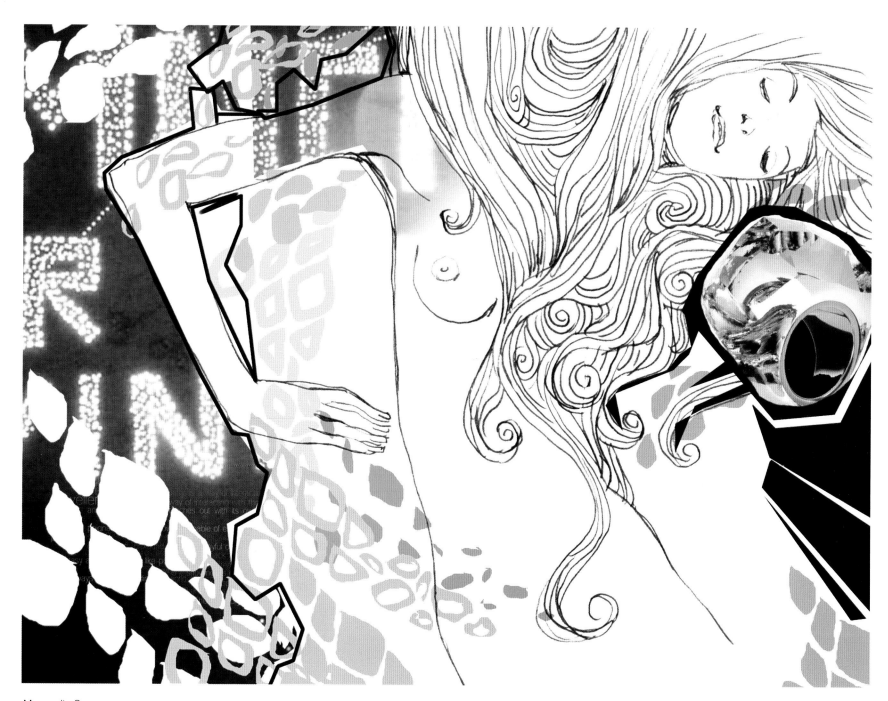

Marguerite Sauvage
Swaroski Movie and Research (2005)
Pencil/Adobe Photoshop

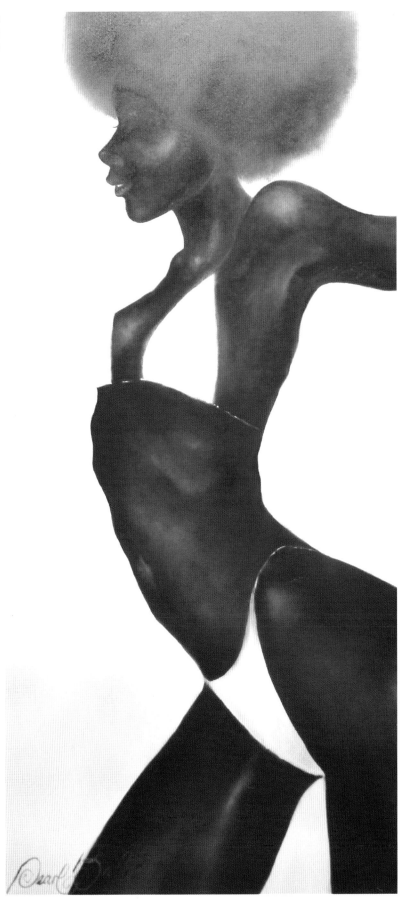

Pearl Bates
Ebony (2005)
Oil on canvas

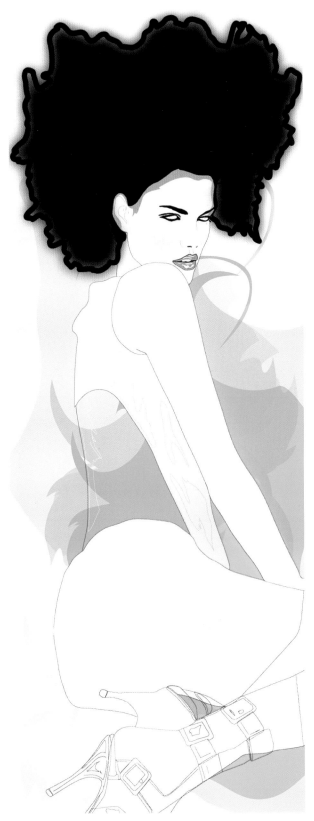

Giulio Iurissevich
Bellissima (2005)
Macromedia FreeHand/Adobe
Photoshop/Adobe Illustrator

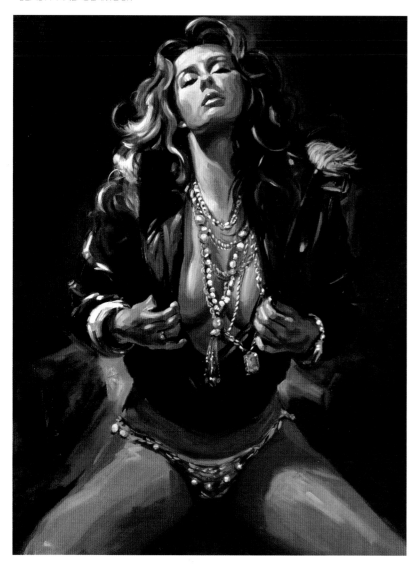

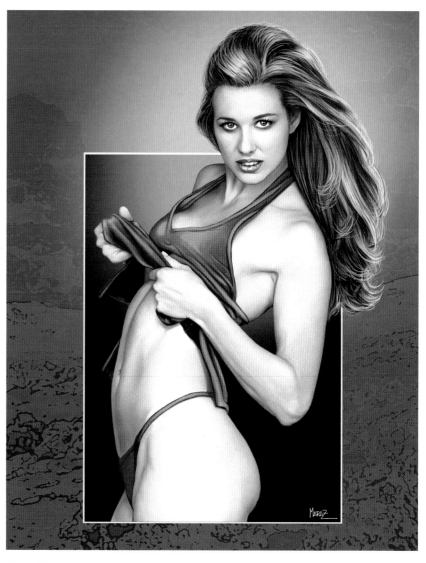

Eric Bailey
Golden (2005)
Oil on Canvas

Carlos Maraz
Calendar Girl (2006)
Corel Painter

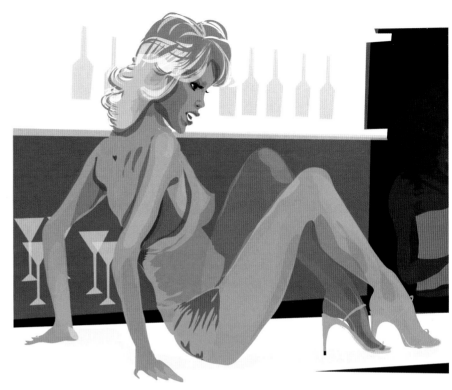

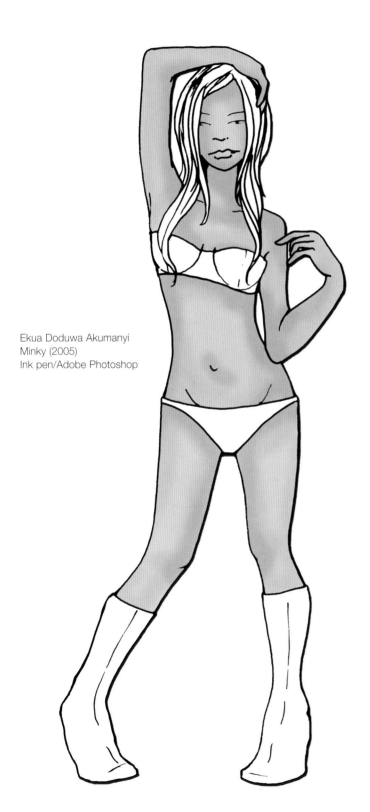

Ekua Doduwa Akumanyi
Minky (2005)
Ink pen/Adobe Photoshop

Kyra Kendall
Dancer (2006)
Adobe Illustrator

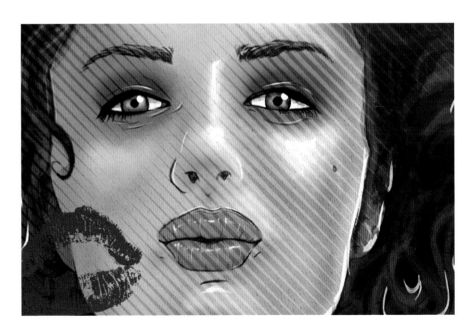

Wingnut Designs
Kiss Face (2005)
Traditional/Adobe Photoshop

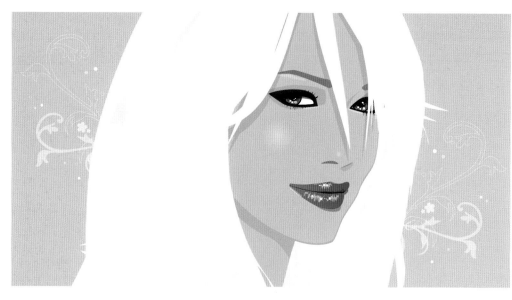

Dilek Peker
Hypnose (2006)
Adobe Photoshop

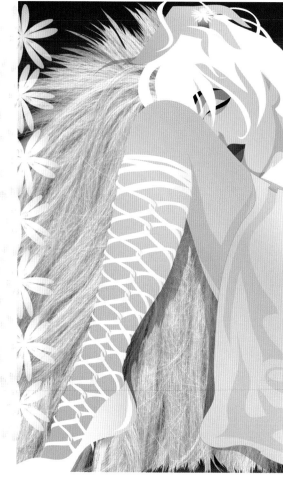

Mats Bergen
Lace-up Leg (2005)
Adobe Photoshop/Adobe Illustrator

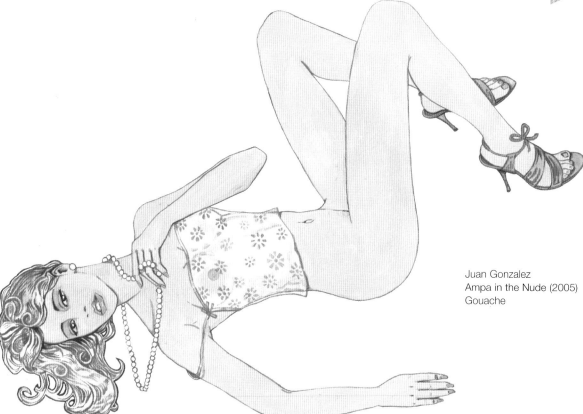

Juan Gonzalez
Ampa in the Nude (2005)
Gouache

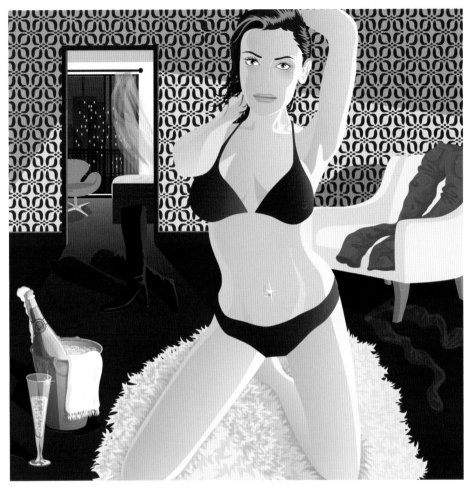

Stuart Holmes
The Brown Room (2002)
Adobe Illustrator

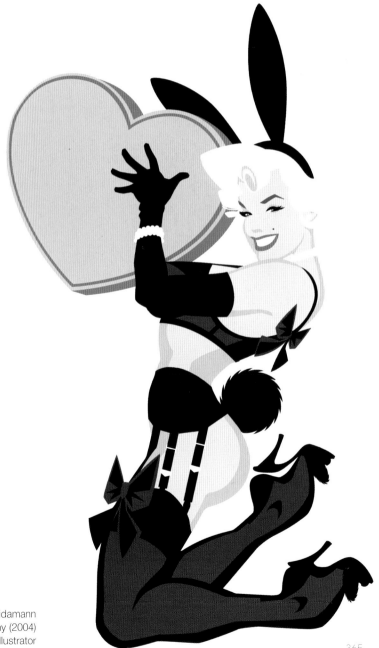

Andrew Bawidamann
Love Bunny (2004)
Adobe Illustrator

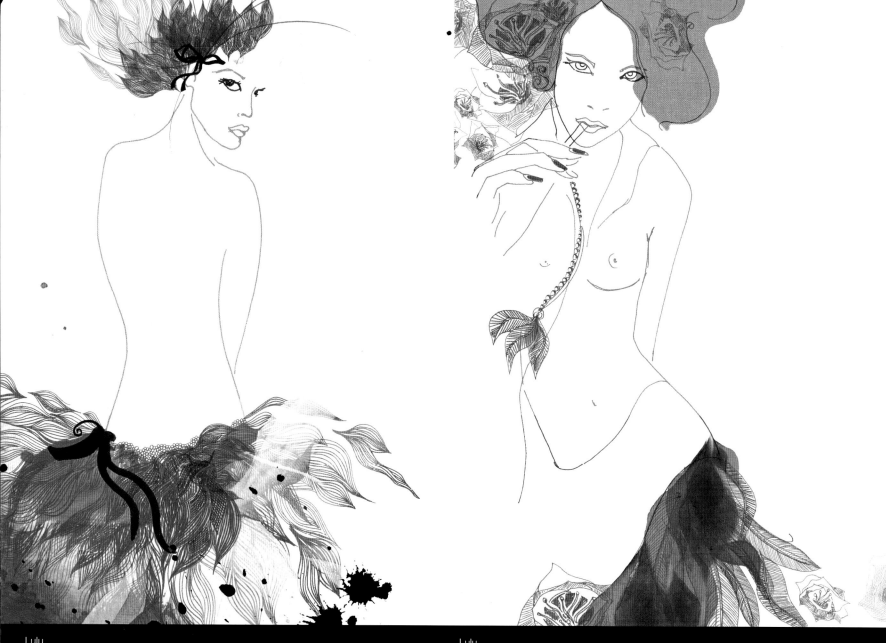

Lulu
Mood (2005)
Adobe Illustrator

Lulu
Lola (2005)
Adobe Illustrator

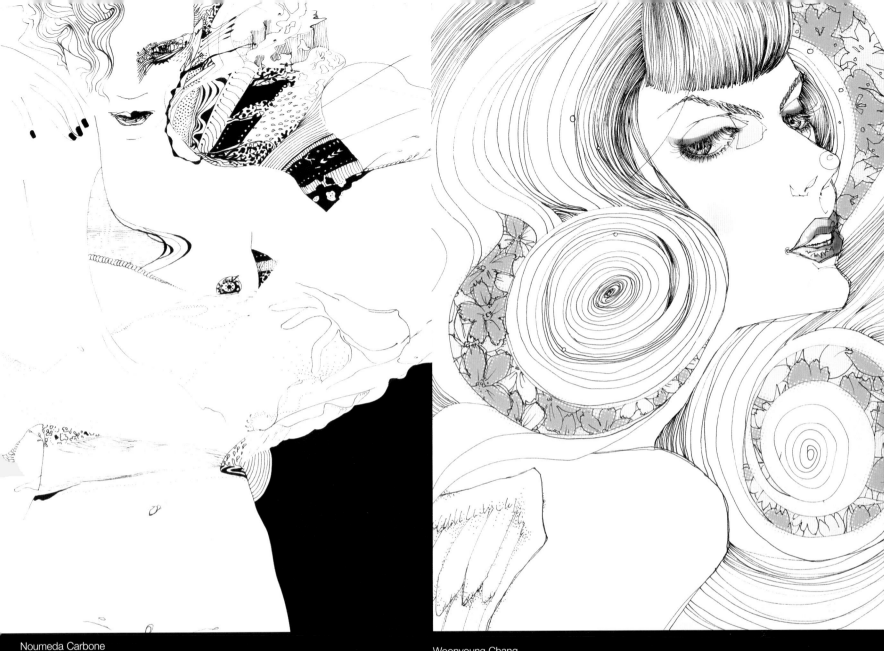

Noumeda Carbone
R#4 (2006)
Ink/Adobe Photoshop

Woonyoung Chang
Femme Fatal of Swallowed Dream (2006)
Micra pigma pen/Adobe Photoshop

367

Fhiona Galloway
Red Lips (2005)
Macromedia FreeHand

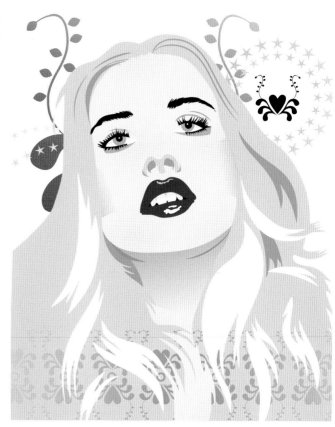

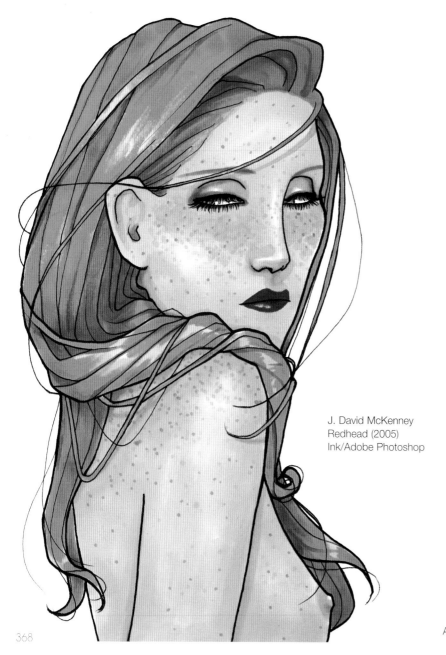

J. David McKenney
Redhead (2005)
Ink/Adobe Photoshop

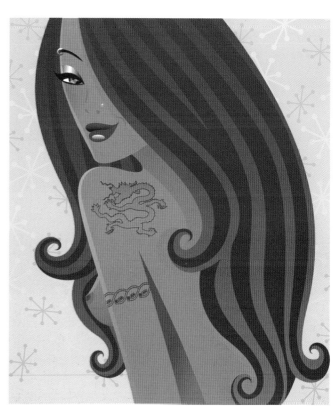

Pinglet
Fetish (2002)
Adobe Illustrator

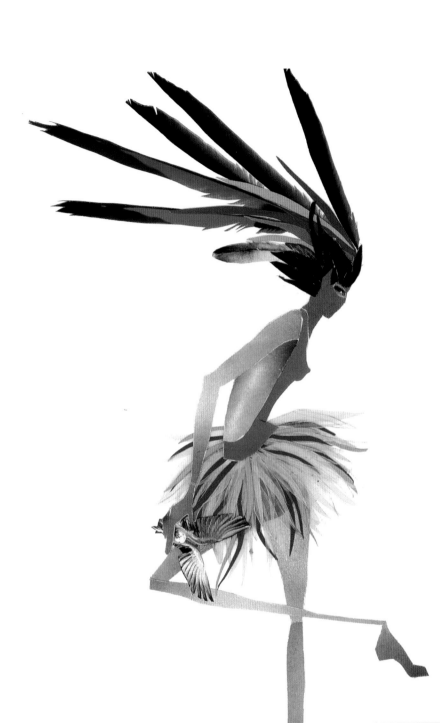

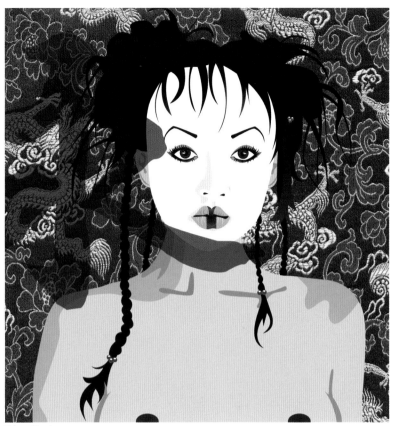

Erica Glasier
Fuuka Sakurai (2002)
Adobe Photoshop/Adobe Illustrator

Marie Gibson
Flamingo Lady (2005)
Photograph/Fabric collage

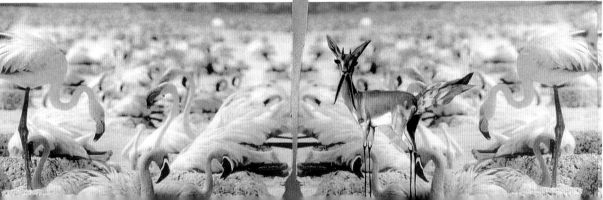

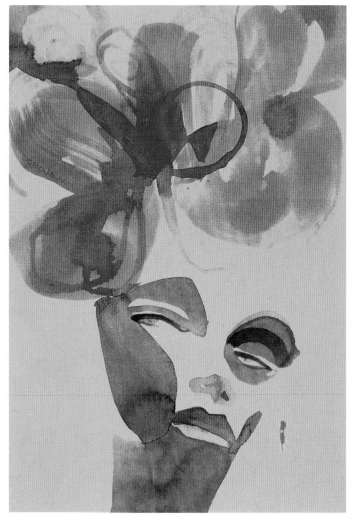

Bil Donovan
Pink Naomi (2003)
Ink

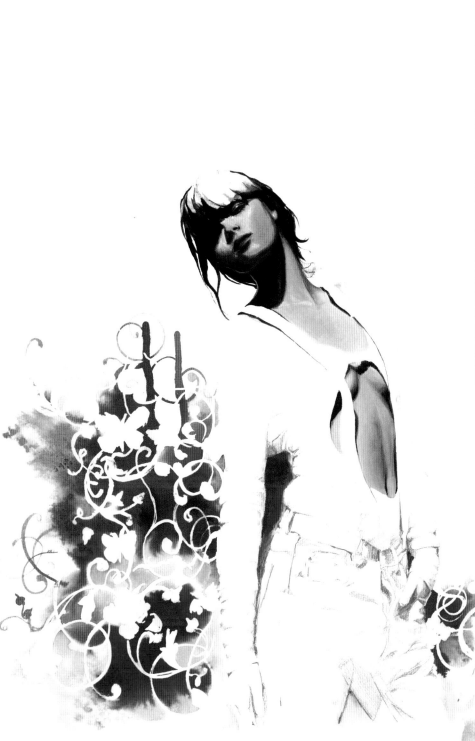

Jennifer Berney
Cabbage Butterfly (2006)
Gouache/Pencil/Ink

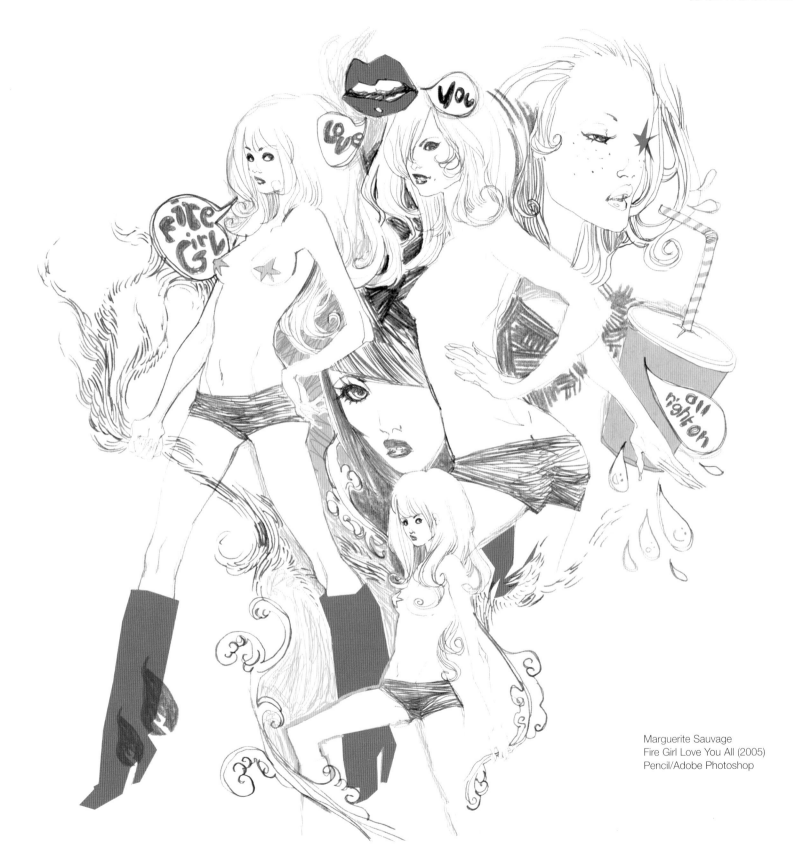

Marguerite Sauvage
Fire Girl Love You All (2005)
Pencil/Adobe Photoshop

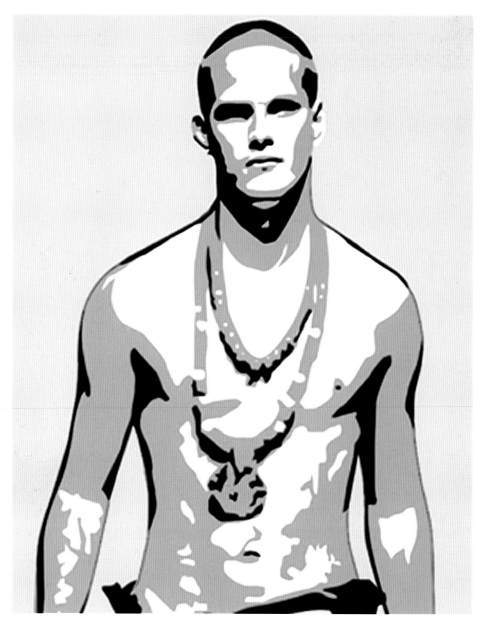

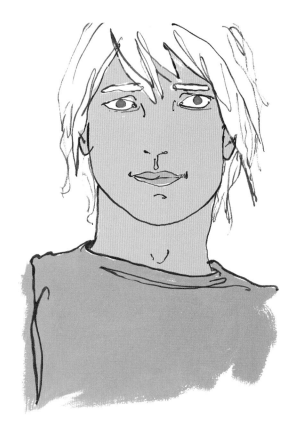

Mel Simone Elliott
Cute Guy (2006)
Gouache/Adobe Illustrator

Naomi Austin
Joey (2005)
Adobe Illustrator

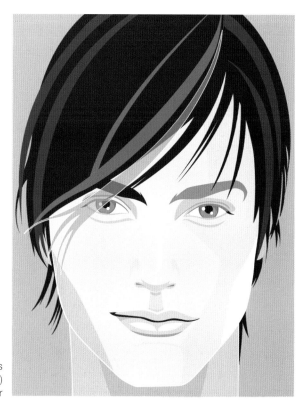

Irene Jacobs
Untitled, for *Man* magazine (2000)
Adobe Illustrator

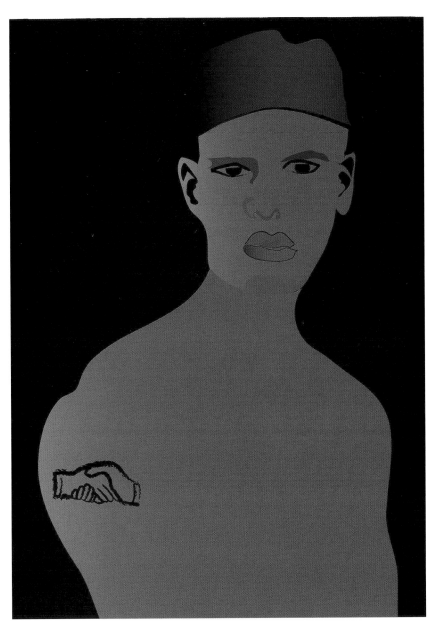

Natascha Engelmann
Tattoo Boy I (2006)
Pencil/Adobe Photoshop

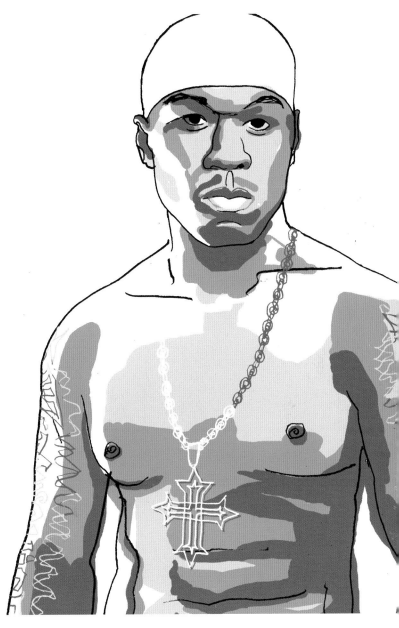

Monica Hellström
50 Cent (2005)
Pencil/Brush/Adobe Photoshop

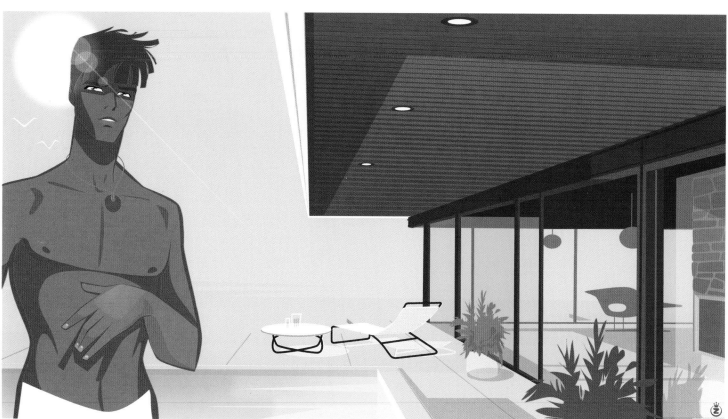

Monsieur Z
Case Study House 22
and Boy (2005)
Adobe Illustrator

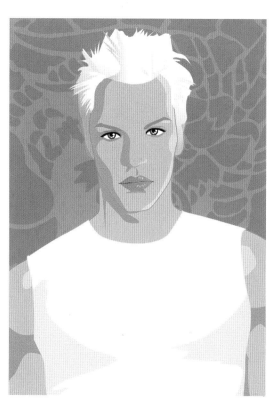

Dilek Peker
Sexy Boy (2006)
Adobe Photoshop

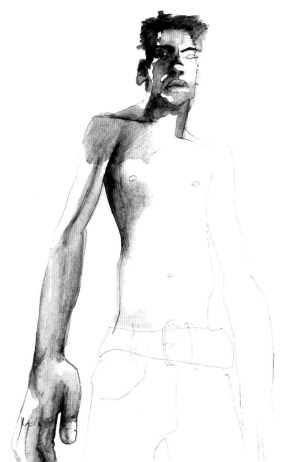

Anna Saunders
I Stop and Stare (2006)
Watercolour pencil/Adobe Photoshop

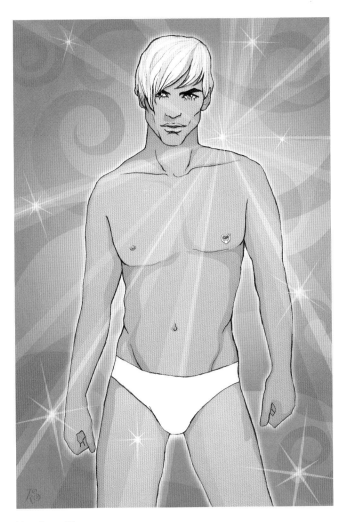

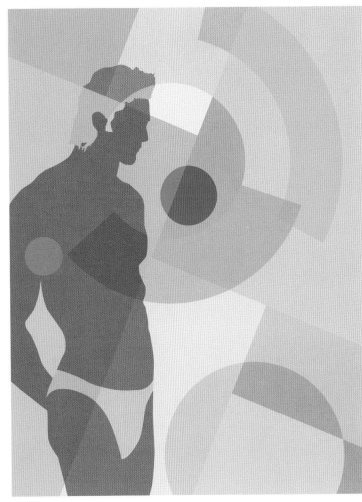

Kun-Sung Chung
Cool Guy (2006)
Adobe Photoshop/Adobe Illustrator

Koichi Fujii
Untitled (2005)
Adobe Illustrator

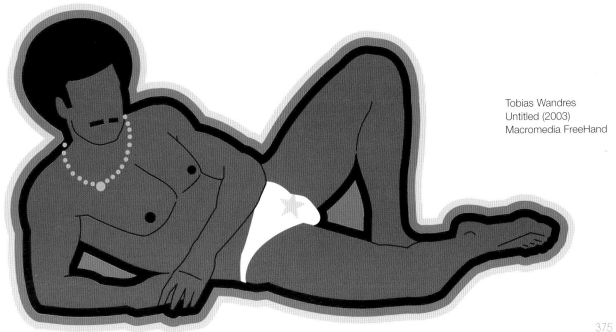

Tobias Wandres
Untitled (2003)
Macromedia FreeHand

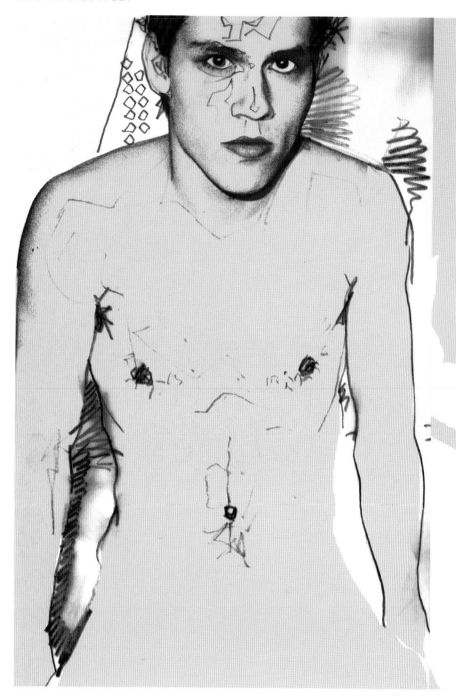

Nick Larrett
Jim, Thinking (2005)
Adobe Photoshop

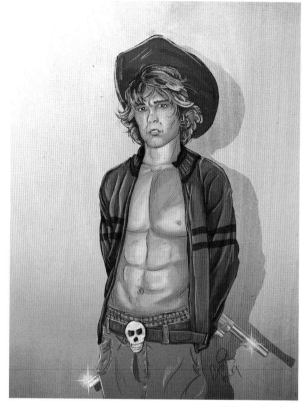

Wingnut Designs
Urban Cowboy (2005)
Traditional/Adobe Photoshop

Arthur Mount
YSL (2003)
Adobe Illustrator

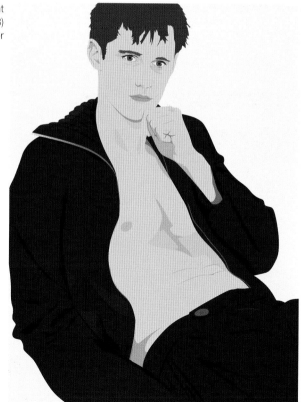

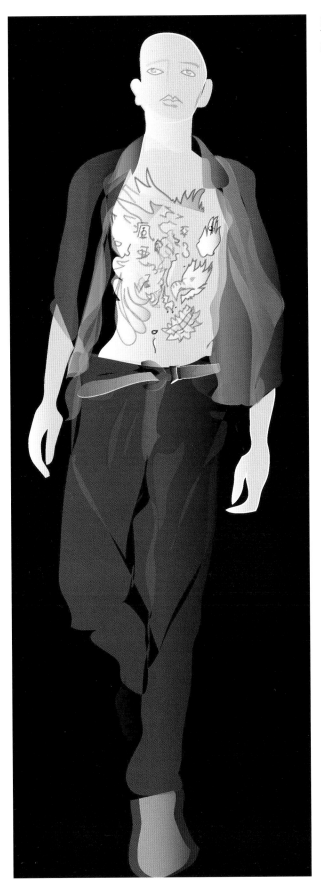

Natascha Engelmann
Tattoo Boy II (2006)
Pencil/Adobe Photoshop

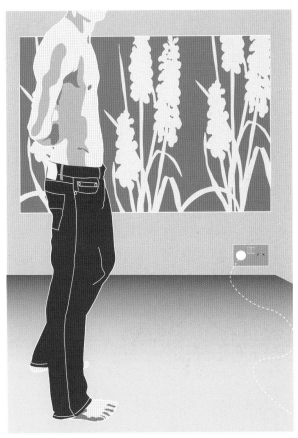

Kristie Jarita Lathbury
Electric Blue (2006)
Adobe Illustrator

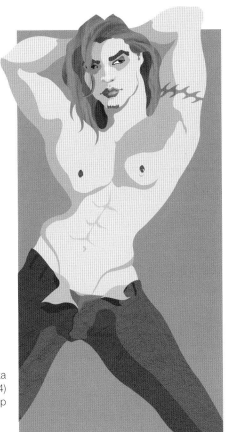

Jeff Mulawka
Rude Boy (2004)
Adobe Photoshop

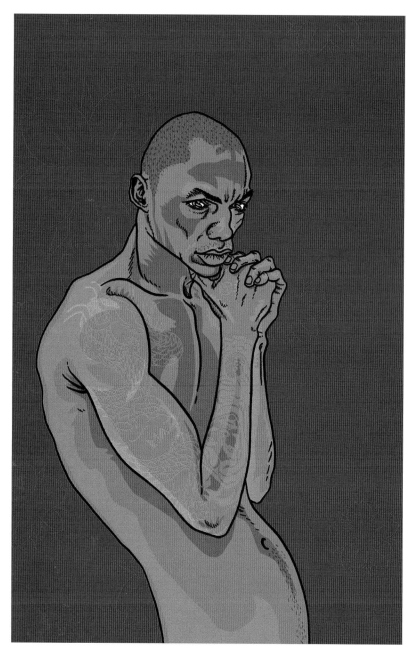

Jan Feindt
Tricky (2002)
Pen/Ink/Adobe Photoshop

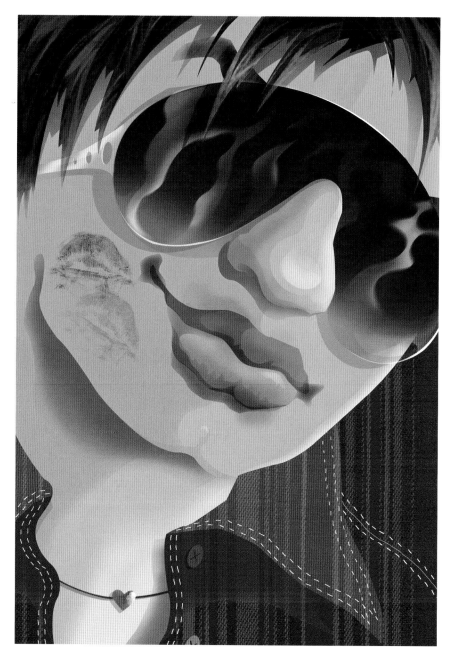

Jeff Mulawka
Flirt (2005)
Adobe Photoshop

Hélène Genevoix
Plurality (2004)
Adobe Photoshop

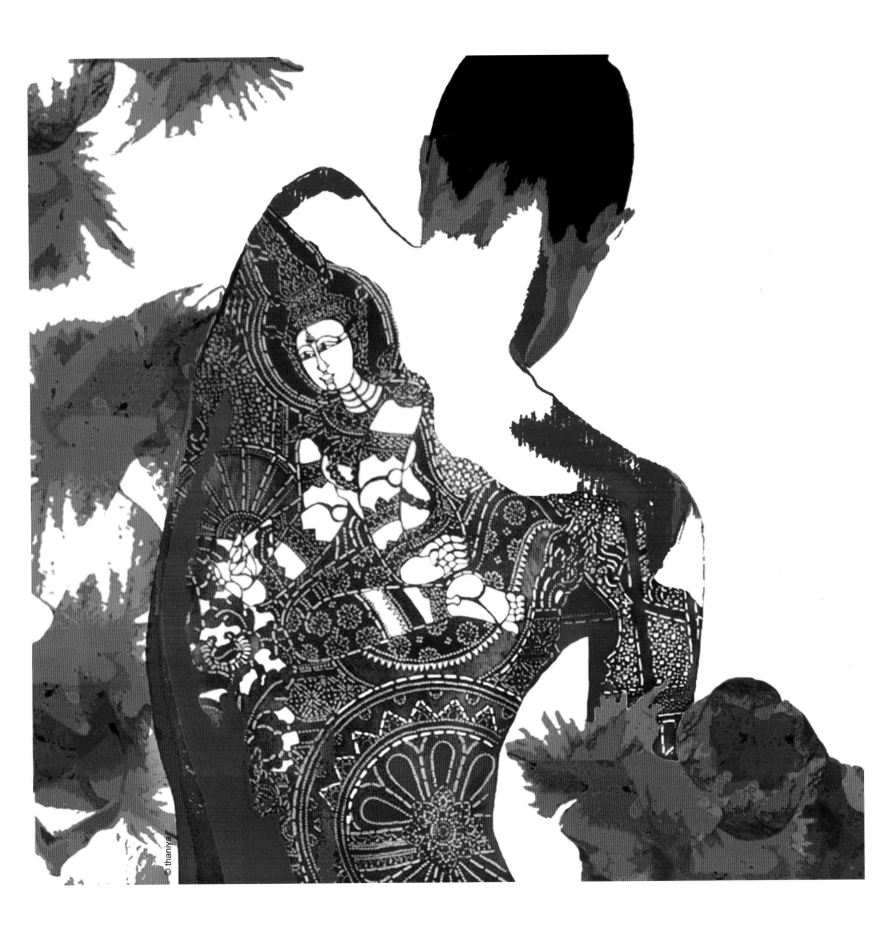

ARTIST CONTACT DETAILS

Agostino, Vincent
email: atomic7@ihug.com.au
www.hottrashstudios.com

Ahmadyar, Wahid
email: Wahid_Ahmadyar@hotmail.co.uk

Akumanyi, Ekua Doduwa
email: equaakum@btinternet.com
www.artwanted.com/strawberry

Allen, Emily
email: emily1allen@hotmail.co.uk

Allen, Lucy
email: lucyallen39@yahoo.co.uk
www.lucyallen.co.uk

Alexander, Louise
email: lou_alexander@hotmail.com
www.artshole.co.uk/louisealexander

Ambotaite, Elena
email: elena.ny@verizon.net
www.elenaambo.com

Amitrano, Marco
email: marcoxamitrano@yahoo.com
www.ArtWanted.com/marco.a

Anderson, Claire
email:
clairefrancesanderson@hotmail.com

Andersson, Kenneth
email: info@kennethandersson.com
www.kennethandersson.com

Apatangelos, Kosmas
email: kommigraphics@gmail.com
www.kommigraphics.gr

Arnow, Rob
email: design@robarnow.com
www.robarnow.com

Arora, Harmind Singh
email: harmind@gmail.com
www.artwanted.com/harmind

Arruda, Joseph S.
email: zeruch@vergenet.net
www.zeruch.net
zeruch.deviantart.com

Aurélie, Margat
email: margataurelie@hotmail.com

Austin, Naomi
email: naomi@naomiaustin.co.uk
www.naomiaustin.co.uk

Austin, Paul
email: austin_paul@hotmail.co.uk

Backhouse, Charlotte Sophie
email: lunadust@hotmail.com

Bailey, Eric
email: eric@birdsandbullets.com
www.birdsandbullets.com

Baker, Claire Ann
email: c.baker5@ntlworld.com
www.myspace.com/edithchick

Baranska, Aga
email: agabaranska@yahoo.com
www.agabaranska.com
www.eyecandy.co.uk

Barthold, Christian
email: weaverofyourdreams@gmx.de
christian-barthold.illustration.de

Bates, Pearl
email: info@pearlbates.com
www.pearlbates.com

Bawidamann, Andrew
email: andrew@bawidamann.com
www.bawidamann.com

Beetson, Sarah
email: sarahbeets@hotmail.com
Represented in Canada by
i2i Art Inc.
20 Maud St. Suite 202
Toronto, ON
Canada M5V 2M5
www.i2iart.com/Beetson
Represented in UK and rest of world
by Illustration Ltd
2 Brooks Court
Cringle Street
London SW8 5BX
email: sarah@illustrationweb.com
www.illustrationweb.com
www.illustrationweb.com/
SarahBeetson

Bergen, Mats
email: matsbergen@t-online.de
www.matsbergen.com
Represented in Austria by
www.weinper.at
Represented in Asia by
www.ua-net.com

Bergstrand, Jonas
email: jonas@jonasbergstrand.com
www.jonasbergstrand.com
Represented by Central Illustration
email: info@centralillustration.com
www.centralillustration.com

Berney, Jennifer
email: jennifer_berney@yahoo.com

Berning, Tina
email: tina@tinaberning.de
Represented by CWC International
611 Broadway, Suite 730
New York, NY 10012 USA
email: agent@cwc-i.com
www.cwc-i.com
Represented in Asia by Cross World
Connections
Tokyo, Japan
www.cwctokyo.com

Billiris, Nicholas
email: nbilliris@hotmail.com

Boberg, Annie
email: info@organisart.co.uk
www.organisart.co.uk

Borgions, Mark
email:
mark.borgions@handmademonsters.com
www.handmademonsters.com

Broadway, Hannah
email: Hbroadway@hotmail.com
www.number40.net/hannah.htm

Brockway, Ewa
email: ewaatusa@aol.com
www.ewabrockway.com

Buckley, Omar
email: URIN1234@yahoo.com

Burns, James
email: info@jamesburnsdesign.com
jamesburnsdesign.com

Byrne, Andrea
email: mail@andreabyrne.com
www.andreabyrne.com

Byrne, Eva
email: email@watsonspierman.com

Cabuay, John Jay
email: johnjay@johnjayart.com
www.johnjayart.com
Represented in USA by
Shannon Associates
email:
newyork@shannonassociates.com

Canales, Iván Solbes
email: ivan@ivansolbes.com
www.ivansolbes.com

Cangialosi, Anna
email: anna@annacangialosi.com
www.annacangialosi.com

Carbone, Noumeda
email: noumeda@tiscali.it
www.noumedacarbone.it
Represented by Private View
email: create@pvuk.com
www.pvuk.com

Cardelli, Maria
email: mcardelli-illustrator@earthlink.net
Represented by Illustration Ltd
2 Brooks Court
Cringle Street
London SW8 5BX
email: team@illustrationweb.com
www.illustrationweb.com/MariaCardelli

Carlstedt, Cecilia
email: mail@ceciliacarlstedt.com
www.art-dept.com
www.agentbauer.com
www.ceciliacarlstedt.com

Castelbarco, Belicta
email: belicta@aol.com
Represented by Die Illustratoren
Güntherstrasse 51
D - 22087 Hamburg
email: kontakt@illustratoren.de
www.illustratoren.de/belictacastelbarco

Chadprajong, Jasper Sinchai
email: jasper_chad@hotmail.com
www.keep-quiet.com

Chang, Woonyoung
email: winnie76@gmail.com
eiti2.com/winnie

Chen, Daniel
Represented by i2i Art Inc
email: info@i2iart.com
www.i2iart.com

Chenna
Studio: PPAINT
email: chenna@ppaint.net
www.ppaint.net
Agent: UNIT
www.unit.nl

Chin, Marcos
email: marcos@marcoschin.com
www.marcoschin.com

Chung, Kun-Sung
email: info@kschung.com
www.kschung.com

Coburn
Represented by Meiklejohn Illustration
5 Risborough Street
London SE1 0HF
email: info@meiklejohn.co.uk
www.meiklejohn.co.uk

Cook, Gillian
email: gillian@gilliancook.co.uk
www.gilliancook.co.uk

Corr, Christopher
email: Chris@Christophercorr.com
www.christophercorr.com

Crampton, Michael
Represented by Meiklejohn Illustration
5 Risborough Street London SE1 0HF
email: info@meiklejohn.co.uk
www.meiklejohn.co.uk

Cunag, Rhiannon
email: rhiannoncunag@gmail.com
rhiannoncunag.com

Cybèle
email: cybele@walkcycle.com
www.walkcycle.com

Darama, Ulis
email: ulisdarama@yahoo.com

Davidson, Megan
email: meg@megan-davidson.co.uk
www.megan-davidson.co.uk

Davis, Nancy
email: nandavis@cox.net
www.nancydavis.org

de la Rosa, Cesar
e-mail: BeleAmi@aol.com
www.CesardelaRosa.com

de Wolfe, Amy
email: amy@amydewolfe.com
www.amydewolfe.com

Detallante, Jeanne
email: jdetallante@gmail.com
www.jeannedetallante.com
Represented by ArtList Paris
email: jonathan@artlistparis.com
www.artlistparis.com

Devil, Naomi
email: naomidevil@naomidevil.com
www.naomidevil.com

Devine, Kat
email: kat_devine@hotmail.co.uk

Dias, Sofia
email: info@sofiadias.com
www.sofiadias.com
Represented by Pict UK
186 Sutton Court Road
Chiswick London W4 3HR
email: ukinfo@pict-web.com
www.pict-web.com

Dix, Steph
Represented by
Graham-Cameron Illustration
The Studio, 23 Holt Road
Sheringham
Norfolk NR26 8NB, UK
email: enquiry@graham-cameron
illustration.com
www.pictureprovider.com

Docampo, Valeria
email: contacto@valeriadocampo.com.ar
www.valeriadocampo.com.ar/editorial

Doerr, Maximilian
email: Maximilian@6in7and8.com
www.6in7and8.com

Donovan, Bil
email: dukedonovan@earthlink.net
Represented by ArtCounsel Inc
853 Broadway New York NY
artscounselinc.com

Edwards, Nina
email: nina@metropolitanmiss.com
www.portfolios.com/ninaedwards
www.metropolitanmiss.com

Egremont, Madeleine
email: maddie@maddieegremont.com

Elena, Arturo
email: arturo@arturoelena.com
www.arturoelena.com

Eley, Natalie
email: nat_eley@yahoo.co.uk

Elliott, Mel Simone
email: mel.elliott@virgin.net

Engel, Christiane
email: chengel@gmx.net
www.desertfriends.com

Engelmann, Natascha
email: illustration@engelworld.com
www.engelworld.com
Represented by Kombinatrotweiss*
Kaiserstrasse 69
60329 Frankfurt, Germany
email: info@kombinatrotweiss.de
www.kombinatrotweiss.de

Evrard, Pascale
www.pascale-evrard.com
Represented by Illustrissimo
email: michel@illustrissmo.com
www.illustrissimo.com

Farrow, Martina
Represented by New Division
5 Risborough Street
London SE1 0HF
email: info@newdivision.com
www.newdivision.com

Fearns, Georgina
email: georgiefearns@hotmail.co.uk

Feindt, Jan
Represented in UK by Illustration Ltd
2 Brooks Court
Cringle Street
London SW8 5BX
email: team@illustrationweb.com
www.illustrationweb.com/JanFeindt

Ferguson, Eleanor
email: lola_in_slacks@hotmail.com
www.artshole.co.uk/eleanorferguson.htm

Freund, Stefan
email: freund@stefanfreund.de
www.stefanfreund.de

Frith, Michael
email: info@michaelfrith.com
m.frith@lineone.net
www.michaelfrith.com

Fujii, Koichi
Represented in by Illustration Ltd
2 Brooks Court
Cringle Street
London SW8 5BX
email: team@illustrationweb.com
www.illustrationweb.com/KoichiFujii

Furukawa, Koichiro
email: koachen@hotmail.com

Gabriel, Raissa
email: raissa@raissagabriel.com
raissagabriel.com

Gagliesi, Malena
email: info@malenagagliesi.com.ar
www.malenagagliesi.com.ar

Gallotta, Marco
email: marcogallotta@yahoo.com
www.marcogallotta.com

Galloway, Fhiona
email: fg.illustration@virgin.net

Genevoix, Helene
email: thaniya@genevoix.com

Gibson, Marie
email: mariegibson_10@hotmail.com

Gimenez, Oscar
email: info@oscargimenez.com
www.oscargimenez.com

Glasier, Erica
email: Erica@EricaGlasier.com
www.EricaGlasier.com

Gonzalez, Juan
email: juanillustrator@msn.com
www.juangonzalez.co.uk

Gonzalez, Yolanda
email: yolanda@yodraws.com
www.yodraws.com

Green, Alex
email: algreen@zoom.co.uk
www.alexgreen-illustration.co.uk

Gross, Sherill
email: art@sagworks.com
www.sagworks.com

Gurevich, Leonid
email: GustavClimt2002@aol.com
www.LeonidGurevich.com

Hansen, Lærke Melgaard
email: l.melgaard-hansen@rca.ac.uk

Hayasaki, Chico
Represented by CWC International
611 Broadway, Suite 730
New York, NY 10012 USA
email: agent@cwc-i.com
www.cwc-i.com

Hellström, Monica
Represented by Anna Goodson
Management Inc.
email: info@agoodson.com
www.agoodson.com

Hollister, Matthew
email: matt@keystonecommonwealth.com
www.keystonecommonwealth.com

Hellovon
email: say@hellovon.com
www.hellovon.com

Holman, James
email: jamesholman1@hotmail.com

Holmes, Stuart
email: sh@stuartholmes.com
www.stuartholmes.com
Represented by Illustration Ltd
2 Brooks Court
Cringle Street
London SW8 5BX
www.illustrationweb.com/stuartholmes

Howells, Tania
email: tania@taniahowells.com
www.taniahowells.com

Hughes, Rian
email address: rian@rianhughes.com
www.rianhughes.com
Represented by Device
email: info@devicefonts.co.uk
www.devicefonts.co.uk

Iurissevich, Giulio
email address: iuri.g@aliceposta.it
www.giulio-iurissevich.com

Jacobs, Irene
email: info@im-jac.com
www.im-jac.com

James, Helen
Represented by New Division
5 Risborough Street
London SE1 0HF
email: info@newdivision.com
www.newdivision.com

Jamtli, Kaja
email: kalijam@hotmail.com

Jaring, Jason V
email: jasonjaring@gmail.com
ccc.1asphost.com/shiftklick

Jeffcoat, Anna Olivia
email: annajeffcoat@hotmail.com

Jensen-Collman, Nina
email: ninakjcollman@hotmail.com

Joaquin, Javier
Represented by The Organisation
Basement, 69 Caledonian Road
London N1 9BT
email: info@organisart.co.uk
www.organisart.co.uk

Jome, Hayato
email: jome@j.email.ne.jp
www.peacecard.com/jome.html

Joshi, Varshesh
email: Varshesh@shoonyadesign.net
www.shoonyadesign.net

Kawahiro, Yurikov
Represented by Asterisk Inc.
#201 5-10-14 Minamiaoyama Minato-ku
Tokyo 107 0062, Japan
email: info@pict-web.com
www.pict-web.com

Kayukawa, Yumiko
email: Yumiko@SweetYumiko.com
www.SweetYumiko.com

Kelly, Genevieve
email: genevieve@rareandwelldone.com
www.rareandwelldone.com

Kendall, Kyra
email: kyrakendall@mac.com
www.kyrakendall.com

King, Christopher
email: chris@antiknowsbest.com
Represented by Illustration Ltd
2 Brooks Court
Cringle Street
London SW8 5BX
email: team@illustrationweb.com
www.illustrationweb.com/ChrisKing/

Kiper, Anna
email: annakip@yahoo.com
www.geocities.com/annakip/

Kloster, Julian
email: juliankloster@hotmail.com

Knight, David
email: dknight1@uclan.ac.uk
vusi@bamstylee.com
www.bamstylee.com

Konstantinova, Elena Lavdovskaya
email: elavdovskaya@tsum.ru

Kuichi, Tatsuro
email: me@tatsurokiuchi.com
sally@heflinreps.com
www.tatsurokiuchi.com
www.heflinreps.com

Lai, Manna
email: mannalai@gmail.com

Laine, Laura
email: laulaine@gmail.com
www.lauralaine.net

Laita, Monica
Represented by New Division
5 Risborough Street
London SE1 0HF
email: info@newdivision.com
www.newdivision.com

Lardot, Christophe
Represented by Chez Antoine – Illustration
Management
45, rue Volta
75003 Paris, France
email: info@chezantoine.com
www.chezantoine.com

Larrett, Nick
email: n.l@fashion-communications.de
www.fashion-communications.de

Lathbury, Kristie Jarita
kristie@adamloveseve.com.au
www.adamloveseve.com.au

Lawlor, Terence
www.lawlorcollage.com
Represented by Meiklejohn Illustration
5 Risborough Street
London SE1 0HF
email: info@meiklejohn.co.uk
www.meiklejohn.co.uk

Lee, Jeeyun
email: jeeyunlee@earthlink.net
www.jeeyunlee.com

Lee, Taryn
email: tarynjlee@hotmail.com
www.coroflot.com/taryn_lee
www.jakandjil.com
www.portfolios.com/taryn

Li, Domanic
Represented by The Organisation
Basement, 69 Caledonian Road
London N1 9BT
email: info@organisart.co.uk
www.organisart.co.uk

Lomax, Liz
email: liz@lizlomax.com
www.lizlomax.com

Long, Xing Jun
email: matahari.kecil@gmail.com
www.artwanted.com/xingjunlong
coffecat-jun.deviantart.com
www.jotterpro.com

Longhurst, Kim
email: kim@ionaccess.co.za

Lopetz:BD
www.lopetz.com
Represented by Büro Destruct
Wasserwerkgasse 7
CH-3011 Bern
Switzerland
email: lopetz@burodestruct.net
www.burodestruct.net

Losana, Amparo
email: aplosana@hotmail.com
www.amparolosana.com

Lui, Janet Pui Kee
email: netlui@hotmail.com

Lulu
email: lulu@plasticpirate.com
www.plasticpirate.com
Represented by CWC International
611 Broadway, Suite 730
New York, NY 10012 USA
email: agent@cwc-i.com
www.cwc-i.com

Lynch, Tiffany
Represented by New Division
5 Risborough Street
London SE1 0HF
email: info@newdivision.com
www.newdivision.com

McCafferty, Laura
email: laura@lauramccafferty.com
www.lauramccafferty.com

McCaffrey, Christy
email: cmac1984@earthlink.net
altpick.com/cmccaffrey

McKenney, J David
email: jdavidmckenney@gmail.com
www.jdavidmckenney.com

McMahon, Claire
email: claire_e_mcmahon@yahoo.co.uk
www.clairemcmahon.com

Mackie, Daniel
email: daniel@danielmackie.co.uk
www.danielmackie.co.uk

Maclean, Fiona
email: fiona@fionamaclean.com
www.fionamaclean.com

MacLeod, Lucy
email: info@lucymacleod.com
www.lucymacleod.com
Represented by PVUK.com Ltd
t/a Private View
17a Swan Hill
Shrewsbury SY1 1NL, UK
www.pvuk.com/news
email: create@pvuk.com

Maraz, Carlos
email: cmaraz@marazdesign.com
www.marazdesign.com

Masa
email: info@masa.com.ve
www.masa.com.ve

Mason, Stuart
email: Stuart14P@aol.com

Masunouchi, Asako
email: mail@asako-masunouchi.com
www.asako-masunouchi.com

Matsubara, Shiho
Represented by Asterisk Inc.
#201 5-10-14 Minamiaoyama Minato-ku
Tokyo 107 0062, Japan
email: info@pict-web.com
www.pict-web.com

Matveeva, Ekaterina
email: info@mambeeba.com
www.mambeeba.com

Mazo, Ariel
email: ariel@ademure.com

Mazzesi, Nicoletta
email: nmazzesi@nmazzesi.com
www.nmazzesi.com

Menisha
Represented by Chez Antoine –
Illustration Management
45, rue Volta
75003 Paris, France
email: info@chezantoine.com
www.chezantoine.com

Messenger, Rachel
email: messenger_rachel@yahoo.co.uk

Modén, Kari
email: kari@moden.se
www.karimoden.se

Mount, Arthur
email: arthur@arthurmount.com
www.arthurmount.com

Mueller, Astrid (Potatomammadesign)
email: info@potatomammadesign.com
www.potatomammadesign.com

Mulawka, Jeff
email: jeffmulawka@hotmail.com
www.jeffmulawka.com
www.altpick.com/jeffmulawka

Murray, Wayne
Represented by Wayne Snooze
email: wayne@snoozelab.com

Nagamiya, Yoco
Represented by Asterisk Inc.
#201 5-10-14 Minamiaoyama Minato-ku
Tokyo 107 0062, Japan
email: info@pict-web.com
www.pict-web.com

Naro, Michinori
Represented by Asterisk Inc.
#201 5-10-14 Minamiaoyama Minato-ku
Tokyo 107 0062, Japan
email: info@pict-web.com
www.pict-web.com

Niles, Laura
email: laura_niles@hotmail.com
www.myspace.com/lauramichelleniles

Nwokedi, David
email: david@insidethecreative.com
www.insidethecreative.com

O'Hora, Zachariah
email: zach@zohora.com
www.zohora.com

O'Malley, Jason
email: aero68@mac.com
www.jasonomalley.com

O'Neill, Jacquie
email: jacquie@jacquieoneill.com
www.jacquieoneill.com

Obasi, Henry
Studio: PPAINT
email: chenna@ppaint.net
www.ppaint.net
Agent: UNIT
email: chenna@ppaint.net
www.unit.nl

Paull, Jacqui & Carl Melegari
www.jpaullmelegari.com
Represented by PVUK.com Ltd
t/a Private View
17a Swan Hill
Shrewsbury SY1 1NL, UK
www.pvuk.com/news
email: create@pvuk.com

Parentela, Claudio
email: c_parentela@libero.it
www.claudioparentela.com

Pariseau, Pierrre-Paul
Represented by The Organisation
Basement, 69 Caledonian Road
London N1 9BT
email: info@organisart.co.uk
www.organisart.co.uk

Peach, Emily
email: emilypeach80@yahoo.co.uk

Peker, Dilek
Represented by d+design
email: info@dpiudesign.com
www.dpiudesign.com

Peluffo, Marcella
email: marcella.peluffo@fastwebnet.it
www.marcella.peluffo.com

Persson, Stina
www.stinapersson.com
Represented by CWC International
611 Broadway, Suite 730
New York, NY 10012 USA
email: agent@cwc-i.com
www.cwc-i.com
Represented in Asia by Cross World
Connections
Tokyo, Japan
www.cwctokyo.com

Pilar, Bella
www.bellapilar.com
Represented by Magnet Reps
email: art@magnetreps.com
www.magnetreps.com

Pinglet
email: pinglet@email.com
www.pinglet.com

Ponce, Diana
email: info@dianaponceart.com
www.dianaponceart.com

Potts, Andy
email: info@andy-potts.com
www.andy-potts.com

Prang, Katherine
email: katprange@yahoo.co.uk
www.myspace.com/prangay

Prikryl, John
email: jprikryl@gmail.com

Pring, Sally
email: mail@sallypring.com
www.sallypring.com

Reece, Gavin
Represented by New Division
5 Risborough Street
London SE1 0HF
email: info@newdivision.com
www.newdivision.com

Renault, Dorothea
Represented by Chez Antoine –
Illustration Management
45, rue Volta
75003 Paris, France
email: info@chezantoine.com
www.chezantoine.com

Rodriguez, Edel
email: edelrodriguez@aol.com
www.altpick.com/edel

Rosen, Kim
email: kim@kimrosen.com
www.kimrosen.com
Represented by Anna Goodson
Management Inc.
email: info@agoodson.com
www.agoodson.com

Rotzsche, Jens
email: jens@adastragrafx.de
www.adastragrafx.de

Saitoh, Yusuke
Represented by Asterisk Inc.
#201 5-10-14 Minamiaoyama Minato-ku
Tokyo 107 0062, Japan
email: info@pict-web.com
www.pict-web.com

Salek, Janis
email: janissalek@verizon.net

Santry, Karen
email: karensantry@verizon.net
www.fashionartbank.com

Saunders, Anna
email: purple_creature@hotmail.com

Sauvage, Marguerite
email: contact@margueritesauvage.com
www.margueritesauvage.com

Scandella, Alessandra
email: alefast@fastwebnet.it
www.alessandrascandella.com

Sharp, Erica
email: info@ericasharp.co.uk
www.ericasharp.co.uk

Shaul, Meirav
email: meiravshaul@hotmail.com
www.meiravshaul.com

Shephard, David
Represented by Illustration Ltd
2 Brooks Court
Cringle Street
London SW8 5BX
email: team@illustrationweb.com
www.illustrationweb.com

Shimizu, Yuko
email: yuko@yukoart.com
www.yukoart.com

Sibley, Michael
email: mich@elsibley.com
www.msibley.com

Silvestri, Marsha
email: msarts@mindspring.com
www.fashionartbank.com

Smith, Andrew
email: andysmithdesign@hotmail.co.uk
eldictator.deviantart.com

Smith, Alexander Brooke
email: alexander@utopiacreative.co.uk
www.utopiacreative.co.uk

Srimekhanond, Prot
email: thisispin@yahoo.com
www.thisispin.com

Stanga, Carlo
email: carlo.stanga@fastwebnet.it
www.carlostanga.com
Represented by Helen Ravenhill
email: hravenhill@earthlink.net

Stolle, Rainer
email: illu@rainerstolle.eu
rainer@brotundbutter.de
www.rainerstolle.eu
www.gotique.de

Storey, Anton
email: antonstorey@mail.nu

Suhariyan, Sonya
email: sonyasuhariyan@gmail.com
www.sonyasuhariyan.com

Symbolon
email: info@symbolon.jp
www.symbolon.jp

Tabib, Lior Yefet
email: liortab@yahoo.com

Tate, Jamal 'Bam'
email: darkreign@mac.com
web.mac.com/darkreign/iWeb/
DARKREIGN/DARKREIGN.html

Teng, LiXan
email: leashapore@gmail.com
leashapore.deviantart.com

Throup, Aitor
email: info@aitorthroup.com
www.aitorthroup.com

Tjader, Ella
Represented by Illustration Ltd
2 Brooks Court
Cringle Street
London SW8 5BX
email: team@illustrationweb.com
www.illustrationweb.com/ellatjader/

Townsend, Claire
email: claire.townsend@hotmail.co.uk

Townsend, Marina A
email: marina_townsend@yahoo.co.uk
marina.artistportfolio.net
www.artshole.co.uk/marinatownsend.htm

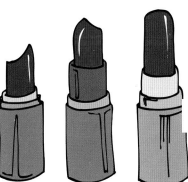
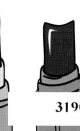
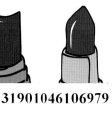
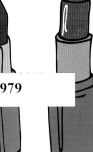
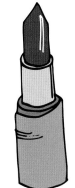
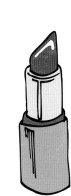

31901046106979

Malena Gagliesi
Lipstick Personality, *Figure*
magazine, NYC (2003)
Adobe Illustrator